Advance Praise

Readers will profit greatly from Hulitt Gloer and Perry Stepp's new commentary, *Reading Paul's Letters to Individuals: A Literary and Theological Commentary on Paul's Letters to Philemon, Titus, and Timothy*. Treating the Pastoral Letters together with Philemon allows the authors to emphasize the commonalities among four letters that are rarely considered together, though they are carefully clustered together in the canon. Gloer and Stepp write well, and the reader will appreciate their clearly presented insights into the historical and literary aspects of the texts. . . .

—*Mark J. Olson*
President, Leland Seminary

The decision to set apart the Pauline letters to individuals is itself immediately interesting and effective in giving these epistles a distinctive place. These commentaries reflect current scholarship such as rhetorical criticism and story/characters and social historical studies. Both primary sources and good modern analyses are interspersed effectively. Words are not wasted, making the commentaries accessible. The reader is rewarded. Clarity and brevity speak well for themselves in these lively commentaries.

—*Peter Rhea Jones*
Gannon Professor of Preaching and
Professor of New Testament
McAfee School of Theology, Mercer University

Hulitt Gloer and Perry Stepp's *Reading Paul's Letters to Individuals* places the letters to Philemon, Titus, and Timothy into much fuller and more informative contexts. This reader-friendly book sheds new light on these four brief letters, illuminating the theological and social richness of Philemon, on the one hand, and the sequence and significance of the Pastoral Letters, whose exegetical treatment for generations has been mired in oversimplified debates revolving around authorship, on the other. Anyone interested in a deeper understanding of Paul as he neared the end of his ministry and life will want to read this book.

—Craig A. Evans
Payzant Distinguished Professor of New Testament
Acadia Divinity College
Nova Scotia, Canada

READING PAUL'S LETTERS TO INDIVIDUALS

Smyth & Helwys Publishing, Inc.
6316 Peake Road
Macon, Georgia 31210-3960
1-800-747-3016
© 2008 by Smyth & Helwys Publishing
All rights reserved.
Printed in the United States of America.

The paper used in this publication meets the minimum
requirements of American National Standard for Information
Sciences—Permanence of Paper for Printed Library Materials.
ANSI Z39.48–1984   (alk. paper)

Library of Congress Cataloging-in-Publication Data

Gloer, Hulitt.

   Reading Paul's Letters to individuals : a literary and
theological commentary on Paul's Letters to Philemon, Titus, and
Timothy / W. Hulitt Gloer and Perry L. Stepp. p. cm. Includes
bibliographical references and index. ISBN 978-1-57312-519-2
(pbk. : alk. paper) 1. Bible. N.T. Pastoral
Epistles—Commentaries. 2. Bible. N.T. Philemon—Commentaries.
I. Stepp, Perry Leon, 1964– II. Title. BS2735.53.G56 2008
227'.807—dc22 2008036638

Disclaimer of Liability: With respect to statements of opinion or fact available in this work of nonfiction, Smyth &
Helwys Publishing Inc. nor any of its employees, makes any warranty, express or implied, or assumes any legal liability
or responsibility for the accuracy or completeness of any information disclosed, or represents that its use would not
infringe privately-owned rights.

Reading Paul's Letters to Individuals

A Literary and Theological Commentary on Paul's Letters to Philemon, Titus, and Timothy

W. Hulitt Gloer and
Perry L. Stepp

Acknowledgments

I owe a debt of gratitude to my wife, Elizabeth, for her gracious support and love. Thanks also to the Disputed Paulines group, Ryan Adams, Trey Anastasio, and Kara Hedges. Several people carefully read and critiqued portions of this manuscript: David Fiensy, Terry Golightly, Errol Stepp, and Rick Brannan of www.pastoralepistles.com. I deeply appreciate their help and sharp eyes. Thanks also to my editor, Leslie Andres, for her sensitive and intelligent work.

Quotations from the Bible are either from the authors' own translations or from the New Revised Standard Version, unless otherwise specified. Generally, material from Greek and Roman sources has been taken from the Loeb Classical Library.

—Perry Stepp
September 2008

To Charles H. Talbert
hodēgos empeiros

Contents

Editor's Foreword xiii

Philemon: The Transforming Power of the Gospel
Introduction to Philemon 3
Salutation (Prescript and Blessing): Affecting a Position
   of Weakness (1-3) 19
Thanksgiving/Exordium: Pointing Back, Pointing Forward (4-7) 24
Body (8-22) 26
   Propositio: Paul's Appeal (8-11) 26
   Probatio: The Gospel's Transforming Power (12-16) 30
   Peroratio: Sealing the Deal (17-21) .36
   Travel Plans (22) 42
Final Greetings and Benediction (23-24) 43
Works Cited 45

The Letters to Titus and Timothy
Introduction to the Pastoral Epistles 49

Titus: The Necessity of Order
1. Salutation and Greeting (1:1-4) 71
2. The Charge Titus Is Given (1:5-9) 77
   A. The Charge: Put Things in Order, Appoint Elders (1:5) 77
   B. Qualifications for Leadership (1:6-9) 79
   C. The Challenge Titus Faces (1:10-16) 84
   D. Summary 90
3. The Way of Life Titus Must Teach (2:1–3:11) 90
   A. Responsibilities in the Household of God (2:1-15) 91
      1. Content (2:1-10) 93
      2. Theological foundation for the instruction (2:11-14) 101

       3. Encouragement and empowerment (2:15) 108
       4. Summary 109
   B. Living as Witnesses (3:1-11) 110
       1. Content (3:1-2) 110
       2. Theological foundation for the instruction (3:3-8a) 112
       3. Encouragement and empowerment (3:8b-11) 119
       4. Summary 123
4. Final Instructions, Travel Plans, and Benediction (3:12-15) 123

1 Timothy: The Nature of True and Faithful Ministry
1. Salutation and Greeting (1:1-2) 131
2. Paul's Charge to Timothy, Part 1 (1:3) 135
3. Description of True Ministry (1:4-20) 136
   A. False Teachers Contrasted with Paul and His People (1:4-11) ...137
      B. Paul's Call to Ministry (1:12-17) 144
      B'. Timothy's Call to Ministry (1:18-19a) 149
   A'. False Teachers Contrasted with Timothy (1:19b-20) 151
4. Paul's Missionary Purposes (2:1–3:16) 153
   A. The Missionary Purpose behind Paul's Teaching (2:1-7) 153
      1. Hymn describing God's grace (2:5-6) 157
      2. Paul's appointment by God (2:7) 158
   B. Behavior in the Household (of God)
      that Supports Paul's Purposes (2:8–3:13) 159
      1. Men (2:8) 159
      2. Women (2:9–3:1a) 159
      3. Elders (3:1b-7) 168
      4. Male and female deacons (3:8-13) 171
   C. Hymn Supporting Missionary Purposes (3:14-16) 174
5. How to Do Ministry in the Last Days (4:1–6:10) 178
   A. False Teachers Contrasted with Paul and Timothy (4:1-5) 179
      B. Ministry in the Last Days (4:6-16) 181
      B'. How to Treat Other Members of the Household of God
        (5:1–6:2) 186
   A'. False Teachers Contrasted with Paul and Timothy (6:3-10) 196
6. Paul's Charge to Timothy, Continued (6:11-16) 199
7. Final Instructions and Reiteration of the Charge (6:17-21) 202

2 Timothy: Triumphant Ministry
1. Salutation, Greeting, and Prayer of Thanksgiving (1:1-5) 207
2. Paul's Charge to Timothy (1:6–4:8) 211

    A. A Model to Emulate: Paul the Sufferer (1:6–2:13) 213
        1. Join in suffering (1:6-18) 213
        2. Be strong (2:1-7) 226
        3. Theological foundation (2:8-13) 230
    B. Images of Ministry (2:14–3:9) 236
        1. A worker who passes the test (2:14-19) 236
        2. A vessel fit for noble use (2:20-26) 241
        3. Theological foundation (3:1-9) 247
    C. A Model to Emulate: Paul the Triumphant (3:10–4:8) 253
        1. What Timothy knows and how it benefits him (3:10-17) . . .253
        2. Paul's charge, Paul's victory (4:1-8) 263
    D. Personal Notes, Final Greetings, and Benediction (4:9-22) 270
Works Cited 281

Editor's Foreword

"Reading the New Testament" is a commentary series that aims to present cutting-edge research in popular form that is accessible to upper-level undergraduates, seminarians, seminary educated pastors, and educated laypeople, as well as to graduate students and professors. The volumes in this series do not follow the word-by-word, phrase-by-phrase, verse-by-verse method of traditional commentaries. Rather they are concerned to understand large thought units and their relationship to an author's thought as a whole. The focus is on a close reading of the final form of the text. The aim is to make one feel at home in the biblical text itself. The approach of these volumes involves a concern both for *how* an author communicates and *what* the religious point of the text is. Care is taken to relate both the *how* and the *what* of the text to its milieu: Christian (New Testament and noncanonical), Jewish (scriptural and postbiblical), and Greco-Roman. This enables both the communication strategies and the religious message of the text to be clarified over against a range of historical and cultural possibilities. Moreover, a section of commentary on a large thought unit will often contain a brief excursus on some topic raised by the material in the unit, sometimes sketching Old Testament, postbiblical Jewish, Greco-Roman, New Testament, and noncanonical Christian views on the subject. Throughout, the basic concern is to treat the New Testament texts as religious documents whose religious message needs to be set forth with compelling clarity. All other concerns are subordinated to this. It is the hope of all participants in this project that our efforts at exposition will enable the New Testament to be understood better and communicated more competently.

—*Charles H. Talbert*,
General Editor

Philemon

Philemon: The Transforming Power of the Gospel

In the century after Paul's death, the letters associated with his ministry were collected, published, and circulated among his (and other) churches. There appear to have been two basic collections, "Paul's Letters to Churches" (which sometimes included Hebrews) and "Paul's Letters to Individuals," the focus of this commentary. As we will see, "Letters to Individuals" is something of a misnomer; the addressees were church leaders, but the congregations were included in the message, and they were meant to overhear the communication. The letters were personal, but not private.

As with the larger collection of Paul's letters to churches, this smaller collection was arranged primarily in order of length rather than chronology. Thus the letter to Titus follows the letters to Timothy in this collection, even though it logically precedes them. Likewise, Philemon—which certainly was written before the Pastoral Epistles (as the letters to Titus and Timothy are collectively known)—was placed at the end of the collection because of its brevity.

In this commentary, rather than following canonical order, we have treated Paul's letters to individuals in their logical order (which we regard as the chronological order), with Philemon coming first. Next, we have treated the letters to Titus and Timothy in the order of the story they presuppose: Titus, 1 Timothy, 2 Timothy. Below we explain our reasons for this reordering of the Pastorals. The commentary on Philemon is meant to stand on its own. The commentaries on the letters to Timothy and Titus stand together as a unified treatment of these three separate but interrelated documents.

Introduction to Philemon

Philemon is often overlooked. It is the shortest of Paul's letters, containing only 335 words in the Greek text, spread over some 25 verses. Due to its brevity, it resides at the end of the Pauline corpus. The story it tells is simple and straightforward: Philemon, a wealthy man from Colossae, became a Christian due to the missionary preaching of the Apostle Paul. After Paul continued on his travels, one of Philemon's slaves, Onesimus, stole money from Philemon and escaped. In his flight, Onesimus traveled to Rome where—it just so happened—Paul himself had been imprisoned for his missionary work. From his house arrest, Paul won Onesimus to Christ. After Onesimus's conversion, he worked for a brief time with Paul. Then Paul, expecting to be released from prison, sent Onesimus back to Colossae, to his master Philemon, along with a letter. In this letter, Paul makes three simple requests. First, he asks Philemon not to punish Onesimus for his theft; Paul had grown quite fond of the lad. Second, Paul asks that Philemon release Onesimus, so that the young man can return to Rome and help Paul with his work. Third, Paul informs Philemon that he will visit Philemon in Colossae soon, and requests that Philemon prepare a place for him to stay.

Prima facie, this letter says little of ethical or theological consequence to modern readers. How can the story of an escaped slave returned to his master hold any meaning for believers today? Indeed, its perceived slightness has resulted in sore neglect by the academy (until recently), the pulpit (except in the period leading up to the American Civil War), and the pew. Too often, Philemon has been seen as little more than an irrelevant, non-theological, canonical interloper.

And yet, Philemon has received increasing attention of late, so much so that one scholar suggests that the letter "is receiving more attention today than at any time in the history of biblical interpretation, with the possible exception of the antebellum abolitionist era in the United States" (Osiek 2000, 125; Still 2005). Indeed, in Philemon we encounter a practical working out of Paul's foundational theological ideas (grace, faith, atonement, reconciliation, freedom in Christ, new creation, and the ethical life that stems from these). Philemon is no less than a case study of the implications of Paul's gospel. Further, this small, oft-neglected letter is perhaps the most subversive and practically theological document in the entire New Testament!

Authorship

The Pauline authorship of Philemon has never been seriously questioned. In the mid-second century CE, Marcion regarded it as Pauline and included it in his "canon" (Tertullian, *Marc.* 5.21; Origen, *Hom. Jer.* 19; *Comm. Matt* 33–34). The Muratorian Fragment (late second or early third century CE) states that Paul wrote the letter to Philemon "out of affection and love," and indicates that the letter was esteemed by the church "for its regulation of ecclesiastical discipline" (Metzger 1997, 305–307). Eusebius lists this letter among the "undisputed" authoritative writings (*Hist. Eccl.* 3.25). New Testament critics have long agreed that the style and vocabulary are thoroughly Pauline. Indeed, it would be difficult to posit a plausible historical or theological context in which an imitator would compose such a document in Paul's name (Dunn 1996, 299–300).

The Letter's Occasion
Slavery in the first century

Our attempts to understand the letter must begin with an understanding of slavery in the first-century Roman world. Thus a brief overview is necessary.

Slavery was an accepted practice in the Roman world. The economy of that predominantly agrarian society depended on the institution of slavery, and few could imagine a world without it. The Stoic philosophers Seneca (c. 4 BCE–CE 65) and Epictetus (c. CE 60–140) denounced slavery, but few voices were raised in protest. Slave revolts aimed at the reform of the institution rather than its abolition (Harrill 2005; Harrill 2003, 575–607).

Roman slavery differed in many ways from the slavery of the American antebellum South. The distinctive nature of Roman slavery can be summarized as follows:

1. Slavery was not based on race or ethnicity.
2. Slavery was an economic issue, not a moral one. Simply put, society "never questioned the morality of enslaving fellow humans . . ." (Harrill 2005, 585).
3. Slaves were legally property, not persons. As far back as Aristotle, slaves were considered property with souls (*Politics* 2.1) and "living tools" (*Eth. Nic.* 8.11).
4. The law allowed owners to mistreat, even kill, their slaves without repercussion.
5. Roman law allowed for slaves to own property such as land, money—and even other slaves!
6. Roman law allowed for the *manumission* of a slave. By means of a legal fiction involving a third party (usually some sort of priest), a slave could buy his or her freedom. Manumission required the owner's consent. Once manumitted, a slave became a client of the former owner and could become a Roman citizen (Harrill 1995).
7. Many slaves were freed by their masters before their thirtieth birthdays (Wiedemann 1981, 51).

8. Slaves could work at a number of jobs and tasks, depending on their skills and abilities or the reason for their enslavement. They might be condemned to the Roman mines or the rowing galleys of Roman ships. Or they might be given positions managing lands and properties, or even a high position in government. Still, "[a]lthough there were some opportunities for high status or resistance for a select group of the most resourceful and fortunate slaves, most slaves lived and died under a brutal system that never questioned the morality of enslaving fellow humans and had no abolitionist movement" (Harrill 2003, 585).
9. A runaway slave was given the status "*fugitivus.*" Runaways were subject to legal action and punishment. The owner of a *fugitivus* could take out a warrant for the slave's arrest. A letter from 298 CE illustrates this well:

> I commission you by this writ to journey to the famous city of Alexandria and search for my slave, by name . . . about 35 years old, known to you. When you have found him you shall place him in custody with authority to shut him up and whip him, and to lay a complaint before the proper authorities against any persons who have harbored him, with a demand for satisfaction. (POxy 14.1643)

Upon capture, these slaves might be resold to harsher masters. They could also be punished by brutal flogging, branding, mutilation, being made to wear an iron collar engraved with the name and address of the owner and the command "Catch me, for I have fled my master," being sold to work on farms or galleys or in the mines, being thrown to the wild beasts in the arena to satisfy the bloodlust of the populace, or even crucifixion or other means of torment and execution (Garland 1998, 327; Bellen 1971, 17–31; POxy 14.164). Further, "bounty hunters" traded in runaway slaves. These might resell the slave for profit or (if properly bribed) even help them gain their freedom.

There were strict laws against harboring runaway slaves (Watson 1987, 49–60). *The Digest of Justinian* states, "Anyone who has hidden a runaway slave is guilty of theft" (11.4.1). However, the Senate decreed that if the runaway were brought forward within twenty days, the person would be free of guilt. Runaways were to be brought forward publicly and handed over to the authorities. The authorities then took responsibility for guarding the captured slave, usually in chains (Garland 1998, 299 n. 23; Watson 1987, 49–60).

But what of the slave owner? Modern readers may have trouble appreciating the difficulties that Philemon faced in this situation. His circumstances are more complex than they first appear to be, and Paul's requests complicate matters further. These are among the issues Philemon faces:

Honor/Shame Issues: On the one hand, Philemon faced the possibility of being shamed in the eyes of his social and economic peers. The escape of a slave might indicate that either he was unable to control his slaves or that he was such a brutal master that escape seemed the only hope. In either case, Philemon would certainly lose face.

On the other hand, Philemon also faced being shamed before his church. Paul's call to welcome Onesimus back "as more than a slave, a beloved brother" was not only a call for a countercultural decision. It was also a call that the whole church "overheard," made public by the reading of the letter. If Philemon accepted Paul's invitation to do something socially unacceptable—treating Onesimus as a brother and releasing him to return to Paul's side—he would lose face among his social class. On the other hand, if he rejected Paul's forceful "request," he would lose face in the eyes of his church. Philemon faced a clear choice between being shamed in the eyes of the world and honored among his fellow Christians, or maintaining his honor before the world at large and being shamed before the church and his dear friend and father in the faith.

Socioeconomic Issues: Philemon had already suffered economic consequences from Onesimus's absence. He had lost the income that Onesimus would have generated by his work. Philemon would likely have had to buy (or rent) another slave to take Onesimus's place. Philemon may also have incurred the cost of bounty hunters, if he chose to send such to find Onesimus and bring him back. Philemon certainly faced the cost of whatever Onesimus stole from him. Finally, Onesimus's successful escape could have been interpreted by Philemon's other slaves as a sign of their master's weakness. This would have encouraged other slaves to make similar attempts at escape. Thus Onesimus's escape presented Philemon with a clear potential for economic trouble, even disaster. Further, in a social structure where the number of slaves one owned determined one's place on the socioeconomic ladder, the loss of even one slave could damage Philemon's social standing.

In the light of these factors, Paul's request for Philemon to accept and release Onesimus becomes much more complex than it first appears. Truly, Philemon is being asked to count the cost of discipleship!

Occasion of the letter: challenges to the traditional view

We can summarize the traditional understanding of the letter's occasion as follows:

- Onesimus is a runaway slave, who stole from his master (v. 18);
- While on the run, Onesimus fled to Rome where he met with Paul;
- This meeting was unintentional, a coincidence or "divine appointment";
- Paul's request, that Philemon receive Onesimus back "no longer as a slave but more than a slave, as a beloved brother" (v. 16), is motivated by the real possibility that Philemon might treat Onesimus harshly, perhaps even refusing to accept his conversion to Christianity (Nordling 1991, 87–119; cf. Garland 1998, 300).

This traditional view has been challenged by several alternative hypotheses:

1. **The dispatched slave hypothesis**: By this reading, Onesimus was not a runaway slave. Instead, Philemon (or Archippus) sent him to Paul on behalf of the Colossian church, just as the Philippian church sent Epaphroditus in a similar situation (Phil 4:10) (Knox 1935; Winter 1987, 1–15). This view provides a plausible explanation for how Onesimus left Philemon and came to meet Paul. However, this hypothesis fails to take seriously Paul's obvious concern that Onesimus may not be welcomed back. It does not explain the possible necessity of Paul "commanding" that Onesimus be received (v. 8), nor does it fit with Onesimus's debt to Philemon (v. 18), or Paul's statement to the effect that Onesimus had previously been "useless" to Philemon (v. 11). As Barclay notes,

> Indeed, the extraordinarily tactful approach that Paul adopts throughout this letter is a clear indication that he recognizes that he is dealing with a delicate situation in which Philemon could well react awkwardly. . . . It is almost inconceivable that Paul should mention such negative details concerning his protégé unless they were a major obstacle in the relationship between Philemon and Onesimus. (Barclay 1991, 164; cf. Artz-Grabner 2001, 589–614)

To salvage this hypothesis, one might suggest that Onesimus had squandered financial aid that he had been sent to deliver to Paul. But why would such a mission be entrusted to a non-Christian slave, who previously had only proven himself to be "useless" to his master?

2. **The *amicus domini* hypothesis**: By this reading, Onesimus was neither a runaway slave nor an envoy sent by Philemon. He rather sought Paul on his own initiative, in fear of his master. His purpose was to ask Paul to play the role of an *amicus domini* ("friend of the master"), thereby to advocate on his (Onesimus's) behalf with Philemon. *The Digest of Justinian*

records the first-century judgment of Proculus that a slave is not considered a fugitive if he flees to a friend of his master for the purpose of asking the friend to intercede on the slave's behalf with the master. This might happen, for example, in cases where a slave was to be punished for something beyond his/her control, or an impending punishment did not fit the crime (21.1.17.4). Indeed, "A slave who takes off to a friend of his master to seek intercession is not a fugitive . . . for flight requires not only the intention but the act of flight" (21.1.43.1; Lampe 1985, 135–37). A clear example of someone acting as *amicus domini* is found in Pliny's letter to Sabinianus (*Letters* 9.4). Here, Pliny follows the rhetorical conventions in regard to *deprecatio,* a plea for mercy.

This hypothesis has the advantage of providing a plausible explanation for Onesimus's meeting with Paul: the meeting was *not* accidental; Onesimus sought Paul and asked him to speak as his (Onesimus's) advocate, perhaps because Philemon was considering punishing his slave for some accident that cost Philemon financially. However, Paul in Philemon does not follow the conventions of *deprecatio,* nor is there any mention of Onesimus's repentance. The two letters are different in both rhetorical tone and strategy.

3. The hypothesis that Onesimus was not a slave but Philemon's estranged younger brother. He sought Paul to arbitrate a family dispute. "Slave" was merely a metaphor for one who was socially dead, who had "no formal enforceable blood ties." Paul writes on the younger brother's behalf, employing familial vocabulary to effect familial reconciliation (Callahan 1993, 357–74; Callahan 1997).

4. The roaming slave (*erro*) hypothesis (Artz-Grabner 2003; Artz-Grabner 2004, 131–43). Philemon was not a runaway slave, but a roaming slave. This suggestion splits semantic hairs, making much of a supposed distinction between types of slaves. As Harrill notes, "This interpretation . . . suffers the methodological mistake of making monolithic claims about Roman slave law and of relying on law exclusively for one's reconstruction of ancient slavery. . . . The distinction between a runaway *fugitivus* and an intercession-seeking *erro* exists only in the jurists" (Harrill 2003, 590).

No view is without its problems. Because it is least problematic, we follow the traditional reading in this commentary.

A brief aside: Paul's attitude toward slavery seems equivocal to many modern readers. The often-asked question is, "Why doesn't Paul just come right out and condemn slavery, and fight aggressively against the system?" In the end, Paul does not attempt sweeping social reforms. Instead, he attacks slavery in "the one place where he could effectively elicit a change, the church. He did so in this letter to Philemon" (Van Dyke 1998, 393; cf. Witherington 2002, 34).

The Nature and Purpose of the Letter

As described above, Paul is sending Onesimus back to his master, and writes to "appeal" that "his child Onesimus" (v. 10), once "useless" but now "useful" (v. 11), be received by Philemon "as you would welcome me" (v. 17). Paul requests further, "Prepare a guest room for me, for I am hoping through your prayers to be restored to you soon" (v. 22).

A careful examination of the language and rhetorical strategy of the letter reveals that, beneath the surface of the letter, there is more going on than first appears. Particularly at issue is the extent of Paul's request with regard to Onesimus: Does Paul want Philemon merely to welcome Onesimus back into his (Philemon's) household? Or does Paul also want Philemon to release the returned Onesimus, giving him freedom to come back and work at Paul's side? If Paul does desire for Onesimus to be sent to join him in Rome, is he asking that Onesimus be sent as a slave on loan, or as a freedman (Taylor 1996, 271)? Awareness of the rhetorical shape of the letter, to which we now turn, may illuminate these issues.

Paul's Rhetoric in Philemon

Paul's world was awash in Graeco-Roman rhetorical conventions and strategies. Just as we make use of the rhetorical conventions and strategies that pervade our lives without even being aware of what we're doing, so Paul would have made use of the rhetorical strategies of his day. He would have been immersed in them and used them both consciously and unconsciously.

As his letters clearly show, Paul was a highly educated citizen of his world. We should not, therefore, be surprised to find evidence of rhetorical training in Paul's letters; in fact, it would be shocking if we did not find such evidence. Rhetoric was the first subject in his education, the foundation on which all other learning was built. Not surprisingly, the conventions and strategies for persuasive speech made their way into written communications as well, becoming literary conventions. These literary strategies then were further developed, so as to enable writers to communicate more effectively.

As we read Philemon, we will encounter a number of rhetorical features. Paul did not need a rhetorical handbook at his side to use these strategies. He may not have been deliberately constructing them. But in his efforts to communicate and persuade, he made use of devices familiar to him. An awareness of these devices can assist us in our efforts to understand what Paul was trying to accomplish. Our survey begins with the overall rhetorical strategy of the letter.

Rhetorical Structure. In his *Rhetoric*, which became the foundation for all subsequent Graeco-Roman rhetoric, Aristotle states that discourses should have four parts: introduction (Lat. *exordium*), presentation (*propositio*), proof (*probatio*), and epilogue (*peroratio*) (3.13). In the *exordium*, the author/speaker seeks to focus the hearer's attention and gain their goodwill. In the *propositio*, the purpose is to present the thesis. In the *probatio*, the author/speaker presents his case employing ethos, pathos, and logos. In the *peroratio*, the author/speaker recapitulates the argument and appeals strongly to the audience's emotions.

Since Paul's letter to Philemon is essentially an oral document, written to be read aloud, we should not be surprised that it follows this structure quite closely:

- *Exordium* (vv. 4-7)
- *Propositio* (vv. 8-11)
- *Probatio* (vv. 12-16)
- *Peroratio* (vv. 17-21)

To this structure, Paul adds a proper epistolary salutation (vv. 1-3), travel plans (v. 22), and final greetings and benediction (v. 23).

Deliberative Rhetoric. Aristotle divided rhetoric into three types: deliberative, forensic, and demonstrative. Deliberative rhetoric urges the audience to adopt or reject some future action. The method is persuasion or dissuasion (*Rhetoric* 1.2.3; cf. Quintilian, *Instituio Oratoria* 3.8.6). In Philemon, Paul employs deliberative rhetoric in his attempt to persuade Philemon to take a particular course of action.

According to Aristotle there are three basic methods of persuasion: ethos, logos, and pathos. Ethos is the establishment of the character of the speaker, his or her credibility and honesty. Logos is the use of reason to develop one's argument. Pathos is the appeal to the emotions of the hearers. Paul employs all three of these methods in his effort to persuade Philemon to do the "good" thing. He works to establish ethos throughout the letter, with his self-description "prisoner of Christ Jesus," his allusion to being Philemon's elder ("an old man"), his decision to appeal rather than to command, his decision not to keep Onesimus without Philemon's consent, his willingness to assume Onesimus's debt, and his confidence in Philemon.

Likewise, Paul works to create pathos by allusions to his imprisonment, his reference to himself as "an old man," his use of emotive language like "heart" and "child," and his allusion to Philemon's debt to him! And he creates logos by the way he appeals to two primary motivations for Philemon to act: advantage ("How will this action be to Philemon's advantage?") and honor ("How will this action bring Philemon honor?") Paul employs both in this letter. If Philemon agrees to Paul's request, then Onesimus will be useful both to him (Philemon) and to Paul. This is a double advantage, because it allows Philemon to help Paul while helping himself. Further, Philemon can at the same time gain honor for himself in the eyes of those who really matter.

Insinuatio. This approach to persuasion involves building one's case gradually and indirectly, avoiding inflammatory or offensive language so as to win a hearing without offending or angering the hearer/reader. In this way, the writer/speaker lays a foundation for making a direct appeal, once sufficient ethos and pathos have been created. According to Cicero,

> We shall derive our greatest supply of openings designed either to conciliate or stimulate the judge from topics contained in the case that are calculated to produce emotions . . . though it will not be proper to develop these fully at the start, but only to give a slight preliminary nudge to the judge, from topics contained in the case that are calculated to produce emotions. (Cicero, *De Oratore* 2.79.324)

In Philemon, Paul appears to be using this approach. He begins to establish his ethos in his self-description (v. 1), gives thanks and praise for Philemon (vv. 4-7), builds an indirect case in vv. 8-14 while also building up the ethos and pathos, makes his appeal in vv. 15-16, then reiterates it in even stronger terms in vv. 17-22. Notice that Onesimus's name is not mentioned until v. 10, almost halfway through the letter!

Garland sums up the linguistic evidence for *insinuatio* as follows:

- Paul uses a pun to describe Onesimus (a name that means "useful") as being formerly "useless" (v. 11).
- Paul does not baldly state that Onesimus ran away, but instead describes his absence with a passive voice, suggesting that God's hand was involved: "He was separated from you for a little while" (v. 15).
- Paul broaches the subject of Onesimus's misdeeds with a conditional sentence, "If he has done you wrong or owes you anything" (v. 18).

- Paul does not explicitly tell Philemon to forgive his slave, but strongly implies that Philemon must take this course of action. Rather than ordering Philemon to do this or that, Paul wants Philemon to discover the appropriate path for himself (Garland 1998, 300–301).

In our context, we might think that Paul as an apostle should simply use his apostolic authority to command Philemon's actions. As noted above, the complexities of the situation require that Paul instead use a delicate, conciliatory approach, a polite strategy that lessens the cost to Philemon of appropriate action (Wilson 1992, 107–19).

Witherington suggests that Philemon also demonstrates characteristics of Asiatic rhetoric, a development of the highly ornamental style cultivated by Isocrates (436–336 BCE). Asiatic rhetoric was noted for its emotionalism, affectation, and redundancy:

> The styles of Asiatic oratory are two, one epigrammatic and pointed full of fine ideas which are not so weighty and serious as neat and graceful, the other with not so many sententious ideas, but voluble and hurried in its flow of language, and marked by an ornamented and elegant diction. (Cicero, *Brutus* 95.325)

Philemon displays elements of this style: redundancy (vv. 10, 16), ornamentation through the wordplay on Onesimus's name in vv. 11 and 20, and pathos and emotion (v. 9). Witherington notes, "This may be a short document but it is a heart-wrenching plea for the freedom of Onesimus ('he is my very heart,' v. 12), using not so subtle attempts at arm-twisting. Philemon is a miniature rhetorical masterpiece in an Asiatic vein" (Witherington 2002, 6).

Paul makes use of several other rhetorical techniques in the letter:

Repetition. Repetition is a device often used in persuasive speech/writing to call attention to key themes and/or emphases. Paul uses this technique frequently in his letter to Philemon. For example, part of the letter's argument is that all Christians are equal in Christ. In this vein, Paul uses the word "brother" four times and scatters the occurrences throughout the letter. In v. 1, Paul refers to Timothy as "the brother." In vv. 7 and 20, Paul refers to Philemon as his "brother." In v. 16 Paul asks Philemon to receive Onesimus as "a beloved brother." The point: as Paul and Philemon and Timothy are brothers, so now Onesimus is a brother to Philemon, and he must be received as such. A second example is Paul's use of the word "heart." It appears first in v. 7 where Paul praises Philemon because "the hearts of the saints have been refreshed through you." It appears next in v. 12 when Paul describes Onesimus as "my own heart."

The final appearance is in v. 20 when Paul asks Philemon to "refresh my heart." These appearances come at the beginning (v. 7), middle (v. 12), and end (v. 20) of the letter. They arguably provide a kind of internal structure. Paul develops the idea across the occurrences, moving from praise of Philemon (v. 7) to request of Philemon (v. 20). The middle appearance identifies Paul's "heart." Both hearers and readers of this short letter would catch this motif.

A third example may be seen in the repetition of Paul's name. Hellenistic letter-writers seldom mentioned their own names after the epistolary opening. Paul, however, features his own name three times in this short missive. As expected, we find it in the salutation (v. 1). However, we find it repeated in v. 9 and a third time in v. 19. As with the references to "heart," the placement of the repeats is interesting: beginning (v. 1), middle (v. 9), and end (v. 19). This repetition clearly demonstrates the urgency of the request in Paul's mind, something hearers/readers would not have missed.

A fourth example is Paul's repetition of the "refreshment" motif in vv. 7 and 20. This motif frames the entire letter. In the introduction, Paul praises Philemon for having "refreshed" the hearts of the saints (v. 7). The letter then ends with the request for Philemon to refresh the heart of a particular saint, Paul himself (v. 20).

Inclusio. Another prominent device Paul uses in the letter is *inclusio*. Notice the placement of the appearances of "brother" in the letter. In v. 1, Paul introduces the term ("Timothy, our brother"). In vv. 7 and 20 he attaches the term to Philemon. In between these two references to Philemon, Paul attaches "brother" to Onesimus. This is a loose example of *inclusio*, or bracketing. *Inclusio* is a device in which a "sandwich" is created by placing story within story or idea within idea, resulting in the following structure:

A
   B
A'

The references to "brother" within the body of Philemon appear as follows:

A. Brother Philemon (v. 7)
    B. Brother Onesimus (v. 16)
A'. Brother Philemon (v. 20)

The reference to brother Onesimus is surrounded by references to brother Philemon; likewise, Paul hopes Philemon's love will surround Onesimus as a "beloved brother."

We can see the same pattern when we look at the appearances of "heart":

A. Philemon refreshed the "hearts" of the saints (v. 7)
    B. "my heart" (Onesimus) (v. 12)
A'. Philemon, "refresh my heart" (v. 20)

On a more implicit level, Paul weaves a similar pattern with his references to obedience. He introduces this motif with the description of Archippus as a "fellow soldier" in v. 2 (soldiers obey those who are in authority over them). Paul brings the motif to the foreground in v. 8, with references to "commanding" and "duty." Paul closes the body of the letter with a final reference in v. 21, when he expresses his confidence in Philemon's "obedience." Once again we see the now-familiar pattern: this motif is found at the beginning (v. 2), middle (v. 8), and end (v. 21) of the letter. Again, we see a discernable progression to the occurrences: Archippus is an obedient "fellow soldier," Philemon too has his "duty" to do, and Paul is confident of his obedience. From beginning to end, there is an underlying call to "obedience."

A. Archippus, the obedient solder
    B. your "duty"
A'. Philemon, the (presumably) obedient soldier

Witherington summarizes his survey of Paul's rhetoric in Philemon:

> What we see in this letter is the limits to which Paul was prepared to go rhetorically to achieve an important aim. While of course he was not prepared to resort to dishonesty or trickery, nor would he conjure up feigned emotions, he was prepared to use all the normal rhetorical conventions, pulling out all the stops, including combining references to persuasion and command and playing the emotion card repeatedly, to give a discourse the necessary weight to achieve its goals. If this makes us uncomfortable because it seems manipulative by modern standards, it is because we do not live in the kind of social and rhetorical environment

Paul did, where this kind of discourse was not only commonplace but actually relished and applauded. And where power inequities in relationships and social inequities such as slavery presented the orator with situations requiring very strident and bold rhetoric to accomplish some purposes. (Witherington 2002, 87)

Likewise Dunn:

> Paul's rhetoric here, as elsewhere, should not be denigrated as manipulative or contrived. It is typical of a leader with a strong personality that he should sincerely want to encourage and leave it open to his audience to respond of their own free will, while at the same time being so convinced of the rightness of his own opinion that he naturally seeks to persuade them to share it. (Dunn 1996, 323)

Provenance

From what location is Paul writing to Philemon? He clearly writes from prison. Twice he refers to himself "a prisoner of Jesus Christ" (vv. 1, 9). He refers to Epaphras as his "fellow prisoner" (v. 23) and speaks twice of his "imprisonment" (vv. 10, 13). Furthermore, he writes in v. 19 that Onesimus was "begotten in chains" (i.e., Onesimus's conversion occurred while Paul was imprisoned). The description of his imprisonment in the letter suggests the kind of house arrest depicted in Acts 28:30. In such a setting, Paul was free to have visitors and send emissaries. He had both the financial resources and the freedom to engage a scribe to write for him, as the letter demonstrates (on the nature of Paul's imprisonments, see Rapske 1994). At the same time, his request for Philemon "to prepare a guest room" for him (v. 22) suggests that he looked forward to an imminent release.

The location of Paul's imprisonment, however, is not clear. The New Testament refers to three Pauline imprisonments: Philippi (Acts 16:16-40; this imprisonment seems too brief to serve as the occasion for writing this letter), Caesarea Maritima (Acts 23:23–26:30), and Rome (Acts 28:16-31). Second Corinthians 11:23 suggests that there were other imprisonments, but gives no specifics. This, taken together with Paul's reference to "fighting the wild beasts in Ephesus" (1 Cor 15:32), has led some to suggest an otherwise unknown imprisonment in Ephesus.

Efforts to locate the place of writing have tended to focus on three strands of evidence: the tradition of the early church, the nature of the relationship between the letter to Philemon and the letter to the Colossians, and Colossae's distance from the locations of Paul's imprisonments.

Paul's Letter to Philemon: The Transforming Power of the Gospel

1. Tradition. Tradition has long held that Philemon (along with the other "Prison epistles") was written from Rome. Early subscriptions support this position, and there was near universal agreement on this until the modern era.

2. Evidence of a close relationship between the letter to Philemon and the letter to the Colossians. Both letters are written from prison (Col 4:10, 18; Phlm 1, 9, 10, 13).

    A. In Colossians 4:9, Paul writes that Onesimus accompanied Tychicus, the bearer of Colossians. Paul describes Onesimus as "the faithful and beloved brother"; this is in keeping with Paul's description of him in Philemon. Furthermore, Paul writes that Onesimus is "one of them" (i.e., someone from Colossae). Onesimus perhaps carried the letter to Philemon at the same time that Tychicus carried the letter to Colossae.

    B. Paul describes Archippus as "our fellow soldier" (Phlm 2). In Colossians 4:17, Paul admonishes Archippus (now in Colossae) to "complete the task you have received in the Lord."

    C. Paul refers to Epaphras as one of the Colossians (Col 4:12). He is apparently the founder of the church in Colossae (Col 1:7), but now is Paul's "fellow prisoner in Christ Jesus," who (along with Paul's coworkers) sends his greetings to the Colossian church (Phlm 23).

    D. The same group of coworkers is mentioned in both letters: Mark, Luke, and Aristarchus (Col 4:10, 14; Phlm 23).

    E. Colossians 4:7-9 suggests that the two letters were written and sent together.

3. The distance between Colossae and the locations of Paul's imprisonment. Given that nothing above rules out Paul writing the letters from Rome, the chief argument against Rome as the place of imprisonment and writing is the distance between Colossae and Rome (about 1,300 miles). Is it reasonable to assume that, upon escaping from his master, Onesimus would have traveled all the way to Rome? Would Paul in Rome have had around him so many residents of Colossae? The arguments run as follows:

    1) Arguments in favor of Rome as the place of imprisonment and writing (the classic presentation of this view is Dodd 1953, 95):

        A. We know that Paul was imprisoned in Rome (Acts 28).

        B. The early tradition placing the writing of these letters in Rome is strong and nearly uncontested.

        C. The distance between Rome and Colossae was never an issue to those who ascribed the letter to Paul in Rome. Apparently, our modern concerns about distance did not trouble those who lived

much closer to the time of writing, who knew firsthand the problems and perils of travel in the ancient world.
   D. As a runaway slave, Onesimus would likely have wanted to get as far away from Colossae, Philemon, and capture as possible. Rome thus likely would have been a safer haven than nearby Ephesus. As the "slave capital" of the empire, Rome was overrun with slaves. It thus provided a perfect place for Onesimus to get lost in the masses, especially since slaves were not distinguishable by race, dress, or occupation. Indeed, Justinian's *Digest* tells of a runaway slave who won election as a magistrate of Rome before being found out (1.14.3)! In Rome, Onesimus could have easily "disappeared" from history had he not met Paul.
2) Arguments in favor of Caesarea Maritima as the place of imprisonment and writing:
   A. We know that Paul was imprisoned there (Acts 23:23–26:30).
   B. Assuming the accuracy of the Acts account, Paul had every hope of being released up until the point where he found it necessary to appeal to Caesar (Acts 25:10).
   C. In Romans 15:22-29, Paul indicates that Rome and the West are his eventual goal. Within the framework of those plans, a visit to Colossae fits nicely into a journey from Caesarea to Rome.
   D. However, if the distance from Colossae is the issue, Caesarea offers no advantages over Rome, being about as far from Colossae as Rome.
3) Arguments in favor of Ephesus as the place of imprisonment and writing (the classic presentation of this view is Duncan 1929, 72–73):
   A. While the New Testament does not explicitly mention any Ephesian imprisonment, passages such as 1 Corinthians 15:32 and 2 Corinthians 1:8-9; 6:5; and 11:23-24 suggest such a possibility.
   B. In his prologue to Colossians, Marcion (c. 150) writes, "the apostle, already in chains, writes to them from Ephesus" (O'Brien 1982, lii).
   C. Ephesus is 100 miles from Colossae. By contrast, Rome is 1,300 miles away, requiring a costlier and riskier journey.
   D. Due to its proximity to Colossae, the presence of so many Colossians with Paul makes great sense if he is imprisoned in Ephesus.

E. Ephesus also makes more sense than Rome due to its proximity, if one accepts the view that Onesimus has sought Paul to mediate between himself and Philemon.

F. If Paul is writing from Ephesus anticipating imminent release, and planning a trip to Colossae to visit Philemon, he could easily continue on to Rome and then to Spain. However, if he is writing from Rome, a trip back east to visit Philemon puts his dream of Rome and Spain on indefinite hold. Similarly, Romans 15:22-29 contains no indication of such a detour to Colossae in Asia Minor.

Weighing the arguments

The case for a Caesarean provenance doesn't really solve any problems, and thus seems unnecessary. The arguments for Ephesus as the place of imprisonment and writing present an interesting option. However, the argument for an Ephesian imprisonment must also explain why the Acts narrative portrays a positive relationship between Paul and those in authority in Ephesus. Acts 19:31 indicates that some of the provincial officials (including the Asiarchs) "were friendly to him" and in the midst of the riot, the town clerk even defended him (Acts 19:35-40)!

In the end, nothing demands that the traditional view of Roman provenance be abandoned. This is the view we adopt in this commentary.

Date

The dating of Philemon (and Colossians) depends on one's decision with regard to provenance. If the letters were written from Ephesus, they likely were written in the mid-50s, during Paul's extended ministry there on his third missionary journey. If the letters were written from Rome, they must have been written during the early to mid 60s, after Paul's arrival there as an appellant to Caesar (Acts 25:10-12; 26:32; 28:16, 30-31).

Salutation (Prescript and Blessing): Affecting a Position of Weakness (vv. 1-3)

The letter begins, as do all Pauline letters, with a standard first-century letter opening: "sender to recipient, greeting." The senders are Paul and Timothy (v. 1). Paul describes himself as "a prisoner of Christ Jesus." With this self-description, Paul emphasizes four things. First, he announces that his imprisonment is on account of his commitment to and service of Christ Jesus. He is being punished for his faithfulness to the call of Christ Jesus in his life. The designation "prisoner" thus has a double meaning: Paul is now physically locked up because of Jesus, but in a larger sense he has been Christ's prisoner since his encounter with the risen Jesus on the Damascus Road (see 2 Cor 2:14-17; Phil 3:12-13) (Wansick 1996; Cassidy 2001).

Second, Paul introduces the theme of his imprisonment. He alludes to this theme again in vv. 9, 10, 13, 22, and 23. Paul does not disclose the exact location of his imprisonment (see the discussion above). Nor does he describe the exact nature of his imprisonment, but the fact that he is free to send and receive letters and visitors suggests a house arrest similar to that described in Acts 28:16, 30-31. As a Roman citizen (Acts 16:38; 22:25-29), Paul had the right to a liberal detention (*custodia libera*) (Rapske 1994). Still, the image of his dear friend and "father" in the faith (v. 19) in chains would no doubt have had a powerful emotional impact on Philemon. This self-descriptor contributes to both the ethos and pathos of the letter. As Witherington points out, "Paul's rhetorical aims have dictated this way of beginning which immediately generates emotion and concern for him" (Witherington 2002, 54; cf. Dunn 1996, 311).

Third, Paul describes himself as a "prisoner of Christ Jesus" rather than "an apostle of Christ Jesus." By this difference, Paul deliberately affects a stance of weakness rather than strength *vis-a-vis* Philemon. He does not posture himself as an apostle, with the accompanying apostolic authority (cf. Rom 1:1; 1 Cor 1:1; 2 Cor 1:1; Gal 1:1; Eph 1:1; Col 1:1; 1 Tim 1:1; 2 Tim 1:1; Titus 1:1). Paul underscores his apostolic authority in every other letter opening, with the exceptions of Philippians (where the sole appellation is "servant") and 1 and 2 Thessalonians (which contain no self-descriptions). Here, Paul begins his appeal to Philemon on a basis other than his apostleship. He temporarily lays aside any power that by right may have been his. Luther has it right: "He empties himself of his rights to compel Philemon also to waive his rights" (Luther, 35.390). The implications of this choice become clear as the letter progresses.

Fourth, by emphasizing his own status as a prisoner, Paul places himself in social solidarity with Onesimus. Both knew social alienation and both knew the experience of having been shackled (Wilson 1992, 113).

Paul's co-sender is Timothy. This is also the case in Philippians 1:1; Colossians 1:1; 1 Thessalonians 1:1; and 2 Thessalonians 1:1. Elsewhere, Paul describes Timothy as a trusted coworker (Phil 2:19-24; 1 Cor 4:27). According to 1 and 2 Timothy, Paul entrusted Timothy with authority over his churches, first to deal with problems in Ephesus and then to carry on Paul's work after Paul's martyrdom. Here Paul simply referred to Timothy as "the brother," a common designation for fellow believers. This term suggests the familial nature of the early Christian community, and such usage may go back to Jesus himself (see Mark 3:31-35; Aasgaard 2004; Frilingos 2000, 91–104). Such familial language will pervade this letter (vv. 7, 10, 16, 20).

Paul does not specify the role that Timothy may have played in the composition of the letter. He may well have contributed to the contents of the letter, or he may have served as Paul's secretary (*amanuensis*). Whatever the case, the fact that Paul acknowledges his presence here indicates that what is being said is not the message of Paul alone. A community stands behind it!

Recipients

Philemon is the primary recipient. We know nothing about Philemon except what can be surmised from this letter. Since Onesimus was from Colossae (Col 4:9), interpreters assume that Philemon also resided in that city. He was apparently a man of some means, for he owned at least one slave (Onesimus). Further, his house was large enough to host a house church (v. 2). Philemon belonged to a group of people scattered over the course of the Pauline missionary travels who hosted house churches: Aquila and Priscilla in Ephesus and Rome (1 Cor 16:19; Rom 16:5); Lydia in Philippi (Acts 16:15); Jason in Thessalonica (Acts 17:5-9); Gaius and Stephanus in Corinth (Rom 16:23; 1 Cor 16:15); and Nympha in Colossae (Col 4:15) (Banks 1994; Branick 1989).

Philemon's house is also large enough to house guests (v. 22). Paul's reference to "a" guest room rather than "the" guest room might indicate multiple guest rooms. Philemon has been an encourager of the "saints" (vv. 5-7). He owes his own soul to Paul (v. 19), a reference to Philemon's conversion to Christ. He is Paul's "fellow worker," together with Mark, Aristarchus, Demas, and Luke (v. 23).

Paul also refers to Philemon as "beloved." This language demonstrates the close relationship between the two while at the same time adding to the creation of pathos. Also note that in v. 16, Paul invites Philemon to accept Onesimus as his "beloved brother." By this language, "Paul lays on the man a hand that is warm and heavy at the same time. Its warmth will be felt when it turns out that love is the main theme of the epistle; its pressure when Paul appeals to Philemon: May he, by receiving Onesimus as a brother, continue and crown the praiseworthy work carried out thus far!" (Barth and Blanke 2000, 253).

Paul describes Apphia as "the sister" (v. 2), a parallel description to that of Timothy ("the brother") in v. 1. Might this be taken to suggest that she was also a fellow worker of Paul's? Might the fact that she receives an appellation separate from Philemon further suggest this possibility? (Cotter 1994, 351) Interestingly, the only other time Paul uses the epithet "sister" in his letters is in reference to Phoebe (Rom 16:12). Of course, the widely held view that Apphia was Philemon's wife still could be true, in any case.

Paul describes Archippus (presumably the same individual addressed in Colossians 4:17) as his "fellow soldier." Elsewhere, this ascription only appears in Philippians 2:25, where Paul applies it to Epaphroditus. Epaphroditus risked his very life in faithful ministry to Paul on behalf of the Philippians; in v. 11, Paul indicates that Onesimus played a similar role in serving him on behalf of Philemon! The ascription "fellow soldier" introduces the language of the military and/or duty motif noted in the introduction above.

The inclusion of "the church in your house" indicates that this letter, while personal, is not private. The whole church was to hear Paul's requests of Philemon in this letter! The implications of this larger audience are huge. Whatever Paul tells Philemon to do will be known by the whole church. Philemon cannot keep this touchy matter private, just between his family and Onesimus. Shame and honor come into play here. If Philemon does not follow Paul's instructions, he will shame himself both at home (his house church) and abroad (with Paul). However, there are further considerations. By this public appeal, Paul "democratizes to some degree the way the Onesimus matter is to be handled if Philemon is not to lose face with his fellow house church members" (Witherington 2002, 55). Paul demands a radical realignment of relationships here, for the house church is the intersection of the natural household and the spiritual household. The whole church, not just Philemon, must accept Onesimus, for if Philemon responds as Paul hopes, Onesimus will be the equal of everyone in the house he once served. Therefore, Paul calls the entire church to ensure that Onesimus is welcomed as a "beloved brother." He not only expects them to hold Philemon accountable, he also calls them to be faithful to the new realities of the gospel.

Paul's standard greeting (v. 3), "grace and peace" (cf. Rom 1:7; 1 Cor 1:3; 2 Cor 1:2; Gal 1:3; Eph 1:2; Phil 1:2) blends the normal Greek epistolary greeting with a standard Jewish salutation. In place of the typical Greek greeting *chairein* (cf. Jas 1:1; Acts 15:23), Paul substitutes *charis* ("grace"). "Peace" is the typical Jewish greeting represented by the Hebrew word *shalom*. And both come "from God our Father and the Lord Jesus Christ." This greeting, which may be built on the priestly benediction of Numbers 6:22-26, is anything but a mere formality. In the twelve carefully chosen words of v. 3, Paul accomplishes five tasks:

First, he introduces the theme of "grace," one of the central ideas of his gospel. "Grace" is God's unmerited favor bestowed on humanity in Jesus Christ (see Rom 3:21-25a; 5:20-21). Both Paul and Philemon have experienced this grace, a grace in which believers live in Christ and by which they must exist for the blessing of others (cf. 2 Cor 8:5-6; Col 4:6). Paul thus reminds Philemon of this central tenet of their faith, preparatory to asking him to extend it to Onesimus. Second, Paul introduces the parallel theme of "peace." Biblically, peace is more than the absence of violence. The Hebrew word *shalom* refers to the wholeness and rest for which God created humanity, which is now available in Jesus Christ (Rom 5:1ff). Like grace, this peace should characterize the Christian's relationships (Gal 5:2; Rom 14:19). This *shalom* does not happen automatically. Jesus called his followers to be "peacemakers" (Matt 5:9, 43-48), to be aggressive in the pursuit of peace. Peter admonished his readers to "seek peace and pursue it" (1 Pet 3:11, quoting Ps 34:14). Paul, in his beautiful summary of the gospel in 2 Corinthians 5:18-19, reminds his readers that, having themselves been reconciled to God, they are called to be "God's ambassadors," agents of reconciliation. In the present letter, Paul offers Philemon an opportunity to put flesh on this ministry of reconciliation.

Third, Paul reminds the recipients that both "grace" and "peace" come from "God our Father." Paul depicts God as "Father" no fewer than thirty-seven times in his letters, alluding to God's parental, providential care. God is both the "Father of our Lord Jesus Christ" (Rom 15:6; 2 Cor 1:3; 11:31) and "our Father," interested and involved in the lives and problems of his children (vv. 15, 22). Fourth, Paul emphasizes the Christocentric nature of the faith by paralleling "God our Father" with "the lord Jesus Christ." Paul mentions Jesus throughout the letter: vv. 1, 3, 6, 8, 9, 16, 20, 23, 25. The fact that he refers to Jesus Christ as *kyrios* ("Lord") is particularly significant in this letter, because of the context of Philemon's relationship with Onesimus. "Lord" here is a loaded term, for it draws a contrast between *kyrios* and *doulos*, "master" and "slave." The implication of "Lord Jesus Christ" is clear: Philemon has a Master who models how he (Philemon) should respond to Onesimus (Fitzmyer 2000, 91).

Fifth, Paul summarizes his gospel in concentrated form. His message is that grace and peace are available to both Jew and Gentile (recall points 1 and 2 above) from God the Father and the Lord Jesus Christ. Paul emphasized the universality of the gospel throughout his ministry: "There is no more Jew or Greek . . . " (Gal 3:28; cf. Col 3:11).

Thanksgiving/*Exordium*: Pointing Back, Pointing Forward (vv. 4-7)

Pauline "thanksgivings" (Rom 1:8-15; 1 Cor 1:4-9; Phil 1:3-11; Col 1:3-8; 1 Thess 1:2-10; 2 Thess 1:3-12; 2 Tim 1:3-7) generally serve a dual purpose. First, Paul uses them to give thanks for the recipients or to offer a prayer on their behalf. Second, Paul uses them to introduce themes from the letter, so that they provide a kind of "table of contents" (not necessarily in a systematic or sequential way). In Philemon, five of the nine themes mentioned in the thanksgiving appear again in the letter: love (vv. 5, 7, 9, 16), Lord/Christ (vv. 5, 6, 16, 20), sharing/partnership (vv. 6, 17), good (vv. 6, 14), and heart/affections (vv. 7, 12, 20) (Mullins 1984, 288–93; Church 1978, 17–33). While Graeco-Roman letters usually contained a thanksgiving or blessing following the greetings, these "previews" of the contents are not characteristic of ancient non-Pauline letters. Thus these Pauline thanksgiving sections are (again) highly rhetorical. Indeed, this thanksgiving serves as an *exordium*, which (according to the standards of Graeco-Roman rhetoric) sought "to establish rapport with the audience, establish the author's ethos, and provide a preview of what is to follow" (Witherington 2002, 58).

Evidence of Paul's understanding of Graeco-Roman rhetoric pervades this section, as it does the letter as a whole. First, in his *Rhetoric*, Aristotle advised that an appeal to the deeper emotions (such as love) created pathos and a receptive frame of mind in the hearer (*Rhet.* 1.2.3). Paul's stirring appeal to the heart and to love (vv. 5, 7) serves to create goodwill and make Philemon more inclined to act as requested (*Rhet.* 2.4–7). Second, Paul employs a *captatio benevolentiae* (another strategy for securing the audience's goodwill), by which he prepares Philemon for the request with regard to Onesimus. He does this by reminding Philemon of his previous generosity toward all the saints (vv. 5, 7). Speaking of this strategy, John Chrysostom says, "nothing so shames us into giving as to bring forward the kindnesses we have bestowed on others" (*Homilia in Philemon* 2.1.7).

These verses parallel the thanksgiving in Paul's letter to the Philippians (Phil 1:3-11) in striking ways. In both cases, remembrance of past benevolence brings thanksgiving and encouragement to Paul. In both cases, Paul sets the stage for further benevolence from the recipients: God is not finished with them yet; their future ministry will yet be more effective (Phlm 6; Phil 1:5-6). In Philemon's case, Paul's prayer is that "the sharing of your faith may promote the knowledge of all the good that is ours in Christ" (v. 6, RSV). The manuscripts are split between the first person ("the good that is ours") and the second person ("the good that is yours"). If the second person is preferred, then (in keeping with the context) the focus here is on Philemon's character and conduct. However, the "you" is not singular but plural, referring to the whole church that meets in Philemon's house and what they may do when committed to sharing the common faith. If the first person ("the good that is ours") is preferred, then the emphasis is the same, but Paul includes himself and others who share the common faith. In either case, Paul is preparing to ask Philemon to treat Onesimus in a way that would make the sharing of his faith "more effective."

Note the parallelism in v. 4:

> your love for all the saints
> your faith toward Jesus Christ.

There is a certain interchangeableness between Christ and his church burned into Paul's psyche, likely from the day on the Damascus Road when Jesus asked, "Saul, Saul, why do you persecute *me?* . . . I am Jesus whom you are persecuting" (Acts 9:4-5). For Paul, faith (faithfulness) and love are the essence of the Christian life, and both are owed to the Lord and to all the saints. Paul underscores this relationship with the chiastic structure in vv. 5-7:

A. Love (v. 5)
    B. Faith (v. 5)
    B'. Faith (v. 6)
A'. Love (v. 7)

Also important is the fact that Paul does not speak of his love "for the saints" but for "*all* the saints" (v. 5). Paul here deliberately reminds Philemon that Christian love is not limited to one or many or even almost all, but is for *all* the saints. Paul is about to present Philemon with an opportunity to demonstrate his acceptance of that truth with regard to Onesimus.

Paul's joy and encouragement stem from his awareness of Philemon's love for all the saints, Philemon's love for him, and the fact that "the hearts of the saints have been refreshed through" Philemon (v. 7). The emphasis here falls on Philemon's refreshment of the saints. Through repetition and the introduction of significant language, Paul moves his case forward. He repeats the reference to Philemon's ministry to "the saints" (twice in sixty-six words) to call Philemon to continue this work. Further, Paul here introduces "heart" language (v. 7; the same term reappears in vv. 12 and 20), which forms a tri-fold frame for the letter. Throughout, the Greek word translated "heart" is *splachna* (lit., "bowels" or "entrails"), a word that refers to the deepest part of a human being. He also introduces references to "refreshment," which will reappear in a significant way in v. 20. Philemon, who has refreshed the "hearts" (the deepest inner being) of the saints in the past, will now have an opportunity to do the same for Paul (if he accepts Onesimus, as Paul requests).

Finally, Paul concludes the thanksgiving by employing familial language for the second time, referring to Philemon as "my brother" (v. 7; cf. v. 1). This term of endearment heightens the sense of *pathos* that Paul works to create in the letter.

Body (vv. 8-22)

Propositio: Paul's Appeal (vv. 8-11)

The *propositio* forms the basic appeal, the main act of persuasion in deliberative rhetoric. Paul follows with the *probatio* (vv. 12-16), in which he supports his appeal, and then a brief but classic *peroratio* (vv. 17-21), in which he summarizes what precedes and makes one final emotional appeal.

Paul begins his plea by referring back to his statements regarding Philemon in vv. 4-7: "For this reason" (v. 8) alludes to Philemon's love "for all the saints," which has already brought joy and encouragement to Paul and refreshment to the saints. Because of these facts, Paul approaches Philemon with an appeal rather than a command.

Some commentators take Paul's language in v. 8 ("bold," "in Christ," "to command," and "duty") to mean that he is waiving his apostolic authority. Lightfoot paraphrases the verse: "My office gives me the authority to dictate thy duty in plain language, but love bids me plead as a suitor" (Lightfoot 1959, 337). Or this could be taken as a veiled threat, by which Paul was saying, "do what I request or I have the authority as an apostle to command you to do it, and may well exercise that authority in Christ!" By this reading, v. 9 becomes but a polite ruse. However, the Greek word for boldness (*parresia*) properly means "free speech." This word originally referred to the democratic right to speak one's opinion openly, candidly, and boldly in the Greek assembly (*ekklesia*, which becomes the word for "church") (cf. Euripides, *Hippolytus* 420–23; Aristotle, *Nichomachean Ethics* 9.2.9; Marrow 1982, 431–46). *Parresia* could also refer to the frank language one might use with a close friend (Plutarch, *Adulat.* 51C). In the New Testament, *parresia* usually means "outspokenness," "courage," or "fearlessness." The word sometimes refers to an unexpected boldness (cf. 2 Cor 3:12; Phil 1:20; Eph 6:19; Acts 4:13). Thus in Christ, Paul has the courage to speak openly, candidly, and boldly to Philemon, to say what needs to be said. He can even "command" (*epitassein*, a strong word, referring to a superior's authority over an inferior) Philemon to do his "duty" in this matter. The "duty" Paul could command is not Philemon's civic duty (which would be punishing Onesimus), but Philemon's duty "in Christ" instead. Philemon would not miss the point of this language. It clearly indicates the gravity of the appeal Paul is about to make. Again, Philemon might even have heard Paul's humble words as a veiled threat.

Paul, perhaps aware of this danger, carefully makes his appeal to Philemon as an equal in Christ rather than treating him as an inferior. Twice he refers to Philemon as a "brother" (vv. 7, 20); Paul also refers to Timothy as "our brother" (i.e., Paul's brother and Philemon's as well); and once he calls Philemon his "partner" (v. 17). Further, Paul states that he will do nothing in this matter without Philemon's consent (v. 14), so if Paul ends up "pulling rank" on Philemon, such is not his first choice of strategies.

Notice also the obvious military language in v. 8, "command" and "duty." It arises from Paul's description of Archippus in v. 2 as a "fellow soldier." Paul applies this same ascription to Epaphroditus in Philippians 2:25, when Paul applauds his sacrificial service. Epaphroditus is Paul's "brother and coworker and fellow soldier." This military motif is a central image for Paul's understanding of his relationship with his coworkers: "fellow soldiers" in the service of their Lord Jesus Christ. Thus, Philemon's "duty" was not to Paul but to Jesus, whose commands were the marching orders for both Philemon and Paul.

Paul refuses to "lord it over" Philemon. He has learned a new kind of leadership from the Lord, whom both he and Philemon serve: "You know that among the Gentiles those whom they recognize as their rulers lord it over them. But it is not so among you; but whoever wishes to become great among you must be your servant, and whoever wishes to be first among you must be slave of all" (Mark 10:42-44). In this vein, Paul begins to make his appeal in v. 9. Speaking to Philemon as a brother, a partner, and a fellow soldier, Paul appeals "on the basis of love" (*dia ten agapēn*). Like all Christian conduct, Philemon's treatment of Onesimus must begin with the love of Christ. Love for a slave was inconceivable in Paul's culture, where slaves were less than human, "living tools," property with souls deservedly consigned to slavery by fate. Runaways deserved nothing but punishment and that punishment might be inhumane. As noted previously, such punishment could range from flogging and branding to death by crucifixion. For Onesimus, the choice of punishments lay solely in Philemon's hands. But by Paul's appeal, "the love of Christ compels" Philemon to follow a different path in his treatment of Onesimus.

Before Paul completes the thought of vv. 8-9a, he begins a new sentence in v. 9b. The way Paul repeats his name in the insertion is striking: this would have captured the audience's attention. The repetition indicates once again that Paul considers this a matter of great importance, and that he is giving himself totally to the coming appeal (v. 10). It reinforces the power of what is to come, all by itself.

Paul further adds to the pathos of his appeal by making two allusions to his own circumstances. First, he refers to his age: Paul is now "an old man." In *On the Creation* 103, Philo (following Hippocrates) lists the seven stages of a man's life, saying that an old man (*presbytes*) is a man aged fifty to fifty-six. Paul's point here goes beyond his specific age, however. It also includes the fact that he is Philemon's elder. In the ancient world, the wisdom of the elders was to be treasured, sought, and deferred to. Paul's remark reminds Philemon of this debt of respect, and echoes the biblical mandate for the younger to "show respect for the elderly and revere God" (Lev 19:32).

Second, Paul alludes to his present imprisoned state. Paul mentions his imprisonment once at the beginning of the letter (v. 1), twice in mid-letter (vv. 10, 13), and once more at the letter's end (v. 23). One might suggest that Paul has framed the letter with these references. Clearly, Philemon will not forget that Paul writes from prison!

Paul is an old man, and he is in prison for his faithfulness to the Lord. These references, taken together with the later references to the fact that Paul was Philemon's "father" in the faith (v. 19) and Onesimus's father in the faith as well (v. 10), constitute a strong emotional appeal to Philemon.

Here then is the progression of thought leading up to the initiation of Paul's appeal:

1. Paul appeals "on the basis of love" (v. 9a);
2. Paul refers to himself as an old man (v. 9b);
3. Paul refers to his imprisonment (v. 9c).

Following this emotional buildup, Paul in v. 10 begins his appeal. Everything Paul has said to this point, roughly halfway through the letter, sets the stage for Paul's request here. The appeal itself is deftly put. Paul asks on behalf of his own "child," a term of endearment par excellence. Once again, familial language comes to the fore (cf. vv. 1, 7, 10, 16, 20). In rabbinic literature, a proselyte is likened to a "child just born" (*b. Yeham.* 22a; Daube 1986, 40). Paul frequently uses this language to speak of his churches (1 Cor 4:14; Gal 4:19; 1 Thess 2:11), Timothy (1 Cor 4:17; Phil 2:22; 1 Tim 1:2, 18; 2 Tim 1:2; 2:1), and Titus (Titus 1:4). Now he includes Onesimus in that number, a statement of the affection that Paul feels for him. Paul became Onesimus's father while "in chains," i.e., during Paul's imprisonment. As a result of his new birth, Onesimus is now numbered among the saints, those whose hearts Philemon is in the habit of refreshing. Paul, as Onesimus's "father" in the faith, was responsible for handing on the truths and traditions of the faith to his new "son," just as he had once done for Philemon, another of his "children" in the faith (v. 19). Philemon would not miss these implications, or the kind of bond that must have existed between Paul and his new "child."

Only at this point, after being told that Onesimus has become both a Christian by his acquaintance with Paul *and* become Paul's own "child" by his conversion, does Paul actually refer to Onesimus by name! The word order in the Greek text delays the name until the very end of the verse: in order, the text reads "I appeal to you on behalf of my child, whose father I became while in chains: Onesimus" (v. 10).

In v. 11, Paul continues to build his case with wordplay on the name Onesimus. Slave names were given by slave dealers to advertise their wares or by slave masters to express their hopes about what the slave might grow up to be. Onesimus means "beneficial, profitable, advantageous" in Greek. However, the name was sometimes considered degrading, appropriate for farm animals. Now Paul says he who was "useless" to Philemon, in spite of his hopeful name, has become "useful" both to Philemon and Paul. In Greek the wordplay is pronounced and powerful. The Greek word *achrēstos* ("useless") and *achristos* ("Christless") were pronounced exactly the same. This trick of pronunciation means that *achrēstos* might also have been heard as *achristos*! Onesimus was "useless" as long as he was "Christless," but now that he is "Christ-full" he is "useful" both to Philemon and to Paul. Paul's wordplay actually serves to advance his argument, because it represents the change in Onesimus's status. Thus Paul adds a second motive for the behavior he desires from Philemon—utility—to the motive of brotherly affection he argued for in vv. 1-10.

Onesimus's usefulness to Paul may have taken many forms. There were the everyday needs of a prisoner under "house arrest": preparing meals, running errands, carrying mail. Depending on his skills and education, Onesimus may also have read to Paul or served as his secretary/scribe. Whatever the case, Onesimus has made himself useful to Paul.

Furthermore (v. 13), Onesimus has exercised usefulness by serving Paul on Philemon's behalf (unbeknownst to Philemon!), ministering to Paul in ways that Philemon would have gladly served had he been close enough. Again, Paul's thought parallels Philippians, where he praises Epaphroditus for risking "his life to make up for those services that you (the Philippians) could not give me" (Phil 2:30). Thus Paul in v. 11 begins laying the foundation for a further request still to come: that Philemon will free Onesimus and send him to Paul's side.

Probatio: The Gospel's Transforming Power (vv. 12-16)

For now, Paul is sending Onesimus—who is Paul's "own heart"—back to Philemon (v. 12). Here is the second appearance of "heart" in the letter. It appeared first in v. 7, where Paul lauded Philemon for refreshing "the hearts of the saints." Now Paul calls Onesimus "my own heart." Once again the word translated "heart' is *splagchna*, the deepest parts of a person's being. Eusebius uses *splagchna* to refer to the self (*Historia Eccesiastica* 7.21.3). Onesimus has become a part of, perhaps even an extension of, Paul's very self. This is an extreme expression of affection and unity. According to Quintilian, an advocate sometimes needs to assume such a closeness with the one for whom he is advocating that any attack on the client becomes an attack on the advocate. Likewise, any good deed done for the client is a good deed done to the advocate (*Inst. Or.* 6.1.24).

By sending Onesimus, his "own heart," back to Philemon, Paul models the actions that he wants Philemon to perform. Paul sacrificially sends Onesimus back to Philemon, in hopes that Philemon will sacrificially send Onesimus back to Paul. Quintilian also advocated modeling for one's hearers the qualities one wants them to exhibit (*Inst. Or.* 2.16.18).

In the final appearance of "heart" (v. 20), Paul will ask Philemon to "refresh" his (Paul's) own heart. Philemon has brought Paul joy and encouragement by refreshing "the hearts of the saints." Now Philemon can bring Paul even greater joy and encouragement by refreshing Paul's own heart. Will Philemon, who refreshed the hearts of the saints, do any less for Paul?

"Refreshing the heart" seems to be a concept unique to early Christianity. Paul may even have coined the phrase. Other Graeco-Roman religions show little concern for refreshing the lives (hearts, spiritual strength) of fellow adherents. Paul's phrase, on the other hand, reflects the Christian conviction that "all of one's actions should be directed to the benefits of others" (Clarke 1996, 277–300).

As noted above, "heart" appears in each of the three major sections of the letter, once near the beginning (v. 7), once in the middle (v. 12), and once at the end (v. 20). These appearances form the framework on which the letter hangs. Ultimately, this letter deals with matters of the heart. Paul is not asking Philemon to do the reasonable or culturally acceptable thing. In the end, the way believers treat one another is not a matter of reason. It is a matter of love.

In vv. 13-14, Paul returns to the fact of Onesimus's "usefulness." In fact, Onesimus has become so useful to Paul that he (Paul) was reluctant to send Onesimus back to Philemon. Paul could have justified keeping Onesimus by considering him to be serving in Philemon's stead, knowing that Philemon would serve at Paul's side were he able to do so. However, Paul does not want to take further advantage of Onesimus's service to him without Philemon's consent, so that Philemon's gift of service "might be voluntary and not forced." By making Onesimus's future service a matter for Philemon to decide, Paul raises a number of matters for consideration.

First, the decision to allow Onesimus to continue his service to Paul must be Philemon's decision. It must be voluntary, not forced. Paul will not seek Onesimus's freedom at the cost of Philemon's captivity. Nor will he stoop to enslaving Philemon so that Onesimus might be free. Origen understood this well:

> God does not tyrannize but rules, and when he rules, he does not coerce but encourages and he wishes that those under him yield themselves willingly to his direction so that the good of someone may not be according to compulsion but according to his free will. This is what Paul with understanding was saying to Philemon in the letter to Philemon . . . . Thus the God of the universe hypothetically might have produced a supposed good in us so that we give alms from "compulsion" and we would be temperate from "compulsion" but he has not wished to do that. (*Homilies on Jeremiah* 20.2, in Gorday 2000, 314)

Or as Barth and Blanke have put it, "when counseling a Christian, and in view of the communal life and order of the Christian congregation, he (Paul) trusts in the power of persuasion, the conscience, and the Spirit" (Barth and Blanke 2000).

Second, Paul could have justified giving sanctuary to Onesimus according to Old Testament law: "If a slave has taken refuge, you do not hand him over to his master . . . Do not oppress him" (Deut 23:15-16). But Roman law forbade offering asylum to runaway slaves. Paul, however, sends Onesimus back to Philemon due to a higher obligation, namely that of doing what is best for both Philemon and Onesimus before he does what is expedient for himself: "Wrongs done between fellow believers had to be sorted out among fellow believers" (Garland 1998, 329; cf. Phlm 16; 1 Cor 6:1-8). Third, while Paul desires to keep Onesimus, he places greater importance on the opportunity for reconciliation between Onesimus and Philemon. Such reconciliation between master and slave required a face-to-face meeting. Furthermore, any official process of manumission required that both slave and master appear together before a magistrate in the province (see Pliny, *Epistles* 7.16). This also required that Onesimus return to Philemon.

Fourth, Paul clearly articulates his understanding of the nature of Christian community in Philippians 2:2-4:

> Make my joy complete: be of the same mind, having the same love, being in full accord and of one mind. Do nothing from selfish ambition or conceit, but in humility regard others as better than yourselves. Let each of you look not to your own interests, but to the interests of others.

By persuading (rather than commanding) Philemon, Paul puts his faith to work and lives out his own teaching in a concrete way. He sacrifices his own desires, even though they are mostly noble in nature, for the sake of Philemon and Onesimus.

Fifth, Paul's mention here of Philemon's opportunity to do his "good deed" (*to agathon*) voluntarily sheds light on the first appearance of "good" in verse 6. There, Paul called on Philemon to perceive "the good" that Christians share and do when they work together from a common commitment to the faith. Now, with his appeal on behalf of Onesimus, Paul makes the "good" concrete as he presents a vision of a momentous good thing that Philemon can do in service to the gospel. In his comments on the law of slavery in Deuteronomy 15:12-18, Philo uses the word "good" with reference to the freeing of slaves after six years of service: "For a slave can have no greater boon ["good," *agathon*] than freedom." Here, Paul speaks of a similar good.

Sixth, Paul joins his desire for Onesimus's service to the service of the gospel. Paul uses the verb *diakoneō* for Christan service in 2 Corinthians 3:3; 8:19, 20; he also uses the noun *diakonia* to refer to service in the gospel ministry in Colossians 1:7, 23, 25; 4:7, 17. Paul's desire for Onesimus's help is not totally personal. He also wants to see Onesimus serving for the sake of the gospel ministry, the needs of which are greater than Paul can meet by working alone.

Seventh, Paul wants to succeed in his advocacy for Onesimus because the very nature of the gospel is at stake. If Christians really are new creations in Christ (2 Cor 5:17), where there is no more Jew nor Greek, slave or free (Gal 3:28; Col 3:11), then this situation provides a textbook case for demonstrating that reality. The truth of Paul's preaching must be fleshed out in practice. He seizes this moment to turn faith statements into substance, rhetoric into reality. Otherwise, Paul's preaching will remain propositional and cognitive with no effect on the lives of his people, "a tale, told by an idiot, full of sound and fury, signifying nothing" (Shakespeare, *Macbeth*, Act 4, Scene 5). Furthermore, as the leader of a house church, Philemon must set a good example for his people of what the implications of the gospel really are. The opportunity for Philemon to demonstrate and live out his faith is at hand. All that remains is for Philemon to rise to the occasion and demonstrate the truth of new creation!

John Chrysostom summarizes Paul's appeal up to this point:

> Be careful to observe how much groundwork is necessary before Paul honorably brought Onesimus before his master. Observe how wisely he has done this. See for how much he makes Philemon answerable and how much he honors Onesimus. You have found, he says, a way by which you through Onesimus repay your service to me. Here Paul shows that he has considered Philemon's advantage more than that of his slave and that he deeply respects him. (*Homilies on Philemon* 2, on v. 13, in Gorday, 314)

In vv. 15-16, Paul offers his perspective on why the current situation has arisen. "Perhaps," he says, "this happened so that . . ." Paul's "speculation" is, in fact, the heart of the matter from his perspective. "He [Onesimus] was separated from you [Philemon] for a while." Paul uses the passive voice ("was separated") rather than the active ("ran away") to imply divine activity. Onesimus did indeed "flee" or "run away" from Philemon, but God was at work in what happened, making his purposes reality. By this argument from providence, Paul frees Onesimus from "the onus of a crime" (Church 1978, 28). Onesimus "was separated" from Philemon, but this temporary separation has eternal and opposite consequences. Now Philemon "may have him back forever." The form of argument here is called *attenustio*, where the advocate lessens the degree of an offense. Onesimus's crime of flight is downgraded to "separation."

And then comes the kicker: Philemon will have Onesimus back, but in a better relationship than they previously had, "no longer [*ouketi hōs*] as a slave but as a brother." Those who argue that Paul is not asking Philemon to free Onesimus seem to miss this phrase. Paul does *not* say, "You might have him back, both as a slave and as a brother." *Ouketi hōs* does not mean "not merely as" or "not only as," but "*no longer as.*" The "no longer . . . but" construction emphasizes that the former condition stops and is replaced by the new condition. Paul says, "You might have him back forever, *no longer as a slave*, but more than a slave, a beloved brother." This is the only time in the New

Testament when a slave is directly called a brother. Here, Onesimus is Philemon's brother both in a spiritual sense ("in the Lord") and also "in the flesh" (i.e., in the personal and social relationship that they will share from this point forward).

It was possible for a slave to become a Christian and remain a slave. Indeed, Paul's instructions to slaves in the household codes of Ephesians (6:5-9), Colossians (3:22–4:1), and 1 Timothy (6:1-2) demonstrate this. However,

> The usual interpretation of vv. 15-16 rightly points both to Paul's primary orientation to brotherly relations and to the fact that Philemon and Onesimus are related as master and slave. However, its concentration on "as a brother" fails to do justice to "no longer as a slave." The interpretation properly emphasizes Paul's expectations about Philemon's new *relations* with his slave, but too hastily dismisses the idea that these relations entail a *structural* change in their relationship as master and slave. (Petersen 1985, 83)

Philemon must receive Onesimus as if the former slave were his own flesh and blood. Thus Onesimus is a brother to Paul spiritually while apart from Paul, but is much more a brother to Philemon, with whom he will be personally and socially. Note at this point the differences between being a *freedman* and a *free man*. Free men had no obligations to their old masters. Freedmen, on the other hand, were not completely free. They owed continuing responsibilities and obligations to the former master. Riders indicating the specific nature of these continuing obligations were sometimes attached to manumission documents.

In this web of relational language (vv. 1, 7, 16, 20), "Paul confronted Philemon with the choice either of continuing to regard himself as Onesimus's owner or of becoming his brother in a new social reality" (Bartchy, 6.71). This new social reality is part of Paul's "new creation" (2 Cor 5:17) where there is "no longer slave nor free . . . for all [believers] are one in Christ Jesus" (Gal 3:28; Col 3:11). In Christ, "the reality of the world as seen from within the world is replaced by the reality seen from within the church" (Petersen 1985, 188 n. 111). Paul's new reality contrasts sharply with the reality humans created for themselves when they "exchanged the truth about God for a lie" (Rom 1:25) and built their lives and societies on that lie. We have come to believe the lie to be the truth, and reject the truth itself because "that's just not the way the real world works." In effect, we have looked at the world upside down for so long that it looks to us to be right side up! Jesus came to "right-wise" the world, and this world right-side-up is a manifestation of the new creation where there are no more slaves and masters, Jew or Greek, black or white or brown, but only brothers and sisters.

Paul's appeal is subtle to be sure, but devastatingly clear. Now Philemon must respond. Consider again the cultural context in which Philemon makes his choice. If Philemon does what Paul asks, he will certainly lose face with other slave owners; who in their right mind would forgive and free a runaway slave? In society where honor and shame are paramount, such an action would perpetuate and compound Philemon's shame. And what of the other slaves in Philemon's household? If Philemon was wealthy enough to host a church in his house, he almost certainly had slaves in addition to Onesimus (Garland 1998, 335 n. 34). Would these other slaves rush to convert or to feign conversion? Would they see Philemon as "soft" on slaves, and then become less productive or perhaps even run away themselves? And what if some of his slaves were already Christians? Should they not expect to be freed as well? For slave owners, manumission served a useful purpose, by motivating the slaves. It was like a carrot, dangling before the slave, a prize prompting them to faithful service and hard work in the hopes of being manumitted. How could the institution of slavery continue to function effectively if the slaves were freed simply because they became Christians? And who in that agrarian world could imagine a world without slavery? It would almost be like an industrial world without machines, or a high-tech world without computers: inconceivable! And what of the economic ramifications of freeing Onesimus? Would Philemon be forced to purchase or at least temporarily rent another slave to take his place? Would the breakdown of the economic structures of his estate lead to financial ruin? Would not the decision to free Onesimus be totally unreasonable, irresponsible, and unfeasible? The complexities of the situation are enormous; one commentator suggests that the reason Paul's request is so indirect and vague is that Paul simply "did not know what to recommend" (Barclay 1991, 175).

But in fact, Paul's appeal is not vague at all. Paul is masterfully employing the rhetorical method of *insinuatio*, which allows him to make a direct appeal indirectly. Look again at the way Paul has developed his appeal up to this point:

- Paul is "a prisoner" of the same Christ Jesus whom Philemon also serves (v. 1);
- Paul is "in chains"(vv. 1, 10) because of his faithful service to Christ Jesus;
- As a prisoner, Paul identifies himself with Onesimus's status as a slave (v. 1);

- Paul refers to Philemon as his "dear friend and "fellow worker," thus identifying with Philemon both in terms of his great affection for him and in terms of the commitment they share to the work of the gospel (v. 1);
- Paul affirms Philemon's love "for all the saints," a love he will call Philemon to extend to the newest saint, the newly converted Onesimus (v. 5);
- Paul implies that there is yet more that Philemon can do to contribute to "all the good that we/you can do" (v. 6);
- Paul celebrates the fact that "the hearts of the saints have been refreshed through" Philemon, a "refreshing" that should continue to extend to the newly converted Onesimus (v. 7);
- Paul describes himself again as an "old man" and "a prisoner of Christ Jesus" (v. 9, second mention) "on the basis of love" for Onesimus his "child" in the faith, whom he has "begotten in chains" (vv. 8-10); in v. 19, we will learn that Philemon stands in the same father-son relationship to Paul as Onesimus, for Philemon owes Paul his "own self");
- Paul announces that Onesimus, once "useless" and Christ-less, has now become "useful" and Christ-full (v. 11);
- Paul asserts that this new Christ-full Onesimus is "useful" to himself as well as to Philemon (v. 11). In fact, he is so useful that Paul would rather keep Onesimus with him during his imprisonment than return him to his master, as Roman law requires. But Paul will take no such action without Philemon's approval (vv. 13-14);
- Paul implies that God is behind all that has happened. He presents his brother Philemon with the opportunity to do a "good " thing of his own free will, by welcoming Onesimus back *no longer as a slave but more than a slave, a beloved brother*" (vv. 15-16). Love for Christ, and love for Paul, can result in nothing less than love for Onesimus.

Peroratio: "Sealing the Deal" (vv. 17-21)

Having set out his appeal in vv. 8-16, Paul strengthens it and brings it to a conclusion in vv. 17-21. Paul follows here the form of a *peroratio*, which typically included

- recapitulation (in this case, a restatement of the request) (v. 17);
- amplification (vv. 18-19);
- emotional appeal (v. 20);
- "sealing the deal," making sure he has secured the hearer's favor (vv. 21) (Arist. *Rhet.* 3.14-19; Bartchy, 5.307).

In v. 17, Paul restates the appeal. He does so in the form of a request prefaced by the statement of a *real condition* (i.e., one that indicates not a possibility nor even a probability but a reality). The text could almost be translated, "since you consider me your partner." Paul calls on Philemon to remember and recommit to the partnership (*koinōnon*) they share in the service of the gospel. Evidence from the papyri demonstrates that *koinōnos* was used to refer to business partnerships. Thus Paul may be telling Philemon (his partner) to receive Onesimus as a representative of the same institution and concerns (Artz-Grabner 2001, 608). Again, the language in this letter parallels Paul's language in Philippians. In Philippians 1:5, Paul gave thanks for the Philippians' "partnership" (*koinōnia*) in the gospel (cf. 2 Cor 8:23, where he refers to Titus as his "partner" [*koinōnos*] in ministry). This venture in which Paul and Philemon are partners requires the recognition and reception of others, who come to be partners in the same venture. As Paul shared this partnership with Philemon, he and Philemon now share it with Onesimus.

Paul appeals to Philemon to "welcome" Onesimus into that partnership, to "welcome" Onesimus "as you would welcome me." Elsewhere, Paul uses the verb "to welcome" (*prosdechomai*) to speak of a Christian's reception of other Christians (Rom 14; 15:7) (see Rom 16:1-2; 1 Cor 16:10-12, 15-18; Phil 2:19-30 for other Pauline instruction on receiving people). But Paul goes even further, by asking Philemon to recognize and welcome Onesimus as a "beloved brother" (v. 16), a member of his own family. He is, after all, Paul's "child" (v. 10)—like Philemon. A father's physical child should be welcomed and treated as the father would be treated; all the more reason for such a welcome for Paul's spiritual child. Onesimus is not only Paul's child in the faith, he is also a "beloved brother" to Timothy, Philemon, sister Apphia, and the church that meets in Philemon's house (vv. 1-2). Furthermore, as Paul's "partner" in the service of the gospel, Onesimus comes to Philemon as an emissary bringing word to Philemon of Paul's hopes and concerns. In any and all of these capacities—child, brother, or partner—Philemon should welcome Onesimus as he would welcome Paul himself. Indeed, through his emissaries, it is as if Paul were actually present in the flesh. To welcome Onesimus *is* to welcome Paul himself.

Like v. 17, v. 18 begins with a *real condition*. The force of the Greek text is not "if" Philemon has been wronged, but "since" he has been wronged, not "if" Onesimus owes Philemon something, but "since" he owes Philemon. Though much speculation has been focused on the nature of the situation, the text gives us no further specifics on this point. By using the aorist tense verb *ēdikēsen* ("wronged"), Paul refers to a particular incident of wrong or injury or unjust treatment. By using the present tense for the next verb (*opheilei,* "owes,") Paul refers to an ongoing, outstanding debt. The logical reading of the language is that Onesimus wronged Philemon at some time in the past, that he owes Philemon an outstanding debt, and that the debt springs from the wrong. Logic compels us to conclude that Onesimus has indeed run away from Philemon his master. After all, Onesimus is with Paul and not with Philemon. And Paul, knowing the case and its circumstances, appeals for Philemon to welcome Onesimus back. The most reasonable conjecture is that Onesimus has stolen from Philemon to underwrite his flight (Stuhlmacher 1975, 49).

Compounding this theft is the fact that Onesimus has also deprived Philemon of his services for however long he has been gone. No matter what Onesimus's role as a slave in Philemon's household may have been, his absence caused financial loss for Philemon. Either Onesimus's work went undone, or Philemon would have had to hire someone (or rent another slave) to do the work until Onesimus could be found: this in itself was considered a form of theft. Add to this the cost of "bounty hunters" that Philemon may have hired to search for and return his runaway slave, and the injury to Philemon becomes even more real and substantial.

Paul, fully cognizant of the damages and ongoing effects of Onesimus's actions against Philemon, makes an incredible offer at the end of v. 18: Whatever the wrong, whatever the debt, Paul says: "charge it to my account!" Indeed, employing typical Roman commercial language of debt and credit, Paul offers to make good on any debt that Onesimus has accrued, putting into practice the reciprocal obligations of friendship ("owes," "charge to my account," "I will pay;" see especially Martin 1992, 321–37; Marshall 1987, 160–64). Paul's pledge demonstrates his concrete commitment to the Christ-full Onesimus, and his recognition of the seriousness of Philemon's situation. Paul is demanding a real change in the relationship between Onesimus and Philemon, and he is willing to sacrifice financially to remove all obstacles to this reconciliation. So, Paul the prisoner offers to pay a well-to-do householder, in order to make good the "debts" owed to the householder by a runaway slave! Rhetorically, this offer is *pathos par excellence*! Here, Paul models the attitude toward possessions that characterized the Christian community from its earliest days in Jerusalem. Luke describes a community where people were willing to say, "What's mine is yours" (Acts 2:41–47; 4:32–5:11; 6:1–7; 11:27–30; 16:11–15:34; cf. Rom 15:25–27; 1 Cor 16:1–3; 2 Cor 8-9). Likewise, Paul is willing to say to Philemon, "what's mine is yours," so that any need caused by Onesimus might be met.

Again, Paul is illustrating the nature of the gospel itself. He will make whatever sacrifices are necessary so that reconciliation might become a reality. This is horizontal atonement, between Philemon and Onesimus. In the same way, God has made a monumental sacrifice so that humankind might be reconciled to him and to one another. This is atonement both horizontal and vertical: "God was in Christ reconciling the world to himself, not counting their trespasses against them, and entrusting to us the message of reconciliation" (2 Cor 5:18-19).

In v. 19, Paul takes the pen into his own hand to write a typical, one-sentence promissory note. This act made the note legally binding (Deissmann 1978, 331–32). The use of the first person personal pronoun, unnecessary in Greek since it is contained in the verb, gives further emphasis to his statement. Paul adds even greater emphasis by adding his own name: again, it was rare for the author of a Graeco-Roman letter to mention his/her name after heading of the letter. Paul places his name in each of the three major sections of the letter (vv. 1, 9, 19). In each instance, the repetition serves a significant purpose: to name the sender of this revolutionary letter (v. 1), to heighten the urgency of the original appeal (v. 9), and to affirm Paul's commitment of all that he is and has to this concrete, revolutionary application of the gospel (v. 19). Paul has said, in effect, "I have signed my name on the dotted line to guarantee that I, myself, will be responsible for anything that Onesimus might owe." For the second time, Paul promises that he will repay.

With Paul's repeated promise, we hear another echo of the gospel: Paul will absorb the wrongs that Onesimus has committed, just as Jesus has absorbed in himself all the wrongs we have committed:

> Surely he has borne our infirmities and carried our diseases . . .
> But he was wounded for our transgressions,
> > crushed for our iniquities;
> upon him was the punishment that made us whole,
> > and by his stripes we are healed.
>
> All we like sheep have gone astray;
> > We have all turned to our own way,
> And the Lord has laid on him the iniquity of us all. (Isa 53:4-6)

Or as Paul himself wrote to the Corinthians, "For our sake, he made him to be sin who knew no sin, so that in him we might become the righteousness of God" (2 Cor 5:21).

At v. 19b, Paul reaches the rhetorical peak of the letter, with a beautiful and devastating piece of understatement. Just to be sure that Philemon doesn't miss the point of the previous verses, Paul reminds him: "I say nothing about your owing me even your own self." This parenthetical reminder is a classic example of a rhetorical device known as *praeteritio* or *paraleipsis*. In this device, the speaker/writer introduces a rhetorical bombshell with a statement such as, "I'm not going to say what I'm now going to say," or "There's really no need for me to say this, but . . . ." Paul, with this last subtle blast (made even more devastating by the fact that the letter—even these "private" reminders—was read aloud to the church in Philemon's house), demolishes every argument Philemon might have had against granting Paul's request for Onesimus.

Philemon, like Onesimus, owes his very self to Paul (cf. Rom 15:27 for a similar application of commercial language to spiritual debt). We know nothing about Philemon's background or past, except that his faith in Jesus Christ was a result of Paul's witness. Paul is essentially saying, "It's not that you owe me anything, Philemon. It's that you owe me everything."

Paul opens v. 20 by again referring to Philemon as "brother," an affirmation that they stand as equals in Christ (v. 7). This occurrence of "brother" is the culmination of the familial language that Paul has been piling up throughout this brief letter (vv. 1, 2, 7, 10 [twice], 16, 20). In the next phrase, "let me have this benefit from you in the Lord," Paul employs yet another word play on Onesimus's name. The verb is *onaimēn* ("Let me have this benefit"), which comes from *oninēmi*, which is in turn the verb from which the name Onesimus ("beneficial, useful") is derived. This is the only New Testament occurrence of *oninēmi*. Grammatically, this sentence is not a command; the verb is in the rare optative mood, making it an entreaty. (In fact, the whole letter is an entreaty, not a command). This "benefit" is not Paul's to command; it is Philemon's to give.

And what is this "benefit" that Paul seeks? Paul asks that Philemon, his brother, welcome Onesimus back "no longer as a slave but as a beloved brother . . . in the Lord." He makes this request "in the Lord"; that is, this response is a natural result of Philemon's relationship with Christ. Further, Paul hopes to have Onesimus back at his side to serve in the work of the gospel. Garland notes, "Simply readmitting him as a slave would provide no real benefit in the Lord to Paul: The apostle will truly have a benefit 'in the Lord' if Onesimus is 'free to serve the gospel, not just his master'" (Garland 1998, 339).

By heeding Paul's appeal, Philemon will "refresh" Paul's "heart in Christ." Here we find the third appearance of "heart." In v. 7, Paul lauded

Philemon for refreshing "the hearts of the saints." In v. 12, Paul referred to Onesimus as "my own heart." Now Paul calls upon Philemon, who had refreshed the hearts of the saints, to refresh his "heart." Paul employs a subtle double entendre here. On an obvious level, Paul speaks of the refreshment of his own heart: Philemon will bring Paul much "joy and encouragement" (v. 7) if he accepts Paul's request. But Paul has also referred to Onesimus as "my own heart," and Philemon's acceptance of Paul's appeal would bring great "joy and encouragement" to Onesimus's heart as well. If Philemon does as Paul requests, his action will be a clear witness to the truth of the gospel, and a clear manifestation of the reality of the community of the new creation. And this powerful testimony is only possible "in Christ," for the new creation in which there is no more slave or free is "in Christ" (2 Cor 5:17; Gal 3:28; Col 3:11).

Paul is "confident" of Philemon's obedience (v. 21). "Obedience" (*hypakoē*) derives from "hear" (*akouō*); thus, obedience is the result of attentive listening and then acting on what is heard (Dunn 1996, 345). This affirmation serves once again to strengthen Paul's appeal. Philemon's obedience is to be to whom or what—to Paul, to Jesus, to the nature of the gospel? At first glance—and after many glances, according to some commentators—Paul has in view Philemon's obedience to Paul the apostle (Wickert 1961, 233; Lohse 1971, 206; Stuhlmacher 1975, 36–37). But Paul's gentleness in this letter, and his reticence to use the heavy hand of apostolic authority, together argue against this view. Instead, Paul here refers to Philemon's obedience to Jesus and his command to love (v. 9), not Philemon's obedience to Paul. Indeed, Philemon's obedience is "the obedience of faith" to which Paul refers elsewhere (Rom 1:5; 16:26; 2 Cor 7:15; 10:5-6; 2 Thess 1:8).

According to v. 20, the "benefit" Paul seeks is "in the Lord," and the refreshment he hopes for, both for himself and Onesimus, is "in Christ." Only Philemon's commitment to his Lord and Christ will be sufficient incentive for him to perform the revolutionary, countercultural, counterintuitive task that Paul asks him to perform. If Philemon accepts that the course Paul calls him to is the will of the Lord, this discovery can move him to an act of obedience that no mere human, not even an apostle, could command. Garland is probably correct in saying, "This perspective mitigates the social problem of freeing Onesimus. [Philemon's] pagan acquaintances would not understand why he should treat his mutinous slave as a brother, but they could grasp how it might be prudent to give way to some god who had made claims on his slave" (Garland 1998, 340 n. 59). But the issue here is not finding a way to mitigate the "peer pressure" Philemon faced. The issue is instead Philemon's obedience to his Lord and Christ, whether the social, economic, and political problems are mitigated or not! Paul's "obedience of faith" considers the cost and finds no price too high to pay for him who gave himself away "so that those who live might no longer live for themselves, but for him who died and was raised for them" (2 Cor 5:15).

This is why Paul can be confident that in the end Philemon will do "even more than I say" (v. 21b). This "even more" might simply refer to Paul's appeal for Philemon to free Onesimus from slavery. However, since Paul has already asked Philemon to welcome Onesimus "no longer as a slave" (v. 16), "even more" may instead refer to Paul's implicit request for Onesimus not only to be freed but also that he be sent back to labor at Paul's side for the sake of the gospel: "Let me have this 'benefit' [*onaimēn*], this Onesimus." Paul appeals for Philemon to send his and the gospel's servant back.

Ultimately, Paul's words cannot bring this reunion to pass. Only a realization that these countercultural acts are indeed the will of Jesus Christ can call Philemon to step further into the "new creation" than he has dared venture before. Thus Paul's "even more" speaks to further ramifications of the good news for Philemon and Onesimus, ramifications that neither of them could have ever imagined. But Paul knows Philemon, and he knows that the explosive nature and power of the gospel that he (Paul) planted in Philemon's life will result in more and greater things than even he can imagine. Paul knows that the Jesus who demands such revolutionary behavior will, "by the power at work" in Philemon, be "able to accomplish abundantly far more" than all Paul asks or imagines (Eph 3:20).

Travel Plans (v. 22)

Verse 22 seems almost frivolous in light of what has come before. The verse tells us a number of things, however, and bears careful attention.

First, it tells us that Paul is hoping to be delivered, spared, or released from his imprisonment, and be able to travel again soon. There is no sense of resignation here to either an impending death or an extended incarceration. Paul is optimistic that he will see Philemon soon, and Philemon needs to start preparing a guest room. Second, Paul's plan, upon his release, is to travel to see Philemon in Colossae. Wherever Paul is imprisoned, this seems to him a logical and reasonable expectation. Third, Paul believes that the prayers of Philemon and his church will help to bring his release to pass. Paul believed in the power of prayer. He practiced it himself (e.g., Phil 3:3-11; 1 Thess 5:17; 2 Cor 12:7-8), and assumed that his fellow Christians did the same.

Finally, Paul veils a warning here. If Philemon is recalcitrant, he may read these words to imply, "When this letter arrives along with Onesimus, I will not be far behind!" Then Paul will see for himself how Philemon has responded to his appeal: "His request that Philemon prepare a guestroom for him . . . is surely designed to make Philemon take the letter seriously: Paul will very soon be on the spot to see how Philemon responded" (Barclay 1991, 171). Perhaps Paul's thinking here is (again) similar to that in the letter to the Philippians:

> Live your life in a manner worthy of the gospel of Christ, so that, whether I come and see you or am absent and hear about you . . . I will know that you are working out your salvation with fear and trembling: for it is God who is at work in you, enabling you both to will and to work for his good pleasure. (Phil 1:27; cf. 2:12d-13)

Final Greetings and Benediction (vv. 23-24)

Paul's final greetings remind us again of the importance of community in the life of the early Christians. Even though he was imprisoned, he was surrounded by Christian brothers and sisters and fellow workers. God does not intend for believers to live in isolation, nor are we able to do so for long. The Spirit dwells within, and the saints surround us, as together we walk the Christian way.

For Philemon, agreeing to Paul's request would bring him a host of problems. However, with the strength that the Spirit gives and the support and accountability that the Christian community provided, Philemon could be faithful even when it cost him dearly. Philemon may well have needed the community's support to deal with repercussions of his decision. Likewise, Onesimus may have needed the community to guide and hold him accountable as he sought to act responsibly in his new status.

Greetings. Paul offers greetings from five people:

1. Epaphras is Paul's "fellow prisoner in Christ Jesus." According to Colossians 1:7-8, Epaphras was the founder of the Colossian church. Colossians 4:12-13 suggests that this relationship continued, as did Epaphras's relationship with the nearby churches of Laodicea and Hieropolis, even after Epaphras moved on to work with other churches. Like Paul, he is both imprisoned because of Jesus Christ and a prisoner of Jesus Christ. It is

likely that he later became bishop of Colossae and a martyr (Fitzmyer 2001, 123).
2. Mark is likely the Mark of Acts 12:12; 19:29. Mark is also mentioned in Colossians 4:10 as the cousin of Barnabas.
3. Paul mentions Aristarchus here; in Colossians 4:10, Paul calls Aristarchus his "fellow prisoner."
4. Paul lists Demas as a coworker here and in Colossians 4:14. In 2 Timothy 4:11, however, Paul states that Demas, because he was "in love with this present world," deserted Paul and left the work. Demas's story is a sad one; even for Paul, not every story was a success story.
5. Paul mentions Luke alongside Demas here and in Colossians 4:14. There, Paul refers to Luke as "the beloved physician." In 2 Timothy 4:11, Paul writes that, during his final imprisonment, Luke was the only coworker who was with him. According to tradition, Luke was the author of Luke–Acts who accompanied Paul on his missionary travels. We can trace part of Luke's work with Paul by examining the "we" passages in Acts, which begin with Acts 16:10 and conclude with Paul in Rome (Acts 28:16). There Paul, under "house arrest," awaited his appeal to Caesar (Acts 25:11-12; 28:30-31).

Benediction (v. 25). This brief benediction would have brought closure to the reading of the letter. These last words, echoing the first words of the letter (v. 3), focus on "the grace of the Lord Jesus Christ." For Paul, "grace" is ever the first and last word. We have been saved by that grace, are being saved by that grace, and will be saved by that grace. By the extension of that grace, Philemon will act in ways that confound the expectations of the culture around him, and Onesimus (who fled in terror and disgrace) will be welcomed back, "no longer a slave but more than a slave, a beloved brother."

How successful was Paul's appeal? The fact that the letter was preserved suggests that Philemon agreed with Paul's request. F. F. Bruce has even suggested that this letter was preserved by Onesimus as his charter of freedom (Bruce 1977, 406).

Works Cited

Aasgaard, Reider. "My Beloved Brothers and Sisters!" *Christian Siblingship in Paul.* ECC; JSNT Sup 265. London/New York: T & T Clarke, 2004.

Artz-Grabner, Peter. "The Case of Onesimus: An Interpretation of Paul's Letter to Philemon Based on Documentary Papyri and Ostraca." *Annali di storia dell'esegesi* 18 (2001): 589–614.

———. *Philemon.* PKNT. Gottingen: Vandenhoeck & Ruprecht, 2003.

———. "Onesimus *erro.*" ZNW 95 (2004): 131–43.

Banks, Robert. *Paul's Idea of Community.* Revised ed. Peabody MA: Hendrickson, 1994.

Barclay, J. M. G. "Paul, Philemon and the Dilemma of Christian Slave Ownership." *NTS* 37 (1991): 164.

Bartchy, Scott. "Philemon." *ABD* 5.307.

———. "Slavery [Greco-Roman]." *ABD* 6.71.

Barth M., and H. Blanke. *The Letter to Philemon.* Grand Rapids: Eerdmans, 2000, 253.

Bellen, Heinz. *Studien zur Sklavenflucht im romischen Kaisserrich.* Wiesbaden: Franz Steiner, 1971.

Branick, Vincent. *The House Church in the Writings of Paul.* Wilmington DE: Michael Glazier, 1989.

Bruce, F. F. *Paul—Apostle of the Heart Set Free.* Grand Rapids: Eerdmans, 1977.

Callahan, Alan. "Paul's Epistle to Philemon: Toward an Alternate *Argumentum.*" *HTR* 86 (1993): 357–74.

———. *Embassy of Onesimus: The Letter of Paul to Philemon.* Valley Forge: TPL, 1997.

Cassidy, Richard. *Paul in Chains: Roman Imprisonment and the Letters of St. Paul.* New York: Crossroads, 2001.

Church, F. F. "Rhetorical Structure and Design in Paul's Letter to Philemon." *HTR* 71 (1978): 17–33.

Clarke, Andrew. "'Refresh the Hearts of the Saints': A Unique Pauline Concept?" *TynB* 47 (1996): 277–300.

Cotter, Wendy. "Women's Authority Roles in Paul's Churches: Countercultural or Conventional?" *NovT* 36 (1994): 350–72.

Daube, D. "Onesimus." *HTR* 79 (1986): 40.

Deissmann, Adolf. *Light from the Ancient East.* Reprint ed. Grand Rapids: Eerdmans, 1978.

Dodd, C. H. *New Testament Studies.* Manchester: University Press, 1953.

Duncan, G. S. *St. Paul's Ephesian Ministry.* London: Hodder & Stoughton, 1929.

Dunn, James D. G. *The Epistles to the Colossians and to Philemon.* NIGTC. Grand Rapids: Eerdmans, 1996.

Fitzmyer, Joseph. *The Letter to Philemon.* AB. New York: Doubleday, 2000.

Frilingos, Chris. "For 'My Child Onesimus': Paul and Domestic Power in Philemon." *JBL* 119 (2000): 91–104.

Garland, David E. *Colossians and Philemon.* NIV Application Commentary. Grand Rapids: Zondervan, 1998.

Gorday, P., ed. *Colossians, 1–2 Thessalonians, 1–2 Timothy, Titus, Philemon.* Ancient Christian Commentary on Scripture, vol. IX. Downers Grove IL: InterVarsity, 2000.

Harrill, J. A. *The Manumission of Slaves in Early Christianity.* HUT 32: Tubingen: Mohr [Siebeck], 1995.

———. "Paul and Slavery," in *Paul in the Greco-Roman World: A Handbook.* Edited by J. Paul Sampley. Harrisburg: Trinity Press International, 2003.

———. *Slaves in the New Testament: Literary, Social and Moral Dimensions*. Minneapolis: Augsburg Press, 2005.
Knox, John. *Philemon Among the Letters of Paul*. Chicago: University of Chicago Press, 1935.
Lampe, Peter. "Keine 'Sklavenflucht' des Onesimus." *ZNW* 76 (1985): 135–37.
Lightfoot, *Saint Paul's Epistles to the Colossians and to Philemon*. Reprint ed. Grand Rapids: Zondervan, 1959.
Lohse, Eduard. *Colossians and Philemon*. Hermeneia. Philadelphia: Fortress, 1971.
Luther, Martin. "Preface to the Epistle of Saint Paul to the Philemon." *Luther's Works*. Philadelphia: Fortress, 1960.
Marrow, S. B. "*Parrhesia* and the New Testament." *NTS* 44 (1982): 431–46.
Marshall, Peter. *Enmity in Corinth: Social Conventions in Paul's Relations with the Corinthians*. WUNT 2/23. Tubingen: J. C. B. Mohr/Paul Sieback, 1987.
Martin, Clarice J. "Commercial Language in Philemon." In *Persuasive Artistry*, ed. D. F. Watson. Sheffield, UK: Sheffield Academic Press, 1992.
Metzger, Bruce M. *The Canon of the New Testament: Its Origin, Development, and Significance*. Oxford: Clarendon Press, 1997.
Mullins, Terence. "The Thanksgivings of Philemon and Colossians." *NTS* 30 (1984): 288–93.
Nordling, John. "Onesimus Fugitivus: A Defense of the Runaway Slave Hypothesis in Philemon." *JSNT* 41 (1991): 87–119.
O'Brien, Peter T. *Colossians, Philemon*. WBC. Waco: Word, 1982.
Osiek, Carolyn. *Philippians and Philemon*. Abingdon New Testament Commentary. Nashville: Abingdon, 2000.
Petersen, Norman. *Rediscovering Paul: Philemon and the Sociology of Paul's Narrative*. Philadelphia: Fortress, 1985.
Rapske, P. *The Book of Acts and Paul in Roman Custody*. Volume 3 of The Book of Acts in Its First Century Setting. Grand Rapids: Eerdmans, 1994.
Still, Todd. "Philemon among the Letters of Paul: Theological and Canonical Considerations." *ResQ* 47 (2005): 133–42.
Stuhlmacher, Peter. *Der Brief an Philemon*. EKKNT. 2nd ed. Zurich: Benzinger/Neukirchen: Neukircher, 1975.
Taylor, Nicholas. "Onesimus: A Case Study of Slave Conversion in Early Christianity." *R&T* 3 (1996): 259–81.
Van Dyke, R. H. "Paul's Letter to Philemon." *Sewanee Theological Review* 41 (1998).
Wansick, Craig. *Chained in Christ: The Experience and Rhetoric of Paul's Imprisonment*. JSNTSup 103. Sheffield: Sheffield Academic Press, 1996.
Watson, A. *Roman Slave Law*. Baltimore: Johns Hopkins University Press, 1987.
Wickert, Ulrich. "Der Philemonbrief—Privatbrief oder apostolisches Schreiben." *ZNW* 52 (1961): 230–38.
Wiedemann, Thomas. *Greek and Roman Slavery*. Baltimore: Johns Hopkins University Press, 1981.
Wilson, Andrew. "The Pragmatics of Politeness and Pauline Epistolography: A Case Study of the Letter to Philemon." *JSNT* 48 (1992): 107–119.
Winter, Sara B. C. "Paul's Letter to Philemon." *NTS* (1987): 1–15.
Witherington, Ben. *The Letters of Paul to Philemon, the Colossians, and the Ephesians: A Socio-Rhetorical Commentary on the Captivity Epistles*. Grand Rapids: Eerdmans, 2002.

The Letters to Timothy and Titus

Introduction to the Pastoral Epistles

Since the early days of the critical study of the Bible, interpreters have noted the similarities shared by Paul's letter to Titus and his two letters to Timothy. These letters are addressed to individuals who were leaders in Pauline congregations, men entrusted with the oversight of some of Paul's churches. The letters center on issues of church leadership and pastoral life. Further, they share a common literary style and approach to argument and theology that, some argue, differentiate them from the other Pauline letters. Thus they have usually been grouped with one another, and together been referred to as the Pastoral Epistles.

At the same time, these letters have often been marginalized and ignored. Their affinities and the differences they appear to share over against the remainder of Paul's letters have led to them being treated as non-Pauline. Currently, the opinion of most critics is that these letters are "pseudonymous." As a result, their authority as Scripture is denied or disregarded, and their witness is frequently deprecated or ignored when summarizing Paul's theology and thought. A couple of examples:

> [The author of the Pastoral Epistles] does not have any doctrine of his own, but makes use of whatever comes to him in the sources which he uses. . . . He is no profound theologian . . . [He] could not do much at an intellectual level. (Easton 1982, 38, 50, 144)

> Organization and development of thought are expected from an author, but the Pastorals are characterized by a remarkable lack of both. (Miller 1997, 139; for these and other examples, see Van Neste 2007)

How then can Christian interpreters deal with the Pastoral Epistles as Scripture? Can we look upon them as faithful transmissions (or depictions) of Paul's thought and theology, practices and life; and if so, how? In this introduction, we seek to answer such questions.

The introduction will proceed as follows. First, to orient the reader, we will offer a narrative reconstruction of the story behind the Pastoral Epistles. Then we will consider several of the components traditionally covered in commentary introductions: issues relating to authorship, dating, the recipients, and the like. The story behind the Pastoral Epistles is the place to begin.

The Story the Pastoral Epistles Tell

Before tracing the story behind the Pastoral Epistles, we must deal with two preliminary issues. First is the question of a starting point: Where (with what letter) does the story begin? Second is the importance of succession to the story, a factor that modern readers, who lack sensitivity to succession language and phenomena that ancient readers possessed, often miss.

Finding the Starting Point

The letters come to us in the canonical order 1 Timothy, 2 Timothy, Titus, but several factors indicate that this is not the best order for reading the letters. First, the Muratorian Fragment (c. 170 CE) mentions the letters in the order Titus, 1 Timothy, 2 Timothy.

Second, Titus's extended introduction (Titus 1:1-4) seems to present themes that go beyond the scope of Titus itself and reach into the letters to Timothy. This is the kind of editorial activity that took place when letters were collected for publication (Trobisch 2000). Hypothetically, Paul or his editors—or the pseudepigrapher(s), if the letters are pseudonymous—would have made such revisions to turn those verses into an introduction not just for Titus but for the three-letter collection.

Third, 1 Timothy takes up and develops themes that Titus introduces; "the content of Titus is repeated and redacted in 1 Timothy" (Quinn 1978, 62–75). The canonical order of 1 Timothy, 2 Timothy, Titus (and then Philemon) comes from a later period, when the small collection of Paul's letters to individuals was gathered, or when it was being added to the larger collection of all his extant letters.

Further, when reading the three letters, the most natural way to reconstruct the story they tell is for the events depicted in Titus to have happened before those in the other letters. In other words, ancient narrative logic, as described by Aristotle (*Poetics* 1450b), demands that the Pastoral Epistles be read in the order Titus, 1 Timothy, 2 Timothy. I will unpack this point more fully after the synopsis below; here it is enough to say that ancient audiences would have understood the letters and the story behind them in the order that I propose.

The Importance of Succession

A second factor that affects our understanding of the story is the prominence of *succession* in the story. I (Stepp) have fully described the ancient understanding of succession and its impact on our reading of the Pastoral Epistles elsewhere (Stepp 2005, *passim*). Here, I summarize briefly.

In modern religious studies, the popular model for understanding succession is the practice of "apostolic succession," where leaders in a religious body trace back their authority and office through an unbroken chain of the laying on of hands, often attempting to build a line all the way back to the Apostles. In this model, two things are assumed when succession takes place: first, the object that is passed on is an office or title (e.g., "Apostle," "Bishop"); second, new leaders are full replacements for their predecessors.

On the other hand, the understanding of succession from the New Testament world was flexible and nuanced. Note the following:

First, texts from this world apply succession to a variety of objects, not just offices. Among the things being passed on in a succession include

- **leadership roles** (official or otherwise) in government, military, philosophical schools, academies;
- **responsibilities and tasks**, such as religious service, work important to the predecessor, the role of prophet, or a ruler's specific agenda;
- **knowledge or craft**, such as magic, medicine, legal expertise, a body of teaching, expertise in fishing;
- **possessions or inheritance**, such as a kingdom, a school, disciples, or the pattern of one's life (Talbert 1998, 154; Stepp 2005, 58–59, 90).

Second, these texts use signs of succession, particularly the Greek *diadochos/diadechomai* word groups, to describe varying degrees of replacement. Ancient authors applied the language and phenomena of succession to several types of predecessor-successor relationships, ranging from what we would think of as *delegation* (a leader gives an agent a limited commission and a limited amount of authority to carry it out: e.g., Mordecai and Ahasuerus in Esther 10:2 LXX) to *full replacement* (where a leader bequeaths his full authority and talent onto the person who follows him in an office or a role: e.g., Elijah and Elisha in 1 Kings 19–2 Kings 2). The best way to picture this phenomenon is to see succession as a continuum that runs from strong succession (full replacement, where the successor is essentially a "reincarnation" of the predecessor) to weak succession (delegation, where the successor receives a limited amount of the predecessor's authority) with various points between these poles.

Third, texts from the New Testament world depict succession as achieving several different objectives. Included among these:

- marking one successor (among several possible successors) as the legitimate heir to the predecessor (see David, Solomon, and Adonijah in 1 Kings 1–2);
- empowering a successor to achieve a goal that he/she might not achieve on his/her own (see Moses and Joshua in Numbers 27 and Joshua 1);
- enabling a predecessor to complete work and achieve objectives after his/her own life and effectiveness have ended (see Alexander's agenda in *Diod Sic* 17–18);
- guaranteeing that an institution will remain healthy and vital after the predecessor's death or retirement (see Diogenes Laertius 4.65–67, 9.115, 10.9; Pliny's *Natural History* 30.2.4–5).

How does an understanding of succession in the New Testament world affect our reading of the Pastoral Epistles? First, the relationships of Paul and Titus and of Paul and Timothy fall within the range of relationships that readers in the New Testament world would have understood as succession. Timothy and Titus do not need to be given the title "Apostle" for them to be Paul's successors. They were given tasks and authority, and the language and phenomena of succession are used; that is enough. Second, Paul's relationship to Titus is a weak type of succession, where a limited commission and a limited amount of authority are passed from leader to agent. Paul's relationship with Timothy is a stronger type of succession, where the leadership of Paul's churches and the care and use of Paul's gospel progressively (over the course of the two letters) pass from Paul to Timothy. Finally, succession in the Pastorals may function in all of the ways listed below:

- to legitimate Titus and (particularly) Timothy as the keepers of Paul's true voice,
- to empower them to accomplish their tasks,
- to continue Paul's work after his death/departure, and
- to ensure the continued health and vitality of Paul's gospel and churches.

The Story

What story, then, do the Pastoral Epistles tell? When examined in chronological order (Titus, 1 Timothy, 2 Timothy), they tell the story of Paul's departure. They depict the ending of Paul's career, as he withdrew from his work, step by step. How would Paul's churches continue in his absence? In each case, Paul provides a successor and delegates to him authority appropriate to the required task.

The beginning of the Pastoral Epistles (Titus) shows Paul withdrawing from direct work with new churches and new areas of mission. Paul is working as a missionary, much in the same way as he is depicted in Acts. He has few restrictions on his movements and can come and go as he pleases. He also has a cadre of coworkers whom he can commission and send here or there as he sees fit.

On the island of Crete, he preaches the gospel and establishes new churches. Before he completes the work of establishing leadership structures for the new churches, he is called away on other business. These churches are not prepared to stand on their own in Paul's absence. Their leadership is not yet firmly established, nor is their training complete. Furthermore, the new Christians don't really know how to act, and they haven't fully broken from their superstitious and hedonistic pasts. They also face external pressures in the opposition of rebellious and malicious people, some of them anti-Christian Jews. These outside antagonists will slander Paul and his people and try to sabotage the faith of the new believers.

To address the dangers raised by his departure and absence, Paul leaves behind Titus, one of his coworkers, to continue the work of establishing leadership in the new churches. To enforce his instructions to Titus, and to enable and empower him to do the necessary work, Paul wrote the letter to Titus. This letter was an open letter, read aloud and available to the people of the churches. It communicated to Titus and the people of the churches what Paul expected of him and of them. It put limits on Titus's authority: he had authority only on Crete, and only until a definite point in the future (Titus 3:12). Paul would soon send Artemis or Tychicus to take Titus's place. At that point, Titus would join Paul in Nicopolis.

The middle of the story of the Pastoral Epistles (1 Timothy) shows Paul withdrawing from direct work with his established churches. This work is personified by the church at Ephesus. In his missionary travels, Paul had spent a significant amount of time with this church, according to Acts.

This part of the story opens with Paul's having left Ephesus. He and Timothy had been working together there, and they had encountered problems of some severity. Then Paul was called away to Macedonia (another area where he did much work), forcing him to leave Timothy in Ephesus. Paul hoped to rejoin Timothy there, but the problems in Macedonia were such that he would not be able to return to Asia at the time of his choosing.

Timothy's task is to face false teachers and recalcitrant church leaders. These antagonists are established leaders in the church; thus Timothy's task is more serious and difficult than the task Titus faces on Crete. This sense of escalating conflict drives the progress of the story's plot. Further, Timothy here appears to be hesitant, unsure of himself, intimidated by his task. Because of Timothy's weakness and the daunting task he faces, the passing on of authority via succession from Paul to Timothy is more marked in 1 Timothy than the passing on of authority in Titus.

Also, Paul's supporting cast has shrunk: among the Pastoral Epistles, only 1 Timothy fails to name any of Paul's coworkers other than the recipient. This lack of resources complicates Timothy's work even further. And Paul is no longer in charge of his itinerary; he *hopes* to return to Ephesus soon, but may not be able to do so.

The end of the story (2 Timothy) shows Paul imprisoned, facing imminent but not immediate execution. He writes from a Roman jail to Timothy, who is presumably still in Ephesus. Paul evidently did not make it back to Asia, as promised in 1 Timothy, or he would have picked up his coat and books along the way.

Paul's supporting cast is conspicuous by their absence. In 4:9ff, Paul describes one coworker (Demas) as having deserted him, another whom he has sent to Ephesus (Tychicus), and two (Crescens and Titus) who simply have left Paul. Are we to understand this cool description as a criticism, and that Titus and Crescens made these trips on their own, rather than under Paul's authority? At any rate, Luke alone is at Paul's side when Paul sends for Timothy and John Mark.

Paul's most pressing concern here is what will happen to his gospel and his churches after his death. He thus makes Timothy his full successor, passing on to him the task of using and administering Paul's gospel. More than a single task is being passed on to Timothy. Timothy must suffer for the gospel, teach the gospel faithfully, and prepare others to receive and care for it after his own death; in all these things, he is Paul's successor. The only thing Paul does not pass on to Timothy is the title and office of Apostle. In every other way, Timothy becomes Paul's replacement, the keeper of the Apostle's true voice.

In 2 Timothy, at the end of the story of the Pastoral Epistles, Paul stands bereft of freedom, followers, and future (at least in this life). There is only one inevitable course for the action to follow: Paul's death. He has not the

Introduction to the Pastoral Epistles

resources or power to affect this fate. Yet he stands triumphant, because he is confident that God has not abandoned him to these travails. He calls Timothy to join him in Rome, hoping that his son in the faith will arrive before the date of his (Paul's) execution.

This is the story that the Pastoral Epistles tell. Surveying the story brings us to another reason for reading the letters in the order Titus, 1 Timothy, 2 Timothy—namely that the narrative logic of the letters demands this order. In his description of narrative plot, Aristotle famously says that a plot is a whole action (one in which there is a change in fortunes from good to bad or from bad to good) "which has a beginning, a middle, and an end." He describes the parts:

> A beginning is that which itself does not follow necessarily from anything else, but some second thing naturally exists or occurs after it. Conversely, an end is that which does itself naturally follow from something else, either necessarily or in general, but there is nothing else after it. A middle is that which itself comes after something else, and some other thing comes after it. (*Poetics* 1450b)

Perhaps a good way to envision the relationship between beginning, middle, and end is in the shape of a funnel. The beginning is the wide end of the funnel, where the main character in the story has many possibilities and resources. The quest is defined, and the hero pursues this goal with few hindrances. As the story progresses from beginning to middle to end, these possibilities narrow and resources dwindle, so that—at the end of the story—the described outcome seems necessary and inevitable.

The Pastoral Epistles fit this understanding of plot quite well, if read in the order proposed. Titus 1:1-3 describe Paul's quest: he is engaged in "furthering the faith of God's elect, and their knowledge of the truth, and the godly life that such knowledge promotes." This introduction thus outlines for the audience the work that Paul will seek to accomplish over the time described by the three letters.

Further, Titus depicts a Paul who is at the top of his game. His options are wide open; he moves freely from place to place, spending the winter where he chooses. He is in charge of his own itinerary, overseeing a group of coworkers and sending them where he thinks they are needed. His supporting cast includes not only Titus and a number of coworkers unknown outside this letter, but also Apollos. These details create a sense of openness and possibility that fits well Aristotle's description of a beginning.

In 1 Timothy and 2 Timothy, Paul's possibilities narrow. In 1 Timothy, he has no coworkers, other than Timothy himself. He has been called away from Ephesus, and wants to return, but circumstances may prevent it. The conflict in Ephesus, which Timothy has been left behind to face, is more serious and more immediate than the conflict on Crete in Titus. These factors—shrinking resources, escalating conflict, and narrowing possibilities—make 1 Timothy the perfect fit for the middle of the story of the Pastoral Epistles, as ancient audiences would have heard it.

In 2 Timothy, Paul has no freedom and no options, and few resources. The only coworker at his side is Luke, and Paul does not even have his books or winter cloak. He calls Timothy to come to him before the inevitable (his execution) takes place. These features fit well Aristotle's description of the ending of a story. And yet this conclusion also contains a reversal (Aristotle, *Poetics* 1451a): Paul's ministry and the effective power of his gospel do not end with his death because Timothy, his successor (and the faithful believers who in turn will be Timothy's successors), will continue to carry on the ministry and to use Paul's gospel as God intended.

Here then is the story of the Pastoral Epistles in a nutshell, as the audience would have reconstructed it: Paul continues his missionary work, in much the same manner as described in the book of Acts. Conflicts internal to his churches escalate as the story progresses, as do external pressures (persecution). These conflicts cause Paul to leave his work behind, step by step. First, he leaves behind his work with new churches, here personified in the church at Crete. Second, he leaves behind his work with established Pauline churches, here personified by the church at Ephesus. Finally, he leaves behind this life itself. With each departure, new problems arise for the churches. In Paul's absence, how will they address these issues? They survive and thrive by trusting the successors that Paul provided for them.

As an aside, I must note something here about pseudepigraphy in letter collections. David Trobisch asserts that pseudepigrapha exist in practically every ancient letter collection. The purpose of these entries in the collections is to "fill in the gaps" by telling readers what happened between and after the established, authentic letters in the collections (Trobisch 2004). Whatever my conclusions below regarding the authorship of the Pastoral Epistles, I must admit that the story of the Pastoral Epistles makes sense in the ways that Trobisch has proposed.

The Characters in the Story, Part 1: The Recipients

In this section of the introduction, I will treat the *prima facie* recipients of the letters, Titus and Timothy, before addressing the authorship of the letters.

Titus

Titus was one of Paul's most trusted coworkers. While not mentioned in Acts, he is prominent in Paul's work as described in Galatians and 2 Corinthians. Early on in Paul's missionary work, Titus (a Gentile, uncircumcised) accompanied Paul to Jerusalem as a "test case" to see whether the Jerusalem church would accept him as a legitimate convert to Christ (Gal 2:1-3). Later, Titus was Paul's right-hand man in dealings with the Corinthian church. He delivered Paul's "tearful" letter to them, and brought back to Paul news of their repentance and readiness to welcome his ministry once again (2 Cor 2:12-13; 7:5-7). Paul also entrusted to Titus the oversight of the Corinthians' participation in the great collection for the Jerusalem church (2 Cor 8:6, 16-17, 23; 12:18).

Now, Paul has left him in charge of the fledgling mission on Crete. Titus must finish work that Paul himself has left unfinished, by raising up and appointing indigenous elders and other leaders according to Paul's normal practice (Acts 15:23). Due to the importance of this work, Paul entrusts it to someone who has previously shown himself to be faithful and effective, time and again. It is not surprising that Paul would write instructions and encouragement to Titus, his faithful delegate/successor.

What evidence is there of Paul's mission work in Crete? Acts makes no mention of a Pauline mission on the Isle of Crete, and no mention of Titus at all. It is not impossible that Paul started a mission on Crete when his ship stopped there on its way to Rome (Acts 27:6-12). But according to the Acts account, Paul's time in Crete seems too brief for the kind of mission envisioned in Titus. The early church thought that Paul's work in Crete occurred after the close of Acts' narrative, when Paul was released from his first Roman imprisonment (Acts 28:28-30), a view supported by the early Christian historian, Eusebius:

> Tradition has it that after defending himself the Apostle was then sent on the ministry of preaching, and coming a second time to the same city suffered martyrdom under Nero. During this imprisonment he wrote the second Epistle to Timothy, indicating at the same time that his first defense had taken place and his martyrdom was at hand. (*Hist Eccl* 2.22; cf. *1 Clement* 5.7; *Acts of Peter* 1.1-3, 49; *Muratorian Canon*)

Although Acts hints at impending martyrdom (20:23-25, 29, 38; 21:13), it is hard to see on what charges Paul could have been executed at the end of the imprisonment of Acts 28 as Luke describes it. Thus it is logical to conclude that Paul likely was released from the Acts 28 imprisonment, then re-arrested and martyred at a later date. Further, both Philippians and Philemon seem to have been written from the Roman imprisonment of Acts 28 (Paul's first). Both reflect Paul's strong hope of release and return to his churches in Asia Minor (Phil 2:24; Phm 22).

Others have tried to place a mission to Crete within the parameters of the Acts narrative (see especially Robinson 1976; Johnson 2001). While there is no unanimity on when this might have occurred, Luke's account is selective (witness Paul's litany of suffering in 2 Corinthians 11:16-33, most of which is not described in Acts). This selectivity means that ample time exists in the story of Acts for Pauline missions to Crete and elsewhere.

Timothy
Timothy is Paul's most prominent coworker. According to Acts 16:1-3, he joined the Pauline mission in Lystra during Paul's second missionary journey, traveling with Paul and his party to Philippi, Thessalonica, Berea, Athens, and Corinth (Acts 17:14-15; 18:5). On Paul's third missionary journey, Timothy appears in Ephesus, from which he is sent ahead to prepare for Paul's upcoming visit to Macedonia and Greece (Acts 19:21-22). Returning with Paul through Macedonia, Timothy went ahead to Troas, and waited there to accompany Paul on the journey to Jerusalem to deliver the collection (Acts 20:1-6).

Evidence from Paul's undisputed letters indicates that Paul frequently sent Timothy as his delegate to "troubled" churches:

- Timothy strengthened the Thessalonian church in Paul's absence (1 Thess 3:1-6);
- He reminded the wayward Corinthian church of Paul's teaching (1 Cor 4:17; 16:10-11);
- He reported Paul's circumstances to supporting churches and took reports of the churches' status back to Paul (Phil 2:19-24; 1 Thess 3:6).

Paul's tribute to Timothy in Philippians 2:19-24 makes clear how much Timothy meant to Paul and his work. Finally, Timothy is named as coauthor/cosender in several of the letters (2 Cor 1:1; Phil 1:1; Col 1:1; 1 Thess 1:1; 2 Thess 1:1; Phlm 1), and sends his greetings to the Roman church in Romans 16:21.

First Timothy presupposes that Paul has left Timothy in Ephesus while he makes a visit to Macedonia. Such a scenario is quite plausible, and might be identified with the trip of Acts 20:1-3 or the separate trip of 2 Corinthians 1:16; 2:12-13; and 7:5-6. Of course, even if those visits do not perfectly fit the circumstances of 1 Timothy, the selectivity of the Acts narrative provides other openings. For example, we know that Paul spent more than two years in Ephesus on his third mission (Acts 19:1; 20:1), yet Luke tells us about only three incidents from this period. Paul certainly might have decided to get back on the road for a few months during this time.

On the other hand, 2 Timothy is written during an imprisonment from which Paul sees little hope of release (2 Tim 4:6-8). Though Timothy's whereabouts are not mentioned, he is close enough to travel to Paul quickly (2 Tim 4:9, 21) and must pass through Troas on the way to pick up Paul's cloak, books, and parchments (2 Tim 4:13).

The Characters in the Story, Part 2: Authorship and Authenticity

Until the time of Schleiermacher (1768–1834), the traditional history as described above was assumed to be factual. Schleiermacher and those who followed argued that the Pastoral Epistles present a fictitious setting and scenario. The author built his story world on the narrative of Acts (or the traditions behind it) and the authentic letters. From this base, he created a fictitious scenario to promote his own understanding of how Paul would address issues in his (the pseudepigrapher's) own time and context.

When discussing the authorship of the Pastorals, three initial observations are in order. *First*, it is important to remember that the Pastoral Epistles present themselves as *three separate letters*. Further, the three differ in important respects (e.g., setting, argumentative strategy, letter type/genre). In discussions of the authorship of these letters, the overwhelming tendency has been to treat them as a single literary unit. Thus the letters are treated as false on three levels: the ascription of authorship is false, the recipients are not the men named in the letters, and the letters are not even really three separate letters, each with its own logic and rhetoric, but something else entirely.

In this approach, the three "Pastorals" are taken as a group and compared to the undisputed letters of Paul (the Pauline "homolegoumena," Romans, 1 and 2 Corinthians, Galatians, 1 Thessalonians, Philippians, and Philemon) as a group. Such an approach fails to consider the important differences between the Pastoral Epistles, and the important differences between the individual members of the undisputed letters. It also fails to account for the striking similarities between individual letters of the Pastoral Epistles and other undisputed letters (e.g., between 2 Timothy and Philippians) when examined letter by letter.

Second, scholars seeking to prove or disprove authenticity must constantly be on guard against the selective use of evidence. Similarities between the Pastorals and the undisputed letters are often muted, and the differences amplified. Criteria for authenticity can cut both ways, as I will show below, and rarely produce unequivocal results.

Third, this discussion is ideologically charged. Proponents of authenticity are often driven by the equation of any type of pseudonymity with deception, by the absence of reliability, or by the desire to support traditional perspectives on familial or societal structures, women's roles in church and family, etc. On the other hand, proponents of pseudonymity may find that such a view allows them to distance themselves from content they regard as questionable or objectionable, such as the traditional perspectives mentioned above. Common to both positions is the presumption that all forms of pseudonymity relegate a text to secondary place in the canon or even undermine its authority entirely.

Is this the historical view of the church or the Graeco-Roman world, however? Several ancient texts point to a more flexible conception of authorship than that to which modern critics hold. In *Atticus* 6.6, for example, Cicero describes writing a letter in a manner quite similar to the way those who view the Pastorals as pseudepigraphy envision (Talbert refers to this as "writing 'as if' by the putative author" [Talbert 2007, 7–8]). Cicero dictated a letter to the secretary of his friend, Atticus (perhaps because the secretary's handwriting was known), in Atticus's name, to a third party. Cicero then read the letter to the third party as if it was from Atticus, without acknowledging in any way (except the correspondence between himself and Atticus) that he (Cicero) and not Atticus was responsible for the content. Talbert continues, "According to ancient sensibilities . . . letters would be perceived as forgeries only if the ideas presented were not in continuity with those of the alleged author" (Talbert 2007, 11; see also Iamblichus, *Life of Pythagoras* 31.198; Metzger 1972; Meade 1986). Due to these differences between modern and ancient views, insisting that authority and authenticity depend on direct authorship is anachronistic.

Further, the original audience received these letters as genuinely Pauline. The Pastorals remain part of the Church's canon of sacred Scripture, recognized as authentic apostolic witness during the second century. They were not and are not secondary texts, deutero-canonical literature, but an important part of the New Testament.

As mentioned above, for the first 1700 years of New Testament study, there is no evidence that anyone questioned the authenticity of these letters. Polycarp of Smyrna (c. 69–155) draws from them extensively, including one clear quotation from 1 Timothy (*To the Philippians* 4, quoting 1 Tim 6:7, 10). Both Irenaeus and Tertullian regarded them as Pauline. The church historian Eusebius, in the early fourth century, lists them among the "undisputed writings" (*Hist Eccl* 3.3.5).

As noted above, Friedrich Schleiermacher was apparently the first to raise the issue of authenticity. In a personal letter to a friend, Schleiermacher suggested that the authenticity of 2 Timothy might be questionable. Over the next 150 years, the Pastoral Epistles were scrutinized for any evidence that might demonstrate that they were, in fact, not Pauline. As the bits of evidence accumulated, scholars began to assume that none of the three was from Paul, and this position became critical orthodoxy. In an ironic twist on Schleiermacher's initial assertion, some today argue that if any of the three were genuinely Pauline, it would be 2 Timothy.

Those who reject Pauline authorship base their conclusion on the following evidence. Note how these arguments run in circles, so that one can usually argue both against and *for* authenticity from similar criteria.

Language and style. Those arguing for pseudonymity note that the Pastorals contain a disproportionately high occurrence of words that are found nowhere else the New Testament. On the pages of the standard critical Greek text, the NA^{27}, the Pastoral Epistles have 13–16 unique words per page, compared to 4–6 per page in the undisputed letters of Paul. Further, the particles and connecting words commonly used by Paul in the undisputed letters (e.g., *since, because, therefore, but now, with the result*) are absent, which give the letters a different flow and a different style.

The Pastorals also differ from the undisputed letters in their vocabulary, which (it is argued) has more in common with second-century writers than with first-century writers. In fact, the vocabulary of the Pastorals appears to have more in common with the ethical compositions of Hellenistic Judaism (e.g., 4 Maccabees or *The Testament of the Twelve Patriarchs*) than with the undisputed Paulines, or even the New Testament as a whole.

The style differs in yet another important way. The author of the Pastorals does not argue with his opponents and their positions in the same way that Paul argues in the undisputed letters. In the genuine letters, Paul displays a rich rhetorical diversity, using many different rhetorical strategies and engaging his opponents as if they were present (Beker 1991, 38–40). The author of the Pastorals, on the other hand, shows little interest in dialogue with his opponents. Instead, he offers a sustained monologue in which belief and behavior are dictated and backed up by tradition, and all other voices are silenced.

Thus, for those who argue on the basis of language and style, the Pastoral Epistles don't sound like Paul because Paul did not write them.

On the other hand, as with all of Paul's letters, the Pastoral Epistles are occasional in nature. We must therefore allow the specifics of the historical situation to affect the language the author (Paul or pseudepigrapher) uses. For example, the Pastorals give a great deal of attention to the specific qualifications of overseers and deacons, the care for and ministry of widows, the management of the household of faith, vice and virtue lists, etc. These obviously require specific vocabulary not needed in other Paulines, which address other concerns. Further, the nature of these letters, addressed first to individuals (and secondarily to congregations and those entrusted with the care of congregations), could require a difference in language and style (over against those letters addressed primarily to congregations). Also, the use of earlier traditional material (such as hymns and confessions) with its own unique vocabulary (as, e.g., 1 Tim 3:16; 2 Tim 2:11-13) is not unique to the Pastorals (see, e.g., Phil 2:5-11; 1 Cor 15:3ff).

Regarding the style of argumentation: the author *does* engage his opponents at some length in 1 Timothy 1:8-11; 4:3-5, 7-8; 6:5-10. Extended argumentation, such as what we see in Galatians 3–4 and 2 Corinthians 10–13, is not necessary because the author in the Pastoral Epistles is not engaging with critics to *persuade*. He is writing to the *persuaded*. "Preaching to the choir" requires a different style and language.

Also under the heading of style: the Pastoral Epistles are dissimilar in another important way from known Graeco-Roman pseudonymous works. Those pseudonymous works tend to lack a concrete setting, and rather create a setting superfluous to the contents of the narrative. This is a sign that the author does not think the readers are familiar with the situation as it can be historically reconstructed. But in the Pastoral Epistles, readers are given a striking amount of detail, and specifics that require explanation. The author presumes the readers will understand things such as personal requests for a cloak and books and a visit before winter and oblique indications of the whereabouts of fifteen workers and coworkers, none of which contradicts what is known from other sources (with the exception of Trophimus) (Bauckham 1988, 490).

Church structure. Those who regard the Pastorals as pseudonymous argue that the church organization evidenced in the Pastorals reflects a post-

Pauline stage of development. The use of titles like "overseer/bishop," "elder," and "deacon" suggest well-defined offices. In such a situation, more attention is being given to institutional structure than to the open, charismatic life of the early decades of the church (Dibelius and Conzelmann 1972, 7). There is even the mention of a "council of elders" in 1 Timothy 4:14 that sounds like an ordination council! In this regard, the church of the Pastorals sounds more like that of the *Didache* (late first century) or the letters of Ignatius of Antioch (early second century) than the church of Paul's day.

On the other hand, Paul begins his undisputed letter to the Philippians addressing the "overseers" and "deacons," obviously assuming that they are an established part of congregational life. Luke indicates that Paul appointed "elders" in his churches from the beginning of his mission (Acts 14:23). And this is not a "structure" that had to be birthed *ex nihilo* by the early Christians. Both the Jewish synagogue and the Graeco-Roman *collegia* (or "club") have similar organizational structures. In fact, Paul in the Pastorals does not deal with the particular duties of these officials, but only the qualities they should possess. There is nothing here by way of structure that could not have existed in Paul's lifetime. Logic dictates that we should be more surprised if the earliest church did *not* develop leadership structures similar to the synagogues and collegia.

Theology. Against Pauline authorship, some note that many theological themes prominent in the undisputed Paulines are surprisingly absent from the Pastorals: God as father, new life "in Christ," the work of the Spirit in the life of the believer, and so on. Some note that the Pastoral Epistles do not share the sense of eschatological expectation that one finds in the nondisputed letters. Further, when the Pastorals do use the same theological terms as the undisputed Paulines, these terms are used with a different meaning. For example, "righteousness" (*dikaiosyne*), a central theme of Paul's gospel in the nondisputed letters, usually refers to "God's redemptive intervention in Christ" (Beker 1991, 42). But in the Pastorals, "righteousness" is an ethical quality. Likewise "faith" (*pistis*): in the nondisputed letters, "faith" refers to trust in God or Christ. In the Pastoral Epistles, "faith" refers to the moral quality of reliability or fidelity, and "*the* faith" refers to the body of teaching that Paul expects his churches to cling to as they navigate the waters of doctrinal uncertainty.

Furthermore, the Pastorals emphasize "good works" (which is *not* a major Pauline theme elsewhere). They describe the Christian life with non-

Pauline terms like "godliness" and "self-control." Such moralistic language is more akin to Hellenistic Judaism than the undisputed Pauline letters.

On the other hand, Paul in the undisputed letters demonstrates an intense concern about the formation of virtuous and ethical behavior in new converts (Gal 5:16–6:10; Rom 12:9-13; 1 Cor 6:9-20; Phil 4:8-9; 1 Thess 4:1-12; 5:14-15). Paul also emphasize the importance of "good works" in texts like Romans 2:6-7; 13:2; 2 Corinthians 5:10; and Colossians 1:10 (the Pauline authorship of Colossians is disputed, but scholarly opinion regarding its genuineness is split fairly evenly).

Further, the Pastoral Epistles do contain a strong sense of eschatological expectation. The author understands the rise of false teachers as a sign of the last days (1 Tim 4:1-5). He anticipates Christ's appearance using the language of epiphany (2 Tim 1:10; Titus 3:4; 2:11; 1 Tim 6:14; 2 Tim 4:8).

Also in favor of the authenticity of the Pastorals is the presence in the letters of key Pauline themes:

- *Salvation is by grace and not works* (2 Tim 1:9; Titus 2:11; 3:5; cf. Rom 3:24; 5:17-21);
- *Present suffering leads to future glory* (2 Tim 2:3-6, 10; 4:6-8; cf. Rom 5:1-5; 2 Cor 4:7-18);
- *The importance of the Gentile mission* (1 Tim 2:7; 3:16; 2 Tim 4:17; cf. Gal 2:8-9; 1 Thess 2:16; Rom 15:15-16);
- *Paul set up as an example for others to follow* (1 Tim 1:15-16; 2 Tim 1:8, 13; 3:10-17; 2 Tim 4:7; 1 Tim 6:12; cf. 1 Cor 3:16; 11:1; Phil 3:17; 2 Thess 3:9)

History. The events in the Pastorals, it is argued, do not fit well with events known to us from other New Testament sources, particularly the book of Acts. Neither Acts nor any other New Testament document mentions a mission of Paul to Crete, or Titus being sent to that island. Neither does Acts nor any other New Testament document mention Paul's entrusting leadership of the Ephesian church to Timothy. And in the Pastoral Epistles, we find no indication of the Jewish-Gentile controversy that plagued Paul's mission in Acts and the nondisputed letters.

Furthermore, the false teachers in the Pastoral Epistles appear to be second-century Gnostics: they refer to their teaching as "knowledge" (*gnōsis*, 1 Tim 6:20); they are infatuated with "myths and endless genealogies" (1 Tim 1:4; Titus 3:9); they believe that the resurrection has already occurred (2 Tim 2:17-18). Obviously, if the false teachers are second-century Christian Gnostics, the letters must post-date Paul.

On the other hand, Acts is a "selective" history. It makes no mention of mission to Illyricum (Rom 15:19). It does not mention the multiple imprisonments or other events in Paul's litany of suffering (1 Cor 11:23-27); Acts mentions only one imprisonment during this period (Acts 16:22-34). In sum, Acts leaves a great deal of Paul's time unaccounted for. The activities and events we read about in the Pastorals are consistent with the Lukan account of Paul's activity, even if they don't neatly match specific events from the book of Acts.

Furthermore, the Pastoral Epistles do indeed show evidence of problems with Jewish or Jewish Christian antagonists, similar to those Paul has dealt with in other letters. His antagonists are said to be obsessed with "endless genealogies" (1 Tim 1–4), the (improper) application of the law (1 Tim 1:7-8), circumcision (Titus 1:10), and "stupid controversies, genealogies, dissensions, and quarrels about the law" (Titus 3:9). Still further, the "Gnostic" elements alluded to are consistent with incipient Gnostic teachings, which Paul may have battled as early as the letter to the Galatians (Gal 4:3, 9-11). Certainly Paul confronted confusion and false teaching about the resurrection in the Thessalonian letters (1 Thess 4:13–5:10; 2 Thess 2:1-12) and 1 Corinthians (15).

And so it goes. Most scholars agree that none of these arguments is conclusive by itself. Their collective weight, however, combined with the fact that most New Testament scholars reflexively reject Pauline authorship, have led to pseudonymity becoming the "default position," something critics automatically assume without testing. Still, a strong minority continues to view the Pastoral Epistles as Pauline; of the seven major English language commentaries published on the Pastorals since the mid-1990s, four argue that the letters are genuinely Pauline, directly or indirectly.

On the basis of these arguments, four basic positions on authorship have developed. I list them here in order of decreasing distance from Paul:

1. Pseudonymity. By this view, the letters are non-Pauline. They were written after Paul's death and independently of Paul's direct associates in an effort to address new developments from a position of "Pauline" authority (Dibelius and Conzelmann, Beker). The author intends to deceive, thus the letters are pseudonymous ("forgeries"), deceptive on three levels. By this view, such deception was a common practice in the ancient world, where standards of literary propriety were different from our own, and an element of deceit was ethically permissible to achieve positive and praiseworthy outcomes.

On the other hand, we must remember that Christians were strongly committed to truth both in theory and practice. Furthermore, the early Christians were quick to reject works that were deemed inauthentic. These were often the works of heretical opponents of developing orthodoxy who sought to pass off their writings as coming from first-century leaders.

2. Allonomymity. By this view, the letters are indirectly Pauline. Here, one of Paul's disciples openly continues to write new materials and applications of Paul's thought, including the Pastoral Epistles, after Paul's death. There is no intention to deceive. Readers were likely aware of the post-Pauline authorship and did not discard the books because of it. The letters may incorporate written fragments left behind by Paul, together with recollections of his teaching. What mattered was to keep the "voice" of Paul alive (Marshall 1999). Over time, the letters came to be seen as proceeding directly from Paul himself.

Many variations of this view exist, as scholars attempt to isolate and work out the materials they think authentic (Harrison 1921, Barrett 1963, Marshall 1999, 59–108, esp. 84, 93). The shortness of proposed authentic fragments, the complexity of fragment hypotheses, and the lack of consensus weigh against this view. Marshall's proposal is the simplest version, and thereby the strongest.

3. Free amanuensis. By this view, the *content* of the letters comes from Paul, but the *articulation* is from the secretary (amanuensis) who composed the letters—thus the content is directly Pauline. The use of an amanuensis, to whom the author would dictate the document, was a common phenomenon. Both strict amanuenses (to whom documents are dictated word for word) and free amanuenses (who possess a degree of control over the wording of documents) are known in ancient Graeco-Roman letterwriting. (For the suggestion that Luke was Paul's amanuensis, see Witherington 2006, 60: "The voice is the voice of Paul, the hand is the hand of Luke.")

The free amanuensis view supposes that, in his earlier letters, Paul exercised specific control over the wording of the manuscripts (see Rom 16:2; Gal 6:11): this explains the apparent uniformity of style in the nondisputed letters. After his first Roman imprisonment, Paul changed his methods, allowing the secretary much more freedom to state the arguments as he saw fit. This new secretary would have been the scribe for the Pastoral Epistles. This explains the uniformity of style between the letters, and the differences in style between the Pastorals and the nondisputed letters.

4. Authentic. By this view, the letters are directly Pauline. They were written by Paul to Timothy and Titus in specific historical circumstances. He

Introduction to the Pastoral Epistles

may have written them with his own hand, or dictated them word to word to an amanuensis.

Conclusion. The position one chooses with regard to authorship will significantly affect the interpretation of the letters. Three convictions guide us in our weighing of the evidence.

First, these letters are an accepted part of the New Testament canon, and as such should not be marginalized or disregarded.

Second, we do not accept the proposal of critical orthodoxy, that canonical documents were written intentionally to deceive. There is nothing noble about these "noble lies," as envisioned.

Third, these canonical documents were written to be read as the apostle's own words and, thus, are best understood in light of all that Paul has written. If we posit that the letters are in some way less than Pauline, we become resistant readers and undermine the authority of the canonical text. Further, if we adopt such views, we are ignoring the way the original audience received the letters. *They* certainly accepted the letters as Pauline, or they would not have preserved and treasured them.

Thus we reject the first hypothesis above, that the letters are pseudonymous and remote from Paul, written deceptively in Paul's name far after his death by people who were not directly associated with Paul. The most serious argument against direct Pauline authorship (the fourth hypothesis) is the argument from language and style. This argument is strong enough to rule out direct Pauline authorship. This leaves us with the second and third hypotheses, or some combination of the two.

Our conclusion is that Paul wrote the letters after his first imprisonment through an amanuensis. He changed his letter-writing practices over against the earlier letters, and gave this amanuensis greater freedom in the wording of the Pastoral Epistles. At a later date, the letters were edited (and perhaps supplemented) into the form (though not the order) in which we currently have them. Thus the letters are real letters, their recipients are real people, and the situations they describe are not ciphers for some later setting. Further, the contents of the letters are Pauline and they bear his *imprimatur* and authority.

Date and Provenance

Obviously, one's conclusions about authorship affect the dating and provenance of the letters. By the scenario we propose above, 2 Timothy is the last of the letters, written from imprisonment in Rome around 66–68 CE. If one places Titus and 1 Timothy in the framework of Acts, they could be dated to the mid-50s. If one places them after release from Paul's first Roman imprisonment, they should be dated c. 63. Paul wrote Titus as he was on his way to Nicopolis for the winter. He wrote 1 Timothy when in Macedonia, a few months later.

Or if one concludes that the letters were written long after Paul's time, then the letters could be dated any time between Paul's death (c. 60 or 68 CE, depending on whether he was executed at the end of Acts 28) until the time of Polycarp (who died in 155). By this view, there is no real way to determine provenance.

Genre

While these documents are often considered to be simply letters, their characteristics demand more careful attention (Richards 2002, 93–97, 129–36, 177–83). First Timothy and Titus share noticeable similarities that set them apart from 2 Timothy. Second Timothy has a nature all its own.

Second Timothy is often likened to a *testament*, an extremely popular genre of literature during and after the intertestamental period (see, e.g., *The Testaments of the Twelve Patriarchs*). The testament was essentially a deathbed speech, the speaker's "last will and testament." In such literature, the speaker looks ahead to his impending death, offers instructions to his children and/or followers, draws moral lessons from his own life experience, and predicts things to come after his death. Second Timothy certainly contains these elements. But we need also note important differences between 2 Timothy and testamentary literature. First, the form of 2 Timothy is a letter, indeed a typical Pauline letter. Second, the plethora of details about Paul, Timothy, and their specific circumstances sets 2 Timothy apart from normal testamentary literature, which is much more vague and timeless in setting. Because of these differences, 2 Timothy should be treated as a "personal paraenetic letter" (Johnson 2001, 322; cf. Richards 2002, 131–33).

Titus and 1 Timothy have often been identified as early "church orders" or "handbooks on church polity" (Dibelius and Conzelmann 1972, 5–7), similar to *The Community Rule (1QS)* (which governed the life of the Qumran community) and *The Damascus Document (CD)* (which governed the lives of Essenes living in towns and villages). Such documents contain ethical instructions, rules of conduct with penalties attached, guidelines for the practice of community rituals, and a delineation of the roles and responsibilities of community officers. The *Didache* is evidence that these documents existed in the church as early as the late first or early second century CE.

However, Titus and 1 Timothy do not really fit this genre. They are addressed first to individuals with oversight responsibilities, and only indirectly to the communities as a whole. They contain direct exhortations to the primary recipients, and instructions about their own personal conduct. True "community rules" address a much wider array of topics and cases than do the Pastorals. They also address the specific duties of leaders. The Pastoral Epistles, by contrast, give no attention to the specific duties of the community leaders, and focus exclusively on their character qualifications.

First Timothy and Titus are, however, very similar in nature to a particular type of royal correspondence known as the *mandata principis*. Such letters contained orders given by a superior to a delegate to be carried out in that delegate's assigned sphere of influence. They described how the delegate should conduct him/herself in the role or office being assumed.

These letters from superior to delegate existed in both private and public forms. The public forms were posted so that the entire community could access them; this was a means of both authorizing the delegate in the eyes of the community and keeping the delegate in check by making public the limits on his commission. In essence, the populace was allowed to "overhear" the delegate's orders!

Clearly, Titus and 1 Timothy are concerned with legitimizing the recipients' authority, particularly as Timothy contends with the false teachers and recalcitrant church leaders in Ephesus. These letters also contain specific orders from Paul, and descriptions of how Timothy and Titus should carry out their duties. The quasi-public nature of these letters helps explain their oft-noted formal nature (e.g., 1 Tim 6:20-21, with its abrupt ending, containing no personal greetings; the extended self-description in Titus 1:1-4). Even though the letters were written primarily to the delegate, they were intended to be overheard by the churches that the delegates were authorized to oversee.

Thus these letters no longer need to be seen as poor attempts at imitating Paul's genuine letters. They are instead examples of Paul's own use of a well-established genre.

Titus: The Necessity of Order

Outline

1. Salutation and Greeting (1:1-4)
2. The Charge Titus Is Given (1:5-9)
    A. The Charge: Put Things in Order, Appoint Elders (1:5)
    B. Qualifications for Leadership (1:6-9)
    C. The Challenge Titus Faces (1:10-16)
    D. Summary
3. The Way of Life Titus Must Teach (2:1–3:11)
    A. Responsibilities in the Household of God (2:1-15)
        1. Content (2:1-10)
        2. Theological foundation for the instruction (2:11-14)
        3. Encouragement and empowerment (2:15)
        4. Summary
    B. Living as Witnesses (3:1-11)
        1. Content (3:1-2)
        2. Theological foundation for the instruction (3:3-8a)
        3. Encouragement and empowerment (3:8b-11)
        4. Summary
4. Final Instructions, Travel Plans, and Benediction (3:12-15)

Salutation and Greeting (1:1-4)

Paul opens the letter in a way that is both standard for him and uniquely his.

The typical Graeco-Roman letter opening consisted of the name of the sender, the name of the recipient, a one-word greeting, and a brief blessing. The openings to Paul's letters are much longer than was customary, and he often used these expansions for rhetorical effect. The opening to Titus is in fact longer than the opening of any other Pauline letter, with the exception of Romans. Paul here adapts the standard format, using it to introduce themes and ideas that will come into play later in the letter. In particular, he expands the description of himself (the name of the sender) to include information about the gospel that he preaches and the source of his authority.

Paul identifies himself as the only sender of the letter (1:1). None of the Pastoral Epistles has a co-sender (co-author?) named in the letter opening, even though Paul in Titus and 2 Timothy names people who are working at his side when the letters are composed. Outside of the Pastorals, only Ephesians and Romans do not name co-senders in the openings. Ephesians and Romans are similar in character in that both are somewhat impersonal. Ephesians appears to be a circular letter, written to be passed from church to church in a particular district in Asia Minor. Romans is the most official and "professional" (and in some ways least personal) of Paul's letters, written to introduce him and his work to a church where people know him by reputation but do not know him personally. Paul here adopts a similar tone, due to the official character of the *mandata principis*.

Paul describes himself as a "slave of God." Paul frequently spoke of his ministry in terms of slavery (1 Cor 4:1; 9:15-19; cf. Rom 1:1; Phil 1:1). In his mind, he had been "bought with a price," so that he no longer belonged to himself. This imagery would resonate powerfully in the ancient Mediterranean world, where slavery was common: in some cities, between one-third and one-half of the populace were slaves.

The idea of being a slave of God/the gods was rare in the pagan world, although Plato does refer to Socrates as God's slave (*Phaedo* 85b). The image is common in the Septuagint, however, where Israel's patriarchs, prophets, and great leaders are referred to as God's slaves:

- Abraham (Ps 105:42)
- Isaac (2 Macc 1:2)
- Jacob (Ezek 28:25)
- Moses (1 Kings 8:53; 2 Kings 18:12; 2 Chr 24:9; Neh 9:14; 10:29; Dan 9:11; Mal 4:4)
- Joshua (Josh 24:29; Judg 2:8)
- David (2 Sam 3:18; 1 Kings 8:24-26; 1 Chr 17:7; Ps 89:3; cf. 1 Chr 17:4; 2 Chr 6:42; Ps 78:70; Ezek 34:23; 27:24-25; 1 Macc 4:30). Also to be associated with David is the slave imagery in the prayer language of the Psalms (19:11, 13; 119:125), which expresses the depth of the psalmist's dedication and submission to God.
- Solomon (1 Kings 3:7-8; 8:52)
- Ahijah (1 Kings 15:29)
- Elijah (1 Kings 18:36; 21:28; 2 Kings 10:10)

- Daniel (Dan 6:20)
- Zerubbabel (Haggai 2:23)
- "the prophets" (2 Kings 17:13, 23; 21:10; 24:2; Ezek 38:17; Zech 1:6)

By describing himself in these terms, Paul points to his obedience to God's plan, by which God brings the gospel and salvation to the Gentiles: this parallels 2 Sam 3:18, where David is God's slave, whose obedience to God's plan will result in salvation for his people Israel.

Paul also refers to himself as "an apostle of Jesus Christ." An apostle was one sent on a mission with a message and the authority to act on behalf of the sender. Paul has been sent by Jesus Christ, bearing authority to do the work Jesus sent him to do (cf. 1:3 and Paul's use of succession language to underscore his authority there).

The purpose for which Paul functions as a slave and an apostle is "to strengthen the faith of God's elect, and their knowledge of the truth which leads to godliness" (1:1b). In the Pastoral Epistles, "faith" (*pistis*) can refer to two things. Subjectively, it can refer to a person's trust in and commitment to Jesus Christ, which results in salvation and a changed life. Objectively, the word can refer to "THE faith," the true teaching of Paul's gospel. Normally, Paul in the Pastoral Epistles places a definite article before "faith" when he uses the word in this objective sense, and there is no definite article in 1:1. Thus here Paul points to the fact that part of his mission is to move his people to deeper trust in and more complete obedience to Jesus Christ. Paul uses the phrase "knowledge of the truth" three times in the Pastoral Epistles: here, in 1 Timothy 4:3, and in 2 Timothy 3:7. "Knowledge" is not limited to cognitive awareness of facts or information. In the Bible, "knowledge" is experiential, something to put into practice. "Truth" here refers to the contents of Paul's gospel and the life the gospel produces.

"Godliness" (*eusebeia*) is a central theme in the Pastoral Epistles: the noun appears ten times in these letters, and the modifier "godly" appears three times. In a Graeco-Roman context, "godliness" refers to a proper attitude and conduct toward the gods. In the Pastoral Epistles, it refers to a life lived in and from reverence toward God. This life of reverence is produced by living out the truth of the gospel: "Truth, to be understood, must be lived" (Peacock 1990).

Paul works to strengthen the faith and knowledge of his people "in the hope of eternal life" (1:2). "Hope" (*elpis*) is not just wishful thinking; it is confident expectation of a future state. Biblically, hope involves elements of both certainty and faith. "Eternal life" (*zōēs aiōniou*, literally "life for/of the ages") refers to both the duration of life (eternal, unending) and the quality of it (an abundant life for the present and future, bestowed by a benevolent God on his people). The focus is both present and future, now and not yet.

Paul ties his slavery and apostleship, and the faith and knowledge his work should produce, to the historic work of God in salvation history. The God who put this plan in motion is "God, who does not lie." In other words, the God who set in motion this plan for saving his people is completely and utterly trustworthy and faithful—he keeps his promises. This description of God contrasts with the traditional characterization of the people of Crete, preparing the way for the quote from Epimenides in 1:12. In the ancient world, Cretans were reputed to regard lying "as culturally acceptable" (Winter 2000, 149–50). "This cultural tendency lies behind the coining of the term '*krētizō*,' meaning 'to play the Cretan,' or 'to lie.'" This description of God also contrasts with the popular picture of Zeus in Cretan folk tales, who used deception to seduce a mortal woman (Towner 2006, 670).

God's plan for saving his people stretches from before creation (*pro chronōn aiōniōn*, literally "before eternal ages," before time existed) into eternity. The promise that his creatures would have fellowship with him, in spite of their sinfulness as he foreknew it, was in God's plans from before creation ("from before eternal ages"). Further, God revealed this eternal life and made it real at a time when the circumstances were exactly right. The Greek word for time (*kairos*) refers to an opportune or appropriate time, a special time, rather than chronological time (*chronos*), a deadline, the ticking of a clock.

At just the right time, God "revealed his plan" (*logos*, "word") through Paul. "Revealed" (*phaneroō*) is a key word in Paul's vocabulary. It functions in the Pauline corpus as "a key term for the revelation of God's salvation in the gospel of Jesus Christ" (EDNT 3.4113). *Phaneroō* was commonly used in the Hellenistic world to refer to the appearance or manifestation of a deity; the birth or ascent to power of a king; a king's royal visit to loyal cities; and the victorious returns from foreign lands of such deified emperors as Claudius, Caligula, and Diocletian. Paul here uses *phaneroō* to refer to the power and presence of Jesus Christ in the preaching (*kerygma*) of the gospel. *Kerygma* refers to the public proclamation of a herald, thus underscoring the official nature of the herald's message.

God entrusted (*pisteuō*) Paul with that message by his own command (*epitagē*) to/regarding Paul. Paul here uses the language of succession (see Introduction to the Pastoral Epistles; Stepp 2005) to describe his conversion and call to ministry. Paul did not appoint himself to the work of the gospel that he describes, nor did he come into this vocation by accident or chance. God chose Paul for this role, so that Paul could play a part in the ongoing ministry of Jesus Christ on earth after his ascension. Paul is Jesus' successor in the care and administration of the gospel and all that it produces. His authority derives from this succession, not from personal power or worth: this is part and parcel with being an apostle. His work and goals and aspirations are dictated by the plan of God, of which he is part, and depend on his continued faithfulness to God's command. For Paul's readers, this succession would have ensured that Paul's gospel continues to produce the results that God designed it to produce—"strengthened faith and knowledge of the truth, which leads to godliness, in hope of eternal life."

To summarize 1:1-3: Paul here adapts the standard letter form by adding a theologically and polemically weighted description of himself, the sender. In this description, he introduces ideas that will be important in the letter that follows. Among them:

- He expresses his pastoral concern for the people in his churches (the purpose of his gospel is to "strengthen the faith" of his people).
- He asserts that knowing God properly leads to a life lived in and from reverence for God ("godliness").
- The goal of this reverent life is eternal life; biblically, this means much more than "going to heaven when you die." Eternal life is an abundant life lived in the presence of God, in this world and in the next.
- God makes this gift of abundant life real and available through the preaching of the gospel.
- Paul's authority to tell people what they should believe and how they should live in the light of those beliefs derives from his place as Jesus' successor in care and use of the gospel.

In a personal letter to Titus, one of Paul's close associates, why would Paul need such a laundry list of descriptors and claims to authority? Many have argued that this lengthy self-description is evidence that Titus is pseudonymous, since Titus would already respect Paul's authority and know these truths about him. Why would Paul make such points if his reader had no need of them?

However, both the opening and the closing (note the plural pronouns in 3:15) of Titus demonstrate that this letter was written to be overheard. The letter is addressed to Titus *as Paul's personal representative in the newly formed churches on Crete*. The churches on Crete would have heard/read and understood these words as instructions from Paul to them, not just to Titus. Thus the long introduction is not primarily for Titus's benefit; it is also meant for those to whom he (or others) read the letter. It reminds them of (and may indeed rebuke them with) Paul's authority, derived from Jesus, mediated through Titus in Paul's absence. However personal this letter may be, it is not a private letter.

In 1:4, Paul names and greets the recipient of the letter, Titus. He refers to Titus as his "true child in common faith." The word translated "true" is used technically to describe "legitimate" children, and by extension refers to a "real" or "genuine" son. By using this term, Paul indicates that he was the one who brought Titus to Christ. Further, Paul has been responsible for instructing Titus in the faith: according to Jewish tradition, the faithful transmission of traditions from father to son was the test of true paternity. The Talmud says, "The father is bound with respect to his son, to circumcise, redeem, teach him Torah, take a wife for him, and teach him a craft" (b. Qidd 22a; b. Sanh 19b). If a man taught Torah to another man's child—since teaching the Torah to male children was a task only open to men in Paul's time—the child became a son to him. For Paul, the gospel replaces (or assumes) the Torah, and he is the father of those who have come to Christ through his preaching (1 Cor 4:15, 17; Phlm 10).

Even though the phrase, "common faith," does not have the direct article, here we should understand "faith" in a blend of the objective and subjective senses. Subjectively, "faith" refers to their shared trust in and submission to Jesus Christ. Objectively, "faith" refers to the gospel to which they have given their lives. In the Greek text, the preposition that links "true child" with "common faith" (usually simply translated "in") is *kata*, which here designates goal or purpose. Thus Titus is Paul's true son for two reasons. First, Paul brought him to Christ and taught him Christ, becoming Titus's spiritual father. Second, as the preposition *kata* indicates, Titus follows Paul in service to the gospel, both of them spending their lives in that calling and vocation.

In the greeting (4b), we see another case of how Paul adapted the standard letter format. The normal Graeco-Roman epistolary greeting was *chairein* ("rejoice!" or "good health!"). Paul baptizes this greeting, expanding it into a statement of his theology in miniature: "Grace and peace from God the Father and the Lord Jesus Christ." For *chairein*, Paul substitutes the related word *charis* ("grace"). Grace is one of the centers of Paul's gospel. It is the unmerited favor that God gives to his people in Jesus Christ, which is the foundation of the gospel message. Here, Paul joins "grace" with "peace." Peace is the typical Jewish greeting, represented by the Hebrew word *shalom*. *Shalom* refers not merely to the absence of open hostility, but to the wholeness and rest for which God created humanity, which is now available in Jesus Christ. Like grace, peace should characterize the Christian's relationships—something that the new Christians in the frontier atmosphere of Crete needed instruction in, as do we all. By joining the two ideas, one Greek and one Hebrew, Paul sounds the note of universality at the heart of his gospel, where there is no more Jew nor Greek, but all are one in Christ.

Further, Paul says that grace and peace come "from God the Father and from Jesus Christ our Savior." By referring to Jesus as the Christ (*christos*, literally "anointed one"), Paul reminds Jewish Christians that Jesus is the Messiah/Christ, foretold in Israel's Scriptures. For Gentile audiences, Paul is setting Jesus in the place of Caesar, the anointed ruler of the world. If Jesus is "the anointed one," then Caesar is not; this is a clear statement of the radical and revolutionary nature of the Christian faith. Paul further emphasizes the radical nature of Christian faith by referring to Jesus as "Savior" (*sōtēr*). In the first-century Graeco-Roman world, "savior" was used as a title both for the pagan gods and for the Roman Emperor. Caesar was proclaimed as the savior of the world, who brought peace and prosperity in the form of the *Pax Romana*. Paul's message is that salvation and safety do not come from pagan gods or human kings. God the Father and Jesus Christ his son are the only source of peace, security, and meaning.

Paul uses the term "savior" twice in the opening of this letter, applying it to Jesus in 1:4 and to God ("by command of God our Savior") in 1:3. In fact, Paul uses "savior" six times in Titus and applies it to Jesus three times and to God three times. Paul's statements in 1:3-4 further underscore Paul's high Christology. He refers to both God and Jesus as "Savior," and asserts that they are together the source of grace and peace. This speaks of the unique status of Jesus in the mind of Paul the monotheist. God is one, and Jesus is not God B, but the Father and the Son together are God.

The Charge Titus Is Given (1:5-9)

The Charge: Put Things in Order, Appoint Elders (1:5)
In 1:5, Paul shifts immediately from the greeting ("grace and peace") into his charge to Titus. He skips altogether the final part of a typical letter opening, the prayer or blessing. Most of Paul's letters contain either a short prayer ("I thank God every time I remember you"—see Rom 1:8-10; 1 Cor 1:4-9; Phil 1:3-6; Col 1:3-4; 1 Thess 1:2; 2 Thess 1:3; 2 Tim 1:3; Phlm 4-6) or a hymnic statement of praise (e.g., "Blessed be the God and Father of our Lord Jesus Christ"—see 2 Cor 1:3-4; Eph 1:3-14). Paul skips this typical part of the opening in three of his letters: Galatians, 1 Timothy, and Titus. In Galatians, the omission has a clear rhetorical purpose. The audience, expecting to hear some kind of pious, benevolent prayer on their behalf from

their beloved Paul, is instead slapped in the face by the exasperated Apostle: "I am astonished that you are so quickly deserting the one who called you by the grace of Christ and are turning to a different gospel!" (Gal 1:6, NIV). In both Titus and 1 Timothy, the omission seems to accentuate the urgency of the charge that Paul makes to his successors.

Paul opens his charge to Titus: "I left you in Crete for this reason . . ." (1:5). The picture the letter draws is that Paul, after his release from his first Roman imprisonment, has been doing new church work on Crete. There were no Christian communities on the island prior to Paul's arrival there. As the work on Crete progressed, Paul was called away to another area, and he left Titus behind to carry on the work. In this letter, Paul describes the next phase of the work to which he has left Titus. Paul has previously communicated these instructions to Titus verbally; notice the last phrase of 1:5, "as I directed you." Paul uses succession language to describe his relationship with Titus: *apoleipō* is used in succession contexts to describe passing on an unfinished task to a successor (most famously Alexander's agenda passed on to his *Diodoxoi, Diod. Sic.* 17.117.3-4, 18.4.1; see Introduction to the Pastoral Epistles; Stepp 2005, 16). Coupled with the common work in service to the gospel that Titus and Paul share, the sense of succession here is clear (contra my earlier and more tentative conclusion in Stepp 2005, 180–81). In this verse, both Titus and the church behind him would hear Paul empowering and endorsing Titus, acting through him to preserve the health of the Cretan churches and the power of Paul's gospel at work there.

Titus's job is "to put the disordered things in order and to appoint elders in every town." "Disordered things" is literally "the things left undone," *ta leiponta*. The things that Paul began during his limited time on Crete now must be completed, and Titus is charged with the task. The phrase "to put things in order" translates the Greek word *epidiorthoō*, and here relates to the proper ordering of the churches and their leadership. In a missionary setting in a frontier culture, where there was no history of Christianity (as short as that history was during Paul's day), strong leaders and clear leadership structure are essential for the health of the church.

Titus will put disordered things in order by appointing elders. "Appoint" translates the Greek *kathistēmi*, a word that refers to selecting and placing people in positions of leadership. *Kathistēmi* is frequently used in succession contexts, and there is a sense of succession of task and authority in 1:5, both from Paul to Titus ("I left") and from Titus to the elders he will appoint. This second succession is marked by the language (*kathistēmi*) and the task that Titus and the elders share—teaching and encouraging (1:9 for the elders; 2:1, 15 for Titus). Again, the sense of succession here is clear (cf. Stepp 2005, 180–81).

As for the elders that Titus will appoint: the term "elder" (*presbyteros*) can simply refer to an older man (see 1 Tim 5:1, Titus 2:2). However, the Jewish communities of the first century referred to leaders in the synagogue and other contexts by the term "elder." These men were well known and respected members of the Jewish community and were expected to lead by example. The character and function of synagogue elders probably served as a template for elders in the Christian communities.

In his missionary work, Paul's practice was to appoint elders to lead the new churches (Acts 14:21-23, 20:28). As Titus 1:6-9 and 1 Timothy 3:1-7 indicate, elders were not chosen simply on the basis of age, nor were their qualifications based primarily on gifting or talent or accomplishments. The primary qualifications were reputation, character, and faithfulness. Other considerations were secondary.

Qualifications for Leadership (1:6-9)
Paul now describes the standards that Titus must use as he searches for elders. He organizes these qualifications into two parallel lists, 1:6 and 1:7-9. The first list (1:6) focuses on the private conduct of the elder with his family; the second list (1:7-9) focuses on the elder and his public conduct. Each list begins with the adjective "blameless" (*anegklētos*), which does not point to sinlessness (an impossibly high standard) but rather to a character that is above reproach, so that nothing from the elders' habits and conduct will damage the work of the gospel.

In the first list (1:6), Paul further defines "blamelessness" with two qualifications relating to the elder and his family. First, the elder must be a "one-woman man" or "a one-wife husband." This qualification has been interpreted in a number of ways:

- An elder cannot be single (Dibelius and Conzelmann 1972, 52); this is often read in conjunction with 1:6b to say that an elder cannot be childless. This reading is unlikely because it would limit Paul from serving as an elder.
- If widowed or divorced, an elder cannot remarry, or an elder cannot be a divorced man (Hanson 1982, 78).
- An elder cannot have more than one wife at a time (Knight 1992, 158); this reading is unlikely, because polygamy was rare (and almost uniformly condemned) in Graeco-Roman society.

- An elder must be faithful to his wife (Towner 2006, 251; Marshall 1999, 156–57).

Arguments can be found supporting and opposing each of these views. The second-century church seems to have favored the second position, and Paul's teaching on widows in 1 Timothy 5 can be seen as supporting a similar position with regard to that office (Kelly 1963, 75). However, when Paul's teaching on marriage in 1 Corinthians 7 and 9 is considered, Paul does not seem to denigrate remarriage after divorce or widowhood: remarriage is a legitimate choice, even if (in a specific context and specific way) it was to Paul a lesser legitimate choice.

The most likely reading is therefore the fourth: Paul here (and in 1 Tim 3:2) is saying that elders must be faithful husbands. Unfaithfulness in marriage was a widespread concern in the first-century Roman world, where stable families were understood to be the foundation of stable cities (e.g., Hierocles, *On Duties*, 22.21). This requirement may well rule out some men who have been divorced and remarried, but Paul is not specifically aiming in that direction.

As for the elder's children, they must be "faithful." "Faithful" likely means both mindfulness of their family responsibilities and faithfulness to Christ and the Christian way. If elders are to be trusted to lead and teach in the church (1:9), which is the household of God (1:7), then what better measure of their fitness than the way they have led their families? One measure of a person's readiness for service as an elder is his ability to manage his own household (cf. 1 Tim 3:4-5).

The elder's children's faithfulness should be evident in conduct that is "not open to the charge of being wasteful or rebellious" (1:6b). Luke applies a form of the word here translated "wasteful" in his description of the lifestyle of the prodigal son (Luke 15:13). In the first-century world, where material goods were believed to exist only in limited quantities, wastefulness was a serious moral failing, bringing suffering and shame to family and community alike. Likewise, rebelliousness disrupted the harmony of family and community, and led to conflict.

The second list of qualifications begins in 1:7. On the surface, Paul here shifts from describing *presbyteroi* ("elders," plural) to describing an *episkopos* ("overseer," singular). The shift in terms and number leads some to conclude that Paul in 1:7 describes the requirements for a different group or office than in 1:6, or an overlapping group (e.g., all *episkopoi* are *presbyteroi*, but not all *presbyteroi* are *episkopoi*). The traditional translation for *episkopos* ("bishop") further muddies the water; being weighted with ecclesiastical tradition, it calls to mind all kinds of church leadership hierarchies. The two terms are usually associated with the leadership of the second-century church, where elders were the priests of individual congregations, and multiple congregations were administered by a single *episkopos*.

In Titus, however, *episkopos* literally means "overseer." In its most basic sense, the word refers to a function rather than an office. If read functionally—as referring to a function that elders fill, rather than to another office—then this sense fits well in context (notice the "for" [*gar*] connecting 1:7 with the requirements for elders in 1:6). So, in 1:7, Paul is not referring to a second or parallel office, but rather to one of the functions of the elders: ". . . the elder, being an overseer, as a steward of God's household, must be blameless." The elders on Crete are to oversee the lives of the new congregations. In short, the "elder" and "overseer" are one and the same. "Elder" is the name of the office; "overseer" (like "steward," which comes later in the verse) refers to a function that the elder fills. This is in keeping with Luke's description of the Ephesian elders (Acts 20:17), to whom Paul spoke at Miletus about their function as "overseers" and protectors of the church (Acts 20:28).

Paul notes that the overseer is "a steward of God's house." With this designation, Paul introduces the image of the church as the household of God and the overseer as a manager, a responsible servant, in that household. "Steward" (*oikonomos*) refers to someone who manages or administers property belonging to someone else, typically a household or an estate (cf. Luke 12:42; 16:1-8). Here, the elder/overseer is a steward of God's property. The implications for leadership are clear. The church does not exist to benefit the leaders; instead, leaders work for the glory of God and the benefit of the church. Nor do the human leaders of the church exercise authority based on personal forcefulness, personality, or giftedness; their authority derives from the one whose precious property they manage, God himself.

Again, the first qualification is "blamelessness." The qualification is repeated here, not because Paul is describing a different group, but because the qualifications in 1:7-8 differ in character from the qualifications in 1:6. The list in 1:6 describes blamelessness in private life (familial conduct); the list in 1:7-8 describes blamelessness in public life. In that public life, the elder is to be

- "Not arrogant" (*mē authadē*), not stubborn, obstinate, contemptuous of others; not insisting on their own way, regardless of consequences;

- "Not quick-tempered" (*mē orgilon*); this word describes people who get angry easily, a person who is prone to angry outbursts, or has a "short fuse";
- "Not a drunkard" (*mē paroinon*); drunkenness was one of the vices of Graeco-Roman society. When cities lacked safe drinking water, wine became the drink of choice and necessity. Excessive drinking led to drunkenness. This text does not command total abstinence, but does warn against drinking to the point of or for the purposes of intoxication.
- "Not violent" (*mē plēktēn*), not a person who is a bully or who is quick to use force or abuse, physical or otherwise, to deal with annoyances and problems;
- "Not greedy" (*mē aischrokerdē*), not a person who is "shamefully greedy, pursuing dishonest money or possession" (LN 25.26).

In 1:8, Paul continues the list with a cluster of positive characteristics. The elder should be someone who is

- "Hospitable" (*philoxenon*), a "friend of strangers." Hospitality was a cardinal virtue in the ancient Mediterranean world, and was frequently emphasized in the early Christian communities, since traveling teachers often needed housing (Matt 10:11; 1 Tim 3:2; 1 Pet 4:9; *Did* 11.2-4; *1 Clem* 12.3). Since local congregations often met in homes, traveling missionaries could use the open home as a base of operations for preaching and teaching. Furthermore, strangers to the faith might also be welcomed for meals or even lodging: "Most early Christians, particularly Gentile ones, likely came to Christian faith not by hearing about it in a synagogue, but by hearing the message over or after a meal in a friend's home" (Witherington 2006, 116). The centrality of this virtue is in keeping with the significance of table fellowship in Jesus' ministry (Lk 5:29; 7:36; 9:12-17; 11:37; 14:1, 7, 15; 15:1; 22:7-23; 24:28-35) and in Acts (2:43-47; 4:32-35; 16:15; 21:7; 28:14; cf. Rom 16:4).
- "A lover of what is good" (*philagathon*, used here for the only time in the New Testament); someone who loves and delights in (and does) what is good, rather than what is corrupt. *Magna Moralia*, attributed to Aristotle, contrasts the person who is *philagathon* with the one who is selfish, mean, or base in character (*TDNT* 1.18);
- "Prudent" (*sōphrōna*); sensible, self-controlled, temperate, moderate, and balanced (see the discussion of *sōphrōn* and its cognates at Titus 2:2);
- "Upright" (*dikaios*) can refer either to behaving in a way that is morally and ethically acceptable or to being impartial and fair in one's dealings with

people. In biblical tradition, *dikaios* can carry the idea of being in a right relationship with God and with others, and—while all are called to exhibit this virtue—it was especially needed in leaders. In the Graeco-Roman world, justice (understood as behavior that conformed to customs or laws) was a cardinal virtue: see Plato, *Euthyphro* 12.c–e; *Gorgias* 507b; *Republic* 1.311a; Polybius, *Histories* 22.10.8; Philo, *Moses* 2.108; *Flight* 63; Josephus, *Antiquities* 8.12.2 §295, 12.2.5 §4315. For Plato, justice was the virtue of promoting order and harmony among people (*Republic* 4.443 c–e).

- "Devout" (*hosion*); literally "pious." This term often occurs alongside *dikaion* in virtue lists. Josephus frequently used *dikaios* and *hosios* together to describe the good kings of Judah, those who were faithful to Yahweh (see, for examples, *Antiquities* 6.87, 8.245, 9.35).
- "Self-controlled" (*egkratēs*); literally "in control," not mastered by desires or hungers. *Barnabas* 2.2 links *egkratēs* with patience and endurance. According to Philo, *egkratēs* is one of the fundamental character traits of statesmanship, and "takes its stand against pleasure, which thinks that it can direct the course of human weakness" (*Allegorical Interpretation* 1.69; *Joseph* 54). Plato specifically says that leaders must be able to master themselves and maintain order and harmony in the community (*Republic* 4.428b–432a; *Laws* 3.697c–e; 6.757a–c).

Paul adds a further requirement in 1:9: the elder must "cling [*antechomenon*] to the faithful message [*pistou logou*] that corresponds [*kata*] with the teaching [*didachēn*]" (i.e., the apostolic teaching). Elders must not only know the true gospel, they must be devoted to it. The formulation *pistos logos* is common in the Pastoral Epistles, often used by Paul to refer to preformed chunks of traditional material (e.g., Titus 3:8; 1 Tim 1:15; 3:1; 4:9; 2 Tim 1:11), where it is usually translated "this is a trustworthy saying" or "this is a reliable saying." These sayings can be and ought to be believed, because they are reliable affirmations of the faith. This message is faithful because it corresponds with the apostolic teaching, which Paul received and passed on to Titus so that Titus may pass it on to the elders he appoints. From the beginning of the church, Christians passed on the traditions of the faith, stories about and teachings of Jesus. (For further discussion of the use of traditional material in early Christianity, see Gerhardsson 1998 and Bauckham 2006.)

The elder's firm grasp on the faithful message has a purpose: it enables him to teach (*parakalein*, often translated "encourage"; here, "instruction with authoritative persuasion" [Towner 2006, 692]) that same message faithfully and effectively, and to use these teachings to refute and correct (*elegchō*) those who oppose or contradict the gospel (1:9b). *Elegchō* is used in contexts relating to church discipline in Matthew 18:15 and 1 Timothy 5:20. Here, Paul's point is that the elder is equipped to defend the true teaching of the church by exposing the weakness of opposing (false) teaching, and "'silencing' the opponents with forceful admonition backed up by apostolic authority" (Towner 2006, 693).

The Challenge Titus Faces (1:10-16)
The elders Titus appoints must be men of strong character, because of the seriousness of the challenge faced by Titus and the Cretan churches. "For there are many rebellious people," Paul writes (1:10). The preposition "for" indicates that the new material (1:10-16) contains the basis for the instructions of 1:5-9. The basis is the existence of false teachers and troublemakers around Titus's churches, perhaps even participating in Titus's churches. These infant congregations need strong and prepared leaders to deal with the threat the troublemakers pose.

This paragraph (1:10-16) works together with the preceding materials (1:5-9) in *synkrisis* ("comparison"), a rhetorical device. Plutarch wrote, "It is not possible to learn better the similarity and the difference between the virtues of man and woman from any other source than by putting lives beside lives and actions beside actions, like great works of art" (*Moralia* 345C–351B). In 1:10-16, Paul paints a colorful picture of those who need immediate correction, in contrast with the faithful elders of 1:5-9.

Who were these troublemakers? Paul describes them as "specifically [*malista*] those of the circumcision" (for *malista* with the sense of "specifically" or "namely," see Towner 2006, 311, 695; Skeat 1979; R. A. Campbell 1995). With "those of the circumcision," Paul could be referring to non-Christian Jews, for Crete had a large Jewish population, and many of them were likely critical of Paul and his work on the island. Paul could also be referring to Jewish Christians, however. Both Acts and Paul's letters indicate that there were Jewish Christians who opposed the acceptance of Gentiles into Christianity. These "Judaizers" concluded that Gentile converts to Christianity must conform to the requirements of Torah, including circumcision, in order to be followers of Jesus (see Rom 4:12; Gal 2:6; Phil 3:2-3; Acts 15). Other Jewish Christians apparently thought that by persuading Gentile Christians to become Jewish in their diets and to accept circumcision, they might minimize the persecution and discrimination they were suffering at the hands of non-Christian Jews around them (Gal 6:12-13). On at least a few occasions, some of these "Judaizers" followed Paul's work, going into his churches in his absence to "straighten them out." Paul therefore is worried that these people, who have dogged his steps throughout his career, are on their way to Crete.

Paul describes these troublemakers as "rebellious" (*anypotaktoi*), "empty-talkers" (*mataiologoi*), and "deceitful" (*phrenapatai*). "Rebellious" indicates that these troublemakers refuse to submit to apostolic authority. The term *could* indicate that they were already at work in the Cretan churches, but the scenario proposed above is more likely. With "empty-talkers," Paul takes aim at their teaching (cf. 1 Tim 1:6); at best, what the troublemakers teach is nonsense, with potential to do great harm. And the end of their teaching is deception and futility, not truth or faith.

Titus must "silence" (or even "muzzle") these people (*epistomizein*, 1:11). The verb *epistomizō* originally referred to the breaking and reigning in of a wild horse, and came to mean silencing a speaker (*LSJ*). The subsequent reference to Cretans as "wild beasts" (1:12) makes this verb an especially appropriate choice. They must be silenced because they are "upsetting the faith [*anatrepousin*] of whole households" (*oikous*). *Anatrepō* refers to undermining or even corrupting someone's faith (cf. Matt 18:6). The troublemakers' teaching is not just affecting a few isolated individuals, rather, they are damaging whole households (or "house churches"?). And worse, their motivation for "teaching the things they should not teach" is a desire "for shameful financial gain" (*aischrou kerdous*). Teachers in first-century Graeco-Roman society made their livelihood in one of four ways. They might be supported by a wealthy patron (e.g., Luke's patron Theophilus, Luke 1:1-4; Acts 1:1-5), work at their own trade and support themselves (e.g., Paul as a leather-worker/"tentmaker," Acts 18:3), beg for alms, or charge their students for the teaching.

The teachers about whom Paul warns Titus fall into this last group; indeed, their "calling" as teachers was simply a way for them to make a living without hard work. The bottom line for these troublemakers was not the faithful lives of their students but the lining of their own pockets. The critique of teachers who charge their students "by the lesson" is at least as old as Socrates (e.g., Plato, *Apology* 19E). Paul echoes this disdain for such practices in 1 Thessalonians 2:5-6, where he reminds his audience that he did not preach or teach to please mortals, nor as a pretext for greed. The false teachers, on the other hand, were pseudo-Christian leaders who threatened the flock like wolves (Acts 20:29-30).

To support his characterization of these troublemakers and the danger that they present, Paul turns to a famous ancient riddle (1:12-13a). Epimenides, an ancient Cretan poet and sage of the seventh century BCE, famously wrote, "Cretans, always liars, evil beasts, idle bellies!" Epimenides is said to have joked that there was no need for wild beasts on the island of Crete because the people were themselves wild animals (Oden 1989, 61). This characterization of Cretans also finds its way into the writings of Callimachus (third century BCE), who wrote in his hymn to Zeus, "Cretans are always liars" (*Hymns* 1.8). Further negative depictions of Cretan character abound in ancient literature. Polybius writes, "So much in fact do sordid love of gain and lust for wealth prevail among them, that the Cretans are the only people in the world in whose eyes no gain is disgraceful" (6:46). Livy asserts that the Cretan's culture of greed made them easy prey for those recruiting mercenaries (*Roman History* 44.45.13). Likewise, Plutarch tells a story of how Aemilius Paulus cheated Cretan mercenaries who served under him by "playing Cretan with the Cretans" (*Aem* 23.4).

As Paul quotes Epimenides' insulting description of Cretans, he conflates it with a paradox usually credited to the philosopher Eubulides. Eubulides was famous for asking a riddle to this effect: if a man says that he is lying, is he telling the truth? Paul ironically asserts that Epimenides was a prophet, and Paul quotes the ancient description of Cretans. He then closes the digression by declaring that the words of Epimenides (the Cretan), which accuse Cretans of always being liars, are in fact the truth (even though spoken by a Cretan!) (Thiselton 1994, 207–23).

The way Paul issues this insult is intentionally ambiguous. On its surface, the rebuke is aimed at the false teachers and troublemakers. By their deceptive teachings, they permitted or endorsed behavior and lifestyles that were at odds with the true gospel, no matter how culturally acceptable these behaviors may have been on Crete. But in another sense, Paul aims his rebuke at the Cretan believers who are overhearing the letter. Paul is challenging them to leave behind the base aspects of their culture and their pagan heritage, and aspire to something more noble and virtuous. The gospel does not leave us as it finds us—it aims to change not only what we believe, but also to transform how we live and who we are.

Due to their cultural heritage, the Cretan believers were likely to be easily swayed by the false teachers, particularly if the teaching they brought was sympathetic to "traditional Cretan values." Because of this cultural weakness, Paul commands Titus to "rebuke them" (*elegchē autous*). Again, Paul is intentionally ambiguous: is Titus supposed to rebuke the troublemakers, or his own people? Of course, Titus is to rebuke the false teachers when they show themselves. But here (unlike 1:12-13a), the primary focus is on the people in Titus's churches, as the purpose clause, "so that they will be sound in the faith," indicates (1:13b). Paul warns Titus that some of his own people will show an interest in or a weakness for these kinds of teachings, and Titus will need to rebuke them back onto safer paths. "*The* faith" here has the definite article, and refers to the body of teaching that Paul had received and handed on to Titus (cf. 1 Cor 15:3). The Cretan believers must adhere to an authentic understanding of the Christian faith. Titus is charged with the responsibility of seeing that this happens.

So they will be sound in the faith, Titus's people must "stop paying attention to Jewish myths and the commands of men who have rejected/turned away from the truth" (1:14). "Stop paying attention" (*mē prosechontes*) is a present participle, which implies that this is an existing problem; some of Titus's people are already fascinated with things that will damage their infant faith in Jesus Christ. And again, Paul's instruction suggests that Jewish elements are involved in the teaching of the troublemakers. Their teachings consist of stories (myths) that originate in Jewish circles or Jewish teachings. In the Graeco-Roman world, "myths" (*mythoi*) could refer to unreal or fabled stories about deities. Pindar (fifth century BCE) refers to myths as the fabrications of mortals, as opposed to stories with divine origins (*Olympian Odes* 1.28–29). Other writers also contrast "myth" with truth (Strabo, *Geography* 10.3.20, 11.5.3; Philo, *Flight* 121; *Rewards* 162; *Giants* 7).

But Paul here describes "*Jewish* myths and commands of men." This is likely a reference to Jewish *haggadah* (stories) and *halakah* (commandments) as used/misused by the troublemakers (Collins 2002, 337). "Commands of men" echoes Isaiah 29:13 ("These people come near to me with their mouth and honor me with their lips, but their hearts are far from me. Their worship of me is made up only of rules taught by men" [NIV]), which Jesus quotes in Mark 7:6-8 in his condemnation of too elevated a view of *halakah*. *Halakah* (derived from the Hebrew root *hlk*, "to walk") refers to legal materials that developed as people tried to understand how the Torah, which set out God's will, applied to daily life. It "focuses on activity in which primarily Jews should be engaged in personal, social, national, and international relationships, as well as other practices and observances of Judaism" (*ABD* 3.26). *Haggadah* (from the Hebrew root *ngd*, "to show," "to tell") refers to narrative non-legal materials that dealt with morals, ethics, and daily life. The purpose of *haggadah* was to help people understand the ways of God and to motivate them to follow these ways. In pursuit of their corrupt ends, however, Paul's opponents on Crete are using these materials to mislead the naïve, build a following for themselves, and line their own pockets. Paul emphasizes the fact that these stories and commands are of human origin and are attractive only to "those who reject the truth" (1:14), in contrast with those who desire "knowledge of the truth which leads to godliness" (1:1).

Paul extends his argument in 1:15, using the language of ritual purity. The maxim in 1:15a is a model of Greek literary artistry: it begins with the word "everything" (*panta*, literally "all things") and ends with "nothing" (*ouden*), creating a sharp contrast. The components of the maxim are organized chiastically, using antithetical parallelism:

A. All things are pure
   B. To the pure
   B'. But to the defiled and faithless
A'. Nothing is pure

The statement is so beautifully crafted that some suggest that Paul is using an existing proverb or saying, into which he has inserted the phrase "and faithless" to make the contrast even stronger.

The first "pure" (*kathara*) refers to ritual or general purity, the second to moral purity; thus to those who are morally pure, all things are pure. In contrast, for those who are "defiled and faithless," nothing is pure—not ascetic pseudo-spiritual self-discipline, not even the rituals and trappings of Jewish religion, commanded though they were by God. Paul continues in 1:15b: "their very minds and consciences are corrupted." The mention of "minds" (*nous*, the thinking and reasoning processes) and "consciences" (*syneidesis*, the center of ethical and moral thinking) suggests that Paul is drawing from Hellenistic anthropological concepts that would be familiar to his audience. The troublemakers are defiled and faithless. Their religious activity, even when it conforms outwardly to the biblical standard, is corrupt. Their thinking, reasoning, responses to moral choices, etc., have been so defiled that they can no longer tell the difference between what is pure and what is impure, right and wrong. They epitomize Paul's descriptions of humanity without God's intervention in Romans 1:18-32 and 3:10-18, where people intentionally and knowingly reject God's truth and exchange it for self-serving self-deception, with the result of human inability even to recognize the truth.

> Mark the sequence that follows: from mind to conscience to words to deeds. The problem begins with the defilement of their minds, which shapes and distorts their moral awareness.... When mental processes are corrupted at the center, then the conscience to some degree loses its power to discern good and evil. Conscience itself becomes polluted. Defilement

has thereby entered into the very citadel of selfhood, so that the defilement colors everything one sees. It is not merely a matter of ignorance but of morally distorted judgment that in time expresses itself outwardly in corrupt actions. If the mind is already corrupted in reason and conscience with a false conception of the Creator, then ascetic practices are hardly going to be sufficient to set one straight. (Oden 1989, 64)

The false teachers "declare [*homologeō*] that they know [*oida*] God" (1:16). They profess faith, allegiance, and dedication to God. They claim that by their teaching they can help people know and experience God more richly, "But they deny [God] with their deeds." Their teaching and its ramifications in their own lives and in the life of the community make it clear that they do not know God.

Scripture throughout points to the dangers of not practicing what one preaches. Isaiah and Amos say much about the hollowness and corrupting nature of hypocritical worship. Jesus addresses the issue in the Sermon on the Mount (Matt 7:21), his pronouncements regarding the Jewish religious leaders of his day (Matt 23), and his depictions of the last judgment (Matt 25:31-46). John deals with this lack of connection between claim and reality in 1 John 1:6, 2:3, 2:9, and 4:20.

Paul closes the chapter with one last description of the troublemakers: they are "detestable" (*bdelyktoi*), "disobedient" (*apeitheis*), and "unfit [*adokimoi*] for any good deed." *Bdelyktos* is a strong word, and can be rendered "abominable," "disgusting," or "repellent." *Adokimoi* can be translated "counterfeit." Because the center of the false teachers' character is disobedience and rebellion, they are repulsive to God, and are not made of "the right stuff" for doing God's work.

Western Christians often separate faith from obedience, much to our detriment. We tend to understand faith simply in terms of mental assent to propositional statements, creeds, or confessions. In the New Testament, however, faith and obedience are inseparably linked, two sides of a single coin—and unless a coin has both sides, it is incomplete and worthless. Paul builds an inclusio around his magnum opus, Romans, with references to the obedience that faith produces (Rom 1:5; 16:26). James famously writes, "Faith, by itself, if it has no works, is dead" (Jas 2:26; see also Matt 7:21; Mark 3:35; Eph 2:8-10; Heb 3:7–4:13; 1 John 1:3-6; Rev 2:1-7; 3:1-2). Bonhoeffer writes, "Only he who believes is obedient, and only he who is obedient believes. . . . Faith is only real when there is obedience, never without it, and faith only becomes faith in the act of obedience" (Bonhoeffer 1963, 69).

Summary

In 1:5-16 (section 2 of our outline), Paul accomplishes several things. First, he commends and condemns sets of virtues and vices, many of which *should* be self-evident. The fact that Paul needs to explicitly praise or condemn some of these items may be evidence of the lawless, perverse character of Cretan society. These descriptions of vice and virtue are not only aimed at those who selected or aspired to leadership; Paul here also endorses character traits that all believers should pursue, and repudiates traits that all believers should flee from.

Second, Paul describes the effects of both good leadership and bad leadership. Good leadership leads to churches full of healthy, productive believers, whose walk matches their talk. Bad leadership leads to churches full of people who are divisive, caught up in minutiae and empty rhetoric, their lives having an appearance of righteousness on the outside but inside full of "dead men's bones," with no grace or love or holiness.

Finally, Paul gives Titus a clear grid for weighing qualifications for leadership in the church, and for identifying false teachers (Witherington 2006, 127):

Faithful Leaders	**False Teachers**
• Faithful manager of the household	• Destroyer of the household
• Blameless in character/reputation	• Defiled conscience, mind, deeds
• Not pursuing dishonest gain	• Motivated by dishonest gain
• Not quick-tempered/intemperate	• Acting like a wild beast, driven by passions and hungers
• Adhering to the true teaching of the gospel	• Liars, embracing and teaching error

The Way of Life Titus Must Teach (2:1–3:11)

The major paraenetic section of the letter covers all of chapter 2 and the first half of chapter three. This section falls into two halves, each following the same outline:

2:1-15

A. Content (2:1-10)
B. Theological basis for the teaching (2:11-14)
C. Encouragement and empowerment (2:15)

3:1-11

A. Content (3:1-2)
B. Theological basis for the teaching (3:3-8a)
C. Encouragement and empowerment (3:8b-11)

Responsibilities in the Household of God (2:1-15)

The first half of the larger section (the whole of chapter 2) is Paul's adaptation of a household code, a type of literature used by the Hellenistic moral philosophers and other teachers to describe the duties, responsibilities, and relationships in a household. Paul does not follow the typical structure of a household code here, however. He takes the old form of the household code and adapts it to apply to the church, the household of God.

Paul's use of the household metaphor for the church is not surprising, for three reasons. First, the metaphor has roots in the Old Testament descriptions of Israel and her relationship with God. Second, the household was the basic unit of Graeco-Roman society. Third, the earliest Christian churches were "house churches."

Old Testament background. The idea that Israel was a family with God as its father is surprisingly rare in the Old Testament. Deuteronomy 32:6 asks, "Do you thus repay the LORD? . . . Is he not your Father?" Isaiah 63:16 declares, "You are our father, though Abraham does not know us and Israel does not acknowledge us; you, O LORD, are our father" (see also Jer 3:4, 19; 31:9; Mal 1:6; 2:10; cf. Exod 4:22-23; Deut 1:31).

The notion that God dwelt among his people goes back to the tradition of the ark of the covenant, which Israel viewed as a physical locus of God's presence (Exod 25–31; 36–40). The tabernacle was built to house the ark until it came to rest in Solomon's temple (1 Kings 8:4; 2 Chr 5:5). The temple was "the house of God," where God dwelt in the midst of his people (2 Sam 7:1-6, 12-13; 1 Kings 5:5; 6:11-14).

In 1 Timothy 3:15, Paul refers to the "household of God, which is the church [*ekklēsia*, lit., "assembly"] of the living God." The notion of Israel as the assembly of God's people also has significant Old Testament roots. In the accounts of Israel's journey from Egyptian bondage to the Promised Land, Israel is referred to as "the assembly of Yahweh" (*qehal YHWH*; Deut 23:2-4, etc.). The Septuagint renders the Hebrew *qahal* as *synagogue* or *ekklēsia*. The community assembled to hear the word of the Lord spoken through Moses (e.g., Deut 4:10). With the temple, the "house of the LORD," these two traditions came together; the temple was the place where God dwelt, and thus the place where God's people met with their God.

Graeco-Roman background. The household was the basic unit of Graeco-Roman society. Households were structured and functioned according to traditional societal patterns. The father, *paterfamilias*, was the undisputed head. The household consisted of his wives, children, slaves, and assorted clients. Each member of the household had a specific place and function. From the time of Plato and Aristotle, "household codes" were used to describe how the members of the household functioned and related to each other. These codes promoted social order, responsibility, and respect within the family. Social critics and moral philosophers also developed catalogs of virtues and vices, which reflected society's expectations for each member of the household. (Paul adapts one such catalog of vices in 3:3-8a; see below.)

House churches. The first Christian assemblies (*ekklēsiais*) met in homes. Paul writes several times of "the church in [name's] house" (Rom 16:5; 1 Cor 16:19; Phlm 2; cf. Col 4:45). In fact, these letters were written to *ekklēsiais* who gathered in someone's home to hear them read. In these house churches, believers listened to the first preachers and teachers, broke bread together and celebrated the Lord's Supper, prayed, cared for each other's needs, and extended hospitality to traveling Christians.

While it is common for interpreters to divide chapter 2 into two units (2:1-10 and 2:11-15), the rhetorical unity of the chapter is striking, and lends persuasive power to what is being taught. The connector "for" (*gar*) in 2:11 links the theological materials in 2:11-15 with the practical instructions of 2:1-10. Indeed, the theological materials provide the foundation for the ethical admonitions. Further, the sentence structures themselves suggest the unity of the chapter: Titus 2:1-5 is actually one long sentence governed by the verb "teach" or "speak" in 2:1. Likewise, vv. 6-14 are governed by the verb "urge" in 2:6.

Also pointing to the unity of the section is Paul's use of enthymemes. An enthymeme is a syllogism in which one of the propositions is understood rather than stated. Ancient teachers of rhetoric taught that enthymemes were especially effective and winning, and their proper use spoke of great rhetorical skill and sophistication (Aristotle, *Rhetoric* 1.2.8-12; Donelson 1986). Paul uses enthymemes throughout Titus 2. In the following list (adapted from Bassler 1996, 192), the propositions that are understood rather than stated are in brackets:

A. [Outsiders will judge believers' faith based on their behavior];
B. Younger women must submit to their husbands, . . .
C. . . . so that the word of God will not be discredited in view of the watching world (2:3-5).

A. [Opponents of the gospel are looking for inconsistencies in the lives of Christian leaders];
B. Titus must set a good moral example and teach with integrity, . . .
C. . . . so that opponents can find nothing to criticize (2:7-8).

A. [Christian slaves want to be good witnesses to their masters];
B. Slaves must submit to their masters and serve in a way that shows their reliability and trustworthiness, . . .
C. . . . so that the true gospel of Jesus Christ will be attractive to outsiders, and win a hearing (2:9-10).

Each enthymeme ends with a purpose clause, which begins with *hina* ("so that") in the Greek text (2:5; 2:8; 2:10). These purpose clauses together build toward the theological explanation that begins in 2:11. Paul's concern is that the lives of believers earn a hearing for the gospel, not discredit it by unseemly behavior—the gospel is scandalous enough, no need to add unnecessary offense!—for it truly is the revelation of the grace of God, which offers salvation to all people.

Content (2:1-10)

This section begins with a heading (2:1), which rules the whole section and provides the finite verb that controls 2:1-5. This opening command also connects what follows back into the preceding materials. In 1:13, Paul told Titus to "rebuke" his people so that they would become "sound" in the faith. Now in 2:1, he commands Titus to "teach what is consistent with sound doctrine," i.e., what is consistent with the teaching Paul received and passed on to Titus. Titus is to pass this teaching on to three groups within the Cretan churches: mature believers (both male and female), young believers (male and female), and slaves.

Titus is to teach the mature men (2:2). The Greek text refers to this group as *presbyteroi* (literally "elders"), but context makes it clear that Paul has age—not church office—in mind. The stages of life were generally thought to run from twenty to twenty-eight ("a young man"), from twenty-nine to forty-nine ("a man"), from fifty to fifty-six ("mature man"), and from fifty-seven on ("old man") (Hippocrates, *De Septimanis* 5; Philo, *Creation* 105). Paul sets forth six virtues that should characterize the lives of these active, mature "fifty-somethings." The virtues are arranged in two groups of three. The first group represents traditional social values: sobriety, respectability, and sensibility. The second group focuses on soundness in classic spiritual virtues: faith, love, and perseverance (cf. 1 Thess 1:3). Paul uses this second grouping in a variety of settings, always keeping "faith" and "love" as part of the list (Gal 5:6; 1 Thess 3:6; 5:8). In 1 Corinthians, writing to a divided church that was struggling with theological confusion about the Parousia, Paul added "hope" as the middle part of the grouping (1 Cor 13:13). In 1 Thessalonians, writing to a community plagued by persecution and suffering, Paul adds "endurance" as the last word—a challenge and an encouragement for them to stay the course in the face of suffering. In the same way, Paul now encourages the new believers on Crete to be marked by steadfastness in the hope of eternal life.

The list of virtues that Paul prescribes begins with "sobriety" (*nēphalous*). This word was originally used to refer to empty vessels set apart for cultic/religious use, but gradually came to be used to refer to restraint in the use of alcohol (Collins 2002, 341). According to Philo, in his treatise on sobriety,

> . . . every evil which has drunkenness as its author has its counterpart in some good which is produced by soberness. Since sobriety is a source of the greatest profit to our bodies, to which the use of wine is a natural practice, how much more is it profitable to our souls, which have no relation to any perishable food? (*Sobriety* 2–3)

Alcoholism, especially among older men and women, was a major problem in the Graeco-Roman world. Dramas from this world make use of the old drunk as a stock figure of ridicule (e.g., Aristophanes, *Nub* 553–55). Paul regularly warns his people away from drunkenness as something incompatible with the Christian lifestyle.

The second virtue is "respectability" (*semnous*). This adjective refers to behaving in a way that is not scandalous or odd, due to a concern for one's reputation and a seriousness of purpose. "The gravitas held in esteem by the ancient Roman was the high seriousness of a person not easily moved but who, when he did move, was deliberate and indeflectable" (Quinn 1990, 130). Philo says, "It is not given to youth but to old age to discern things precious and worthy of reference, particularly those who are judged, not by unreasoning and deceitful sense but by mind when absolutely pure and unalloyed" (*Eternity of the World* 77). In 4 Maccabees, Eleazar ("an old man," *presbyta*, 5:6) says to Antiochus, "You shall not defile the reverent lips of my old age nor my lifelong service to the law" (5:36; see Collins 2002, 341).

The final virtue in the first trio is sensibility (*sōprhonos*). Graeco-Roman society held this to be one of the four cardinal virtues associated with respectability and venerability. Both women and men were expected to exhibit this virtue. It relates both to character and to conduct. Ultimately, *sōphrōn* is the practical sense of knowing what to do and what not to do; we might translate it "sanity" or "prudence." Louw and Nida suggest the word be understood in the sense of having "'right thoughts about what one should do' or 'to let one's mind guide one's body'" (*LN* 88.94). According to Philo, this virtue refers to the health of the soul, that which makes one's thinking sane (*Virtues* 14). Since the time of Aristotle, *sōphrōn* was understood to be expressed differently in the lives of men and the lives of women (*Politics* 1.5.8; 3.2.10). Thus, Paul encourages both men and women to exhibit this virtue in ways appropriate to their genders. Athenaeus, citing Homer, states that *sōphrōn* is to be taught to children as "the virtue that is most appropriate for young people and the first of all virtues, an element of harmony, and productive of good" (*Deipnosophists* 1.8[e]).

Each member of this first group of virtues was highly esteemed in Graeco-Roman society. The list here demonstrates "a deliberate and reflective integration of Christian life with some of the qualities that Hellenistic society and its spokesmen considered the most important in human life" (Quinn 1990, 315).

The second group of virtues, "faith, love, and perseverance" (*tē pistei, tē agapē, tē hypomonē*) appears as a classic Pauline description of the Christian life as early as 1 Thessalonians (1:3) and Galatians ("faith and love," 5:6). "Faith" here, in spite of the definite article, refers to the believer's trust in God that produces obedience and commitment. "Love" is a self-surrendering love for God and a self-sacrificing love for others. "Perseverance" refers to the Christian's commitment to following the way of Christ, regardless of circumstances and consequences, peril and persecution. The middle member of the grouping helps define the other members; here, Christians must exercise faith and perseverance in a context of love.

Paul next outlines Titus's teaching for mature women, *presbytidas* (2:3). Again, he has in mind the "fifty-somethings" of the church, mature but active Christian women. These women are to be "reverent in their behavior" (*en katastēmati hieroprepeis*). In Hellenistic literature, *katastēmati* refers to a person's behavior or disposition, and *hieropropeis* describes priests and priestesses, sacred possessions, etc., as "holy and venerable." Philo used *hieropropeis* to refer to the way that, when devout people dedicate their talents and abilities to God, these abilities become "sanctified and holy" (*Heir.* 110). Philo also used the word to describe the Essenes, because they viewed everyday life as a kind of sacred liturgy (*Every Good Man Is Free* 75; see Collins 2002, 343). Thus the lifestyle that Paul prescribes is one that exhibits worshipfulness and reverence in its conduct.

Second, these women are "not to be slanderers" (*mē diabolous*). In biblical tradition, the devil is the great slanderer, accusing the faithful of crimes imagined and real. But unlike a prophetic rebuke (e.g., Nathan with David in 2 Samuel 12), which aims for repentance, the purpose of slanderous accusations is to tear down rather than to restore. Third, these women are not to be "slaves to much wine." The emphasis on sobriety here parallels the instruction to mature men in the preceding verse; this attests to the problem of drunkenness for both women and men in Paul's world.

Finally, these women are "to teach what is good." With this prescription, Paul turns from Titus's direct instruction for the mature women to the things Titus was to teach indirectly, through the mature women, to the younger women (2:4-5). The fact that these women had a teaching/mentoring role in the church seems parallel to the description of elders in 1:10. This suggests the existence of a quasi-office in the early church, "the widows," who shepherded and taught younger women just as elders were responsible for shepherding and teaching younger men (see Thurston 1989).

Why does Paul tell Titus to teach these things to the young women indirectly, through the older women, rather than teaching them directly? Paul is conscious of the potential for jealousy, temptation, and scandal. He wants to be sure that no accusations, with or without foundation, keep the gospel from earning a hearing in Cretan society. Therefore, he has Titus approach the instruction of young women with great caution.

The mature women are to teach what is good, so that they can "teach modesty [*sōphronizōsi*, a verb related to *sōphrōn*, see the discussion at 2:2] to the younger women [*neas*]" (2:4). *Neas* refers to women in their twenties. The essential feminine virtue in the Hellenistic world was modesty (here self-restraint and propriety in all matters, sexual and otherwise). Modesty was thought to be especially important for younger women.

What does the life of a modest Christian woman look like? Paul describes it: these women "love their husbands." "Love" here has the force of respect and loyalty, rather than romance. In a culture where arranged marriages were standard, this is a striking and important teaching. They also "love their children"; in the Graeco-Roman world, children had little value and were often viewed as little more than a drain on a family's already-stretched resources. Good wives were expected to love (rather than resent or neglect) their children. An inscription on a woman's tomb from the third century CE reads, "Julius Basus for Otacilia Polla, his sweetest wife. Loving to her husband [*philandrō*] and loving to her children [*philoteknō*], she lived with him unblamably [*amemptōs*] for thirty years" (Deismann 1965, 315).

Further, the younger women are to be

- "sensible" (*sōphronas*), as the mature men were to be in 2:2;
- "pure" (*hagnas*), or chaste; Paul shared the view of many Jews of his day that the Gentiles among whom they lived were sexual reprobates (cf. Lev 18; Rom 1:24-27; 1 Cor 5:1; 1 Thess 4:5). Here he admonishes the young women in his churches to be free from moral defect in thought, word, and deed.
- "busy in the home," (*oikourgous*, "fulfilling their duties at home" [NET]);
- "generous" or "kind" (*agathas*);
- "submissive to their own husbands"; because Paul here specifies "their own husbands" (*tois idiois andrasin*), he clearly is not saying that women are subject to men in general, but rather describing the relationship in their own households. "Submission" (*hypotassō*) implies a recognition of and support of a husband's authority. In the Hellenistic world, the husband was the unchallenged head of the household. If Christian teaching challenged that status, people would see that challenge as deeply subversive, damaging the church's witness.

The instruction for wives to submit to husbands is found elsewhere in the New Testament: 1 Peter 3:1; Colossians 3:18. The most developed New Testament teaching on the topic is in Ephesians 5:21–6:9, where the call for wives to submit to their husbands is prefaced by a call for all members of the church to submit to one another. The instructions for various members of the household follow that overarching command: wives, submit (*hypotassō*, understood from the preceding verse) to husbands; husbands, love your wives as Christ loved the church; children obey (*hypakouō*, not *hypotassō*!) your parents; parents, slaves, masters, etc. The instructions to the various members of the household show what "submission to one another out of reverence for Christ" looked like.

Polycarp's description of the life that Christian wives should live is similar to Paul's, although he does not use the term "submission." Christian wives are "to walk in the faith that has been given to them and in love and purity, cherishing their own husbands in all truth and loving everyone equally in all chastity, and to train their children in the training of the fear of God" (Polycarp, *Phil* 4.2).

Paul commands that the young women demonstrate these qualities in their lives "so that the word of God may not be blasphemed" (or "may not be discredited"). The church gave nearly unprecedented freedoms and respect to women. Because of these freedoms and respect, Christian families must live with order and propriety, so that the pagan culture around the church would not have grounds for accusing it of promoting disorder in home or community. Christians must not live in ways that cause non-Christians to despise the faith and blaspheme the word of God. In other words, Paul's concerns are (again) missionary. He calls on Christians to live in ways that earn a hearing for the gospel. The way we live our lives determines the nature and effectiveness of our witness to the world.

Paul next turns to the "young men" (*neōterous*, 2:6), men in their twenties. Titus must "urge" (*parakalei*) these men to act with discretion (*sōphronein*): in other words, they should exhibit a kind of wisdom that enables them to know what to do and what not to do, how to act and how *not* to act. Paul insists

- that mature men be sensible (*sōphronas*, 2:2);
- that mature women teach modesty (*sōphronizōsin*, 2:4) to the younger women;
- so that the younger women would be sensible (*sōphronas*, 2:5); and
- that young men act with propriety and discretion (*sōphronein*, 2:6).

But Titus is to do more than teach; he must also practice what he preaches. Paul commands him to be a model for the young men in the Cretan churches. Indeed, "imitation" plays a significant role in the teaching/learning process in the ancient world. Paul clearly understood its importance and employed it regularly:

- 1 Corinthians 11:1—"Be imitators of me, as I am an imitator of Christ."
- Philippians 3:17—"Be imitators of me, . . ."
- Ephesians 5:1—"Like dearly loved children, be imitators of God."
- 2 Thessalonians 3:9—Paul and his companions supported themselves rather than depend on the support of the Christians in Thessalonica, "not because we do not have the right to such support, but in order to give ourselves to you as an example, so you could imitate us."

Paul's call for his people to imitate him is not an indication of an inflated ego. It rather speaks of his understanding of his responsibility as a teacher to live in such a way that he becomes a living example of what he teaches. In Judaism, "the life of the rabbi was itself Torah" (Davies 1977, 455). Likewise, in Hellenistic culture, the teacher was to be a living demonstration of his teaching.

Titus's example must show evidence of the "good works" that characterize the healthy Christian life (e.g., Eph 2:8-10; Matt 5:13). His example and his teaching must complement one another, demonstrating the truth of what is said and lived. Thus in his teaching, Titus must "show integrity." The content of Titus's teaching should be morally sound and pure, and the manner of his teaching must be characteristically honest, sincere, and pure in motive—all in contrast to the teaching of the false teachers (1:10-16). Titus's teaching should also reflect "gravity" or "dignity" (*semnotēta*, cf. 2:2, where mature men are to be *semnous*, "respectable"). This word "suggests . . . a quality that inspires respect, fear, or reverence" (*TLNT* 3.244; see also Moulton and Milligan, 4587). Titus's teaching should be respectful and respectable in every way. Further, it must be "a message so sound that it is above criticism." "Sound" (*hygiēs*) is a word drawn from the world of health and medicine, which can mean "accurate," "right," or "useful." "Above criticism" is literally "cannot be censured" (*akatagnōstos*); this is a courtroom image, describing the innocence of a person acquitted of a crime. *Akatagnōstos* appears once in the Septuagint in 2 Maccabees 4:47. Unfortunate men were condemned to death "who would have been freed uncondemned [*akatagnōstoi*] if they had pleaded even before the Scythians" (Collins 2002, 346).

Note also how Paul personifies Titus's speech in 2:8; compare his personification of love in 1 Corinthians 13:4-7. This personification of speech reflects Paul's conviction that it is not human rhetoric but the presence of God in the message that provides the power of the gospel (1 Cor 1:18–2:5).

If Titus's teaching lives up to these high expectations, the result will be that opponents of the gospel "will be put to shame" (*entrapē*). This verb carries the picture of "turning around" or "reversing." When used in a positive sense, it means "to change one's attitude to respect." When used in a negative sense, it means "to put to shame." Here, the idea is reflexive: "may be ashamed of their position." Shame will be the result of "having nothing evil to say about us." "Evil" here translates a word that Paul uses as the opposite of "good" in Romans 9:11 and 2 Corinthians 5:10.

Paul returns to the content of Titus's teaching in 2:9: "Slaves are to subject themselves [*hypotassō*, here in the middle voice] to their masters."

Instructions to slaves were a standard part of household codes, and Paul includes them in the household codes of Ephesians (6:5-8) and Colossians (3:22-25). Coupled with the evidence of the letter to Philemon, the inclusion of slaves in the household codes indicates that slaves were an integral part of the early Christian communities. This is not surprising, since nearly half of the population in some urban centers were slaves. Furthermore, the basic unit of Roman society was the household (*oikos, oikia*), which included slaves, and we read in the New Testament of entire households being baptized (e.g., Acts 16:15). Christian slaves, like Christian wives, were to recognize and respect the authority structure in the household, although their respect took different forms.

Although "in all things" can be taken with the phrase that precedes it ("subject themselves"), it is better read with the phrase that follows ("be pleasing"). This clarifies the fact that, while the slave submits to a master, the slave also serves a higher master—Jesus Christ.

Thus Paul here instructs slaves "to please their masters in all things." The adjective "pleasing" (*euarestos*) was commonly used in Hellenistic moral teaching to describe an attitude of sensitivity to the will of one's master in any situation (Collins 2002, 347). It is used frequently in the New Testament to describe the Christian as one who pleases God by doing God's will (see Rom 12:1-2; 14:8; 2 Cor 5:9; Phil 4:18; Eph 5:10; Col 3:20; Heb 13:21). Slaves are also "not to talk back" (*mē antilegontas*). The command cannot be limited to arguing with direct orders; *antilegontas* refers to "speaking against someone," "talking in opposition to someone," and so on. Therefore, the command refers to speech disrespectful of or detrimental to the master's authority, such as gossip and complaining designed to promote unrest and rebelliousness among fellow slaves.

Further, slaves are not to steal (*mē nosphizomenous*) from their masters (2:10). This verb was commonly used to refer to the misappropriation of funds for one's own benefit through fraud or embezzlement. Philo tells the story of Capito, a poor man who was appointed tax collector in Judea and became rich by embezzlement (*Gaius* 199). *Nosphizomai* is used twice in the story of Ananias and Sapphira in Acts 5. Ananias "kept back part of the money for himself" (Acts 5:2). In Graeco-Roman culture, it was not uncommon for slaves to have more education than their masters, and to be more capable of handling business matters. Embezzlement was an ever-present temptation for those slaves who were entrusted with the tasks of managing large sums of money or buying for the household or estate. Stealing from one's master violates the loyalty expected of slaves, whom Paul commands to "demonstrate all good faith." "Faith" here is "trustworthiness," the "dependability" that Christian slaves should show to their masters. Paul commands them to be completely honest and faithful. In 1 Corinthians 4:2, Paul writes that such loyalty and faithfulness are the primary responsibilities of the slaves who manage their masters' households (Collins 2002, 348).

Paul concludes his instructions to slaves by providing the rationale behind the instruction. As with the instructions to younger women (2:5) and Titus's teaching and example (2:8), the goal is to live in ways that make the gospel attractive to outsiders. Slaves are to obey and demonstrate all good faith "so that in all things they may enhance the beauty of the teaching of God our Savior." "Enhance the beauty" (*kosmōsi*) refers to arranging things, putting things in order, or decorating something. It was commonly used in a cosmetic sense to speak of beautifying a person or a building by adding ornamentation. Metaphorically, the Hellenistic world viewed virtues as a kind of personal ornamentation or adornment: in 3 Maccabees 6:1, Eleazar adorns himself with his life's virtues. By the first century, *kosmeō* had also come to mean "to honor": for example, exemplary behavior brought honor to one's ancestors. Likewise, the faithful slave brings honor to the gospel (Collins 2002, 348).

In the phrase, "the teaching of God our Savior," the relationship between "teaching" and "of God" can be understood in two ways. This phrase can refer to the teaching that comes from God (a subjective genitive, emphasizing the origins of the teaching), or it can refer to the teaching about God (an objective genitive or genitive of content, emphasizing the central topic and purpose of the teaching; see the discussion in Collins 2002, 349). Here, it seems best to follow the second reading. Thus Paul is referring to "the teaching about God our Savior." Again, Paul aims for Christian slaves—indeed, all Christians, every member of the household—to live in such a way that their lives give positive witness to the gospel in their community. The way that Christians live and conduct themselves, regardless of their station in life, can be a prophetic witness to the message of the gospel and its authenticity and power.

Theological foundation for the instruction (2:11-14)

Paul follows the affirmation in 2:10 with a summary reflection on the nature of the gospel (2:11-14). This reflection takes the form of a tightly knit unit, structured chiastically. The themes Paul introduces in 2:11—God, salvation, appearing—are repeated in 2:13, when he describes "the glorious appearing of our great God and Savior, Jesus Christ." Sandwiched between these parts is a description of the life Christians are to live.

First appearance of Jesus (his earthly ministry) (2:11)
> How to live in the last days, between the first and second appearances (2:12)

Second appearance of Jesus ("second coming") (2:13)

This beautifully structured piece sends the message that, as Christians, we live lives determined by memory and hope, past and future, first appearance and second coming. In his first appearance, Jesus showed us how to live (and empowered us to live as he showed us) so that we would be ready to welcome his second appearance.

The "for" in 2:11 connects what follows with what precedes; Paul here is describing the theological basis for the instructions to the household of God in 2:1-10. Why should Christians live the kind of restrained, respectable, exemplary lives Paul has just prescribed? They should live this way because "the grace of God, which brings salvation to all people, has appeared." "Grace" (*charis*) is a central theme in Paul's letters: see above, the comment on 1:4. In its most basic sense, *charis* means "gift," something that is not deserved or earned. This grace "has appeared" (*epiphainō*). *Epiphainō* was commonly used in the Hellenistic world to speak of the way gods and deities sometimes appeared to intervene in human history on behalf of humankind. For example, the word was often connected with the appearance/presence of Asclepius, the god of healing, when people were healed from serious illnesses or injuries. The belief that deities sometimes walked among mortals was common: witness Acts 14:8-20, where the people of Lystra mistakenly identify Paul and Barnabas as Hermes and Zeus. Further, *epiphainō* came to be used in reference to the presence of human emperors when they intervened in beneficent ways in the lives of their subjects. The emperor's actions were often seen as an expression or manifestation of the saving presence of the gods. Julius Caesar was said to be "god made manifest, born of Ares and Aphrodite, the common savior of human life" (*SIG* 347.760.6; see Collins 2002, 351).

The Roman poet Virgil was a client of Caesar Augustus. His *Aeneid*, an epic account of the founding of Rome, with Roman imperial ideology woven throughout, is the story of Aeneus, a character from Homer's *Illiad*. As Virgil crafts the story, Aeneus wanders from Troy to Italy, and becomes one of the founders of Rome by defeating the native Latins. Virgil depicts the rise of the emperors as the dawning of the Roman Golden Age.

Similarly, the Priene Inscription praises the birthday of Augustus as a holiday,

> Since Providence, which has ordered all things and is deeply interested in our life, has set in most perfect order by giving us Augustus, whom she filled with virtue that he might benefit humankind, sending him as a savior [*sōtēra*], both for us and for our descendants, that he might end war and arrange all things, and since he, Caesar, by his appearance [*epiphanies*] (excelled even our anticipations), surpassing all previous benefactors, and not even leaving to posterity any hope of surpassing what he has done, and since the birthday of the god Augustus was the beginning of the good tidings [*euangeliōn*] for the world that came by reason of him . . . . (Danker 1982, 215–18; the translation is from Evans 2000, 69)

So, Augustus was a savior for the present and the future who brought peace to the empire. His birthday, the birthday of a god, is proclaimed as "the beginning of the good news" for the world. And all this is tied to his appearing!

For the Christian, however, the "good news" is all about the God and Savior Jesus Christ, and *his* appearing, *his* incarnation in human history. For Paul, the "grace of God" appeared not in the person of a Graeco-Roman deity or emperor, but in the person of Jesus Christ. The purpose of Jesus' appearance in history was to bring salvation to all people; here is a central tenet of Paul's theology, namely that salvation is for all people, Jew and Gentile alike. The affirmation "which brings salvation to all people" is polemical (Collins 2002, 352); Paul is concerned with the influence of ethnocentric Judaizing Christianity, which asserted that Gentiles could not become Christians without first becoming Jews (see 1:10-11; 1:13-16; 3:9). Paul adamantly asserts that the grace of God and the salvation this grace makes possible are offered to all people, without discrimination or favoritism.

In 2:12, Paul describes the effect that the first appearance of Jesus Christ (i.e., his earthly ministry) should have on the daily lives of his followers. Jesus' ministry (his words and example) "teaches us to reject godlessness and worldly passions." The word "teaches" (*paideuousa*) refers to the educating and disciplining of a child. The writer of Hebrews, drawing on Proverbs 3:12, describes God as a father who disciplines (*paideuei*) his children (Heb 12:6; 12:7; 12:10). And Clement, in his letter to the Corinthian church, exhorts his readers to "Let our children share in the instruction that is in Christ" (*en Christō paideias*, 1 Clem 21.8).

In his description of the life produced by the teaching of Christ, Paul contrasts two ages and the ways of life that characterize each (cf. Rom 5:12-21; 8:5-11). The instruction consists of negative and positive admonitions.

Negatively, Christians are to "reject godlessness and worldly passions." "Godlessness" (*asebeian*) is the opposite of godliness (*eusebei*). "Godlessness" can be understood as that which is opposite God's character, or it can refer to a lifestyle/attitude that has no regard for God. Remember, in the Pastoral Epistles, godliness refers to a life lived in and from reverence for God. *Asebeia* would then be a life that has no thought of or reverence toward God.

"Worldly" (*kosmikas*) refers to the systems or standards of this world. Paul here joins "worldly" with "passions" to speak of desires that follow worldly standards and result in immoral behavior, that which is against the character and will of God. Paul looks at the world through an apocalyptic prism: the present age, characterized by godlessness and lives driven by worldly passions, is evil and destined for destruction (Gal 1:4). In the midst of the present evil age, Christians must live lives that are "sensible" (*sōphronōs*), "upright" (*dikaiōs*), and "godly" (*eusebōs*). All three of these positive characteristics have appeared previously in Titus. "Sensibility" (or "self-control") was a cardinal virtue in Hellenistic culture. In contrast with "worldly desires," Paul here may be building on his own Jewish abhorrence of the sexual behavior of Gentiles, whom the Jews viewed as being driven by worldly, animalistic passions. "Uprightness" probably points to the Jewish notion of righteousness, which includes living in a right relationship with God and others. And as noted above, "godliness" refers to a life lived in and from reverence for God. The three virtues work together, each producing the others. Self-control and reverence produce a life of healthy relationships; healthy relationships and reverence help produce self-control; and so on.

Christians are to live this kind of life "while we wait for the blessed hope, which is the glorious appearing of our great God and Savior, Jesus Christ" (2:13). Living as we do between the earthly ministry of Jesus (his first appearance) and the second coming of Jesus (his second appearing), we "wait" (*prosdechomenoi*). *Prosdechomai* refers to remaining "in a place and/or state, with expectancy concerning a future event" (*LN* 85.60). We look for and await this event, with confidence that our waiting will be fruitful (cf. 1 Thess 1:10; 1 Cor 16:22). This expectation is the "blessed hope," which Paul explains with the next phrase, "which is the glorious appearing," the second coming of Jesus Christ. The "and" (*kai*) that connects these phrases in the Greek text is epexegetic, so that the second phrase explains and defines the first. Paul focuses his audience's attention on the future appearing "of the glorious appearing of our great God and Savior, Jesus Christ."

To this point in the letter, Paul has twice referred to God as "Savior" (1:3; 2:10). In this place, Paul seems to be referring to Jesus as both God (i.e., equal to God) and Savior. As the footnote in the NRSV shows, this phrase can be rendered "the glory of our great God and of our Savior, Jesus Christ," thus not suggesting any equality between God and Jesus. However, the following factors suggest that the entire phrase is referring to Jesus:

- Grammatically, the phrase has only one definite article, placed before "God." The article should be assumed before "Savior," but it is not written in the text. In Greek grammar, the construction falls under the Granville Sharp rule: if two nouns are singular (not plural), personal, and *not* proper names, and the construction is article–noun–"and" (*kai*)–noun (this phrase meets all these qualifications), then the nouns *always* refer to the same thing (see *GGBB*, 270-90).
- The expression "God and Savior" exists as a definite formula in both the mystery religions and the Septuagint.
- If 2:13 does indeed refer to the second coming of Christ, it is rather unlikely that Paul would speak of God the Father returning with his Son.

These factors taken together suggest that Paul here refers to Jesus as our great God and Savior. This verse then is a powerful affirmation of the oneness and equality of God the Father and Jesus Christ, God the Son.

This coming appearance will demonstrate or manifest Jesus' glory (*doxēs*). Paul refers to the glory of God more than any other writer in the New Testament. Non-Jewish Hellenistic writers do not use *doxa* with reference to the gods; for them, the word referred to "fame" or "reputation." Writers in Hellenistic Judaism, however, use *doxa* to translate the Hebrew word *kabod*, which refers to the manifestation of the presence and activity of Yahweh in some sort of perceivable experience (Collins 2002, 354).

Paul follows the reference to Jesus' second coming with further elaboration on what Jesus accomplished during his earthly ministry, his first appearance. This elaboration takes the form of an early Christian hymn or creed, material that believers would have memorized and then chanted or sung as part of worship. The poetic and formal characteristics of these materials aided in memorization; this is how the early Christians, many of whom were illiterate, learned their theology. In fact, the hymn that Paul quotes here likely was known and used in worship in the Cretan churches.

Early Christian confessions began as short, simple statements: "Jesus Christ is Lord" (Rom 10:9) or "I believe that Jesus Christ is the Son of God" (the variant reading at Acts 8:37, footnoted in most modern English translations). Gradually, these confessions were extended with the addition of descriptions of Jesus' life and work (e.g., 1 Cor 15:3ff). Early Christian hymns were patterned after the Old Testament psalms, and/or the hymns of

Hellenistic religions. Hymns were longer and broader in scope than confessions; examples of early hymns include Philippians 2:6-11 and Colossians 1:15-20. (A full discussion of the nature of these hymns and confessions, and the criteria by which they can be identified, can be found in Gloer 1996, 209–17.)

As with the christological hymns of Philippians 2 and Colossians 1, this hymn focuses on interpreting the death of Jesus. The passage's hymnic qualities clearly stand out in the beginning of 2:14, which opens with a complex relative clause that has a Semitic character. The first three phrases, each of which begins with its verb (also a Semitic construction), form a complete three-line stanza, picking up from the "Jesus Christ" at the end of 2:13:

> Who gave himself for us (2:14a),
> That he might redeem us from all wickedness (2:14b)
> And cleanse for himself a people of his very own, eager to do good works (2:14c).

The verse begins with the relative pronoun "who" (*hōs*), as do the christological hymns in Philippians 2, Colossians 1, and 1 Timothy 3:16. The relative pronoun marks the transition between one form of material and another. Paul reminds his audience that Jesus "gave himself for us"; compare Galatians 1:4 and Jesus' words in the Lukan account of the Last Supper, "This is my body, which is given for you" (Luke 22:19). The verb "gave" (*edōken*) was frequently used to refer both to sacrificial offerings and to self-sacrifice/martyrdom (Thucydides, *History* 2.43.2; 1 Macc 2:50, 6:44; Mark 10:45; Ignatius, *Smyrn.* 4.2). Jesus gave himself "for us" (*hyper hēmōn*); we are the reason for his sacrificial death.

- The New Testament writers commonly use *hyper* to describe the effects of Jesus' death (Rom 5:6, 8; 14:15; 1 Cor 11:24; 15:3; 2 Cor 5:14-15; 1 Thess 5:10; Mark 14:24; Luke 22:19-20; John 6:51; 11:50-51; 18:14; Heb 2:9; 1 Peter 2:21; 3:18; cf. Judas Maccabeus's death "for them," *hyper autōn*, Josephus, *Ant* 13.1.1 §1.6; Collins 2002, 356).
- Paul and the synoptic writers use *hyper* in each of the accounts of Jesus' words at the Last Supper (1 Cor 11:23; Mark 14:22-25; Matt 26:26-29; Luke 22:15-20), and in Paul's recitation of the tradition that had been passed on to him (1 Cor 15:3ff)—all of which suggest that Jesus' death was a vicarious death or atoning sacrifice.

This view of Jesus' death as a substitutionary sacrifice grows out of the meeting of three streams:

- the developing notion of sacrifice in Judaism, which was grounded in the idea of collective and individual representation common in Semitic thinking, represented in the Old Testament concept of the Suffering Servant (Isa 52–53);
- Christian application of the Suffering Servant motif to the death of Jesus; and
- the widespread acceptance in Judaism of the Hellenistic concept of the violent death of the righteous as vicarious, which by the first century had become the standard way of interpreting the deaths of martyrs (e.g., 2 Macc 7; 4 Macc).

The two phrases that follow are controlled by *hina* ("that"), indicating purpose. These phrases reflect the Semitic style of synthetic parallelism. The key thoughts—redemption, cleansing, wickedness, being Jesus'/God's own people, eagerness ("zeal") for good works—all reflect a thought world permeated by the Old Testament.

First, Jesus gave himself for us "that he might redeem us from all wickedness." The word translated "redeem" (*lytrōsētai*) is used only three times in the New Testament: here, Luke 24:21, and 1 Peter 1:18. It can be translated "set free" or "rescue." In non-biblical writings, it refers to the price of manumission, a payment of money to secure the freedom of slaves or prisoners of war. In the Hellenistic world, slaves were manumitted by means of paying a prescribed amount of money to a deity. After that payment, the slave was freed from the old master and became a servant of the god to whom he/she was manumitted. More than one thousand deeds inscribed on temple walls between 201 BCE and 90 CE attest to the practice of slaves who were freed by being "sold" into the service of the Pythian Apollos at Delphi. This Graeco-Roman concept is paralleled in the Old Testament by passages that describe the powerful deeds God did to free the Israelites from bondage in Egypt (see Exod 6:6; 15:13; Deut 7:6-8; 9:26; 13:5; 15:15; 24:18).

What the believer has been redeemed ("set free," "rescued") from is "all wickedness." "Wickedness" (*anomies*) refers to living with no regard for moral or ethical law. In Christ, the believer is set free to enjoy an ironic freedom: freedom to be obedient, freedom to be a slave of Jesus Christ (cf. Paul in 1:1), freedom from all those things that would interfere with living in a right relationship with God and others. Indeed, "it is for freedom that Christ has set us free" (Gal 5:1). The believer now has freedom to be obedient to the call of God rather than remain in bondage to the self and the desire to be *of* the world, not just *in* the world.

Second, Jesus gave himself in order to "cleanse for himself a people of his very own." "Cleanse" (or "purify," *katharisē*) is a ritual term that refers to the act of making someone or something free from contamination, and therefore acceptable as an instrument for worship. By extension, the word refers to making someone morally clean, free from moral impurity or any act not worthy of God. "People of his own" evokes the idea of a "chosen people." This idea is central to the Old and New Testaments: for example, in Exodus 19:5, God says to Israel, "You shall be my chosen people out of all the nations" (e.g., see also Exod 23:22; Deut 7:6; 14:2; 26:18). First Peter describes believers as "a chosen race" (1 Pet 2:9; see also Rom 8:33; Col 3:12; 1 Tim 5:21; 2 Tim 2:10). At the close of the first century, Clement writes of how God "chose the Lord Jesus Christ and us through him as a chosen people" (*1 Clem* 64.1). Paul links being chosen with cleansing in Ephesians 5:25-26. After describing Christ as Savior in 5:23, Paul writes that Christ chose the church as his bride, and "gave himself up for her in order to make her holy by cleansing her with the washing of water."

This rescued, purified, and chosen people is to be "eager to do good works." Freed slaves in the Hellenistic world entered the service of the god for whom they were manumitted; the chosen people of Israel entered the service of their redeemer, Yahweh. Likewise, those who have been redeemed by Jesus Christ enter his service. They are to live in a state of readiness to serve and obey. As in Ephesians 2:10, "good works" serves as a Pauline summary description of the Christian life (see also Titus 1:16; 2:7; 3:8; 3:14; 1 Tim 5:10; 5:25; 6:18; 2 Tim 2:21; 3:17).

Encouragement and empowerment (2:15)

Paul returns to personal exhortation and encouragement in 2:15. Titus must faithfully carry out Paul's commands; he is not only to deliver these instructions, he must also make sure that they are followed. Paul refers to the instructions as "these things [*tauta*]," the things he has described in 2:1-14. For the use of *tauta* as a summary term at the end of a body of teaching, see also Titus 3:8; 1 Timothy 3:14; 4:6, 11, 15; 5:7, 21; 6:2, 11; 2 Timothy 2:14.

Titus administers these things by "teaching" (*lalei*; cf. 2:1), "encouraging" (*parakalei*), and "rebuking" (*elegche*), all words that have appeared previously in the letter (1:9, 13; 2:1, 6, 9). Together, these terms paint a picture of the pastoral care that Titus must provide. He must teach, explaining the *what* and the *why* of the Christian life that Paul describes. He must encourage his people to live according to these truths. And he must rebuke or correct those who stray from or reject these truths. All of these elements are essential to the healthy witness of the church.

Titus must teach, encourage, and rebuke "with all authority." The word translated "authority" (*epitagēs*) is a strong word. It refers to the right or authority to issue an order, and was used in the Hellenistic world to describe commands from kings and gods. Paul used it in 1:1 to describe the command of God that made him an apostle, setting the course of his life and death. Thus Titus, when he teaches and encourages and rebukes, is acting not on his own authority but on the authority of Paul and the God who sent him. Further, the reference to "all authority" echoes Jesus' announcement that he had been given all authority, and that by that authority he was sending his disciples out to make disciples in every nation (Matt 28:18-20). Paul has carried out his mission according to this authority, and now gives Titus a mission to carry out according to this authority.

In keeping with this authority, Paul encourages Titus to "let no one look down" on him. Paul was no doubt aware that some in the churches would not receive his representatives and welcome their work as leaders in the church; see 1 Corinthians 16:11, where Paul tells the Corinthian church to respect Timothy, and the similar encouragement directed at Timothy in 1 Timothy 4:12. Titus was to carry out his work with full confidence in the authority Paul had given to him (Titus) as Paul's successor in the care of the gospel in Crete, and the chain of empowerment that had passed from Jesus to Paul and then to himself (Titus).

Summary

In Titus 2 (the first half of section 3 in our outline), Paul describes the responsibilities of members of Titus's churches. He takes the household code, a type of literature familiar from the work of the Hellenistic moral philosophers, and adapts it to the household of God. Throughout, Paul's concern is that his people in Crete live the kinds of lives that will earn a hearing for the gospel. The proverbial lawlessness of Cretan society posed special problems for the church as it sought to witness. The kinds of ecstatic, amorphous Christianity that some people see in the earliest Pauline churches would have proven disastrous in such a setting. So, on Crete, in the specific situation Titus faced, Paul commanded that his people live settled, conservative lives that did not unnecessarily contradict traditional Roman values.

Living as Witnesses (3:1-11)

As with Titus 2, Titus 3 contains practical instructions for Titus's church. Its structure parallels the structure of chapter 2: paraenesis, or practical instruction (3:1-2), followed by a theological foundation for the paraenesis (3:3-8a), followed by a direct statement of encouragement and commissioning to Titus (3:8b-11).

Content (3:1-2)

Titus must "remind" (*hypomimnēske*) the Cretan believers of the kind of lives they are called to live (3:1). This language suggests that the instruction Paul describes here is not new information to the audience; these are characteristics they already know should be reflected in their lives, likely through previous teaching from Paul. Using five infinitives, Paul describes seven virtues/characteristics of the Christian life.

First, Titus's people should "be subject to rulers and authorities." The terms "rulers" (*archais*) and "authorities" (*exousiais*) sit here without a conjunction between them. This construction suggests that the two terms refer to a single group of governing authorities, rather than to two separate groups; so also the more generic command "to be obedient" that follows. The New Testament uses *archais* and *exousiais* together ten times, and Paul uses them together with the same verb (*hypotassesthai*, "be subject to") in Romans 13:1-7. In each case, governmental authorities are in view. "Being subject" includes recognition of authority, subordination, and obedience. Submission to legitimate governmental authorities was a cardinal virtue in the Roman world, and such submission would no doubt enhance the church's reputation in the community. Paul encourages such behavior elsewhere in the Pastoral Epistles: in 1 Timothy 2:1-2, he urges Christians to pray for kings and all people in authority "so that we may live peaceful and quiet lives, in all godliness and dignity."

We should not be surprised that Paul would take such a position. On many occasions, the Roman Empire was a help to Paul in his work. He used Roman citizenship to his advantage more than once. His life was saved several times by Roman authorities. He used Roman roads and seaways to spread the gospel, and his travels were made safe (or safer) by the presence of Roman soldiers along these ways. Apart from the *Pax Romana*, he never could have traveled so freely and extensively. Even when imprisoned, Paul's rights were protected to the point that he was able to continue his ministry; Acts ends with Paul under house arrest, guarded by Roman soldiers but able to welcome "all who came to him, proclaiming the Kingdom of God and teaching about the Lord Jesus Christ with all boldness, unhindered" (Acts 28:30-31). Given all of this, it is easy to see how Paul would write that the governing authorities have been "instituted by God . . . for your good" (Rom 13:1, 4), and how he here can say that Christians should "be subject to rulers and authorities." He would have prescribed this same attitude whether the letter was written before or after his first imprisonment in Rome: keep in mind that he chose to be imprisoned in Rome by appealing to Caesar (a privilege offered to him as a Roman citizen). (For further evidence of how Christians worked out submitting to the empire, see Athenagoras, *Legatio* 37.2–3.)

Of course, Christian submission to governmental authority was not absolute. In Acts 4, Peter and John are arrested by the Jewish Sanhedrin (both a civil and religious authority in Judea) for preaching and teaching in the name of Jesus. After being ordered to "cease and desist" in their activities, Peter and John replied, "whether it is right in God's sight to obey you rather than to obey God, you must decide; for we cannot keep from speaking about what we have seen and heard" (Acts 4:19-20). After their release, they resumed preaching and were arrested again (Acts 5:12-18). Then they miraculously escaped, returned to preaching, and were arrested again (Acts 5:19-26). When brought before the Sanhedrin and reminded that they had been ordered not to preach in Jesus' name anymore, "Peter and the apostles answered, 'We must obey God rather than any human authority'" (Acts 5:29). Clearly, the apostles here were *not* "being subject to rulers and authorities" (Titus 3:1a); their refusal to quit preaching and teaching about Jesus was an act of civil disobedience. This act suggests that believers will face situations where we must pledge our allegiance to an authority higher than earthly rulers and authorities. At the same time, the clear New Testament witness is that Christians should support and submit to earthly rulers and authorities as far as they are able to do so, even when such obedience is inconvenient or costly, as long as the earthly rulers and authorities do not command things antithetical to the Christian's allegiance to God.

Second, Titus's people are "to be obedient" (*peitharchein*). The verb here is a compound, joining *peithō* ("obey") and *archē* ("rulers"), and probably refers to obedience to all legitimate authorities, in contrast to the more limited scope of *archais* and *exousiais* mentioned earlier in the verse. Again, orderliness and stability in the churches and in the lives of Christians would win a hearing for the gospel; chaos and insurrection would shut people's ears.

Third, the believers are "to be ready for every good work." "Ready" (*etoimous*) refers to being fully prepared, a state of readiness. According to 2:14, only those who have been purified are fully prepared for good works in service of God. According to 1:16, those who have not been purified are unsuitable for any good works.

Fourth, Titus's people are "to speak evil [*blasphēmein*] of no one" (3:2). While we tend to think of blasphemy as speaking evil of or toward God, the word was used in Hellenistic society to refer to slandering other people. Paul uses it in this sense here; see also the similar sense in 2:5. The broad nature of the command is reflected by the object "no one." Christians are not to speak evil of anyone, even those who oppose the faith, because the adversary is not other people but the spiritual forces of darkness (Eph 6:12).

Paul follows this list with another group of three characteristics, governed by the verb "to be" (*einai*). Christians are to be "not quarrelsome" (*amachous*); the adjective is formed from a verb that means "to fight or quarrel," to be contentious, either by words or actions. Christians are also to be "gentle" (*epieikeis*); this word describes a person who is fair, patient, and considerate in dealing with others. Finally, Christians are "to demonstrate full courtesy [*prautēta*] to everyone." *Prautēs* was a way of dealing with people that was the opposite of harshness (*LN* 88.59). Paul heightens the importance of this virtue by insisting that believers demonstrate "full" (or "every," *pasan*) courtesy "to everyone" (*pros pantas anthrōpous*). Again, Paul's language allows for no exceptions. He calls Christians to be respectful of all authority (Christian and non-Christian) and kind, gentle, and courteous to all people (Christians and non-Christians). Greek writers valued these last three characteristics, considering them cardinal virtues. The appearance of such characteristics in the lives of Christians would serve both to flesh out the gospel in the believers' lives and to win favor in the Hellenistic world.

Theological foundation for the instruction (3:3-8a)

The instructions in 3:1-2 remind Titus's people of how they are to live as those redeemed and purified (2:14). To contrast this new life with the life of the society around the audience, Paul tells Titus to remind them also that this is not how they once lived (3:3). This reminder provides a rationale for the instructions that preceded it, as shown by the word "for" (*gar*) that begins the thought in 3:3.

At this point, Paul inverts the "once–now" formula found throughout the New Testament:

- "once heathen, now illuminated/cleansed" (Rom 6:17-18; 7:5-6; 11:20-32; Gal 4:3-9; 1 Cor 6:9-11; Col 3:5-10; Eph 3:1-10; 1 Pet 2:25; 4:3-4)
- "once hidden, now revealed" (Titus 1:2-3; 2 Tim 1:9-10; Rom 16:25-27; 1 Cor 2:7-10; Col 1:26-27; Eph 3:5-6; 1 Pet 1:20) (Collins 2002, 360).

Here, having described the "now," Paul turns to the "once" with a catalog of eight vices that characterized the non-Christian life. "We ourselves" captures the emphatic nature of the Greek text. "Were once" (*ēmen pote*) points to a state of being in the past, which is no longer true in the present. The first-person plural "we" refers to humanity in general, outside of God's intervention in Christ. Thus the list of vices that follows reflects the general condition of people who have not yet been redeemed and purified, a group to which Paul and Titus, and the group to whom Titus will minister, once belonged. This list resembles other vice lists in which Paul seeks to characterize humanity apart from God's salvation in Christ (e.g., Rom 1:29-31; 1 Cor 6:9-11). The list appears to be organized to show a logical progression from spiritual insensitivity and disobedience to spiritual deception, etc., to living a life controlled by hatred (Arichea and Hatton 1995, 299). "We once were . . .," Paul asserts,

- "foolish" (*anoētoi*): this word can have a generic sense (stupidity, silliness), but in this context probably refers to ignorance or disregard of the Christian message and its demands ("the knowledge of the truth that leads to godliness," 1:1);
- "disobedient" (*apeitheis*): this word refers to a pattern or attitude of disobedience (*LN* 36.24);
- "deceived" (*planōmenoi*): literally "led astray" or "misled." "Don't go astray" was a popular Hellenistic moral exhortation (e.g., Epictetus, *Discourses* 4.6.23). The progression in the first three vices is clear: disregard for the truth leads to disobedience and moral confusion.
- "slaves to various lusts and pleasures": "pleasures" (*hēdonais*, the root of our word "hedonism") and "lusts" (*epithumiais*) refer to physical and sexual pleasures, but can also refer to any negative thing that gives enjoyment. Sensuality can become obsessive and addictive, and can dominate a person's life until that person is enslaved, completely under the control of the behavior. Paradoxically, the hedonistic exercise of freedom does not result in greater freedom; it results in bondage and a lack of freedom. The Stoics taught that the ideal moral life was a life without passions.
- "living lives of wickedness and envy": "living lives" (*diagontes*) refers to a pattern of behavior, the way one lives life (*LN* 41.3). "Wickedness" (*kakia*) is a comprehensive term for evil activity. "Envy" (*phthonos*) is a negative attitude toward someone perceived to be in a more advantageous position (*LN* 88.160); envy leads to resentment and covetousness.
- "hated by [*stygētoi*] and hating [*misountes*] one another": *stygētos* refers to something that is hated, abominable, or despicable (Aeschylus, *Prometheus*

592a; Philo, *Decalogue* 131; *1 Clem* 35.6; Heliodorus 5.29.4). Clement describes the tormenters of Hananiah, Azariah, and Mishael (Shadrach, Meshach, and Abednego) as "abominable [*stygētoi*] men and full of all wickedness" (*1 Clem* 45.7). Taken together, the two terms depict a life far from the Christian ideal of loving one another.

Paul's description of the old life in 3:3, juxtaposed with his description of the new life in 3:1-2, is a powerful reminder of how we should live in stark contrast with how we once lived.

NOW	THEN
Subject to rulers and authorities	Foolish
Obedient	Disobedient
Ready for every good work	Deceived
Speaking evil of no one	Slaves to various lusts and pleasures
Not quarrelsome	Living lives of wickedness and envy
Gentle	Hated
Showing full courtesy to everyone	Hating one another

This reminder is not merely descriptive; it is also prescriptive, challenging us to examine our own lives. Do we demonstrate evidence that a new person has taken residence, or do we manifest the characteristics of the old life? This list and others like it allow us to ask if we are living as new creations in Christ.

In 3:4-7, Paul uses an early Christian hymn that speaks of baptism as an act of rebirth and renewal. As with 2:14, the hymnic nature of the present text is clearly indicated by the rhythmic, poetic structure of the Greek text and the hymnic vocabulary. The passage, which is one sentence in Greek, divides naturally into three stanzas:

> When the kindness and benevolence of God our Savior appeared,
>   Not because of any righteous works we had done (3:4-5a),
> But according to his mercy he saved us
>   Through the washing of rebirth and renewal by the Holy Spirit (3:5b),
> Whom he poured out on us richly through Jesus Christ our Savior
>   So that, being justified by his grace,
>   We might become heirs according to the hope of eternal life (3:6-7).

The two hymns also parallel one another thematically. In 3:4, Paul returns to the same motif—epiphany, Jesus' appearing—which he used in 2:11-14. In fact, each of the key words from 2:11 are repeated in 3:4:

- "salvation" (2:11), "our Savior" (3:4);
- "grace" (*hē charis*), "kindness" (*hē chrēstotēs*);
- "God";
- "appearing" (*epephanē*);
- "humanity" (*anthrōpois*), "benevolence" (lit., "love for humanity," *philanthrōpia*, 3:4).

In the earlier passage, Paul depicted present-day Christian existence (2:12) as living between Christ's first appearance (2:11) and his second coming (2:13). There, Paul focused on the effect that the first appearance should have on life in the in-between times. In those verses, Paul alludes to baptism in the use of purification language (2:14), which he makes more explicit here in reference to the water of rebirth.

In 2:11, Paul referred to the appearance of the grace of God our Savior. In 3:4, Paul refers to appearance of the "kindness and benevolence of God our Savior." Paul frequently uses "kindness" (*chrēstotēs*) to describe an attribute of God's mercy (Rom 2:4; 11:22; Eph 2:7) or to refer to a Christian virtue (2 Cor 6:6; Gal 5:22; Col 3:12). The word refers to goodness of character in action, "to provide something beneficial for someone as an act of kindness" (*LN* 88.67). "Benevolence" (*philanthrōpia*) is similar, in that it speaks not only of a feeling or emotion but of positive acts of kindness toward others. These two terms appear together often in Hellenistic literature.

- The emperor Gaius was said to be "good and benevolent" (*chrēstos kai philanthrōpos*; Philo, *Gaius* 67);
- Gedaliah, a Judean governor showed "goodness and benevolence" (*chrēstotēta kai philanthrōpian*; Josephus, *Ant* 10.9.3 §164; cf. Jer 40:8);
- The emperor Pertinax ruled with *philanthrōpia* ("benevolence") and *chrēstotēs* ("goodness"; Dio Cassius, *History* 73.5.2);
- When a conquered city opens its gates and surrenders, the conquering generals should treat its citizens with benevolence and goodness (*philanthrōpos kai chrēstos*; Onasander, *General* 18.1).

In fact,

> Benevolence was widely viewed as the quintessential quality of a good king. . . .
> In sum, manifestations of goodness and benevolence were to be expected when a king, his governor, or his general arrived for a solemn visit to a city, evidence that the arriving personage was indeed a Savior [*sōtēr*] or benefactor [*euergetēs*]. Since the royal sovereign was often considered to represent the deity—sometimes to the point of being deified himself—these expressions of goodness and benevolence were a manifestation of the goodness and benevolence of the gods. (Collins 2002, 364)

In 3:5a-b, Paul associates the manifestation of God's kindness and benevolence with God's mercy. In 3:4, Paul captures the rich Hellenistic image of the formal arrival of an emperor or god. The manifestation of benevolence that accompanied such a solemn arrival was associated with clemency. Philo links both clemency (*Moses* 1.198) and mercy (*Cherubim* 99) with the royal and divine attribute of benevolence. Likewise, Paul here writes that we have been saved "not because of any righteous works that we had done, but according to his mercy." "Works of righteousness" (*ergōn tōn en dikaiosunē*) refers to the kind of life and conduct that God requires. "We had done" is literally "we ourselves had done"; the first person verb (*epoiēsomen*) together with the first person plural pronoun (*hēmeis*) makes the statement emphatic. Paul wants this message to be clear: our salvation is the result of God's mercy, not the righteous things we have done. At the same time, our salvation produces righteous actions (rather than us producing them by our own goodness); these are the result, not the basis, of our salvation (cf. Rom 8:1-4; Eph 2:8-10).

This activity defines "mercy" (*eleos*); it is not pity, but compassion and love, both of which are undeserved. As always, the initiative in salvation is God's. This has been the case since he sought out Noah and Abraham, to initiate covenant relationships with them and make them his agents (Gen 6:8; 12:1-3). God both initiates and accomplishes the work of salvation; from beginning to end, it has been and is and ever will be a work of grace.

We have been saved "through the washing of rebirth and renewal by the Holy Spirit" (3:5c). "Washing" (*loutrou*) "can refer to a bath, the water in which one bathes, or the act of bathing" (Collins 2002, 366). This word was used to refer to ceremonial washings, whether of the whole body or particular parts of the body, which functioned as a passage from one state of life to another. These washings "symbolized the transition from the secular to the sacred" (Collins 2002, 366). In Titus 3:5, the washing is one of "rebirth" (*palingenesia*, a compound of *palin* ["again"] and *ginomai* ["to become," "to come into being"]). This word was used in reference to a wide range of experiences, including healing and restoration of health, return from exile, the beginning of new life, the restoration of souls, new life for a people, and the anticipated restoration of the world. The notion of "rebirth" is found in Jesus' discussion with Nicodemus (John 3:3-8), which uses the same cluster of ideas: water, new birth, Spirit. Jesus tells Nicodemus that he must be "born again," rebirth in water and Spirit. Such rituals were familiar both to Jews and Greeks. Jewish proselytes were initiated into Judaism through a ritual washing of the entire body.

Paul here joins rebirth with "renewal" (*anakainōseōs*). This word refers to improving something by making it new: "to cause something to become new and different, with the implication of becoming superior" (*LN* 58.72). It appears also in Romans 12:2: "be transformed by the *renewing* of your mind." *Anakainōsis* is not found outside of Christian literature. Throughout the New Testament, "new" generally indicates the kind of conversion that is necessary as the second coming of Jesus Christ approaches (Collins 2002, 367).

What does Paul mean by this reference to "rebirth" and "renewal"? Interpreters have suggested several possibilities:

- Rebirth and renewal are two separate things, with rebirth relating to the initiatory rite of baptism and renewal relating to the ongoing work of the Holy Spirit. This is the clearest reading of the text, and is to be favored. Thus we have here two ways in which God saves us: through the rebirth that comes at conversion, metonymized in Paul's reference to baptism; and through the renewal that the Holy Spirit brings to the day-to-day life of the baptized believer.
- Rebirth and renewal are two sides of the same thing, and the *kai* ("and") that connects them is epexegetic; in this case, "renewal" is an explanation of "rebirth," and rebirth *is* renewal.
- Both rebirth and renewal are explanatory to "washing": in this case, the sentence would be translated, "He saved us through the washing, that is, the rebirth and renewal, which are done by the Holy Spirit."
- Washing/baptism is a sign of rebirth and renewal: thus, "He saved us by means of the washing, which is a sign that we have experienced rebirth and renewal from the Holy Spirit."

The picture of the Holy Spirit being "poured out" (3:6) on believers is used in Acts 2:17-18, 33, and 10:45. It originates in the Greek translation of Joel 2:28-30. All these passages speak of the fact that the eschatological age of the Spirit has begun, and that the Spirit is at work. Even as the Spirit of God was present and working in the creation of the universe and humankind (Gen 1–2), so also the Spirit is at work in the new creation (2 Cor 5:17). Paul says that God has poured his Spirit on us "richly" (*plousiōs*); the focus is on the abundance and lavishness of God's gift of the Spirit that comes "through Jesus Christ our Savior." The New Testament writers several times refer to Jesus as the giver of the Holy Spirit (John 1:26-27; 4:10-11; 20:22-23; Matt 3:11; Mark 1:8; Luke 3:16). The work of the Holy Spirit is front and center in Titus 3:5-6, and must also be front and center in the believer's life. He (the Spirit) brings rebirth through his action in conversion and continuing renewal through his ongoing presence in the Christian's day-to-day walk.

"So that" (*hina*, 3:7) points the reader to the purpose of the grace, rebirth, and renewal: we may inherit eternal life. "Being justified" (*dikaiōthentes*) refers to God's work in moving people into a right relationship with himself. This statement is pure Paul, echoing his disputes with the Judaizers in Romans and Galatians. We are not justified by our good works but by God's grace. This verb is a divine passive, indicating that the action is God's (see the discussion of Philemon 1:15-16). Again, we see hints of the Judaizing opposition that Titus and Paul faced on Crete.

We who have been "washed" by the Spirit (3:5) are "justified by his grace" (3:7). "Being justified" means that God has turned right side up everything that was turned upside down by sin. In Romans 1:23, Paul succinctly summarized the Fall (Gen 3), where people first chose Satan's lies over God's truth: humanity "exchanged the truth of God for a lie and worshipped and served the creature rather than the Creator." Ever since, humans have built their lives, individually and corporately, on a lie. We by nature see the world upside down, but in Christ we catch a glimpse of what right side up really looks like. Further, through Jesus and the Spirit, we are reborn and continually being renewed so that we can begin to live life right side up.

All this happens by God's grace, so that "we might become heirs according to the hope of eternal life." Paul makes use of inheritance as a theological motif in Romans, 1 Corinthians, and Galatians. To the Jew in the first century, "inheritance" was a reminder of God's promise to give Israel the promised land of Canaan, and what God did to fulfill that promise. The theme was extended to refer to God's blessings in general. By its very nature, "inheritance" looks to a future fulfillment. "According to the hope" refers to the Christian's confident expectation of that which is hoped for: remember, in the Bible, "hope" is *never* just wishful thinking! In this case, the inheritance that we confidently expect is "eternal life" (*zōēs aiōniou*), the "in Christ" relationship that is both now and in the future, "already" and "not yet." The "now" experience of eternal life points toward, results in, and gives us confidence that we will possess the "future" experience of eternal life (Eph 1:3-14): "Now we see in a mirror dimly, but then we shall see face to face. Now I know only in part; then I will know fully even as I have been known fully" (1 Cor 13:12). According to Ephesians 1:13-14, the Holy Spirit's presence is God's guarantee to us of our inheritance.

Paul closes the section by stating, "the saying is sure" (*pistos ho logos,* literally, "the saying is faithful.") This affirmation points back to the hymnic materials in 3:4-7: *Pistos ho logos* appears three times in 1 Timothy (1:15; 3:1; 4:9) and once in 2 Timothy (2:11), and confirms that Paul is faithfully reproducing the traditions he received and has handed on to his readers.

Encouragement and empowerment (3:8b-11)

Having assured Titus (and the church, overhearing the letter) of the trustworthiness of the teaching he has just presented, Paul does three things in 3:8b-11. He charges Titus to teach these things for the good of the faithful; he urges Titus to avoid foolish arguments; and he urges Titus to avoid divisive people.

Paul begins, "I want you to insist on these things" (3:8b), pointing back to all that he has written in 3:1-8a. The scope of "these things" is made clear by the repetition of "good works" later on in the verse (cf. 3:1), and the parallelism with 2:15. "Insist" (*diabebaioomai*) refers to speaking with confidence, firmness, and certainty, and implies the importance of what was being said. Hellenistic writers frequently used this term to refer to their paraenesis (for examples, see Aristotle, *Rhet* 2.13.1; Demosthenes, *On the Treaty with Alexander* 17.30; Polybius, *Histories* 12.12.6). Titus is to speak of these things in this way "so that those who have come to believe in God may be careful to devote themselves to good works." "Those who have come to believe" translates a perfect participle (*pepisteukotes*), which indicates an action that occurred in the past though its effect continues into the present. Their trust is "in God" ("our Savior," 3:4). Some suggest that this verse reflects the Gentile nature of these congregations, since Jews would already believe in God. However, the faith that Paul here describes is faith according to the Christian gospel to which Titus's people have entrusted themselves, and which Titus is to affirm. "May be careful" (*phrontizō*) refers to fixing one's attention on something, taking something to heart and actively pursuing it to completion, "making every effort" toward some goal. They are to be careful "to devote themselves to good works." "Devote" (*proistasthai*) has the sense of making something one's primary concern, engaging in something with intense fervor. The object of this devotion is "good works," a Pauline expression for the various facets of Christian life (Titus 1:16; 2:6, 14; 3:1, 14).

In support of devotion to good works, Paul makes a standard rhetorical argument from advantage (i.e., he tells how this practice is advantageous): "These things are good and profitable for everyone." Good works are "good" or "fitting" for everyone; they are also "profitable" (*ōphelima*); this second adjective refers to things that are beneficial or advantageous.

Things that are not part of good works may be unprofitable and worthless, however. In 3:9, Paul lists such things. Titus's people are to avoid (*periistaso*) such things as "stupid controversies" (*mōras zēteseis*) (3:9). "Stupid" (or "foolish") refers to things that are nonsensical or without reason. "Controversies" refers to arguing, forcefully expressing differences of opinion without interest in seeking a solution. Further, they are to avoid "genealogies." Scholars have proposed several ways of understanding this warning:

- The term refers to traditional Jewish ancestral lists, by which a person's Jewish identity and place among the Jewish people (e.g., priest, Levite, relationships to royalty) could be determined. These lists were important to Diaspora Jews.
- It refers to Jewish stories and legends built around Hebrew ancestors. These stories became popular among Jews influenced by Greek culture. They often included attention to the meaning and interpretation of even the minutest details of the biblical record, such as numbers and the spelling of names. Some of these legends are included in Jewish writings, such as the Book of Jubilees.
- It refers to the lists of demigods found in various Gnostic movements. Since the Gnostics believed that anything material was evil, they held that the universe was not created by the Supreme God but by demigods who came between the Supreme God and the physical universe. Their genealogies contained lists of these semi-divine beings.

Paul's list of things that are unprofitable and useless continues. Titus's people are to avoid "quarrels" (*ereis*); Paul normally uses this word to refer to the selfish arguments and behaviors that arise from jealousy or rivalry (Rom

13:13; 1 Cor 1:11; 3:3; 2 Cor 12:20; Gal 5:20). *Ereis* points to the act of separating from one another or causing divisions and schisms in the church through jealous behavior that damages the unity of the group. The Cretan believers are also to avoid "disputes about the law" (*machas nomikas*); the large Jewish population on Crete and the presence of Jewish Christians in the community (1:14-15; 3:5, 7) suggest that what is being disputed here is most likely the Law of Moses.

With regard to each of these points, Paul's desire for Titus is clear: he is to avoid them and teach his people to do likewise. Spending time on these things is "unprofitable" (*anōpheleis*, the negative form of *ōphelima* from 3:8c) and "worthless" (*mataioi*, "futile" or even "senseless" due to a lack of content). No advantage is to be gained through pursuing them, but much can be lost. The Church must major in major things, rather than becoming embroiled in controversies, quarrels, and dissensions that divert us from our mission and lead to unchristian behavior. Legion are the sad and devastating stories of churches and Christian groups who have ruined their witness and completely lost sight of their mission due to selfish behavior and minor quibbles that were allowed to metastasize.

Having discussed the things that may lead to division, Paul turns to the church's response to those who cause such divisions (3:10). Titus must warn (*nouthesian*) twice ("once and then twice") anyone who causes divisions (*hairetikon antrhōpon*, lit., "divisive person"). *Nouthesian* implies some kind of instruction or correction beyond a bare rebuke. One ancient Greek writer described such correction: "admonition is the instilling of sense in the person who is being admonished, and teaching him what should and what shouldn't be done" (Pseudo-Demetrius, *Epistolary Types* 7). *Hairetikos* refers to being divisive or causing divisions/splits within a group. Though the modern English word "heretic" is derived from *hairetikos*, the emphasis here is on the negative behavior that causes splits rather than false teachings or beliefs specifically.

If the divisive person does not respond appropriately after one or two admonitions, Titus is to "reject" or "ignore" (*paraitou*) this person, having nothing more to do with him/her. Paul asserts that this action is necessary because "such a person is perverted and sinful, being self-condemned" (3:11). "Perverted" (*exestraptai*), which carries the image of "turned inside out," refers to a person who is warped or distorted in their thinking and behavior. "Sinful" refers to those who act in a way that is "contrary to the will and law of God" (*LN* 88.289). Finally, Paul says that such a person is "self-condemned" (*autokatakritos*), judged by his/her own actions. Apart from one appearance in Philo, this word is found only in Christian literature.

Thus when the church removed this person from fellowship, essentially saying "We no longer regard you as a brother/sister," this statement was the official recognition of the truth of the person's actions, recognizing a decision that the person had already made by his/her behavior.

Both Jesus and Paul address the matter of church discipline. In Matthew 18:15-35, Jesus outlines a three-step process for disciplining a member of the church who sins against another:

1. The offended party must gently and humbly discuss the matter with the offender, one on one.
2. If the first step does not bring a resolution, the offended party must again approach the offender, this time bringing along two or three other respected members of the church community; Jesus promises that he will be present in this gathering, acting to bring the offender to repentance and restore the relationships. "I tell you that if two of you on earth agree about anything you ask for, it will be done for you by my Father in heaven. For where two or three come together in my name, there am I with them" (Matt 18:18-19).
3. If the second step does not result in reconciliation, then bring the matter to the whole church. If the offender refuses to listen to the counsel of the entire community, "let such a one be to you as a Gentile and a tax collector" (Matt 18:17; of course, we must note that Jesus offered forgiveness to Gentiles and tax collectors).

Immediately after this passage, Matthew has Jesus admonish Peter to forgive his brother or sister seventy-seven times. Matthew immediately follows that admonition with the parable of the unforgiving servant. Jesus' teaching on this matter (and everything else) must always be read in context.

Paul addresses church discipline in the Corinthian correspondence. In 1 Corinthians 5, he calls upon the Corinthian church to discipline a member of the congregation for inappropriate sexual behavior. The aim of this action is redemptive in nature (1 Cor 5:5) as all such discipline should be. In 2 Corinthians 2:5-11, Paul calls upon the church to forgive an offender (perhaps the same man as in 1 Corinthians 5, but most likely not) who has been disciplined by the congregation. The pattern here is the same as in Jesus' discussion of discipline in Matthew. The purpose of church discipline is always redemptive. The goal is always to forgive and restore (not to remove or be rid of) the offender.

Instead of becoming embroiled in "stupid controversies and quarrels," Titus and those he teaches must attend to good works. One of those good works is the effort to bring errant members of the congregation back into the fold (see also 2 Tim 2:25-26).

Summary

In 2:1–3:11, Paul commands Titus to teach and advocate a Christian lifestyle that will result in healthy relationships with God, healthy relationships in the church, and a good reputation in the community around the church. Paul describes this lifestyle in two parallel sections, 2:1-15 and 3:1-11. The two sections are balanced: both begin with the content of teaching that Titus is to impart, followed by the theological rationale behind the teaching, followed by a statement charging and empowering Titus to deliver and implement the teaching. Titus is to put this system of beliefs and practices into place through a community/household structure, where the mature take responsibility for mentoring the immature, and where all "submit to one another out of reverence for Christ."

Running throughout is Paul's conviction that right living (orthopraxy) is inextricably joined to right beliefs (orthodoxy): we cannot separate what we believe from what we are.

Final Instructions, Travel Plans, and Benediction (3:12-15)

As in other letters, Paul's final instructions give details about his travel plans and companions. He usually mentions his desire to visit the recipients (Rom 1:11; 15:22-24, 28-29; 1 Cor 11:34; 2 Cor 1:15-16; 12:20-21; 13:10; Phil 2:24; 1 Thess 2:17-18; Phlm 1:22) and occasionally gives specific details of his travel plans (Rom 15:22-29; 1 Cor 16:5-9). His instructions to Titus here are in keeping with his practice of sending trusted coworkers to act in his stead when he is not able to visit. He sent Titus and a companion to Corinth (2 Cor 12:18; cf. 7:13; 8:6, 18, 23) and perhaps Troas (2 Cor 2:13); Timothy to Corinth (1 Cor 4:17; 16:10), Thessalonica (1 Thess 3:2, 6), and probably to Philippi (Phil 2:19-30); and Epaphras, Tychicus, and Onesimus to Colossae (Col 1:7; 4:7-9).

Here, Paul's plan is to send Artemas or Tychicus to replace Titus on Crete, so that Titus can join him at Nicopolis (3:12). Artemas is not mentioned elsewhere in the New Testament. Tychicus is a companion of Paul's in Acts 20:4, the bearer of the Pauline letters to Colossae (Col 4:7) and Ephesus (Eph 6:21), and Paul's delegate to Ephesus in 2 Timothy 4:12. Clearly, Paul has confidence in both of these representatives. They are capable of replacing Titus and carrying on the work on Crete. As for Titus, Paul instructs him: "Do your best to come to me soon." "Do your best" (*spoudason*) means putting the utmost effort into some activity, "try as hard as you can" or "make every effort."

Titus was to join Paul in Nicopolis. At the time, there were seven cities bearing this name, built to commemorate Roman victories (the name "Nicopolis" means "city of victory.") Most scholars agree that the Nicopolis mentioned here was in Epirus, located on the isthmus of the Bay of Actium northwest of Corinth and Athens. This city was built by Augustus to celebrate his naval victory over the forces of Mark Antony in 31 BCE. Nicopolis of Epirus was ideally located for sea travel between Italy and Achaia, and was an important commercial center due to its place on a major trade route. The much-revered Stoic philosopher Epictetus was exiled there in 89 CE. Nicopolis was exactly the kind of city that Paul would have wanted for a ministry base: a commercial center, a transportation hub, with important links to Achaia and Italy. Furthermore, as a seaport it would have been an ideal place to spend a winter, the season of the year when sea travel was most dangerous (1 Cor 16:6; Acts 27:9-12; see Collins 2002, 373–74). At Nicopolis, Paul would be perfectly positioned for further travels when spring came and the seas were less treacherous. These details clearly indicate that, wherever Paul may have been writing from, he was not in prison but rather free to make his own plans.

Titus is also to "make every effort to send Zenas the lawyer and Apollos on their way" (3:13). "Make every effort" is the adverbial form of *spoudazō*, the verb from 3:12a. Like Artemas, Zenas is mentioned only here in the New Testament. Apollos, on the other hand, is a well-known figure from early Christianity. According to Acts 18:24–19:1, he was an Alexandrian, well versed in Scripture, who was instructed in the ways of the Lord by Priscilla and Aquila. Paul's frequent mention of Apollos in 1 Corinthians (1:12; 3:4-6; 4:6; 16:12) indicates that he was well known in Achaia. Titus must make every effort to send them on their way, by providing whatever they need: money, food, clothing, means of transportation (see Rom 15:24; 1 Cor 16:6; 2 Cor 1:16). This is further emphasized by the next phrase, "see that they lack nothing." Titus must supply them adequately for the journey, and involve his people in this task, so that they can "learn to devote themselves to good works, so as to meet pressing needs." "Pressing" (*anagkaias*) carries the idea of urgency or necessity; these are real needs. Titus's people are to participate in this work "so that they will not be unproductive." "Unproductive" (*akarpoi*, lit., "fruitless") is part of the agricultural imagery Paul uses when describing ministry (e.g., 1 Cor 3:5-9; 9:10-11). The image of bearing fruit seems to have been a common term for good works in the early church (Matt 3:8, 10; 7:16-20; 12:33; Luke 3:8-9; 6:43-44; 8:8).

Finally, Paul's letters typically end with various greetings. Third-person greetings, where Paul names his coworkers and companions in the format "[Name] greets you," are characteristic (Rom 16:21-23; 1 Cor 16:19-20a; 2 Cor 13:12b; Phil 4:21b-22; Phlm 23-24; Col 4:14; 2 Tim 4:21b). Here, "all who are with me send greetings." Paul follows this with a second-person greeting, where he asks his correspondents to convey his greetings to others. These are also common in Paul's letters. "Greet those who love us in the faith" is similar to Paul's second-person greetings in Romans 16:3-16a, 1 Corinthians 16:20b, 2 Corinthians 13:12a, Philippians 4:21a, 1 Thessalonians 5:26, and 2 Timothy 4:19. "In the faith" can be read several different ways:

- "In faith" could be adverbial, describing their love for Paul, thus "those who faithfully love us."
- "Faith" could mean "right belief." Then we could render the phrase "those who love us and believe as we do."
- "Faith" could refer to trust in Christ. Then the phrase might be translated, "those who love us and trust in Christ as we do."
- "Faith" could be a shorthand expression for the Christian faith. Then the phrase would be translated, "our fellow Christians who love us."

Each of these possible readings expresses a genuine dimension of the Christian faith.

Paul understood ministry to be a team effort. These verses give us a glimpse of some of those who were "on Paul's team." He did not work as a lone ranger; rather, he was part of an extensive network of people, who were together committed to the mission of proclaiming the gospel and building the church. This is part of the New Testament pattern for missions and ministry. The mission was a community affair, and Paul expected the community of faith to support those on the mission, both with their prayers and their financial and material gifts. Furthermore, Paul believed the community should meet the needs of its own people. Nowhere is this clearer than in his admonitions about the collection for the saints in Jerusalem, which was at the center of his third missionary journey (Rom 15:22-29; 1 Cor 16:1-4; 2 Cor 8–9). In the Gospel, Acts, and Paul's letters, Christians are called to be generous and say, "that which is mine is also yours."

"Grace be with all of you" is the shortest benediction in all the Pauline letters; we have moved from one of the longest salutations to the shortest benediction. It serves to bless the whole community on Crete, a fact highlighted by the plural "all of you." Again, even though Titus was the addressee and primary recipient of the letter, Paul was addressing the whole congregation, all the new congregations on Crete. The letter would have been read to them, referred to by them when questions arose, perhaps even waved in the faces of some when disputes occurred. As it blessed and encouraged Titus, so it blessed and encouraged all those with whom he faithfully shared it and to whom he taught the instructions it contained.

And indeed, the letter to Titus continues to bless all who read and heed it today.

1 Timothy

1 Timothy: The Nature of True and Faithful Ministry

Outline

1. Salutation and Greeting (1:1-2)
2. Paul's Charge to Timothy, Part 1 (1:3)
3. Description of True Ministry (1:4-20)
    A. False Teachers Contrasted with Paul and His People (1:4-11)
        B. Paul's Call to Ministry (1:12-17)
        B'. Timothy's Call to Ministry (1:18-19a)
    A'. False Teachers Contrasted with Timothy (1:19b-20)
4. Paul's Missionary Purposes (2:1–3:16)
    A. The Missionary Purpose behind Paul's Teaching (2:1-7)
        1. Hymn describing God's grace (2:5-6)
        2. Paul's appointment by God (2:7)
    B. Behavior in the Household (of God) that Supports Paul's Purposes (2:8–3:13)
        1. Men (2:8)
        2. Women (2:9–3:1a)
        3. Elders (3:1b-7)
        4. Male and female deacons (3:8-13)
    C. Hymn supporting missionary purposes (3:14-16)
5. How to do Ministry in the Last Days (4:1–6:10)
    A. False Teachers Contrasted with Paul and Timothy (4:1-5)
        B. Ministry in the Last Days (4:6-16)
        B'. How to Treat Other Members of the Household of God (5:1–6:2)
    A'. False Teachers Contrasted with Paul and Timothy (6:3-10)
6. Paul's Charge to Timothy, Continued (6:11-16)
7. Final Instructions and Reiteration of the Charge (6:17-21)

The body of 1 Timothy follows a roughly chiastic structure. This structure is discernable in the detailed outline above, but a less detailed outline will make it obvious:

1. Opening (1:1-2)
    2. Paul's charge to Timothy: stop the false teachers! (1:3)
        3. Description of true ministry (1:4-20)
            4. The purpose of Paul's instructions: his people need to live lives that win a hearing for the gospel (2:1–3:16)
        3'. How to do ministry in the last days (4:1–6:10)
    2'. Paul's charge to Timothy: faithfully keep, use, pass on, and protect the teaching entrusted to you (6:11-16)
1'. Closing (6:17-21): final instructions, reiteration of the charge

In both this outline and the more detailed outline at the beginning of this chapter, section 2 segues into 3 without a break. Using this less detailed outline, note that the body of the letter begins (2) and ends (2') with Paul charging Timothy to accomplish specific tasks (1:3; 6:11-16). Sections 3 (1:4-20) and 3' (4:1–6:10) contain descriptions of the ministry to which God called Paul and Timothy. Section 4, the long middle section (2:1–3:16), focuses on the motivation that lies behind Paul's paraenesis (practical instructions).

Note also that sections 3 (1:4-20) and 3' (4:1–6:10) are themselves structured chiastically:

3. Description of true ministry (1:4-20)
    A. False teachers contrasted with Paul and Timothy (1:4-11)
        B. Paul's call to ministry (1:12-17)
        B'. Timothy's call to ministry (1:18-19a)
    A'. False teachers contrasted with Timothy (1:19b-20)

3'. How to minister in the last days (4:1–6:10)
    A. False teachers contrasted with Paul and Timothy (4:1-5)
        B. Ministry in the last days: what Timothy should pursue, what he should flee (4:6-16)
        B'. Reverse *Haustafel*: how Timothy should treat other members of the household of God (5:1–6:2)
    A'. False teachers contrasted with Paul and Timothy (6:2-10)

One other structural feature deserves comment here. In the first four large sections of the letter (1:1–3:16), which amounts to 45 percent of its length, the Greek text contains only eight second-person substantives (second-person pronouns or verbs, addressing "you.") None of these are found in chapter 2. In the final three large sections of the letter (4:1–6:20), which amounts to 55 percent of the book, the Greek text contains fifty-two second-person substantives. The point of this observation is to say that the character of the second half of the book (4:1–6:20) is much more personal and less generic than that of the first half of the book (1:1–3:16).

Salutation and Greeting (1:1-2)

The opening of this letter follows the standard Graeco-Roman format: sender's name, recipient's name, greetings. As was his practice, Paul follows the standard form but adapts the parts of the opening to advance his rhetorical purposes.

Here, Paul describes himself as "an apostle" (1:1). An apostle (*apostolos*) was a person sent on a mission, carrying a particular message, wielding the authority of the sender. In a generic sense, "apostle" refers to Christian missionaries, those who went into new cultures to spread the gospel and plant churches. Used in this way, the title may have been restricted to those missionaries sent out by the Jerusalem church. In a proper sense, the word refers to the twelve leaders among the earliest followers of Jesus, minus Judas, plus Matthias (Acts 1:15-26). Paul does not number himself among the twelve, but he considers himself their equal (1 Cor 9:1). "Apostle" is his customary way of referring to himself (Rom 1:7; 1 Cor 1:3; 2 Cor 1:2; Gal 1:2; Phil 1:2; 1 Thess 1:1; Phlm 3). Paul further describes himself as an "apostle of Christ Jesus." "Christ" translates the Greek *christos*, which means "anointed one." The equivalent Hebrew term is "Messiah." By placing the title "Christ" before the name Jesus (as is often the practice in his letters), Paul emphasizes Jesus' messianic role. This emphasis is especially appropriate if his readers are dealing with matters related to Judaism and Jewish Christianity—as is the case in 1 Timothy (see 1:7). Thus Paul makes it clear from the outset that he is the authorized ambassador of the Jewish Messiah, Jesus Christ.

Further, Paul undertakes his work "by the command of God our Savior and of Christ Jesus our hope." Paul's mission is not one of his own choosing; he was selected for this task by God. On the Damascus Road, Paul encountered the risen Christ and was called to take the good news to the nations (Acts 9:1-9; 22:6-21; 26:2-18). He originally met Timothy while obeying this command, and he and Timothy came to share the mission together while carrying out this God-given work (Acts 16:1-5). This mission first brought Paul to Ephesus (Acts 19), and it was to further this mission that Paul now left Timothy in Ephesus to shepherd the church there. Paul's words here remind Timothy and those he works with in Ephesus that all these things—their church and faith, the work of Paul and Timothy—are the result of "the command of God our Savior and of Christ Jesus our hope."

"God our Savior" and "Christ Jesus our hope" stand in striking parallelism. Clearly, the two act as one. Paul identifies both parties by attaching terms that describe their functions (Savior, hope). The command that Paul received was aimed at bringing his people salvation and hope. Paul describes God as "Savior" three times in this letter (1:1; 2:3; 4:10). "God the Savior" is an idea with clear roots in the Old Testament and the Judaism in which Paul was raised. In the Hellenistic world, deities (and even emperors) who were thought to rescue people from all kinds of evils (including death) could be referred to as "savior." But for Paul, there is only one savior, the one true and living God of Israel.

Salvation brings hope (*elpis*). In the Old Testament and Judaism, God is the source of hope. The *elpis* word group plays a prominent role in 1 Timothy. In addition to this occurrence of the noun (*elpis*), the verb *elpizō* appears four times. Paul uses this verb to affirm that God is the object of hope because he is the Savior of all people (4:10). All people are called to live with their hope centered in God (5:5; 6:17). Paul further designates Christ Jesus as our hope (see Titus 2:13; 3:7; cf. Titus 1:2; Col 1:27, where Paul refers to Jesus as "the hope of glory"). Referring to Jesus as our "hope" indicates that hope comes to the believer in Christ Jesus.

In 1:1, Paul uses this two-part expression ("God our Savior" and "Christ Jesus our hope") to say that God is the Savior, the foundation and source of the Christian's hope. Jesus personifies that hope (cf. Ignatius of Antioch, *Magn* 11.1; *Eph* 21.2; *Phld* 11.2; Polycarp, *Phld* 8.1). Paul clarifies this relationship further in his letter to Titus. There, God is the Savior (Titus 2:10) who is faithful to keep his promises (Titus 1:2). God demonstrates his faithfulness in the two appearances (the first coming and the second coming) of Christ Jesus, who gave himself to redeem his people (Titus 2:14). His people's salvation results from God's mercy, not from their own good works. This mercy of God is made available to them through Christ Jesus, realized in them by rebirth and renewal, as enacted in baptism (Titus 3:4-6). This salvation, rebirth, and renewal will be fully realized in them at the time of Jesus' second coming (Titus 2:11-14) (Collins 2002, 23).

In 1:2, Paul names the recipient of the letter. Timothy is the best known of Paul's travel companions. The son of a Gentile father and a Jewish mother, Timothy was likely born and raised in Lystra, the city where he first met Paul and became Paul's "child in the faith." After his baptism, Timothy became Paul's trusted coworker, accompanying Paul to the provinces of Asia, Achaia, and Macedonia. In this letter, Paul has placed Timothy in Ephesus, the capital city of the province of Asia, to give leadership to Paul's churches there and throughout the region. Paul had previously established Ephesus as his own headquarters for ministry in Asia, and spent almost three years there (Acts 19).

In 1:2, Timothy is Paul's "true [*gnēsiō*] child in the faith." The adjective *gnēsios* could indicate that Timothy was Paul's "legitimate" child, in contrast with others who might (falsely) claim to be Paul's children in the faith. Perhaps there were other teachers in Ephesus who contradicted or opposed Timothy, but claimed to have Paul's approval. *Gnēsiō* could also point to Timothy's character, in which case we would translate the word "faithful." Both readings are legitimate, and both may be in view here. In 1 Corinthians 4:17, Paul describes the relationship he shares with Timothy as a relationship of love and shared service, referring to Timothy as "my beloved and faithful child in the Lord, who will remind you of my ways in Christ Jesus." Likewise, in Philippians 2:22, Paul reminds the believers in Philippi of "how like a son with a father he [Timothy] has served with me in the service of the gospel." Timothy was loyal both to Paul's message and method. Paul here praises him as a legitimate and faithful proclaimer of the gospel, and demands that the Ephesians (to whom this letter would have been read aloud, perhaps by Timothy himself) receive him as such. Timothy's ministry in Ephesus is an extension of Paul's.

Paul follows the name of the letter's recipient with the greeting. The standard greeting in a Graeco-Roman letter was *chairein*, "rejoice!" or "good health!" Paul greatly expands and Christianizes this greeting, turning *chairein* ("rejoice") into *charis* ("grace"), and loading other theological material together with it. Here, the greeting is "Grace, peace, and mercy from God our Father and Christ Jesus our Lord." Each element of this greeting is significant. "Grace" refers to something that is a gift; in the New Testament, it most often refers to God's unmerited favor and love for humanity. Here, as in most of his letter openings, Paul joins "grace" with "peace" (*eirēnē*). "Peace" represents the typical Hebrew greeting *shalom*. This peace is more than the absence of violence or overt hostility. It refers to total well-being, a life where everything is good and right and healthy, the sum total of God's blessings bestowed on a human being, enabling that person to live life to the fullest. Thus in this greeting, Paul combines a slightly altered (but familiar sounding) Hellenistic greeting and the typical Hebrew greeting. In so doing, he points to the fact that (according to his gospel) in Christ Jesus, there is no more Jew nor Greek (Gal 3:28). The greeting is a compact, concentrated statement of the nature of Paul's gospel itself.

In this verse, Paul inserts "mercy" (*eleos*) between grace and peace. Biblically, "mercy" is an attribute of God, an expression of his benevolence to his people (Jer 3:12; 9:34). The translators of the Septuagint used *eleos* to render the Hebrew word *chesed*, which is often translated into English as "steadfast love" or "covenantal love." First Chronicles 16:34 presents a typical use of this word: "Give thanks to the Lord, for he is good; for his steadfast love [*chesed*] endures forever." Paul uses the grouping of "grace, mercy, and peace" here and in 2 Timothy 1:2. God's mercy, which is available to all, results in grace, which brings peace.

The source of these blessings is "God the Father and Christ Jesus our Lord." "Father" reminds Timothy of the intimate relationship that God desires with every person. He is the God to whom believers cry, "Abba." The Christian's relationship with this God is like the parent-child relationship, a relationship of love and concern. (Incidentally, the parent-child relationship is a central picture in the Old Testament's use of *chesed*. God's love is a parental love, stubborn, sometimes hard, sometimes expressed in discipline or correction). Speaking of Christ Jesus as "Lord" attaches to Jesus the title used for God in Judaism. To speak of him as "*our* Lord" reminds believers that they know him in community, even as Jesus taught them to pray, "Our Father . . . ." For Paul, God and Jesus stand together as the source of grace, mercy, and peace, which are available to any and all.

Graeco-Roman letters *usually* had a prayer or blessing following the greeting, although this practice was not universal. This prayer or blessing was usually a single simple sentence, expressing thankfulness to the gods for the recipient or praying for the gods' blessing, etc. Paul included such prayers in all but three of his letters. When Paul omits the prayer of thanksgiving, he does so for rhetorical effect.

The Pauline letters that do not have the prayer are Galatians, Titus, and 1 Timothy. In Galatians, the omission seems to be motivated by Paul's exasperation with the readers. The audience, expecting to hear some kind of pious, benevolent prayer on their behalf from their beloved Paul, is instead slapped in the face by the angry Apostle: "I am astonished that you are so quickly deserting the one who called you by the grace of Christ and are turning to a different gospel!" (Gal 1:6, NIV). In both Titus and 1 Timothy, the omission accentuates the urgency of the charge that Paul makes to his protégés/successors. On the other hand, 2 Timothy, which has the prayer of thanksgiving, is much more personal than 1 Timothy and Titus, and 1 Timothy and Titus are more official in tone than 2 Timothy.

Paul's Charge to Timothy, Part 1 (1:3)

As noted above, Paul here moves directly from greeting to charge, skipping the customary prayer or blessing, signaling both the gravity and urgency of what follows. The charge in turn elides (without even a break in the sentence) into the next section, where Paul offers a description of true ministry.

In 1:3, Paul writes, "As I urged you when I left for Macedonia, stay in Ephesus . . . ." Paul here indicates that the instructions in this letter repeat instructions that he had previously given to Timothy. Apparently, Paul and Timothy have been working together in Ephesus. Paul left Ephesus to deal with an emergency in Macedonia, and left Timothy behind to face a developing situation of his own, a serious problem with false teachers in the church. Meanwhile, the problem in Macedonia was not easily dealt with (see 3:14-15a, "I hope to come to you soon, but if I am delayed . . ."). This is the apparent situation behind the writing of the letter.

In Acts, Luke records two Pauline trips to Macedonia. Macedonia was a mountainous Roman province in the northwest part of the Greek peninsula. This area includes parts of modern-day northern Greece, southern Yugoslavia, and southwest Bulgaria. On Paul's first visit to this area (Acts 16:6–17:9), Timothy accompanied him as they established churches in the important cities of Philippi and Thessalonica (the provincial capital). Timothy also accompanied Paul on his second visit to Macedonia (Acts 20:1-6; cf. 2 Cor 2:12-13). Timothy's presence on this visit is confirmed by Paul's mention of him in the salutation of 2 Corinthians (1:1), written after Paul's arrival in Macedonia. Neither of these trips to Macedonia fit the circumstances reflected in 1 Timothy.

The fact that the text of Acts does not provide circumstances that match the scenario assumed in 1 Timothy has troubled some interpreters. Three explanations have been offered.

1. Some interpreters regard this as evidence that Paul did not write 1 Timothy. The scenario proposed in 1:3 is fictitious, created by a pseudepigrapher, who simply did not notice (or care) that the details did not match up with what was known about Paul's movements from other sources. People who follow this hypothesis may also assert this pseudepig-

2. Some interpreters, arguing that the letter was written by Paul, follow the early church tradition of Paul's release from the imprisonment at the end of Acts and his subsequent missionary activity (*1 Clem* 5). Most who follow this line argue that all events in the Pastoral Epistles are from Paul's career during this time.
3. Other interpreters, also arguing that Paul wrote the letter, point to the three years that Paul spent in Ephesus (Acts 19). Luke only records three events from this time, leaving ample time for the problems and movements described in 1 Timothy 1:3.

Our position is that Paul is behind the material in 1 Timothy, and that the scenario presented in 1 Timothy 1:3 is not fictitious. Therefore, we reject the first explanation. Either of the other explanations will suffice. The differences between them do not change the way the final form of the text is read. (For more on authorship, see Introduction to the Pastoral Epistles above.)

The verb translated "urge" (*parakalesa*) here means "to urge strongly" (BDAG). It was used in diplomatic correspondence when a delegate (someone sent by a person of higher authority) wanted to express tactfully an order from the person above the delegate to someone beneath the delegate on the chain of authority. Here, Paul is the delegate, or representative, acting on behalf of God and Christ Jesus (1:1). Timothy's orders, from God through Paul, are to remain in Ephesus, a city where he had a long history. He was a natural choice to oversee the affairs of the church there.

Paul left Timothy in Ephesus so that he would "command certain people to stop teaching false doctrines." The word translated "teaching false doctrines" (*heterodidaskalein*), which only appears in early Christian literature, summarizes Paul's concerns and Timothy's task. Paul does not identify the people who are teaching the troubling doctrines. They remain an anonymous "someone" throughout the letter. They appear to present a more serious and immediate threat than the false teachers and troublemakers in Titus: here, the false teachers appear to be leaders in the churches, attacking Paul's work from the inside rather than the outside (as seems to have been the case in Crete).

Description of True Ministry (1:4-20)

In 1:4-20, Paul segues without a break from his charge to Timothy to a description of the life of ministry that he has lived, and that Timothy should also live. This section opens and closes with descriptions of the false teachers and opponents who stand against Paul and bedevil the church at Ephesus. Between these descriptions, Paul inserts a description of his own call to ministry and a description of Timothy's call to ministry. Both descriptions draw sharp contrasts between the false teachers and Paul/Timothy:

- Paul was appointed to ministry by God (1:1, 11). The false teachers, on the other hand, appoint themselves, "wishing to be teachers of the law" (1:7).
- Timothy was also selected for ministry by God (articulated through prophecy, 1:18) and can carry out Paul's orders if he clings to and depends on his relationship with Jesus Christ, according to Paul's teachings. The false teachers, on the other hand, have rejected this relationship to follow and propagate other teachings, and have shipwrecked their faith (1:19-20).

This section following the charge can be outlined as follows:

A. False Teachers Contrasted with Paul and His People (1:4-11)
    B. Paul's Call to Ministry (1:12-17)
    B'. Timothy's Call to Ministry (1:18-19a)
A'. False Teachers Contrasted with Timothy (1:19b-20)

False Teachers Contrasted with Paul and His People (1:4-11)

In 1:4, Paul describes some of the elements of the false teaching. The false teachers are wrapped up in "myths and endless genealogies." "Myths" (*mythois*) originally referred to any story or statement. By the fifth century BCE, however, the word was used for fabricated stories (such as Aesop's Fables), "fictional narrative (as opposed to *logos*, the truth of history)" (BDAG). Sometimes myths served didactic or moral purposes; other times, their function seems to have been etiological (i.e., an explanation of some natural phenomenon or historical event). By the Hellenistic period, Greek writers distinguished between reality and "myth" (Plato, *Timaeus* 26e; Plutarch, *Obsolescence of Oracles* 46; *Moralia* 435D. The word *mythos* appears in each of the Pastoral Epistles (1 Tim 4:7; 2 Tim 4:4; Titus 1:4) and again in 2 Peter 1:16. Paul here is not specific about the kinds of myths he has in mind. He could be referring to the stories found in Graeco-Roman religions, or he could be referring to the misuse of Jewish *haggadah* (on *haggadah* and *halakah*, see the commentary on Titus 1:14; for "genealogies," see the discussion at Titus 3:9). The genealogies Paul here condemns are "endless" (*aperantois*); the adjective describes something that has no limit (BDAG); it just keeps going on and on and on.

The problem with these genealogies is that they lead to "useless disputes" (*ekzēteseis*). The false teachers and their myths and endless genealogies produced angry disputes in the church, "rather than the proper administration of the household of God, which comes by teaching the faith." Paul contrasts the result of the false teaching with the results of teaching the true gospel. "The faith" refers to Paul's gospel, which he received from Jesus Christ. "Administration of the household of God" translates *oikonomian theou*. *Oikonomia* refers to the responsibility of managing property that belongs to someone else, particularly the management of a household or estate. Throughout the Pastoral Epistles, Paul refers to the church as the household of God. Good church leadership is properly caring for God's household, the church (1 Tim 1:4; 3:15; 2 Tim 2:20; Titus 1:7). Myths and speculations don't lead people to salvation, nor do they build healthy churches. The faithful teaching of the gospel accomplishes both.

Paul continues in 1:5, "The goal of this command is love," one of the features of a healthy and well-led church. While certain people in the church at Ephesus are causing arguments by their speculations and irresponsible teaching, Timothy's task is to foster love and harmony in the church. This love comes "from a pure heart and good conscience and genuine faith." The heart (*kardia*) was seen as the deepest depths of a person's being, the center of thought and will and emotions. It represents the whole person who can think and feel and choose. A pure (*katharas*) heart is one untainted by foreign alloy or alien allegiance. It is an undivided heart, turned totally toward God, focused on God alone. According to Jesus, those who are "pure in heart" will see God (Matt 5:8), because their attention will be where it is supposed to be. Such people are faithful to "seek first the kingdom of God and his righteousness" (Matt 6:33); "first" here refers to priority.

"A good conscience" is a Hellenistic notion. In Hellenistic thought, the conscience (*sunedēsis*) enabled a person to distinguish between right and wrong. Through thinking and self-examination, the conscience guided moral decisions based on certain accepted norms. The Stoics gave a great deal of attention to the function of the conscience (e.g., Seneca, *Happy Life* 20.3–5; *Tranquility of Mind* 3.4; *Epistles* 43.4–5; Collins 2002, 28). In Paul's thought, the conscience has been renewed in Christ, so that right and wrong are determined by a new set of standards; life is lived by these new norms. "If anyone is in Christ, there is a new creation" (2 Cor 5:17). Paul is using language that will resonate with Hellenistic readers, but he fills it with new meanings. "A genuine faith" (*pisteōs anypokritou*) can refer to two things. It could here mean "holding on to the accepted contents of the Pauline gospel" (i.e., "the unadulterated truths of the faith"), in contrast to false teachings.

But it more likely refers to personal faith that is not polluted by pretense or hypocrisy, believers who entrust themselves to Christ Jesus in a way that produces repentance and obedience (cf. 2 Tim 1:5, where Paul commends Timothy's "sincere faith").

Paul continues: "Some people have gone astray, turning to meaningless talk" (1:6). The verb translated "gone astray" (*astochēsantes*) refers to missing a mark, abandoning or deviating from truth; Paul uses this word again in his final description of the false teachers (6:21). The people Paul writes about have missed—or intentionally avoided—the point. Instead of the love, pure heart, clean conscience, and genuine faith that the gospel should produce, they pursue "meaningless talk" (*mataiologian*, a compound of *mataios* ["empty," "futile"] and *logos*). Paul draws a devastating picture of the teaching spread by the false teachers. It is composed of myths and endless genealogies, useless speculations that produce angry disputes, meaningless talk (cf. Titus 1:10).

Further, alongside their meaningless talk, "they want to be teachers of the law, but do not understand the things they are saying, about which they so confidently insist" (1:7). The word translated "they want" or "they desire" can refer to claiming to be something one is not. "Teachers of the law" (*nomodidaskaloi*) is a word coined by early Christian writers to distinguish between Jewish teachers and Christian teachers (Luke 5:17; Acts 5:34). It implies a level of expertise and education in the Law of Moses. The mention of the law here suggests that the troublemakers are from a Jewish background, and bring a Jewish orientation to Christianity. Paul may have in mind here the Judaizers, a group of legalistic Christians who caused him trouble throughout his ministry (see discussion of under Titus 1:10).

This reference to the false teachers' desire to be *nomodidaskaloi* leads to a brief reflection on the nature and function of the law. Paul writes: "But we know that the law is good, if one uses it legitimately" (1:8). The "we" is inclusive, referring to all Christians who follow Paul's gospel, particularly Timothy and those who work at his side. "Good" translates *kalos*, which usually refers to pleasant outward appearance (i.e., "beautiful"). Here, however its focus falls on the character of the law as a valid guide for moral and ethical conduct—which is not what the false teachers have in mind when they use it.

As elsewhere (Rom 3:31; 7:12, 16; Gal 3:21), Paul affirms the goodness of the Old Testament law. For Paul, the purpose of the law, now that the new covenant has come through Christ, is to make people conscious of their sin and thereby their need for a Savior (Rom 3:19-20; Gal 3:19-25). Here he writes: "The law [*nomos*] is good if it is used legitimately [*nomimōs*, lit., "according to the law," according to its purpose]." But the false teachers are not using the law according to its legitimate purpose. Their purpose is legalistic or ethnocentric (i.e., to make everyone acceptable to God by making everyone like them in habits, diet, and so on), which rules out the proper use. The misguided purpose behind their approach to the law demonstrates that it was not given for their use.

Paul continues in 1:9-10 with a classic vice list. Vice lists are found in the works of many Hellenistic writers, including Dio Chrysostom, Diogenes Laertius, Lucian, Onasander, and Seneca. Customarily, such lists included five vices; Philo's list in *Sacrifices of Cain and Abel* 32 includes 146 vices (Collins 2002, 30). Such lists were useful for moral teachers because they took abstract precepts and made them concrete in terms of specific behaviors and attitudes (Malherbe 1986, 138). The New Testament contains more than twenty vice lists: Matthew 15:19; Mark 7:21-22; Romans 1:29-31; 13:13; 1 Corinthians 5:10-11; 6:9-10; 2 Corinthians 6:9-10; 12:20-21; Galatians 5:19-21; Ephesians 4:31; 5:3-5; Colossians 3:5, 8; 1 Timothy 1:9-10; 2 Timothy 3:2-5; Titus 3:3; James 3:15; 1 Peter 2:1; 4:3, 15; Revelation 9:21; 21:8; 22:15 (Charles 2000). The extensive use of this form suggests that these were part of a large body of material used in the early church. Lists were meant to be illustrative, not exhaustive. Writers selected or rejected vices for the list by what most serious and threatening in their particular context.

Paul's list has fourteen vices, plus a generalizing "*et cetera* clause" at the end. Notice how the list is organized:

- Paul begins with four pairs of vices connected with the conjunction "and" (*kai*).
- He follows these pairs with six single vices, each standing stark and alone, not surrounded by conjunctions. This strategy ("asyndeton," the omission of conjunctions for effect) was thought to add force and momentum to the presentation of a list. This would be especially powerful and persuasive to those who heard the letter read aloud.
- Paul uses several words with synonymous or overlapping meaning; the lack of clear and logical progression between some of the vices adds to an overwhelming impression of chaotic and sinful behavior.
- The cumulative effect of the list is increased by the use of alliteration; each of the first five vices begins with the letter alpha.
- As a whole, the list reflects the order of the Ten Commandments (as does the vice list in Matthew 15:19).

Paul writes, "We know that the law was not given for the righteous person, but for the lawless and rebellious, for the ungodly and sinful, for the godless and irreligious, those who kill their fathers and mothers, for murderers, sexually immoral people, homosexuals, slave traders, liars, perjurers—and whatever else opposes sound teaching" (1:9-10). The first eight vices are paired (e.g., "lawless *and* rebellious . . .").

- "Lawless" (*anomois*) indicates that these people who seek to use the law for their own purposes have rejected God's purpose for the law. A truly "legitimate" use of the law requires a proper understanding of the law and its purpose. Paul pairs this vice with "rebellious" (*anypotaktois*), which refers to people who by nature rebel against authority (cf. Titus 1:6, 10). Thus in the first pair we find an attitude of defiance toward law and authority.
- "Ungodly" (*asebesi*) is the vice opposite the virtue "godliness" (*eusebeia*); in the Pastoral Epistles, "godliness" refers to people who live in and from reverence for God. Thus ungodly people have no proper respect for God or the things of God. Paul pairs this vice with "sinful" (*hamartolois*), which refers to people who habitually violate God's law. Where the first pair focused on defiance toward authority, this pair focuses more specifically on attitudes toward God—irreverence and unconcern for spiritual things, paired with the habit of making moral choices that reject God's way.
- "Godless" (*anosiois*) refers to corrupting or neglecting things that are holy or devoted to God. These people have no room for the things of God in their lives. Paul pairs this vice with a near synonym, *bebēlois* ("irreligious"), which refers to treating spiritual realities with contempt and ridicule, making such things profane (see the use of these words at 2 Tim 2:16 and 3:2 and the discussion below).

The first six vices (the three pairs discussed to this point) all relate to a person's relationship with God, as do the first of the Ten Commandments (no other gods; no idols; do not take the Lord's name in vain; respect the Sabbath and other such holy things). The remaining vices, including the next pair, describe specific acts that speak of a person's relationship with other people. The parallels between these vices and specific parts of the Ten Commandments are easy to identify.

- "Those who kill their fathers" (lit., "fratricides" [*patroloais*]) is paired with *metroloais* ("matricides" or "those who kill their mothers"). These vices correspond with "Honor your father and mother" (Exod 20:12). For the

Jews, killing either parent was a particularly egregious and horrifying sin (Exod 21:15, 17; cf. Marcus Aurelius, *Meditations* 6.34). This is the last pair in the vice list. Every vice that follows stands without partner or conjunction.

- "Murderers" (*androphonois*) corresponds with "You shall not murder" (Exod 20:13). *Androphonos* was used in Greek and Hellenistic Jewish writings to refer to anyone who deliberately killed another person (2 Macc 9:28; 4 Macc 9:15).
- "Sexually immoral people" (*pornois*) corresponds with "You shall not commit adultery" (Exod 20:14). This word is found more frequently than any other in New Testament vice lists. It refers to a wide variety of sexual misbehaviors.
- "Homosexuals" (*arsenokoitais*) refers to active or "practicing" homosexuals. This vice also corresponds with Exodus 20:14. The earliest occurrence of this *arsenokoitēs* is 1 Corinthians 6:9, where Paul adapts language from the Septuagint of Leviticus 18:22, "You shall not sleep with a man [*arsenos*] as if lying [*koitēn*] with a woman." In Paul's mind, homosexuality was one of the results of choosing to worship idols and refusing to worship God; one type of confusion led to another (Rom 1:18-32; cf. 1 Cor 6:9).
- "Slave traders" (*andrapodistais*) refers to someone "who acquires persons for use by others" (BDAG), thus "kidnapper," etc. Such acts were strongly condemned in both Greek and Jewish culture (e.g., Philo, *Special Laws* 4.14). This vice corresponds with "You shall not steal" (Exod 20:15). In fact, some rabbis taught that Exodus 20:15 referred specifically to kidnapping (Collins 2002, 34).
- "Liars" (*pseustais*) is a generic term for those who do not tell the truth. This vice corresponds to "You shall not give false testimony against your neighbor" (Exod 20:16), as does the next vice in the list.
- "Perjurers" (*epiorkois*) refers specifically to those who lie under oath. The Jews viewed perjurers as the most heinous of liars, since perjury aggravates the offense of speaking untruth about another (Philo, *Special Laws* 4.48). Combined with the fact that oaths often involved the Lord's name, perjury was seen as an attempt to manipulate God, a direct offense against him.

Paul brings this long list to a close with a catchall clause: ". . . and whatever else opposes sound teaching." "Sound teaching" (*hygiainousē didaskalia*) is the faithful exposition of the gospel. This teaching included elements of lifestyle alongside narrative and theological reflection on the life of Jesus.

Sound teaching is not just about what people believe, it is also concerned with how they live; not just what Christians think but also how they act.

Further, this sound teaching is that which conforms "to the gospel which declares the glory of the blessed God, which he entrusted to me." "The gospel" (*to euangelion*) refers to the good news of Jesus Christ; that is, the story of his life, his teachings, suffering, death, resurrection, *and* what he accomplished through them. "Glory" (*doxēs*) is an attribute of God, an extension of his power, present in the gospel. "Blessed" (*makariou*) is not normally a term associated with God in the Greek Bible; it is used in the New Testament only here and at 6:15. *Eulogētos*, "praised," or "blessed" is the norm (Eph 1:3; 2 Cor 1:3). However, Hellenistic writers commonly applied *makarios* to the gods as far back as Homer, and both Josephus (*Ant* 10.278) and Philo (*Special Laws* 1.209; 2.53) applied *makarios* to Yahweh.

This gospel was "entrusted" to Paul by God (cf. 1 Thess 2:4). "Entrusted" (*episteuthēn*) is a term used in succession contexts to refer to the act of passing on responsibility to a successor (Dio Cassius 53.31.3; see the discussion of succession in Introduction to the Pastoral Epistles). God is the one who entrusts the gospel to Paul; the verb is a divine passive (see the discussion of divine passive verbs in Philemon 15-16). Paul is Jesus' successor, chosen by God's command (1 Tim 1:1) to carry on a vital aspect of Jesus' ministry (the care and use of the gospel) when Jesus' specific physical presence was gone from the earth (Stepp 2005, 113, 117).

The fact of this succession—that Paul was chosen by God and entrusted with the gospel, which formerly had been in the direct care of Jesus himself—separates Paul from the false teachers. The false teachers want to be teachers of the law, but they have no calling or commission beyond their own ambitions. They have appointed themselves to be teachers (as opposed to Paul, appointed to his place of ministry by God [1:1, 12]). The result of this self-appointment is the teaching of myths and endless genealogies, nonsense that produces angry, hairsplitting disputes, meaningless talk, unhealthy churches, and the like. Paul, on the other hand, knows how the gospel is to be used, as do all his people with him ("But WE know . . . ," 1:8). He possesses this knowledge because he stands in a line of succession from Jesus Christ. Jesus bequeathed the gospel to him, entrusting it to Paul as his successor (a succession of tradition; cf. 2 Tim 2:2, the discussion at that passage below). This succession legitimates Paul and his own successor, Timothy, over against their opponents: compare the way 1 Kings 1–2 uses succession to show that Solomon, not Adonijah, is the legitimate successor of King David. It also supernaturally enables Paul and his people to handle the gospel in ways that are proper and beneficial for his churches. Indeed, because he is Jesus' successor, when Paul speaks regarding the matters that Jesus has entrusted to him, he does not speak with his own voice or authority. His words are backed by the authority of the one who chose him and bequeathed the gospel into his care, Jesus Christ.

Compare the results of the false teaching—disputes, futile talk, lives characterized by vice—with the result of the true teaching of the gospel, "the proper administration of the household of God"(*oikonomian theou*, 1:4). Good teaching and sound doctrine produce healthy churches, churches that are properly led, fed, and cared for.

Paul's Call to Ministry (1:12-17)

In 1:12-17, Paul turns to thanksgiving. His thanksgiving develops naturally from the mention of God entrusting the gospel into his care. Rhetorically, this section serves to affirm Paul's *ethos*, his image, integrity, and authority. This section is not parallel in form to the normal prayers of thanksgiving in Paul's letters (e.g., Rom 1:8-10; 2 Cor 1:4-9; Phil 1:3-6), although it may serve some of the same functions. Several differences are clear at first glance. Paul is not giving thanks for the letter's recipient (Timothy)—as would be the norm—but for God's grace in Paul's own personal story. Further, the thanks are addressed to Jesus (not to God), and the language also differs from the normal "I give thanks" (*eucharisteō*, Rom 1:8; 1 Cor 1:4) or the less common "Praise be to God" (*eulogētos*, 2 Cor 1:3; Eph 1:3). Paul here uses a weaker term, *charin echō*, "I am thankful" or "I have thanks."

Paul writes, "I am thankful to the one who empowered me, Christ Jesus our Lord" (1:12). In the light of the succession ideas in 1:1 and 1:11, the audience would have understood this to be a specific reference to spiritual power for preaching and administering the gospel and all it involves and produces, which Paul received in his succession from Jesus Christ. The same Lord who entrusted the gospel message and ministry to Paul has also empowered and enabled him to carry out this ministry. "Empowering" refers to both an initial act of empowering (at Paul's conversion and call to ministry) and to an ongoing enabling, a day-by-day gift of strength and wisdom.

Paul is grateful because Christ has "judged [him] faithful, appointing [him] to ministry." "Judged" (*hēgēsato*) refers to thinking a certain thing about someone. "Faithful" (*piston*) can refer here to being trustworthy, reliable, or dependable. It can also refer to Paul entrusting himself to Jesus Christ, so that this relationship determined the course of his life. *Diakonia* is Paul's favorite word for ministry. It can refer to any type of help or assistance. The word became a technical term for service in the Christian community

(Matt 20:24-28). Second Corinthians is Paul's most extensive description of the nature of ministry. Paul uses *diakonia* to refer to Christian ministry twelve times in that letter alone.

In 1:13-14, Paul employs a "once–now" scheme, which was a familiar part of Hellenistic rhetoric (Collins 2002, 37). God appointed him to ministry, "even though I was a blasphemer and persecutor and a violent man" (1:13). Paul here draws a stark contrast between his life before and after conversion. Before his conversion, Paul's life was characterized by ignorant unbelief. In the Bible, "blasphemy" usually refers to speaking evil of God. "Violent man" translates *hubristēn*, "arrogant," "violent," "insolent." From this word, we get our English word for overwhelming arrogance, "hubris." The three nouns describing this life interpret one another. How was Paul a "blasphemer"? He was a blasphemer because he was a persecutor of Christ and the church, treating the body of Christ violently; he spoke evil of, opposed, and persecuted Jesus Christ and his people (Acts 8:3; 9:1; 22:4-5; 26:11; 1 Cor 15:9; Gal 1:13; Phil 3:6).

But "I was shown mercy, because I acted ignorantly, in unbelief." Paul's ignorance was his lack of understanding of who Jesus was and what God was doing through him, thus through the church. The Old Testament differentiates between sins committed out of ignorance (e.g., Lev 22:14; cf. Lev 5:18; Num 15:22-29) and those committed maliciously and intentionally (Num 15:30). Sacrifices can be made for the former, but not the latter (Num 15:30-31). Paul's "unbelief" was his failure to believe that Jesus was God's Messiah. In Romans, Paul speaks of the unbelief of some Jews; he was once of their number. So it was that Paul was himself "shown mercy" (*eleēthēn*); this verb is a "divine passive," indicating that the mercy came from God (for "divine passives," see the discussion at Philemon 15-16).

As God showed his mercy to Paul, "the grace of the Lord overflowed, producing faith and love in Christ Jesus" (1:14). This verse is a nexus of central ideas from Pauline theology. "Grace" (*charis*) is a central attribute of God; God treats people better than they deserve. The word "overflowed" presents the image of a container filled and spilling over; it is a picture of abundance and richness. This overflowing grace produced "faith and love [*agapēs*]" in Paul's life. "Faith" is a pervasive idea in Paul's letters; he uses the noun *pistis* 142 times and the verb *pisteuō* another 54 times. Here, *pistis* refers to Paul's deep trust in God through Jesus Christ. "Love" is likewise a pervasive idea; Paul uses the noun *agapē* 75 times, the verb *agapaō* another 35—and that's to say nothing of the synonym *phileō* (common in compounds). Love is central to Pauline thought; in 1 Corinthians 13, it even trumps faith!

So here is Paul's description of his conversion: where once was ignorant unbelief, now is faith; where once was violent persecution and arrogance, now is self-sacrificing love. This change, this overflowing grace producing faith and love, is only found "in Christ Jesus." Paul uses "in/with Christ" language to express the deep, intimate relationship that exists between the Lord and his people. It speaks of the believer's loyalty to Jesus, because being "in Christ" involves recognizing that Christ is the Lord to be honored and obeyed, and that they are subservient to him, his possessions. Being "in Christ" also means that Christians are so identified with Jesus' death that his death becomes their death, his life becomes their life, his righteousness their righteousness, his glorification their glorification (Rom 6:3; Col 2:11-12; Gal 2:20; Eph 2:1-7). Because of this identification, even the Paul who was once faithless (*apistia*, 1:13) is judged faithful (*piston*, 1:12).

This truth, realized in Paul's own experiences, leads in 1:15 to the first "faithful saying." These sayings are spread throughout the Pastoral Epistles. Paul uses the formula *pistos ho logos*, "the saying is faithful," five times (here; 1 Tim 3:1; 4:9; 2 Tim 2:11; Titus 3:8). It is found nowhere else in the New Testament. The formula marks traditional material that Paul has taught his churches, of which he is reminding the recipient. It emphasizes both the importance and the reliability of the material to which it refers: "this statement can be believed, and deserves to be believed." Paul here enhances the formula by adding a second phrase: "The saying is sure, *worthy of full acceptance*." "Worthy" (*axios*) denotes something deserving recognition because of merit or value. "Acceptance" (*apodochēs*) carries the idea of approval, believing something to be true and deserving recognition.

The faithful saying that deserves full acceptance is this: "Christ Jesus came [*ēlthen*] into the world to save sinners." This statement has all the earmarks of an early Christian confessional statement (Gloer 1996, 209–17):

- It has a formulaic introduction ("the saying is sure").
- It is introduced by the Greek word *hoti*, usually translated "that" but commonly used to introduce quotations ("*hoti* recitative": the text literally reads, "the saying is sure, that [*hoti*] Christ Jesus came . . .").
- The verb *ēlthen* (from *erchomai*) is commonly used in New Testament statements referring to the mission of Jesus (Matt 5:17; 9:13; John 18:37). With the exception of 1 Timothy 6:7 and Romans 5:12, the phrase, "to come into the world," is used in the New Testament only to refer to the mission of Jesus (see Bultmann 1963, 152–56).
- The word order in the phrase "Christ Jesus" reflects the early Jewish/Christian emphasis on Jesus as Messiah.

This traditional statement announces that Jesus is the Messiah who came into the world to "save sinners" (*hamartōlous sōsai*). "Sinners" are those who violate God's law and live in opposition to God's purposes—as Paul once did. The verb, "save," can refer to rescue from danger, restoration to a state of well-being in the present, or preservation after death. Here, salvation refers to deliverance from the effects of sin, such as death, lives characterized by strife and vice, and hostility and animosity toward God and other people. The term echoes Paul's earlier characterization of God as Savior (*Sōtēr*) in 1:1 (see also 2:3; 4:10; cf. 2:15; 4:16; 2 Tim 1:9; Titus 3:5). Here, it is Christ Jesus who acts to save sinners. The christological implications of referring to both God and Jesus as Savior cannot be missed.

After the saying, Paul returns to his own experience: "'Christ Jesus came into the world to save sinners'—of whom I am the first." Paul sees himself as the foremost of sinners. He uses "first" (*prōtos*) here not in a chronological sense, but either to designate rank ("the worst of sinners") or to indicate that his salvation is a model case of an undeserving sinner, saved by grace through Jesus Christ. As a persecutor of the church, Paul was the model of those who reject God's truth in Christ Jesus. Thus *prōtos* expresses Paul's sense of helplessness because of his earlier rejection of Christ, and his amazement at the wideness of God's mercy which gave him a new life, completely undeserved and unexpected. Through skillful use of literary and rhetorical techniques, Paul thus identifies himself both with the common lot of humanity and with the common faith of the church. He is a model of the gospel incarnate. "But I was shown mercy for this reason: so that in me, the first of sinners, Christ Jesus might demonstrate his full patience" (1:16). This sentence continues the once/now contrast from earlier in the paragraph. The model sinner has now become a demonstration, an advertisement, for the depth of God's mercy. If Christ can and does save the worst of sinners, then he can and does want to save any and all sinners. The passive "I was shown" is again a divine passive, emphasizing God's action. "Full patience" translates *hapasan makrothymian*, "all patience." God's patience includes both the notion of never giving up, in spite of numerous opportunities and reasons to do so, and the idea of perseverance in a determined effort to achieve a particular goal. Here, the goal is saving Paul, the "first" of sinners. "Full" carries the idea of "all-encompassing," "unlimited." "Full patience" is synonymous with grace.

God showed Paul mercy so that Christ could demonstrate his full patience by using Paul "as an example [*hypotypōsin*] for those who are about to believe in him, receiving eternal life." *Hypotyposis* refers to a prototype, a model; the word was used to refer to the preliminary sketches an artist made before undertaking a large project. Paul's conversion is more than an example. It is in fact the model case of conversion: God can take a violent, blasphemous opponent and turn him into an obedient servant, faithful to the point of death. Paul is saying that, if others come to see how graciously God dealt with him, this will give them hope that Christ can and will deal with them graciously also. This will lead them to believe. "Believe" (*pisteuein*) refers to trusting in Christ to the point of obedience. This kind of belief results in "eternal life," an expression that refers both to the continuity of life in Christ (i.e., it is eternal, unending) and the quality of life in Christ (abundance; "I came so that they might have life, and have it to the fullest extent" [John 10:10]). Paul is a model of this belief and the reward it brings.

In 1:17, motivated by his explanation of God's saving grace, Paul erupts into praise in a doxology. "Now to the King eternal, immortal, invisible, the one and only God, be honor and glory for ever and ever, amen." The form of this passage resembles other doxologies in the New Testament (e.g., Rom 16:27; see the discussion of doxologies at 2 Tim 4:18 below). "The King eternal" reflects traditional Jewish praise, and evokes the biblical understanding of God as a king whose kingdom is the central focus of history. The preaching of Jesus focused on this kingdom (e.g., Mark 1:14-15), as did the preaching of John the Baptist before him. Paul writes of this kingdom in 1 Corinthians 4:20; 6:9-10; 15:24, 50; Galatians 5:21; Romans 14:17. The proclamation that God is the King of the Ages establishes his superiority to the Roman emperor, and to any other human ruler whose reign is limited to a single age. "Immortal" (*aphthartō*) refers to something that will not rot or grow corrupt, or decay with time. God is not affected by the power of death and decay. That God is "invisible," and therefore not to be represented by figures or idols, is a central tenet of Jewish beliefs (see Exod 33:20; John 1:18; Col 1:15; Josephus, *J.W.* 7.346). According to Colossians 1:15, Jesus Christ is the unseen God made visible. In Judaism, the belief that God is "the one and only God" was affirmed daily in the recitation of the Shema (Deut 6:4): "The LORD is our God, the LORD alone." The Septuagint renders the second phrase, "the LORD is one." "Alone" speaks of the exclusivity of God, while "one" speaks of God's uniqueness. Both readings reflect the central tenet of the Jewish understanding of God, and inform our understanding of Paul's phrase. Israel was different from other nations because of its monotheism; other nations were polytheistic and henotheistic. From the beginning, Israelites were called to be loyal to their God, and were strictly forbidden to worship any other, for this was the one true and living God, not only of Israel but also of the whole world.

Having described the attributes of God that motivate his praise, Paul now offers that praise: "honor and glory forever and ever." In the New Testament, "honor" (*timē*) and glory (*doxa*) are often companions (Rom 2:7, 10; Heb 2:7, 9; 1 Pet 1:7; 2 Pet 1:17; Rev 4:9, 11; 5:12, 13; 21:26; cf. Rev 7:12). The two terms are synonymous. "Honor" refers to showing reverence and respect to God. "Glory" refers to praising God by declaring his greatness. The language is performative; in other words, by pronouncing the doxology, the worshiper gives glory and honor to God. "Forever and ever" (lit., "to ages of ages") is found in several other New Testament doxologies (Gal 1:5; Phil 4:20; 2 Tim 4:18; Heb 13:21; 1 Pet 4:11; Rev 1:6; 5:13; 7:12). The phrase points to a God who—being eternal and immortal—lives and reigns forever. "Amen" is the traditional response to a doxology. In liturgical settings, this is the group's response to the confession, by which they claim it as their own. Citing 1QS 2.10, Collins notes, "'Amen' was the congregation's response to each of the three parts of the Aaronic blessing (Num 6:24-26) pronounced in the synagogue" (Collins 2002, 47).

Timothy's Call to Ministry (1:18-19a)

In 1:18-19a, Paul turns from his own experiences, his own call to ministry as an example of God's transformative power, and turns to Timothy's call to ministry. These verses are a single sentence in the Greek text. Paul here addresses Timothy by name, which is unusual; in Graeco-Roman letters, the names of sender and recipient were normally confined to the opening and closing (see the discussion on Philemon 19). Directly addressing Timothy in this setting serves to underscore the seriousness of what Paul is saying to him, and the gravity of the situation Timothy faces.

"I am entrusting [*paratithemai*] this command [*parangelian*] to you, Timothy my son" (1:18). *Parangelian* refers back to 1:3: "*command [parangeilēs]* certain people to stop teaching false doctrines." This word is frequently used in reference to orders in the military (1 Macc 5:58; 2 Macc 5:25; 13:10; Onasander, *General* 25; *POxy* 1411.16; 2268.5). Paul now entrusts (*paratithemai*, from *paratithēmi*) this command into Timothy's care. *Paratithēmi* is a succession term, used to refer to passing an object on in a succession. Paul earlier described his call to ministry as a succession of tradition from Christ (1:11). Now he describes Timothy's call to this particular task (dealing with the false teachers in Ephesus, 1:3) as a limited succession of tradition and authority from himself. As Jesus made Paul his successor, so Paul makes Timothy his (Paul's) successor; as Jesus empowered Paul through the succession, so Paul empowers Timothy.

Paul has entrusted this command to Timothy "in keeping with the prophecies once spoken about" him. This phrase highlights the fact that, even though Paul chose Timothy to be his coworker and successor, God chose him for ministry, and for this specific task, first. This parallel between Paul and Timothy—the fact that both of them were chosen for their roles by God—is characteristic of succession in ancient Mediterranean literature. Paul makes Timothy his successor, empowering him, entrusting the command to him so that he "can fight the good fight, holding on to faith and a clear conscience" (1:18-19). For Paul, the struggle to protect the gospel and its teaching is "the good fight." Paul was willing to tolerate opposition and ignorant attacks, as long as the pure gospel was being taught (Phil 1:15-18). But he responded aggressively and decisively when the teaching of the gospel was corrupted (Gal 1:6-9; "Even if we or an angel from heaven should preach to you something other than what we preached to you, let him be accursed" [Gal 1:8]). In reflecting on his own life and ministry, Paul wrote, "I have fought the good fight" (2 Tim 4:7). Timothy is to carry out his mission in keeping with the word of God spoken in these prophecies, for they are of such a nature that he, by following them, will be able to fight for the purity and integrity of the gospel. (For military metaphors applied to ministry, see 1 Cor 9:7; 2 Cor 10:3-4; 1 Thess 5:8; Phlm 2; 1 Tim 6:12; 2 Tim 2:4; 4:7.)

The next phrase describes the means by which Timothy fights this fight: he does so by "holding on to faith and a clear conscience." His dependence on and trust in Jesus Christ will give him strength for the struggle. So also the purity of his behavior: "conscience" was seen as the compass that guided moral choice and action. Compromise in any area would weaken Timothy's resolve and spiritual strength. If his life and ministry were characterized by faith and integrity, then Timothy would be strong for the struggle.

Paul here highlights the significance of the community of faith. He refers to the prophecies made earlier about Timothy (1:18). This reference points to the role of the community of faith in recognizing and affirming those who are called by God to ministry (Acts 6:1-6; 13:1-3). God works through the life of the community to accomplish his purposes in the lives of its members. Paul does not here specify what these prophecies were, who uttered them, or when they were spoken. Prophecy refers to speaking for God, as God's mouthpiece. It is the only spiritual gift to appear in all of Paul's lists of gifts (Rom 12:6; 1 Cor 12:10, 28-29; cf. 1 Cor 13:2; 14:6, 22).

False Teachers Contrasted with Timothy (1:19b-20)

Paul next points to a negative example from the community of faith: "Some have rejected these things [faith and a clear conscience, 1:19a], making a shipwreck of their faith. This includes Hymenaeus and Alexander, whom I have handed over to Satan, in order that they might learn not to blaspheme" (1:19b-20). "Making a shipwreck" translates *enauagēsan*. Hellenistic literature used his nautical metaphor to describe negative or disastrous experiences (Diogenes Laertius 5.55; Philo, *Dreams* 2.147; *Change of Names* 215; Josephus, *Ant* 5.183; 12.355). These false teachers, by their rejection of faith and a clear conscience, made a shipwreck of "the faith." Here, Paul is saying one of two things. Either these two have damaged or destroyed their own faith and dependence on Christ, implying that whatever faith they once had is gone; or he is saying that they have corrupted the teaching of the faith, the gospel, damaging both their standing in the church and the church's standing in the world.

Paul names two examples of this tragic phenomenon, Hymenaeus and Alexander. He mentions these men—or other men of the same names—elsewhere. Paul mentions a Hymenaeus in 2 Timothy 2:17-18, a false teacher who damaged the faith of others by teaching that the resurrection was already past. Paul also mentions an Alexander in 2 Timothy 4:14, a coppersmith who did great damage to Paul and his work by slandering Paul and his message. The way Paul mentions these men indicates that his audience knows them and their story. Paul exercises church discipline over these men by "handing them over [*paredōka*, from *paradidōmi*] to Satan." The expression is drawn from courtroom language, where *paradidōmi* referred to remanding or "handing someone over" for some kind of punishment. This verb is used with reference to Jesus' betrayal, arrest, and being handed over for crucifixion (Matt 26:2, 15; 27:2; John 19:16). "Turning them over to Satan" refers to the church withdrawing fellowship and spiritual support from these two, praying that God will allow them to experience the full effects and consequences of their actions. This echoes the language of 1 Corinthians 5:5, where Paul commanded the Corinthian church to punish a man guilty of scandalous sexual behavior by expelling him from the church. By teaching their own ideas as God's truth, Hymenaeus and Alexander are actually misrepresenting and opposing God, which is equivalent to blasphemy. But even blasphemers can repent and be forgiven (as in the case of Paul, 1:13). Implicit in the working of church discipline is the aim of restoration. Both here and in 1 Corinthians 5, the point of the punishment is to bring people to repentance and reinstatement in the community of faith.

Paul's image of shipwrecked faith is a stark picture indeed. This shipwreck was caused by the intentional rejection of conscience, the compass that shows people the right course. To intentionally choose the wrong course is to follow a road to ruin. This is especially true for the Christian, because the Christian conscience is part of the mind, made new and being continually renewed in Christ (Rom 12:2; 2 Cor 5:17). For the believer, "true north" is no longer located in the self—"There is a way that seems right to a person, but its end is the way to death" (Prov 14:12, NRSV)—but in the rule of God.

Summary. In 1:3-11, Paul charges Timothy with an important task, and empowers him to accomplish that task. Using his own calling to ministry (a succession of tradition from Jesus Christ) as an example, he empowers Timothy to do this work, making Timothy his (Paul's) successor in care of and authority over the teaching in the church at Ephesus. Just as Paul and his people are empowered by Jesus Christ to know how to use the law properly, so also Paul empowers Timothy to stop the false teachers who bedevil the Ephesian church.

In 1:12-17, Paul weaves his own testimony around a statement of traditional material, "Christ came to save sinners" (1:15). The traditional material echoes Jesus' own language for describing his mission (Luke 19:10). Paul considered himself to be the worst of sinners, and therefore a perfect example of God's patience and saving grace: "If God could save me—blasphemer, persecutor, man of violence—then he can save anyone." This reminds believers of the power of personal testimony, for all have experienced God's saving grace. Paul finishes this paragraph with a magnificent benediction; it is not unusual for Paul to break out in praise after a discussion of the salvation God has made available in the gospel (e.g., Rom 11:33-36; Eph 3:20-21). God's saving work deserves to be celebrated, and throughout the Bible we find his people attempting to give him his due (Exod 15:1-18, 20-21; Luke 1:46-55, 68-79; Rev 19:1-9; 21:3-4).

In 1:18-20, Paul describes Timothy's own call to ministry. Like Paul, Timothy was singled out for his work by God. Paul contrasts the way Timothy will carry out his ministry with the way false teachers in Ephesus were doing their work. Again, the methods, message, and results are drastically different.

Throughout this passage, Paul contrasts false teachers—their character and the character of their teachings, and the rotten fruit their teaching produces—with teachers of the true gospel, like himself and Timothy.

False Teachers/Teaching Person	Faithful Teachers/Teaching Person
• Self-appointed (1:7)	• Chosen by God, stand in a line of authority commissioned by God (1:1, 11, 18)
• Do not understand what they teach (1:7)	• Understand what they teach and how it should be used (1:8)
	• Fighting the good fight (for the purity of the gospel)
• Reject faith and conscience (1:19)	• Hold to faith and clear conscience (1:19)

Teachings	Teachings
• Myths and endless genealogies (1:4)	• Legitimate; use law according to God's purpose for it (1:8)
• Empty talk (1:6)	• Healthy teaching (1:10)
• Blasphemy (1:20)	• Declare the glory of the blessed God (1:11)
	• Trustworthy and deserving of acceptance everywhere (1:15)

Results	Results
• Useless disputes (1:5)	• Proper administration of the household of God (1:4)
	• Love from pure heart, good conscience, genuine faith (1:5)
	• Transformed life (1:12-16)
• Shipwrecked lives, witness, faith (1:19)	• Faith and clear conscience (1:18-19)

Paul's Missionary Purposes (2:1–3:16)

The Missionary Purpose behind Paul's Teaching (2:1-7)

First Timothy 2:1 begins the long middle section of the book. This section consists of paraenesis (practical instruction about daily life). Paul here describes the kind of life God wants his people to live. A single goal lies behind the practical instruction: Paul wants his people to live out their faith in ways that make the gospel appealing to people in the pagan society around them. He hopes to do this by adopting three strategies:

- when Christian values agreed with prevalent Graeco-Roman values, he promoted them;
- when Christian values disagreed with prevalent Graeco-Roman values, he treated them cautiously;
- when the exercise of freedom led to disorder and loss of reputation, he restrained that freedom.

Paul writes: "First of all, then, I urge that requests, prayers, petitions, and thanksgivings be made for all people" (2:1). The phrase "first of all" (*prōton pantōn*) indicates that this is the first instruction in this section of the letter. It also indicates the significance of this particular instruction, and might be rendered "above all." "Then" (*oun*) connects this material with the material that precedes it; these instructions are part of (or flow from) the command of 1:3, 18, and the proper administration of the household of God (1:4). "I urge" translates the same verb as in 1:3 (*parakaleō*). In both instances, it reflects a polite but authoritative tone.

Paul communicates the content of the first command through four different words for prayer. These words are largely synonymous with one another:

- "Requests" (*deēseis*), urgent petitions based on personal need;
- "Prayers" (*proseuchas*), a generic term for all kinds of prayer;
- "Petitions" (*enteuxeis*), requests on behalf of others;
- "Thanksgivings" (*eucharistias*), expressions of gratitude for blessings or benefits.

The overlap between these terms indicates that Paul, rather than attempting to give his readers a systematic theology of prayer, is simply commanding that all kinds of prayers be offered. He wants prayer to be a prominent element in the worship of the Ephesian church, and expects it to be practiced in a way that reflects positively on the message of the gospel. As in 1 Corinthians 11, Paul's concerns center on the manner in which prayer is offered, partly because of the public nature of worship in the Christian house congregations (see 2:8-9, below).

Furthermore, these prayers are to be made "for everyone" (*hyper pantōn anthrōpōn*). Here, Paul's missionary purposes move to the front. Notice the repetitions of "all" in 2:1-7: make prayers for all people (2:1), for kings and all those in authority (2:2), because God our Savior wants all people to be saved (2:4), for Christ Jesus the mediator gave himself as a ransom for all

(2:6). With these repetitions, Paul points to the universal nature of God's grace, and the universal aim of the gospel.

Here, Paul is responding to a facet of the false teaching in Ephesus. His opponents seem to have aimed at stopping support for Paul's missionary activity in other places. This attitude of "charity begins at home," this lack of concern for people outside their circle or "in-group," may have been motivated by ethnocentric (perhaps Judaizing) elements in the false teaching. Or it may have begun with the same kinds of elitism and over-realized eschatology that troubled the church in Corinth (e.g., 1 Cor 4:8-13). Whatever the case, the believers who were under the sway of the false teaching were ignoring their responsibility to live as God's ambassadors in a pagan world: "The prayer practice Paul sought to reinstate in Ephesus had the evangelistic mission to the Gentiles as its target" (Towner 2006, 165). Thus in 2:1-7 (and again in 3:14-16), Paul clearly asserts that God is the universal God and Savior, that the gospel aims at offering salvation to everyone, and that the Ephesian church needs to support this endeavor. They will show their support through financial backing for Paul's work, prayer support, and living in ways that win a hearing for the gospel.

In 2:2, Paul moves from the general (the command to pray for all people) to the specific (prayers for particular persons). Prayers should be offered "for kings and all those in authority." "Kings" (*basileōn*) translates the word used to refer to the Roman emperor, although the plural form may indicate that others are also in view. "Those in authority" (*hyperochē*) refers to people holding rank or position, civil and governmental authorities. Throughout the history of the Church, Christians have prayed for those who ruled over them—and for much of that history, those governments were not at all Christian. Around 175 CE, Athenagorus wrote an open letter to Marcus Aurelius, emphasizing Christians' loyalty to the empire and their desire for peaceful coexistence with those around them. He closed the letter by praying, in language that echoes 1 Timothy 2:2, for the emperors to be blessed by an orderly succession of rule and continued prosperity. "[We] pray . . . that the succession to the kingdom may proceed from father to son, as is most just, and that your reign may grow and increase as all men become subject to you. . . . This is also to our advantage, that we may lead a quiet and peaceable life" (*Legatio* 37.2–3). The structures of governments may change, and the titles and names of governing officials will change along with those structures, but the need to pray for those officials remains the same. Indeed, whether Christians agree with those in authority over them or not, those who work in government are God's servants, established by God to achieve good purposes (Rom 13:1-7). Throughout Christian history, believers have prayed for the government they lived under, even when they didn't agree with it, especially when they didn't agree with it.

Paul's goal for these prayers for governing authorities is "so that we might live quiet and peaceful lives in all godliness and dignity." "Quiet" (*ēremon*) and "peaceable" (*hēsuchion*) are synonyms, referring to a life that is calm, orderly, and free from danger and trouble. Such a life is not a given, but may result from the Christian's prayers on behalf of others. This life is lived "in all godliness and dignity." "Godliness" (*eusebeia*) refers to a life lived in and from reverence for God. However, *eusebeia* can also serve as a technical term for religious activity. Here, then, the implication may be that, because of the Christian's prayers, governmental interference in the practice of their religion may be lessened, which would make it easier to share the gospel with and minister to the culture. "Dignity" (*semnotēti*) refers to behavior that is good and proper, above reproach or worthy of respect, especially in relation to other people. Taken together, these two words describe the essence of the Christian life in terms readily recognizable to Hellenistic audiences. They demonstrate obedience to the great commandments of love toward God and toward one's neighbor.

Paul continues, "Praying such prayers is good and pleasing to God our Savior, who wants all people to be saved and come to a knowledge of the truth" (2:3-4). "Good" (*kalos*) here refers to behavior that is right or correct. "Pleasing" (*apodekton*) points to a thing that is acceptable to God; this may echo the idea that Old Testament sacrifices needed to be pleasing to God. God "wants all people to be saved." The word translated "wants" refers to God's purpose: God is the motivator behind Paul's missionary work; indeed, Paul is a missionary to the Gentiles because of God's direct command. "All people" refers again to the universal scope of God's plan of salvation. Some groups in Paul's world preached an inherently exclusive, elitist message. The message of the Judaizers excluded people who were non-Jews. Early Gnostics limited salvation only to those who had received secret knowledge, the "elect" or truly spiritual. For Paul, however, God's salvation is available to all, without exception.

Paul uses the phrase "knowledge of the truth" elsewhere in the Pastoral Epistles as shorthand for the content of the gospel (see 4:3; 2 Tim 3:7; Titus 1:1). People "came to this knowledge" at conversion, when their beliefs and behaviors were no longer based on the lie of pagan beliefs (Rom 1:24), but the truth that is found in Jesus, himself the way, truth, and life.

Hymn describing God's grace (2:5-6)

In 2:5-6, Paul presents supporting evidence for his claims regarding the universality of the gospel (2:4). This material is likely part of an early Christian confession or hymn. It is a succinct statement of faith. Such statements are found throughout the New Testament, and demonstrate the early Christian practice of developing "capsule" statements of the basic elements of the faith. In a world where many people were illiterate, such statements provided an easy way for people to learn, remember, and pass on theological information.

The statement reads,

> For there is one God,
> And one mediator for God and humanity,
> The human, Jesus Christ,
> Who gave himself as a ransom for all,
> The witness at its appointed time. (2:5-6)

The statement affirms three things. First, "there is one God." As noted in the discussion of 1:17 above, this conviction historically sets Israel apart from other nations. In the New Testament world, monotheism continued to distinguish Jews and Christians from the polytheism of the surrounding cultures. Here, Paul stresses that there is only one God, both Creator and Savior of all people, Jews and Gentiles. Second, "there is one mediator for God and humanity." "Mediator" (*mesitēs*) is a Hellenistic term, found in diplomatic, legal, and commercial language. Philo refers to Moses as a mediator between God and the people of Israel (*Moses* 2.166; *Dreams* 1.143; cf. *TDan* 6.2). This word refers to someone who acts as an intermediary to reconcile two parties, or to someone who helps to bring an agreement between two parties and guarantees such an agreement. Jesus Christ, "himself human," is the one who makes peace between humanity and God. The stress on Jesus' humanity sets him apart from the mediators of popular Graeco-Roman religion. It also reminds the audience of Jesus' suffering and death, which prepares for the next phrase, the third affirmation.

Third, the man Christ Jesus "gave himself as a ransom for all." "Ransom" (*antilytron*) refers to a means or an instrument by which people are set free. In the first-century world, where slavery was seen as both acceptable and necessary, "ransom" referred to the money paid to a slave owner in order to free a slave, the means by which deliverance was made available. Jesus himself uses this language to speak of his death in Mark 10:45.

Christ Jesus "gave himself" by his self-sacrifice on the cross. In so doing, he became the means by which all people might be delivered. He offered himself "for all people" (*hyper pantōn*: for this formula, see the discussion at Titus 1:14). Further, Jesus' death is "the witness at the appropriate time." In other words, Jesus' death is convincing testimony of the true character of God, as described in 2:4—he wants all people to be saved and come to the knowledge of the truth. ("Witness" *could* refer to Paul's ministry. In that case, the phrase would be pointing ahead to 2:7, but the reading adopted above is more likely.) This testimony comes at the appropriate time (Rom 5:6; Gal 4:4).

Paul's appointment by God (2:7)

Because of his desire that all people be saved and come to knowledge of the truth, God called Paul to ministry. "For this witness, I was appointed preacher and apostle—I speak the truth, I am not lying—and teacher of the true faith for the Gentiles" (2:7). The verb "appointed" (*tithēmi*) refers to selecting someone for a special task or function. Again, this verb is used in succession contexts. Paul's appointment is threefold: preacher (*kērux*), apostle, and teacher (*didaskalos*). The same series of tasks appears in the same order in 2 Timothy 1:11; cf. 1 Timothy 4:13, where Timothy devotes himself to preaching and teaching. Paul is appointed all these things for the benefit of the Gentiles, "in faith and truth." This last phrase can refer to the spirit and manner of the teacher, "faithful and true." It can also refer to the content of the teaching; if this is the case, then "faith" and "truth" are a hendiadys, two expressions pointing to one idea, thus "in the true faith." Paul inserts a parenthesis into this description of his calling: "I am telling the truth, I am not lying." This statement contains both a positive and negative assertion. This kind of contrast-based assertion was a common rhetorical device. Paul uses it here to make the statement regarding his appointment emphatic; we should not assume it indicates defensiveness on Paul's part (or skepticism on Timothy's).

Throughout the remainder of chapters 2 and 3 (or at least through 3:13), Paul builds on the metaphor of the church as the "household of God" (3:15). He uses a modified household code (*Haustafel*) to structure his paraenesis. "Household codes" were a type of literature used by the Hellenistic moral philosophers and other teachers to describe the duties, responsibilities, and relationships in a household. Paul does not follow the typical structure of a household code here, however. Both here and in 5:1–6:2, he takes the old form of the household code and adapts it to apply to the church, the household of God.

Behavior in the Household (of God) that Supports Paul's Purposes (2:8–3:13)

In 2:8–3:1a, Paul addresses conduct during the public worship service. This paragraph is one of the most controversial in all the New Testament. Over the years, because of his statements regarding women and their roles in the church in this paragraph, Paul has been ignored, rebelled against, championed, and vilified. He begins with a non-controversial command, however, picking up the theme of prayer from 2:1-4.

Men (2:8)

Paul writes: "Therefore, I want men to pray in every place, lifting up holy hands, without anger and argument" (2:8). "Therefore" ties this command back to the missionary purposes behind 2:1-7: in essence, "God wants all people to come to a knowledge of the truth, therefore pray everywhere." Paul focuses his attention here on men; the word *andras* ("the men") is gender specific (unlike *anthrōpos* in 2:1, 5). The men are to pray "in every place"; the Greek word translated "place" (*topos*) was used in Hellenistic Judaism to refer to places of worship or prayer (Ferguson 1991, 65–73). Thus this reference is to prayer in public worship, wherever the Ephesian Christians gather. The posture of lifted hands during prayer was common for both Jews and Gentiles in Paul's world (see Pss 141:2; 143:6). "Holy hands" may be cultic language, referring to the way priests purified themselves before sacrifices, symbolized by the ritual washing of hands. Here, it refers to hands (and by metonymy, lives) set apart to belong to God, to be used for his purposes (rather than selfish ones). These holy hands are to be accompanied by holy, unselfish attitudes; prayer is not consistent with anger and argument. People in the Ephesian church may have been using public prayers to air their grievances or debates, something along the lines of publicly praying, "Lord, we ask that you will show our brother the error of his ways and make him agree with us." Paul places great value on living in ways that make the gospel attractive to outsiders; it's easy to imagine how such prayers would have affected non-Christians who witnessed the believers at worship, giving them a false impression of the nature of the gospel and the church.

Women (2:9–3:1a)

More controversial is the remainder of the chapter, where Paul addresses the conduct of the Ephesian women in public worship. He writes: "Likewise, I want the women to dress in appropriate clothing, making themselves beautiful with modesty and self-control, rather than with elaborate hairstyles and gold, or pearls or expensive clothes, but through good deeds, which are fitting for women who profess to worship God" (2:9-10).

Several issues come together here. First, as with 2:8, Paul's overriding concern was that the gospel be attractive to outsiders. This concern grew out of the missionary purpose articulated in 2:1-7: Christianity gave women dignity, self-actualization, and freedom that they did not find in more traditional areas of society. If anyone in the church, man or woman, was exercising these freedoms in ways that scandalized outsiders, keeping them from giving the gospel a hearing, Paul would have stepped in and limited those behaviors. He would have done this even if the behaviors were not specifically sinful, or if they sprang from legitimate freedoms that the gospel and Spirit gave (cf. Paul's instruction regarding freedoms and stumbling blocks in Rom 14 and 1 Cor 8:1–11:1).

Paul's concern with the church's witness and reputation focuses here on conduct in the worship service, and is heightened by the fact that "private" homes in the cramped cities of the Graeco-Roman world were not all that private. The only parts of the home that were truly private were the rooms reserved for sleeping and bathing. The rooms where early Christians met to worship—the entryways, courtyards, atriums, etc.—were open to anyone who walked by (Vitruvius, *De Architectura* 6.5.1; Osiek and Balch 1997, 17). Thus public worship was truly *public*, out in the open for everyone in the world to see (cf. 1 Cor 11 and 14, especially 14:16, 24).

Second, Roman society at this time was engaged in a serious conversation about the roles and behavior of women. This discussion centered on what is now referred to as "the new Roman woman."

> Some women of means and position (married and widowed), supported in some cases by free-thinking males, flouted traditional values governing adornment and dress and sexual propriety. The emergence of this movement was so disturbing to the status quo that Augustus issued legislation against it. (Towner 2006, 196)

As an example from this discussion, consider a letter that Seneca wrote to his mother during the 40s CE, commending her for her beauty and nobility:

> Unlike the great majority of women you never succumbed to immorality, the worst evil of our time; jewels and pearls have not moved you; you never thought of wealth as the greatest gift to the human race . . . you have never blushed for the number of children, as if it taunted you with your years; never have you, in the manner of other women whose only recommendation lies in their beauty, tried to conceal your pregnancy as though it were

indecent; . . . you have not defiled your face with paints and cosmetics; never have you fancied the kind of dress that exposed no greater nakedness by being removed. Your only ornament, the kind of beauty that time does not tarnish, is the great honor of modesty. (Seneca, *ad Helviam* 16.3–4, quoted in Winter 2003, 60)

The parallels between Seneca's description of his mother's virtue and Paul's prescription for Christian women in Ephesus are striking. Women of this time were judged on the basis of the clothing that they wore. If a woman wore stylish clothes and elaborate jewelry and hairstyles, people assumed that she was more likely to be promiscuous and to rebel against her husband.

Roman society deeply valued stability and tradition. Women in that society were pushing against the traditional boundaries of propriety. Powerful forces were troubled by these changes and the instability that accompanied them. Paul reasoned that if pagan society associated the church with these changes, these behaviors that scandalized, then they would not have been willing to listen to the gospel. Both here and in 1 Corinthians 11 and 14, Paul restricts women in the use of their gifts, and for the same reasons. These restrictions were situational, not universal. They sprang from Paul's missionary purposes. Paul wanted the gospel to have as wide a hearing as possible, and any exercise of freedom that he judged unwise, which might have kept people from listening, was to be prohibited.

Third, the false teaching in Ephesus apparently involved gender roles and the devaluing of childbearing and marriage (1 Tim 4:3). The Christian women in Ephesus seem to have found the heresy especially appealing (see 2 Tim 3:6-7). Here as in Corinth, the heresy resulted in over-realized eschatology and elitism. Some women may have been involved in teaching heresy. Even if these women were not active partners in false teaching, the heresy itself made the possibility of scandal based on attitudes toward gender roles—already a touchy subject in the Roman cities, as seen above—an even more explosive issue. (For a detailed discussion of the background to this passage, see Towner 2006, 190–200.)

Against this background, Paul instructed the women to dress in clothing that is "appropriate" (*kosmiō*); the word refers to something that is not excessive, but respectable. They are to "make themselves beautiful" (lit., "adorn [*kosmein*] themselves") with modesty (*aidous*) and self-control (*sōphrosunēs*). *Sōphrosunē* implies that a person knows what is appropriate and helpful in a given situation. Further, they were not to make themselves beautiful by ostentatious jewelry or scandalously stylish clothes or elaborate hairstyles (*plegmasin*, lit., "braided hair"). In Graeco-Roman culture, a woman's lavishly braided hair was considered a work of art. The hair often rose several inches above the head, intertwined with chains of gold or strings of pearls.

Instead, the women were to make themselves beautiful with "good deeds" or "good works." "Good works" are a central focus in the Pastoral Epistles, appearing no fewer than ten times. Paul uses the phrase as a shorthand expression referring to the Christian life (cf. Eph 2:8-10). "Good works" are works for the benefit of other people. Such works, along with modesty and self-control, are the proper adornment for demonstrating the beauty of women who claim to be Christians, "who profess to worship God." Notice again the parallels with Seneca's letter, quoted above. The lives people live and the way they demonstrate their values are the clearest signs of their character. As with the qualifications for leadership below (1 Tim 3), Paul urges believers to look below the surface and to be people of true character, living lives of reverence toward God, seeking to bless others.

Paul continued: "Women must learn in quietness, with all submissiveness" (2:11). His instructions here suggest a radical departure from the traditional synagogue. There, the instruction was limited to men and boys. Jesus set this tradition aside during his ministry (Luke 10:38-42). Thus from the beginning of the church, women were included in the instruction together with men. In the light of the concerns outlined above, Paul established parameters for that learning. "Quietness" (*hēsuchia*) can refer to absolute silence, but here points to a quiet, non-argumentative demeanor. "Submissiveness" (*hypotagē*) commanded the Ephesian women to respect the authority of the teacher, not arguing disputable points or advocating for the positions of the false teachers. The need for these attitudes cannot be restricted to women, for they represent the demeanor that any learner should assume, male or female.

Further, Paul did not "permit women to teach or to give orders to a man" (2:12). "I do not permit" (*ouk epitrepō*) speaks of Paul's authority as apostle and successor of Jesus Christ in the care and use of the gospel (as did "I urge" in 2:1). Paul unpacks "I do not permit" with three infinitive clauses. The first clause prohibited the women in Ephesus from teaching. In the context of this chapter, with its concern for the public worship service, this prescription specifically applied to the authoritative, public teaching of Scripture. Further, this prescription aimed at heart of the circumstances in Ephesus. Women in that church had fallen under the influence of false teaching that promoted nontraditional values and denigrated marriage and childbearing, apparently due to some kind of over-realized eschatology. The false teachers in the church were encouraging the women to bring up these readings of Scripture in discussions, or while the teacher was speaking during public worship. Due in part to their society's concern with the new Roman woman, these attitudes and activities gave the church a bad reputation with the community around it, causing people to refuse to listen to the gospel.

As he does throughout the Pastoral Epistles, Paul responded to the heresy by appealing to succession. The gospel, initiated by God, passed from Jesus to Paul to Timothy and Titus to the faithful people (*anthrōpos*, not *anēr*, which refers specifically to "men"), who would then teach it to others (2 Tim 2:2). As these faithful men and women taught the gospel correctly and without compromise or deviation (2 Tim 2:15), the heresy would be defeated. Talbert notes, in the context of 1 Corinthians, "the defense of the tradition [the gospel] would not be committed to those most swayed by the heresy (the women). Such people would rather be prohibited from exercising authority and from teaching" (Talbert 2002, 118).

By way of contrast with the Ephesian women, note the way Luke commends Priscilla (together with her husband) as an example of one who taught the true gospel (Acts 18:24-26). She not only taught the gospel, she taught it to Apollos, who was seen by some in the first-century church as equal to (if not surpassing) Paul in importance (cf. 1 Cor 1:12; 3:4, 5, 6, 22; 4:6)! Talbert notes, "In this context where the woman is a representative of the true tradition there is no reluctance to depict her as the teacher of a male preacher" (Talbert 2002, 118). What makes the difference between the women in Ephesus—whom Paul commanded not to teach—and Priscilla, who is commended for teaching? The difference is that Priscilla was faithful to the gospel that Paul preached. The women in Ephesus—having fallen under the influence of the false teachers—were not. Thus the overriding issue in 1 Timothy 2:9-15 is not gender but orthodoxy and heresy.

In the middle clause, "give orders" translates *authentein*. *Authenteō* referred to usurping authority, taking authority for oneself, often with selfish motives or violent consequences. In this literary and social context, *authenteō* did not universally prohibit the exercise of authority or leadership by women in the church. Luke and Paul commended Priscilla and Phoebe, for example, who were strong and gifted women (Acts 18:18, 19, 26 [notice the order of Priscilla and Aquila's names]; Rom 16:1, 3; 2 Tim 4:19). Rather, Paul here was condemning the way some women in Ephesus were seeking leadership, their motivations, and the rebellious and irresponsible way they exercised the freedoms and responsibilities Christianity afforded them. (For discussion of *authenteō*, see Baldwin 1995, 65–80, 269–305, who discusses the relevant bibliography, ancient and modern; Winter 2003, 116-19.)

The final clause of the three ("she is to be in quietness," or "she is to have a quiet demeanor") reiterates the attitudes commended in 2:11. Again, this was not a command to complete silence; such an injunction would have contradicted Paul's thinking and the practices of the early church (Acts 2:17-18; 18:18, 19, 26; 21:9; Gal 3:28; 1 Cor 11:2-16).

In 2:13-15, Paul supports his prescriptions for the Ephesian women by a theological argument (2:13-14) and a traditional saying (2:15). "For Adam was formed first, then Eve. And Adam was not deceived, but the woman, being thoroughly deceived, became a sinner" (2:13-14). These verses present a conclusion drawn from the order of creation in Genesis 2 and the circumstances of the fall (Gen 3). The argument resembles the argument Paul makes in 1 Corinthians 11:3, 8-9. "Formed" translates *eplasthē*, the same word used in the Septuagint to describe God forming Adam from the dust (Gen 2:7; cf. Gen 2:19). "Deceived" translates *ēpatēthē*, which refers to being misled into believing something that is not true. Paul says because of the tempter, and her own weaknesses, Eve ("the woman") was "thoroughly deceived" (*exapatētheisa*, an intensive form of *ēpatēthē*). As a result, Eve "became [*gegonen*] a sinner [*parabasei*]." *Parabasis* is often translated "transgression." It refers to stepping outside a boundary, willfully acting against established rules or laws.

These verses reflect the prevalent view in Judaism. The woman was first deceived, and her deception led to the fall of the human race. Therefore, it was by her disobedience that sin and death came into the world. Furthermore, people in the ancient world generally believed that women were more easily deceived than men, more easily swayed by passions and emotions. For example, Philo wrote,

> Why did the serpent accost the woman and not the man? . . . The woman was more accustomed to being deceived than the man; For his counsels as well as his body are of a masculine sort, and competent to disentangle the notions of seduction; but the mind of the woman is more effeminate, so that through her softness she easily yields and is easily caught by the persuasions of falsehood, which imitate the resemblance of truth. (*Questions and Answers on Genesis* 1.33)

Such views are part of Paul's background, and may play a part in his instructions here. They are not the foundation of the prohibitions, however. Paul's central concerns (thus the foundation of the prescriptions and prohibitions he made) were practices in the Ephesian church, and how those practices were "turning people off" to the gospel.

Paul's revolutionary attitude toward women is evident in several passages, beyond those mentioned in connection with Phoebe and Priscilla:

"In Christ there is no Jew nor Greek, male nor female, slave nor free, for you are all one in Christ" (Gal 3:28) and "If any person is in Christ, that person is a new creation; the old things are passing away, and look! new things have come" (2 Cor 5:17). Paul also endorsed prayer and prophecy from the Corinthian women in public worship, as long as they did it with propriety (1 Cor 11:5, 12). For Paul, the effects of the fall—including the struggle for dominion between men and women, husbands and wives (Gen 3:16b)—are being reversed and done away with in the gospel.

But that reversal is not yet complete; renewal is still partial. Christians still live and witness in a world that has not yet come fully right-side-up, and have in fact not fully come right-side-up themselves. Thus the exercise of freedoms found in that reversal is not the priority. Instead, the priority is witness, faithfulness, love. Here, as elsewhere (Rom 14; Eph 5:21–6:9; 1 Cor 8–11; 12–14), Paul demands that Christians restrain the exercise of individual freedoms to do what is best for the church and her testimony before the watching world. Only then do they "submit to one another out of reverence for Christ" (Eph 5:21).

Seen in this light, the specific restrictions Paul placed on women in 1 Timothy 2:9-15 and elsewhere (e.g., 1 Cor 14:34-35, if that passage contains Paul's words, rather than a Corinthian slogan that Paul refutes) were specific prescriptions for a particular situation, place, and time. They are not universal or timeless. Medicine that helps to heal the sick may cause a healthy person to become ill; likewise, Paul's prescriptions for dealing with the problems of a sick church should not be universalized.

Verse 2:15 is the most difficult of all: "'Women will be saved through childbearing'—if they continue in faith and love and holiness with self control." The verb "will be saved" is singular, and no subject is stated. A literal translation of the phrase then would be, "[She] will be saved," which appears to single out Eve (an echo of Gen 3:16 and perhaps even 3:15). It is better to take the first half of 2:15 as traditional or gnomic material; this is born out by 3:1, "This saying is sure," which points back to the trustworthy saying, "Women will be saved through childbearing."

What does it mean to say that women will be saved through bearing children? At least four readings have been suggested; the first two can be rejected out of hand:

- This verse promises that Christian women will be kept safe (physical "salvation," safety or deliverance from danger) when giving birth. This view points back to Genesis 3:16, where Eve's punishment is pain in childbearing. The preposition "through" (*dia*) is taken in the sense, "in the

experience of" (cf. the use of *dia* in 1 Cor 3:15), rather than the more customary "by means of."
- This verse refers to Mary giving birth to Jesus. Women are thereby saved by Jesus' birth, which begins the undoing of the effects of the fall. Many of the early church fathers adopted this reading.

Two other readings have more to commend them.

- "Childbearing" is a metaphor for producing virtues (see Plato, *Symp* 206C, 209A–E; Philo, *Leg* 2.82; 3.3, 180–81). By this reading, Paul was not specifically affirming traditional roles (although he was certainly not excluding them). His point was specifically to endorse the pursuit of virtues, "faith and love and holiness with self-control," on the part of the Ephesian women. Thus women would be saved if they pursued the proper virtues, character traits that blessed both them and the people around them, winning a hearing for the gospel (Waters 2004, 703–35, especially 716–22). This reading of 2:15 is consistent with the instructions of 2:1-2, 9-10.
- "Childbearing" refers to the Ephesian women finding salvation (in some sense) in embracing traditional familial roles, because in so doing they strengthened the witness of the church and rejected both the new Roman woman and the heresy, with their attendant potential for scandal. "Childbearing" is a generic shorthand expression for those traditional roles. Paul was not commanding that every woman be married (cf. 1 Cor 7:8-9), nor was he excluding faithful women who did not have children.

In the context of this chapter, and the sociological context described above, the fourth reading seems best. The piece of tradition Paul quotes here would have been understood by the Ephesian church as an affirmation of traditional, Augustan roles for women. Again, Paul was aiming at aspects of the false teaching that denigrated traditional roles. He affirmed: women will be saved by bearing children, i.e., by embracing traditional, societally acceptable roles, and rejecting the false teaching and societal trends that push them in the other direction. The last half of the verse confirms this reading, as does 3:1a. Women must also "continue in faith and love and holiness with self-control." "Continue" translates *meinōsin*, which refers to continuing in some activity or state, to live a life characterized by certain things. Here, the things they were to pursue are faith (their commitment to Christ), love (for God and others, rather than selfishness), holiness (being dedicated and set apart for God and his purposes), and self-control. This is a powerful description of the Christian life that ultimately applies to all Christians, both men and women.

For much of recent history, Christians have struggled to apply 1 Timothy 2:9-15. Some regard the restrictions from this passage as universal commands from God, orders to be enforced in every church for all time. Others dismiss these verses as chauvinistic relics, or non-Pauline (or sub-Pauline) ranting, often assuming 1 Timothy is pseudonymous, and that pseudonymity means the text contains less authority. Neither approach is faithful to this passage in its contexts, its place in the Pastoral Epistles and its place in Paul's gospel, and the teaching that flows from it. To be faithful to those contexts, we must read and apply this text against two concerns, two backdrops. First, we must read this text against the entirety of 1 Timothy (and indeed the entirety of the Pastoral Epistles), and Paul's concern for the purity of the gospel as voiced here. Plainly, Paul is motivated by heresy, not gender. Second, we must read this text against other Pauline passages that describe the appropriate use of Christian freedom (Rom 14; Gal 5:13; Eph 5:21–6:9; 1 Cor 8–11; 12–14). When read together, these texts remind us that things that are permissible are not inevitably beneficial. When the witness of the church or the purity and effectiveness of the gospel are at stake, Christians must be willing to give up their rights, curtail the exercise of freedom, and do what is best for others and for the community. This follows the example of Christ (Phil 2:1-8).

Summary. In 2:1–3:1a, Paul focuses on the testimony of the church. The believers in Ephesus were hurting their witness, particularly by the way they acted during their worship services. Paul here commands them to fix certain problems:

- To stop refusing to pray for people outside their circle, because God wants people everywhere to hear the gospel and come to know him;
- To stop praying prayers filled with polemic and personal agendas;
- To stop dressing and acting in ways or taking on attitudes that the community around them would find scandalous and unsettling. "Freedom in Christ" does not mean freedom to sin or to offend unnecessarily.

The gospel is countercultural and counter-intuitive. As such, it is offensive enough on its own. Paul says *do not add to the offense.*

Elders (3:1b-7)

In 1 Timothy 3, Paul continues to use the household code format to describe life in the church, the household of God. Here he moves from public worship (the setting of the instructions in chapter 2) to questions regarding the leadership of the church. Paul writes: "If anyone aspires to serve as an overseer, he desires a good work. Because of this, the overseer . . . " (3:1-2). "Serve as an overseer" translates *episkopēs*, a verbal noun that refers to the work of overseeing. "Overseer" in 3:2 translates *episkopon* (a term related to *episkopēs*), which refers to the person doing the work of overseeing. "Overseer" and "elder" appear to be interchangeable terms in the New Testament, both referring to a single office/function in the New Testament church (Titus 1:5-7; Acts 20:17, 28; 1 Pet 5:1-3). In the second century, these terms came to refer to separate but overlapping offices (see the discussion under Titus 1:5).

Elders/overseers were responsible for nurturing and shepherding the members of the congregation (1 Pet 5:2), visiting and praying for the sick (Jas 5:14), protecting the church from false teaching (Acts 20:29-31), and living as examples for other Christians to follow (1 Pet 5:3). Here, Paul focuses on the character of the overseer, rather than duties and responsibilities. He affirms that the work of oversight in the church is "a good work," a noble (or important) task, worthy of being aspired to. Because this task is good, noble, and important, overseers must possess the following character qualities (3:2-7; several of these characteristics are paralleled in Titus 1:6-9, see the longer discussion there):

- "Irreproachable" (*anepilēmpton*) refers to having a good reputation with others; synonymous with *anegklētos* (Titus 1:6).
- "The husband of one wife" (Titus 1:6, see the discussion there).
- "Sober-minded" (*nēphalion*) is the first of five positive virtues on the list, qualities that describe an ordered life. *Nēphalios* generally referred to abstaining from drunkenness, but was often used metaphorically to refer to freedom from excess (see the discussion under Titus 2:3).
- "Self-controlled" (*sōphrona*; see the discussions at Titus 1:8; 2:2, 5).
- "Appropriate" (*kosmion*); often appears together with *sōphrona* in non-Christian writings. This word was used in 2:9 to describe respectable clothing for women. Here, the focus is on behavior, a life that is orderly and free from confusion.
- "Hospitable" (*philoxenon*, literally "friend of strangers," used in Titus 1:8). Christians were a minority group within a larger and sometimes hostile society. Thus they needed to welcome and show hospitality to one

another, especially traveling missionaries. In Acts, one sign of genuine conversion was the willingness to open one's home and share resources with other believers (Acts 16:15, 34; cf. John 4:40; Luke 19:1-10).
- "Able to teach" (*didaktikon*); one of the chief responsibilities of the overseer was to teach and to watch over the teaching in the church. In Timothy's setting, where false teaching was a clear and present danger, this ability was especially needed. Titus 1:9 reads, "[The overseer] must adhere firmly to the faithful message, as it has been taught, so that he is able to encourage by sound teaching and rebuke those who oppose it."
- "Not addicted to wine" (*mē paroinon*) is the first in a series of four virtues described with a negative. Drunkenness was one of the pervasive vices of ancient society. Wine was the liquid of preference, because safe drinking water was rare. Biblical admonitions aim at drunkenness, not drinking wine *per se* (see the discussion at Titus 1:7).
- "Not a bully" translates *mē plēktēn* (see the discussion at Titus 1:7). This virtue appears to go together with the two that follow, describing a single facet of character. Notice the contrast between these virtues and the descriptions of the false teachers in 1 Timothy 6:3-5 and 2 Timothy 2:22-26.
- "Courteous" (*epieikē*) refers to treating people with patience, tolerance, and kindness (see the discussion at Titus 3:2).
- "Not argumentative" (*amachon*) refers to someone who is not contentious or quick to argue or pick a fight (see the discussion at Titus 3:2).
- "Not a lover of money" (*aphilargyron*); "lover of money" refers to someone motivated primarily by a desire for monetary rewards. Greed is one of the sins of the false teachers (1 Tim 6:5). Titus 1:7 says that an overseer must not be *aischrokerdē*, "greedy" (see the discussion there).
- "Ruling well over his own household, with children who submit to his authority with all respect (for if someone cannot lead his own household, how will he care for the church of God?)" The family/household was the basic unit of Graeco-Roman society, and the proper management of one's household and family obligations was a cardinal virtue. "Ruling" translates *proistamenon*, from *proistēmi*. This word refers to governing, directing, or caring for or being devoted to something. "Ruling well" carries the idea of leading and caring for the family in a way that promotes health, virtue, and happiness. One sign of such a household was children who respectfully submit to authority. Thus the overseer must be able to lead in a way that produces respect, so that people will follow where he leads. The parenthetical question underscores the importance of this characteristic for the church, where people are best motivated by loyalty and altruism

(as opposed to a business, where profit and self-interest motivate). See the discussion at Titus 1:6, where the overseer's children must be "faithful" and "not open to the charge of being wasteful or rebellious."

- "Not a new convert, or he may become conceited, falling into the judgment of the devil"; "new convert" translates *neophyton*, from which we get our English word "neophyte." New converts thrust into positions of leadership "become conceited" (*typhōtheis*; see the discussion of the form *tetyphōmenoi* at 2 Tim 3:14 below), thereby incurring "the judgment of the devil." This last phrase may refer to the same judgment that the devil will suffer, thus "he will be condemned as the devil was." Or it may refer to a punishment that the devil executes, something akin to being "handed over to Satan" (1:20; see the discussion there).
- "It is particularly important that he have a good witness with outsiders, so that he will not fall into disgrace and the snare of the devil." The faith and practices of the overseer should be such that even those outside the household of faith are impressed by his irreproachable behavior. If his behavior is not irreproachable, then the overseer will "fall into disgrace." Again, Paul is centrally concerned with the witness of the church; overseers should conduct themselves so that outsiders will respect the church, and thereby be more open to hearing the gospel. When outsiders correctly accuse the church of wrongdoing, the gospel itself suffers a loss of honor. This is the "snare of the devil"; as with the previous point, the phrase is ambiguous.

Noteworthy is the fact that Paul here gives no attention to job descriptions, but focuses entirely on qualifications. Three areas of life must be considered, and the candidate must prove blameless in all three: faithfulness in the family, faithfulness in the church, and faithfulness in the community. The specific qualities mentioned add up to being "above reproach" in these areas. The fact that Paul pays no attention to job descriptions suggests that Timothy already knew what the overseers (and deacons) were supposed to do; of course, he also already knew what kinds of people they should be. Likely, Paul has in mind here leaders (or potential leaders) in the Ephesian congregations who do not measure up. The congregations, as Timothy or others read these instructions to them, would be taking the measure of these people, and considering the positive and negative effects that their leadership might have on the church and her witness.

Male and female deacons (3:8-13)

The New Testament church practiced a "division of labor" in their leadership. One group of leaders (the elders/overseers, apparently exclusively male) were in authority over the spiritual health of the church, and another group (the deacons, men and women) "served" the first group by carrying out their instructions and attending to more practical matters. The model for this division of labor is Acts 6:1-7, where the Apostles ask the church to choose seven men (Luke does not refer to them as "deacons") to oversee a particular benevolent ministry. This allowed the Apostles to devote themselves to prayer and preaching/teaching ("the ministry of the word," Acts 6:4). The roles of elders/overseers and deacons appear to have divided in much the same way.

"Deacon" comes from the Greek *diakonos*, "servant" or "minister" or "helper." Paul uses this word to describe himself and his coworkers (1 Cor 3:5; 2 Cor 3:6; Rom 16:1; Col 1:23; 4:7; cf. 1 Tim 4:6; 2 Tim 4:5). Again, as with "overseer," the word seems to refer to a function within the life of the church more than a specific office. And, as with "overseer," the word "deacon" came to refer to specific offices in the church at some point in the second century CE. As with the overseer, Paul gives no specific job description other than that suggested by the term itself. He assumes that the readers will know the function of deacons. His concern is with the qualifications that ensure faithful fulfillment of that function. "Deacons likewise [*hōsautōs*, referring back to the qualifications for elder/overseer] must be . . ." (3:8):

- "Respectful" (*semnous*): refers to something that is dignified, serious; related to *semnotēs*, 3:4.
- "Not insincere" (*mē dilogous*; *dilogos* would literally refer to "double speak"): they must mean what they say. As Jesus commanded, "Let your 'yes' mean 'yes,' and your 'no' mean 'no'" (Matt 5:37).
- "Not heavy drinkers"; not commanding abstinence, but moderation (cf. 3:3 and the discussion there).
- "Not greedy" (*mē aischrokerdeis*); this term refers to dishonest gain. Deacons were involved in practical areas of ministry, which may have included the administration of church money for ministry to needy persons. The temptation for embezzlement or other forms of "self-help" would present themselves. (Compare with 3:3 and Titus 1:7.)
- "Adhering to the mystery of the faith with clear conscience" (3:9). Here, Paul's focus shifts from personal qualities to matters of faith. Deacons must be wholly committed to (not just acquainted with) the teaching of the gospel. "Mystery" (*mysterion*) refers to something once hidden, now

revealed. "Of the faith" points to the gospel, the teaching of the church (*not* personal faith). The "mystery of the faith," what is revealed in the gospel, is God's plan for saving all people, Jews and Gentiles together, through Jesus Christ. "Clear conscience" here may refer to pure motivations (i.e., not serving for selfish reasons, self-aggrandizement, or financial gain). Or the phrase may be the equivalent of "without reservation."

As with the overseer, the deacon should have demonstrated readiness to assume such a role. Paul directs, "Examine them before letting them serve" (3:10). "Examine them" translates the imperative verb *dokimazesthōsan* (lit., "Let them be tested"). This testing/examination is a command, not an option. It may have taken the form of a period of observation and probation, or being shepherded by established leaders who walked the candidates through different situations and kinds of ministry. Paul continues, "Then let the ones who are blameless [*anegklētoi*] serve as deacons." *Anegklētoi* is synonymous with *anepilēmpton* (3:2; cf. Titus 1:6).

In 3:11, Paul changes topics to speak of "the women." A literal translation reads, "The women [*gynaikas*] likewise must be respectful, not slanderers . . ." (3:11). This verse has prompted great discussion and debate (Stiefel 1995, 442–57). The confusion springs from the fact that *gynē* can refer either to women in general or specifically to wives. The central question is whether *gynē* refers to

- the wives of the deacons (3:8-10);
- female deacons (women who are part of the same group as 3:8-10 but not necessarily married to the men in those verses); or
- a distinct group of female leaders, separate from the group in 3:8-10.

Some argue that the wives of deacons (and not a group of female leaders) are in view. They base their view on the following:

- Paul mentions deacons in 3:8 and again in 3:12; thus it seems more natural for 3:11 to speak of women attached to the men in 3:8-10 and 3:12ff, rather than a separate group.
- If this is a separate group/office, one would expect a more detailed description than this short sentence, nine words in length.
- Some argue further that (at least for the Pastoral Epistles) women are not allowed to exercise leadership or authority in the church (2:12). This letter would not commend women for a particular office in the church. This view is based on a misreading of *authenteō* in 2:12.

1 Timothy: The Nature of True and Faithful Ministry

Others argue that the wives of the deacons cannot be in view. They either argue that this verse refers to women serving as deacons, members of the same group as in 3:8-10; or they argue that these are women leaders who were part of a separate group. The argument against 3:11 referring to the wives of the deacons:

- Paul does not give any indication of the relationship between the women in 3:11 and the men in 3:8-10. For example, there is no possessive pronoun (such as *autōn*) or other marker attached to *gynē* to indicate that these women go along with these men in 3:8-10.
- No special qualifications are prescribed for the wives of overseers.
- The word "deacon" (*diakonos*) apparently did not have a feminine form or equivalent at this time. In Romans 16:1-2, Paul refers to Phoebe using the male form of the word, *diakonos*.

Those who argue that a separate group—not wives, not female deacons—is in view also point out the following:

- The word "likewise" (*hōsautōs*) has been used previously in the letter to change topics from one group of people to another (2:9; 3:8; cf. Titus 2:3, 6). Thus its presence here signals a similar change.

The argument against 3:11 referring to deacons' wives is persuasive. Thus option 1 above is ruled out. Paul here is talking about a group of women leaders in the church, and not just the wives of male leaders. The difference between options 2 and 3 depends too heavily on a later concept of church office, where titles and job descriptions became more official than functional. Thus we have translated the verse, "Likewise, the female deacons must be respectful, not slanderers, sober-minded, faithful in all things" (3:11). Because 3:8-10 and 3:12-13 deal with male deacons, the verse should be treated as a parenthesis.

These women must be

- "respectful"; translates *semnous*, the same word is applied to male deacons in 3:8;
- "not slanderers"; translates *mē diabolous* (see the discussion of this word at Titus 2:3 and 2 Tim 3:3).
- "sober-minded"; translates *nēphalious* (see the discussion of this word at Titus 2:2);

- "faithful in all things" here refers to having character that is dependable and trustworthy.

In 3:12, Paul applies qualifications to the deacons that he has already applied to the overseers, in much the same wording: "Deacons must be the husbands of one wife [cf. 3:2], ruling well over their children and their households" (cf. 3:4). He continues, "For those who serve well as deacons gain a good standing for themselves, along with much boldness in the faith which is in Christ Jesus" (3:13). Those who serve well receive two benefits. First, they "gain a good standing for themselves." Some take this to refer to advancement or promotion to a higher rank, such as becoming an overseer. It more likely refers to honor, influence, reputation and esteem within the church, although a shift from serving as a deacon to serving as an elder would be possible for some, depending on gifts and personality. Second, they gain "much boldness in the faith." The experience of serving God through serving the church, seeing God work and minister through their efforts, will give them confidence as they live lives of witness and as they continue in a faith relationship with Jesus Christ.

Faithful service produces a good standing. This standing may be in the sight of other people, or of God. The two are not necessarily the same. The kind of faithful service that God requires sometimes puts believers at odds with the world around them; witness Paul's persecutions and suffering (e.g., 2 Cor 11:23ff; 2 Tim 3:10-13; 4:5-8). For this reason, the New Testament teaches that praise from people is deceptive (John 12:42-43). But faithful service gives boldness, even in the face of hardship. Paul writes to the Philippians that his faithfulness, even when he was imprisoned, was giving his people "confidence in the Lord, because of my bonds, to speak the word even more fearlessly" (Phil 1:14).

Hymn Supporting Missionary Purposes (3:14-16)
In these verses, Paul further explains his purposes for the letter. He points back to 1:3 and the problem Timothy was left in Ephesus to face, explaining the rationale behind his paraenesis. He also inserts another hymn fragment that supports his missionary purposes.

Paul writes, "Hoping to come to you soon, I am writing these things to you so that, if I am delayed, you will know how our people should conduct themselves in the household of God" (3:14-15a). As noted in 1:3, Paul has been called away from Ephesus to deal with a problem in Macedonia. He hopes to return to Ephesus soon (or to be reunited with Timothy elsewhere?), but the problem in Macedonia has not yet been settled. Because his plans for the near future are still not clear, Paul writes "these things" (*tauta*) to Timothy. In the Pastoral Epistles, Paul uses *tauta* thirteen times, always to refer to instructions that he has just articulated (i.e., it is anaphoric, pointing back to what precedes; here, 4:6; 4:11; 4:15; 5:7; 5:21; 6:2; 6:11; 2 Tim 1:12; 2:2; 2:14; Titus 2:15; 3:8). "These things" (Paul's instructions in 2:1–3:13) relate to the way Paul's people "should conduct themselves in the household of God." Household language, applied to the church, emphasizes the likeness of the church with the human family. It stresses the close relationships between people in the community; they are an "in-group" to one another, and must bless and help and favor one another.

This household is "the church of the living God." The expression "living God" is used fifteen times in the Old Testament and another thirteen in the New Testament. Initially, it was used to distinguish the God of Israel from the lifeless idols worshiped by the surrounding nations. It describes a God who is both alive and at work in the world. Even more specifically, for Paul the phrase indicates that God is not only alive and at work in the world, he is also alive and at work in the lives of his people (Gal 2:20; Rom 8:5-14). Furthermore, the church is the "pillar and foundation of the truth" (3:15b). Paul moves from the family/household image to the closely related image of a house or building. Pillar (*stylos*) and foundation (*hedraiōma*) are architectural images. *Hedraiōma* is related to *hedra*, "sitting place," and the adjective *hedraios*, "fixed" or "immovable" (*TDNT*; cf. Paul's use of *themelios*, "foundation," in 1 Cor 3:10-15 and Eph 2:20). "Pillar" and "foundation" are both used metaphorically for something (or someone) that gives solidity, security, and stability. For Paul, the church, the household of faith, is essential to the proclamation and preservation of "the truth" (*alētheias*). Paul uses *alētheia* fourteen times in the Pastoral Epistles (1 Tim 2:4, 7 [twice]; here; 4:3; 6:5; 2 Tim 2:15, 18, 25; 3:7, 8; 4:4; Titus 1:1, 14). The word always refers to the gospel, either generically or specifically. Paul and Timothy are engaged in a critical struggle, in which false teachers challenge the truth of the gospel.

Next, Paul articulates key items of this truth: "By confession of all, great is the mystery of godliness" (3:16). "By confession of all" translates *homologoumenōs*, an adverb derived from *homologeō*. It refers to something that an entire group of people agree to or confess. In a liturgical setting (such as what is provided by the material that follows), the word could introduce a confession or creed. "Mystery of godliness" refers here to that which is revealed in the gospel; in biblical Greek, the word *mystarion* (lit., "mystery") focuses on the act of revealing, not concealing. Paul next expresses the mystery in the form of a creed or hymn:

> He was revealed in the flesh,
> Vindicated by the Spirit,
> Seen by angels,
> Preached among Gentiles,
> Believed on in the world,
> Taken up in glory

The middle lines of this poetic text—"seen by angels, preached among the Gentiles, believed on in the world"—support Paul's missionary purposes, the central motivation behind this large section (2:1–3:16). Paul is here using a creed or hymn, material that his people in Ephesus knew and sang or chanted together in worship regularly, to remind them of their commitment to supporting the spread of the gospel to people who were not like them or part of their circle.

As with most New Testament hymns, the subject is Christology. These lines share many of the characteristics of Graeco-Roman hymnody. The first line begins with the relative pronoun *hos*, translated more literally as "who was revealed" than "he was revealed." Further, the structure of the lines is repetitive:

- Every line begins with an aorist passive verb, and all the verbs end with the same *–thē* sound.
- In every line but one, the verb is followed by the preposition *en* ("in," "by," "among," "on," "with.") The exception is "Seen by angels."
- Every line ends with a dative case noun.

Notice also the topical movement from line to line:

- Incarnation ("He was revealed in the flesh");
- Resurrection ("Vindicated by the Spirit");
- The beginning of the gospel witness (or Jesus' heavenly reign; "Seen by angels");
- Working through the church ("Preached among Gentiles");
- Emergence of the community that bears his name ("Believed on in the world");
- Ascension ("Taken up in glory").

"Was revealed" translates *ephanerōthē*, a verb that refers to showing or revealing something. "In the flesh" points to Jesus' earthly ministry. Jesus' incarnation revealed the character of God, his plan for offering salvation to the world, now contained in the gospel.

"Vindicated by the Spirit" refers to the resurrection, which vindicated Jesus; in other words, it proved that Jesus was right all along, and those who opposed him were wrong. "By the Spirit" could also be translated "in the Spirit/spirit." We have translated this phrase to refer to the Holy Spirit, the power that raised Jesus from the dead (Rom 8:11; see also the Holy Spirit's presence in Jesus' baptism, Mark 1:9-11 par). This phrase could also be taken as a reference to Jesus' divine nature, which was proven through his resurrection (Rom 1:3-4), or it could be read to refer to Jesus' divine nature in contrast with his humanity (which would be the center of the preceding line). Thus Paul in these two lines would intend a contrast something like, "He was God incarnate" (Jesus' physical nature, his humanity), "Vindicated over all his enemies" (Jesus' divine/spiritual nature).

"Seen by angels" may be better translated "appeared to angels." "Angels" (*angelois*) translates the Greek word for messenger. By the first century, the word had come to be used to refer to heavenly messengers, messengers from God. The passive verb here translated "[was] seen" (*ōphthē*) is used throughout the New Testament to refer to some kind of heavenly appearance (the only exception is Acts 7:26). The passive verb is used in the following New Testament passages:

- Moses and Elijah appeared before the disciples at the transfiguration (Matt 17:3; Mark 9:4);
- "There appeared to them Moses and Elijah . . .";
- Angels appeared to Zechariah in the Temple (Luke 1:11), to Jesus in the garden (Luke 22:43), to Moses in the desert (Stephen's speech, Acts 7:30);
- Things appear in prophetic visions (Acts 16:9; Rev 11:19; 12:1, 3);
- God appeared to Abraham (Stephen's speech, Acts 7:2);
- The passive verb is most commonly used to refer to Jesus' appearances after his resurrection (Luke 24:34; Acts 13:31; 1 Cor 15:5, 6, 7, 8).

So then, what does Paul mean by "seen by angels"?

- He may be referring to the resurrection, the role angels played in announcing the event (Matt 28:1-7; Mark 16:5-8; Luke 24:4-7; John 20:12-13), and by extension the way the earliest church carried on the angels' witness to the resurrection (Acts 1:22; 2:32; 3:15; 4:33; 5:32; 10:41). This is the most likely reading.
- He may be referring to Jesus' ascension; on the heavenly throne, Jesus would be surrounded by the angelic court, ruling over all other powers (e.g., Col 2:10, 15; 1 Pet 3:22; Heb 1:4-6).

- He may be referring again to Jesus' earthly ministry, thus to the presence of angels at various events in Jesus' life—birth, baptism, temptation, etc.

"Preached among Gentiles" and "Believed on in the world" refer to the center of Paul's calling—apostle to the Gentiles (2:7). The witness of Jesus' resurrection, and the faith and transformation that it produces, were spreading over the world due to the faithful ministry of Paul and others like him.

"Taken up in glory" refers to Jesus' ascension. His ascension is into glory; in other words, at his ascension, Jesus returned to the privilege of sharing in the very nature and greatness of God himself, so that he is worthy of praise and adoration. During Jesus' prayer on the night of his arrest, he asks, "Father, now glorify me in your presence, with the glory I shared with you before the creation of the world" (John 17:5).

Summary. In the long section that runs from 2:1–3:16, Paul's central concern is the effectiveness of the message of the gospel. Nothing—no elitist or ethnocentric teaching (2:1-7), no private agendas or grudges (2:8), no "edgy" or potentially scandalous exercises of freedom (2:9-15), no poor or thoughtless choices as to who will lead (3:2-12, especially 3:7)—*nothing* can be allowed to stand in the way of that message reaching the largest number of people with integrity and effectiveness.

Related to Paul's concern for the effectiveness of the gospel and the church's witness is his concern for how his people live. Christian belief (orthodoxy) and behavior (orthopraxy) go hand in hand, two sides of the same coin (Matt 7:21; Mark 3:35; John 3:36; 13:17; 14:15, 23; Rom 1:5; 16:26; Eph 2:8-10; Heb 13:20-21; Jas 2:17; Rev 22:12-13). When the two are separated, or when one is emphasized to the detriment of the other, then the truth of the faith is obscured, and the believers' own devotion to God suffers shipwreck (1:19).

How to Do Ministry in the Last Days (4:1–6:10)

In this long section, Paul returns to his description of true and false teachers, true and false ministry (also the topic of 1:4-20). As with 1:4-20, the present section is structured around a chiasm:

A. False Teachers Contrasted with Paul and Timothy (4:1-5)
   B. How to Minister in the Last Days (4:6-16)

1 Timothy: The Nature of True and Faithful Ministry

B'. How to Treat Other Members of the Household of God (reverse *Haustafel*) (5:1–6:2)

A'. False Teachers Contrasted with Paul and Timothy (6:3-10)

False Teachers Contrasted with Paul and Timothy (4:1-5)

Here, Paul denounces the false teachers and their techniques and doctrines: "The Spirit explicitly says that, in the last times, some people will desert the faith by devoting themselves to deceitful spirits and demonic teachings" (4:1). "In the last times" refers to the entire age between Jesus' resurrection and his return. Biblically, the phrase "the last days" does not refer to some specific period immediately prior to the end. Rather, Jesus by his resurrection inaugurated the last days, and they continue until he returns, the *last* day (Heb 1:1). Christians now and always live in the last days. "Times" translates *kairos* rather than *chronos* (*kairos* focuses more on the nature of an event, e.g., "an opportune time"; *chronos* focuses more on the timing of the event). Thus Paul is concerned not with the calendar but with the season or era in which these things happen.

As Paul describes these last days, he focuses on their character. "Some people will desert the faith"; apostasy and tribulation characterize these days, and can be seen in the activities of those led astray by the false teachers (cf. 1:3-7). The verb "will desert" is future tense, but it refers to events both contemporary and future to the writer. "Desert" translates *apostēsontai* (from which we get the word, "apostasy"), which refers to "[distancing] oneself from some person or thing" (BDAG). Here, it refers to turning away from what is accepted by the church as good and true. Paul uses this same word in a positive sense in 2 Timothy 2:19, "Everyone who claims the name of the Lord must turn away from evil" (see the discussion of 2 Tim 2:19 below). Instead of deserting (repenting of) evil, these people will desert "the faith," the truths of the gospel, which Paul summarizes throughout these letters (e.g., 2:5-6 and 3:16).

In renouncing the truths of the Christian faith, these people are instead "devoting themselves to deceitful spirits and demonic teachings." "Devoting themselves" translates *prosechō*, which includes both mental assent and active adherence—they don't just listen or accept, they live out these teachings. The spirits are "deceitful" (*planois*), and the teachings have a demonic source. "Spirits" and "demons" may be parallel, thus rendering the phrase "the deceitful teachings of demonic spirits." Further, these people devote themselves to these teachings because of the false teachers, "the hypocrisy of liars who have seared their own consciences" (4:2). Hypocrites are "play actors," pretending to be what they are not (cf. 1:7). "Conscience" (*suneidēsin*) refers to the moral compass, the ability to distinguish between right and wrong, acceptable and unacceptable. "Seared" translates *kekaustēriasmenōn*, from which the English verb "cauterize" is taken. The image here is that these people's consciences once operated properly, so that they knew the difference between right and wrong. But through constant choosing of the wrong, they have rendered their consciences inoperative. Another possible reading of this verb is that their consciences are branded, either to indicate their guilt (criminals were sometimes branded as punishment) or to show the mark of their true owner and master, Satan (Knight 1992, 189).

Paul spotlights two of the false teachers' teachings: "prohibiting marriage and teaching abstinence from foods" (4:3). The specific nature of these teachings is impossible to discern; "abstinence from foods" could refer to strict vegetarianism, or eating as little food as possible, or refraining from eating at particular times or seasons. As is evident in other letters, Paul's churches dealt from time to time with pseudo-spiritual asceticism (e.g., Col 2:16; 1 Cor 7:1-7). Paul does recommend abstinence from some foods in certain situations, so as not to offend the weaker members of the church (Rom 14:13-23; 1 Cor 6:7-13; cf. Col 2:20-23). He likewise commends abstinence from marriage or marital sex in certain settings (1 Cor 7:5, 8-9). The false teachings about diet may have been based on Old Testament dietary laws, but there is no clear indication. Or they may have been based on popular Hellenistic thought, which denigrated the physical in favor of the spiritual, and so sometimes taught extreme physical self-discipline. The reasoning ran, if the physical universe is evil in and of itself, then truly spiritual people should avoid involvement with it as much as they can. Thus the more one withdraws from the world into an ascetic life, the closer one is to the life that God intended. Abstinence from foods and marriage (therefore from sex) would be practical results of such a view.

But "those who believe and know the truth" know that God created such things "to be received with thanksgiving." The repetitiveness in 4:3b-4 is emphatic. Paul here alludes to Genesis 1, where God declares seven times that what he has made is good (see especially Gen 1:31). Everything God created is good; therefore, nothing is to be "rejected" (4:4). "Rejected" (*apoblēton*) refers to "throwing something away." Paul continues, "nothing is to be rejected if received with thanksgiving; for it is sanctified by God's word and prayer" (4:4-5). The reiteration of "thanksgiving" (*eucharistias*, 4:3 and 4:4) emphasizes the importance of gratitude as a motivator and guide for good behavior.

Paul's view of creation is thoroughly Jewish. The material world is not evil; and while asceticism may not be wrong in and of itself, the denial of creation's goodness that often accompanies it is wrong, for "everything God created is good." Biblical cosmology calls on believers to celebrate God's good creation, and to treat it responsibly as stewards of God's possession (Gen 2:15).

In 4:5, Paul gives a second reason why everything created by God is good. "It is sanctified by God's word and prayer" (4:5). To be "sanctified" is to be set apart for God's use; *hagiazō* ("sanctify") comes from *hagios* ("holy"), which primarily refers not to "super-saintliness" but to being set apart to belong to God, usually with some kind of sacrificial sense in the background. "God's word" refers to Genesis and the pronouncements of goodness there (Gen 1, all creation; 2:23-25, marriage and marital sexuality).

The mention of the "last times" (4:1) introduces an eschatological, even apocalyptic, note into Paul's instructions. Paul believed that he and his fellow believers were living in the last days, the period preceding the return of Christ. This time would be marked by a great apostasy, when false teachers would lead many people astray (e.g., see 2 Tim 3:1-5; 4:3-4). In these verses, Paul speaks of some who have renounced the faith by following evil, deceitful teachings of demonic origin, led by hypocritical liars whose consciences are so scarred that they no longer function. The deceptive nature of rebellion against God is in view here; as Paul describes it, humanity has "exchanged the truth of God for a lie" (Rom 1:25) and chosen to live on the basis of that lie. As a result, the foundation on which human lives and societies are built is an illusion, the truth turned upside down. In Christ, God came to turn things right-side-up again.

Ministry in the Last Days (4:6-16)

The apocalyptic tone of 4:1-5 gives urgency to Paul's continuing instructions to Timothy. "By teaching these things to the brothers and sisters, you will be a good minister of Christ Jesus" (4:6). Again, "these things" (*tauta*) is anaphoric (cf. 3:14). "Teaching" translates *hypotithemenos*, which is literally "to lay something down" (e.g., Priscilla and Aquila "risked [*hypethēkan*] their lives" for Paul, Rom 16:4); here, the word refers to "laying down" (or explaining) teaching or instruction (as in Plato, *Hipp Maj* 286b; BDAG). For "minister" (*diakonos*), see the discussion above at 3:8-13.

To be a good minister of Christ Jesus, Timothy needs to be "trained in the words of the faith and the good teaching which [he had] followed." "Trained" (*entrephomenos*) refers to raising children, and includes all the activities that have to do with raising a child. The word is a present participle, implying that this training is an ongoing process (lifelong learning) rather than something in the past, or something one can finish. In the expression, "words of the faith," a definite article precedes *pistis* ("faith"); this suggests that Paul is referring to Timothy's knowledge of the content of the gospel, the essence of the Christian message, and all it implies and produces, rather than his personal devotion to Christ. "Good teaching" (*kalēs didaskalias*) also refers to the Christian message. The two phrases work together; "words of the faith" focuses on the content of the gospel message, and "good teaching" may emphasize the way the message is delivered and administered. Paul here again highlights the importance of the community of faith; Timothy received the sound teaching from those who were in Christ before him, and now hands that teaching on to others (2 Tim 2:2; 3:14-17). Church leaders cannot function apart from the communion of the saints.

Paul further instructs Timothy: "Reject those myths, profane and old-womanly" (4:7). "Profane" (*bebēlous*) refers to being devoid of anything divine or religious (see the discussion above at 1 Timothy 1:9). Paul further denigrates these myths by referring to them as "old-womanly" (*graōdeis*). This expression was frequently used by the philosophers to describe empty teaching or speech. For example, Plato describes shallow, superficial, "pop-psychology" reasoning about virtue and vice as *graōn hythlos*, "old woman's chatter" (*Theat* 176b; see also *Rep* 1.3501; *Gorgias* 527a; *Strabo* 1.2.3). In this way, Paul describes the false teachers' myths (and other teachings that might distract Timothy from the true gospel and the work that accompanies it) as irreligious (profane) and without value. Timothy must reject these myths, and instead "train [himself] in godliness." "Train" translates *gymnaze*, which can refer to athletic exercise and preparation, or metaphorically to discipline in a particular area of life. The verb is a present imperative, which stresses the necessity of ongoing, continuous action. Thus training in godliness is not a short-term project; it is a lifelong endeavor. "Godliness" is a major theme in the Pastoral Epistles. It refers to a proper attitude toward God, and the life that results from this attitude. A godly life is a life lived in and from reverence for God.

"For training the body has some value, but godliness has great value, holding promise for the present life and the life to come" (4:8). This comparison employs a traditional "from the lesser to the greater" argument. "Training the body has some value"; indeed, physical training and perfection were highly prized in the Graeco-Roman world. But their value was limited, holding promise only for this life. Thus they cannot compare to the value of exercise that leads to godliness, the value of which is not limited, for it benefits a person both in this life and the next. This "life" is the kind of eternal, abundant life that God has promised to his people. It begins in this life and continues into eternity.

In 4:9-10, Paul gives a theological foundation for his claims regarding the benefits of spiritual training. He writes, "This saying is faithful, and worthy of full acceptance; for this we labor and struggle: 'We have put our hope in the living God, who is the Savior of all people,' namely all who believe" (4:9-10). The introductory formula is identical to 1:15. There is some debate over whether the phrase points ahead to 4:10 or back to 4:8. Towner argues that it points back to 4:8, and that the faithful saying is "Training of the body has some value, but godliness has great value" (Towner 2006, 309; cf. J. B. Phillips, NET). Roloff argues that all of 4:10 is in view, based on the use of *gar* ("for") in that verse (compare 2 Tim 2:11; Roloff 1998, 240). But more likely, the *hoti* in 4:10 (after "struggle") introduces the quotation ("we have put"), which is 4:10b. Further, the saying in 4:10b fits the thematic patterns of the "faithful sayings" better than any part of 4:8.

Thus "for this [i.e., on the basis of the following truth] we labor and struggle: 'We have put our hope in the living God.'" "Labor" (*kopiōmen*) and "struggle" (*agōnizometha*) are synonyms, the first referring to hard work and the second to intense effort spent against some obstacle or opponent. The labor and struggle Paul has in mind are his work for the church (cf. Col 1:24, "I rejoice in my sufferings on your behalf, and by them am completing in my body what was lacking in the sufferings of Christ on behalf of his body, the church"). Labor and struggle were (and remain) part of the calling to ministry; a quick glance at Paul's litany of sufferings (2 Cor 11:22-28) makes this clear. Nevertheless, he and those who struggled at his side (including Timothy) had placed "put [their] hope" in God. "We have put our hope" translates *ēlpikamen*, a perfect tense form of *elpizō*. The perfect tense emphasizes an action in the past that continues to be in effect. "Hope" is a confident expectation for the future, an expectation based in evidence and experience—not just wishful thinking. Paul's confidence is based in his experience with the object of his hope, "'the living God, who is the Savior of all people,' especially all who believe." The focus in Paul's description of God is on the universality of his (God's) saving action; in Judaism, the phrase "living God" emphasized that there was only one real God and creator of the whole earth, of every tribe and nation. Now this one God wants to offer his salvation to everyone. Yet this salvation must be accepted by making a faith commitment to God through Jesus Christ, acceptance of the offer is not automatic.

In 4:11-16, Paul continues his instructions to Timothy with a series of ten imperatives. "Command and teach these things" (4:11). "Command" translates *parangelle* (cf. the same word in 1:3, "Remain in Ephesus so that you may command certain people to stop teaching false doctrines"). Both "command" and "teach" are present imperatives, which refer to an ongoing, continuing task. "These things" (*tauta*) could refer to the entire letter to this point, or 4:1-10 (or 4:7-10, etc.).

The next verse reminds Timothy of how big his task is: "Do not let anyone treat you with contempt because you are young" (4:12). Timothy's task in Ephesus is to face down false teachers who seem to be entrenched in the church, with broad support in the church (as opposed to Titus, where the false teachers appear to be outsiders or on the fringe). As Timothy teaches and commands the instructions Paul is handing to him, his opponents may well belittle him. We have no way of knowing Timothy's age, but he was younger than Paul and also (no doubt) younger than many of the believers in Ephesus. In the first-century culture, young people were expected to defer to the wisdom of older people—even when the older people were wrong, or deceived by false teachers, and so on. Thus Paul writes to shore up Timothy's authority, as both Timothy and the members of the Ephesian church who listened to this letter being read would have understood. Paul challenges them to support Timothy, and Timothy to refuse to let the rebels scoff at him. Further, Timothy must set an example that fleshes out his message for all to see. Talk is cheap until realized and made concrete. Age is not, in and of itself, the criterion for leadership. As the qualifications lists show, character was most highly to be prized, above even age and talents. Timothy must live out that character, be an "example in words, in behavior, in love, in faithfulness, and in purity." "Example" (*typos*) originally referred to an identifying mark, perhaps something that indicated ownership. It comes to refer to a model or pattern to be followed (BDAG). Timothy is to offer such a pattern in:

- the words he speaks; no careless or thoughtless words;
- his conduct, the life he lives, and the way he interacts with others;
- his love for God and others;
- his faithfulness and dependability, both with Paul's commands and with the secrets and best interests of others;
- his purity, the uprightness and moral character of his life.

If Timothy was slack in any of these areas, or let down his guard, he would harm the people to whom he ministered. He would also be inviting rebellion against and opposition to the corrections Paul wanted to make in Ephesus.

The words people speak and the claims they make are fleshed out in the lives they live. In a world where scandal was entertainment, believers' words and actions were to be characterized by love, faithfulness, and purity. In a letter that focuses so centrally on the example that Christians set, and how that example affects the hearing the gospel receives, we should not be surprised to see Timothy commanded to live a life of example that does not hurt his own work and witness.

Until Paul arrives, he commands Timothy to "devote" himself to three activities that characterize the minister's role in worship (4:13). "Devote" translates *proseche*, "to pay close attention to" or "apply oneself to" something. The things Timothy is to devote himself to include

- "the public reading of scripture," the use of the Old Testament in corporate worship. At this time, the only opportunity most people had to encounter Scripture was when it was read publicly. It was and remains important for believers to be biblically literate: "Faith comes from what is heard, and what is heard comes through the speaking of the word of Christ" (Rom 10:17; see also 2 Tim 3:14-17).
- "exhortation" (*paraklēsei*), encouragement that involves challenge, instruction, and practical admonition aimed at faithfulness.
- "teaching," guiding others to grow in faith by explaining and applying the Scriptures that have been read.

Timothy is not without resources in these pursuits. "Do not neglect the spiritual gift that is in you" (4:14). "Gift" (*charismatos*) refers to Timothy's spiritual gift. The specific gift is not mentioned, although it no doubt relates directly to his ministry in Ephesus; teaching or prophecy or encouragement would make sense. This gift was given to Timothy "through [or confirmed by] prophecy, accompanied by the laying on of hands by the elders." The parallel with 1:18 (and similarities and differences with 2 Tim 1:6) suggests that Timothy was "ordained" on at least two different occasions. The event this passage speaks of was the first, when he was ordained by a group of elders (perhaps from his home church, Lystra) when he began his ministry. Subsequently, Timothy was set apart again, for a deeper or more specific ministry; this is the event of 2 Timothy 1:6. Ancient Mediterranean readers would have seen this as a succession event, where both task and power to accomplish it pass from leader to successor. In Numbers 27:18-23, Moses (in obedience to direction from God) laid hands on Joshua in the presence of all the congregation of Israel to indicate that Joshua was to succeed him in leading the people. After this event, Joshua was filled with the spirit of wisdom (Deut 34:9). From this and other examples (see Stepp, 2005), early Christians adopted a similar ceremony that marked their acceptance of God's choice of persons for specific roles and asked for the Spirit to enable and guide them (Acts 6:6; 13:3; cf. 8:16-19; 9:17; 14:23; 19:5-6). The Spirit through the church has gifted Timothy in the same way, and Paul's admonition to him is clear; he must not "neglect" (*amelei*, lit., "disregard," "ignore," "pay no attention to") his gift, but must continually use and depend on it as he carries out his ministry.

The opening of 4:15 repeats the verb from 4:14 (*ameleō*, "neglect") in a positive form: Timothy must "continue to do these things" (4:15). "Continue" translates *meleta*, an imperative form of *ameleō*'s opposite. *Meletaō* refers to meditating on something, continuing to think about or practice something. The word implies more than a casual occupation with something; it refers to an ongoing pattern of behavior or action. Timothy must "wrap [himself] up in them"; this phrase translates *en toutois isthi*, literally "be in them," "become immersed in them," "become absorbed in these things." Timothy must make Paul's priorities and teachings his obsession and constant focus "so that [his] progress in them will be evident to everyone." This repeats the idea of example from 4:12. People will be watching Timothy, waiting to see if he is true or false. His life must be a model of what becomes of a person who is obsessed with pleasing and serving God: how much love, grace, and faithfulness God can produce.

One final pair of admonitions rounds out the section. The first is, "Be very careful about your own conduct and what you teach" (4:16). This admonition repeats the language and theme of 4:11. Again, both Timothy's teaching (and ministry) and his way of life are the test of his faithfulness and the basis of his credibility. He must walk the walk as well as talk the talk. This instruction bears repeating because, if Timothy perseveres in "these things . . . [he] will save both [himself] and those who listen to [him]." Timothy's immediate "salvation" is from false teachers and the dangers posed by their teachings, but in the end the phrase does refer to the ultimate salvation of both Timothy and his people. Timothy is not the agent of salvation, but he is the means by which God continues his saving work. "Those who listen" (*tous akouontas*) was a technical term referring to the devoted followers of a teacher, his disciples. If Timothy is faithful with the instructions Paul has given, then those who attack the church (cf. Acts 20:28-32) will fail in their attempts to pull people away from salvation. God will work through Timothy's faithfulness to guard and keep them.

How to Treat Other Members of the Household of God (5:1–6:2)

The next part of this large section resembles the adaptation of the household code above (2:8–3:13). A unique feature of 5:1–6:2 is that the code is "reversed"; instead of focusing on what Timothy should teach to the other members of the household of God (*their* actions and responsibilities; see 2:8–3:13; Titus 2:1-10), this section focuses on Timothy's own actions and responsibilities toward different groups in the household. Church leaders must serve and minister to all the people under their care; thus Paul's instructions for Timothy focus on a broad spectrum of people. The groups addressed are

- Older and younger believers, male and female (5:1-2);
- Widows (5:3-16);
- Elders (5:17-25);
- Slaves (6:1-2).

Older and younger believers, male and female (5:1-2). Paul begins: "Do not speak harshly to an older man, but encourage him as a father" (5:1). "Older man" (*presbyterō*) uses the same word translated "elder" in Titus 1, but here refers to any man in (or around) his fifties (see the age ranges for *presbyteros* described in the discussion of Titus 2:1). Timothy is to not "speak harshly" to such men when they are in the wrong. "Speak harshly" translates *epiplēxēs*, which can refer to physically striking out, or striking out with words (BDAG). Timothy must instead "encourage" (*parakalei*) these men, gently correcting and exhorting them toward the right path. Timothy must also treat these men like a son would treat his father; the wisdom that they have gleaned from their experiences can be a source of support and direction for Timothy, if he is willing to listen and use it wisely. Likewise the older women in 5:2a, whom Timothy must view as mothers: in both cases, Timothy is to consider them "family" and treat them with care and respect. Toward the younger men, Timothy is to act like a brother (compare the directions to Titus in 2:6-9). Timothy is further to treat the younger women like sisters. Ever mindful of the potential for scandal, Paul admonishes Timothy to act toward these women "in absolute purity." "Purity" (*hagneia*) refers to propriety and moral cleanness in actions and intentions. Timothy is to take care that nothing impure or questionable passes between him and the younger women of his churches.

Widows (5:3-16). Timothy must see that the church "honors the widows who truly are widows" (5:3). "Honor" (*tima*) has a double meaning, implying both respect and financial support. The "widows who truly are widows" are those who are left alone, with no means of support outside the Christian community. The care for such widows was a prominent concern throughout the Old Testament. As Acts 6 makes clear, the earliest church also took this responsibility seriously; in fact, questions about how widows were to be cared for led to the first major crisis in the life of the Jerusalem church.

Paul restricts such care to widows who have no hope of support from their families; either they have no families, or their families disregard them due to their faith in Christ. If the widow has family who are Christians, then the family "must first practice their religion toward their own household" by caring for the widow. "Practice religion" translates *eusebeō*, the verbal form of *eusebeia*, "godliness." The verb refers to honoring God and fulfilling one's obligations to him. In this case, the first obligation of a believer is to honor God by honoring and caring for family members who are in need. In so doing, children "repay their parents what they owe them." In many cultures, the idea of repaying parents is prominent, since it is believed that the children owe their lives to their parents. For Paul, fulfilling this obligation to parents is part of fulfilling one's obligation to God, and thus "is pleasing to God," in the same way as an acceptable sacrifice or appropriate act of worship.

In 5:5, Paul returns to the "real widow." Because she has no family to provide for her, and is truly left all alone, she "sets her hope on God, and continues in her petitions and prayers night and day" (5:5). She has come to trust in God completely and depend on him alone. This is evidenced by a life of regular and continuous prayer; prayer has become a regular part of her nights and days. In the Greek text, the words translated "petitions" (*deēsesin*) and "prayers" (*proseuchais*) both have the definite article, which suggests that they represent two separate but related aspects of prayer. Perhaps "prayers" is used in a generic sense and "petitions" refers specifically to requests made on behalf of others (cf. 2:1). In the New Testament, dependence on God and dependence on the community of faith are synonymous, for the church is God's presence in the world (cf. the story of Ruth, where God's primary means of acting is through the faithfulness of his people). Paul here highlights the church's responsibility to care for the needs of its own (cf. Acts 2:34-37; 4:32-34; 6:1-6).

In contrast to the godly widow, Paul describes the self-indulgent widow. She "lives indulgently" (*spatalōsa*): this word is used again in James 5:5 to describe the sins of wealthy people who live without regard for God or the needs of others (cf. Ezek 16:49 LXX, Sir 21.15). Paul continues, "Even though she lives, she has already died" (5:6). The goal of these commands is that "they may be beyond reproach" (5:7). *Tauta* here points back to the commands that precede it, although Paul will add other instruction on this same topic in the following verses. "They" could refer to the widows; thus Timothy is to admonish them so that they will live in ways that honor God.

Or it could refer to the church that offers support to the godly widows. Again, Paul's concern is that the church's reputation be such that the world around it is willing to hear its witness. Or "they" could even refer to the families of the widows; the next verse appears to point in this direction.

"If someone does not provide for his own, especially his immediate family, he has denied the faith and is worse than a nonbeliever" (5:8). "Provide" translates *phronoei*, and refers to being materially responsible for someone's care. When a believer refuses to provide materially for family members who are in need, they have "denied the faith" by making a mockery of their claim to belong to Jesus Christ. They do this by refusing to show the same kind of sacrificial love that Jesus showed, and in a particularly egregious way—again, one that would damage the witness of the church, since Graeco-Roman society viewed caring for one's family as a grave responsibility. The one who refuses this responsibility is, therefore, "worse than a nonbeliever." Paul uses the word translated "nonbeliever," *apistos*, to refer to those who do not trust Christ and refuse to acknowledge his lordship (1 Cor 6:6; 7:15; 10:27; 14:22, 23; 2 Cor 4:4; 6:14-15; cf. Luke 12:46). Here, Paul says that even worse than a nonbeliever are so-called believers who do not fulfill their responsibilities to their families.

Paul returns to the widows to whom the church should offer support. "Do not put a widow on the list for support unless . . ." (5:9). This appears to be a reference to a group of older women in the church who not only received financial support from the church but also functioned in some leadership capacity in the congregation. As with overseers and deacons (1 Tim 3), Paul focuses on the character of these women; Titus 2:3-5 may offer a partial description of their responsibilities. (For a full study of the office of widows, see Thurston 1989; Winter 1988, 83–99; Winter 2003, 123–40). Paul sets out the criteria for enrollment. The first four items are specific activities, the last a generalized summary.

- "At least sixty years old," regarded here as past the age for remarriage and raising children (see 5:11, 14);
- "The wife of one husband"; this criterion may be taken to rule out remarriage after divorce or the death of an earlier spouse. It more likely focuses on her faithfulness to her husband rather than the number of husbands she has had. In the new Roman cities, it was customary for men to be fifteen to twenty years older than their wives; consequently, there were many widows of marriageable age (Witherington 1995, 173–81; Winter 2003, 125).
- "With a reputation for good works"; see the discussion at 2:10.

- Having "raised children"; her demonstrated ability to provide for the needs of her children, material or otherwise, shows her fitness for service in the church (cf. 1 Tim 3:4-5).
- Having shown hospitality; *exenodochēsen* refers to treating a stranger as a guest, either during her life prior to widowhood or even in her poverty since. Hospitality was a cardinal virtue in the earliest church; see the discussion at 1 Timothy 3:2.
- Having served the saints (lit., "if she washes the feet of the saints"); washing feet was a task usually relegated to a servant or slave. If taken literally, this qualification indicates that these women were willing to perform this service for other Christians. If understood figuratively, it means that the widow in question was willing to perform menial tasks in service of her fellow believers.
- "Helping [*epērkesen*] those in trouble"; this word likely refers to giving materially to help others, either before becoming a widow or even in her poverty since.
- "Having devoted herself to good works"; this qualification seems to be a summary of the preceding characteristics. The verb *epēkolouthēsen* ("devoted oneself to") implies a serious pursuit.

Timothy must refuse to enroll younger widows onto the list for support and responsibility, for several reasons. They may be overcome by their desires so that they want to marry. The Greek verb *katastrēniaō* refers to being "governed by strong physical desire" (BDAG), and speaks particularly of sexual desires. These desires alienate them from their pledge to Christ (assuming they were enrolled on the list) and cause them to want to marry. To marry would violate their commitment to staying single in return for the church's support and their full-time service (5:11-12). They also "learn to be idle" (5:13). The verb translated "learn" (*manthanousin*) is a present indicative verb, which may imply that this was an ongoing concern; perhaps it could be translated "they are learning," i.e., such activity is already going on and must be dealt with, the situation has already arisen. Paul is not hypothesizing here, this situation is already a problem in the Ephesian church. "Idle" (*argai*) refers to deliberate wasting of time, habitual refusal to engage in meaningful activity. Furthermore, these women are already apparently running around "from house to house" rather than focusing their time and attention on their own households or on the important work of the church. They had become "gossips [*phlyaroi*] and meddlers [*periergoi*], talking about things they should not talk about." "Gossip" (*phlyaros*) refers to meaningless talk, nonsensical and irrational; *phlyō* refers to bubbling over or "overflowing with words" (LSJ), babbling. "Meddling" refers to someone insinuating themselves into someone else's life, where they don't belong. It implies a kind of manipulation. Further, their talk itself is destructive, and has a negative effect on the life of the church community by damaging relationships, in and outside the church.

Paul would prefer for young widows "to marry and have children and manage a household" (5:14). These would be appropriate and acceptable activities for women in the first-century Graeco-Roman world, enabling the young widows to contribute to society, in a way that helps (and does not harm) the church's witness. Paul again voices the motivation behind such instructions: this would "give those who oppose us no opportunity for slander" (cf. 2:1-15, 3:14-16). Next, Paul makes clear how serious this possibility is: "some have already turned aside to follow after Satan" (5:15). A group of women from the church has turned away from the faith, rejecting the gospel, and are influencing people to follow the same course, saying things they should not be saying.

The instructions in 5:15 and 2:11-15 arise from a single issue, a real (not hypothetical or potential) problem in the Ephesian church. The basis of these instructions is not gender. The problems Paul is addressing have been exacerbated and promulgated by young women, but the tendencies and attitudes at the root of the problem are not female, they are human. The influence of false teachers has caused "some to turn away to follow Satan." These people are spreading deception based on the false teaching, "saying what they should not say." They have essentially become mouthpieces of the false teachers. And remember also that "false teachers" seldom would apply that term to themselves. Perhaps these young women were busy, running around "from house to house," in service of the false truths they had learned.

In the final verse in the paragraph, Paul returns to the topic of caring for the widows. He focuses on the widows' families, and particularly the adult females who are believers in the widows' families. He writes, "If any believing woman has widows in her family, then she must provide for them" (5:16). Providing for family members in need is not a suggestion or recommendation; it is a command. Providing for family members who are truly in need assures that the church is "not burdened," so that it may focus on assisting those who do *not* have families or other means of support, those who truly are widows and all alone.

Elders (5:17-25). Next, Paul takes up several matters concerning elders (*presbyteroi*, which we regard as interchangeable with "overseer" [*episkopos*]; see the discussion at Titus 1:7). The New Testament uses this term several times to refer to leaders in the church (Acts 11:30; 14:23; Titus 1:5; 2 John

1; 3 John 1). In Acts 14:23, Paul and Barnabas appointed elders in every church established on their first missionary journey (Acts 13–14). In Titus 1:5, Paul urges his delegate to "appoint elders in every town." The role was borrowed from Judaism, where leaders in secular or religious roles were designated by this title (cf. Mark 8:31; 11:27; 14:23; 14:1). The title was applied to these leaders because they were normally chosen from among the older members of the community. While age (which normally brought respect) was a factor in the Christian use of the term, the primary idea is that of occupying a responsible position of leadership rather than chronological age.

The verb translated "rule" in 5:17 (*proestōtes*, from *proistēmi*) more properly refers to guiding, directing, leading. Those elders who carry out this charge well deserve "double honor" (*diplēs timēs*): this expression refers to financial support, as shown by the quotes in 5:18 and the use of *timē* in 5:3 to refer to financial support for the widows. "Double honor" might imply greater financial support than they currently receive, or it might imply that though they were being compensated, they were not receiving the honor and respect due to them. This double honor is especially due those who "labor in preaching [lit., "the word," *logos*] and teaching." "Preaching" here refers to proclaiming the gospel message, both to believers (for encouragement, etc.) and especially to nonbelievers. "Teaching" refers more specifically to instructing believers in matters of faith and practice. Both practices are essential for healthy churches. The fact that Paul mentions these specific practices may indicate that other elders had other responsibilities in the church (administration, pastoral care, etc.).

Paul supports this admonition with two quotations, one from the Old Testament and one from the words of Jesus in Luke. The introductory phrase, "the scripture says," which governs both quotes, indicates that by the time of writing the words of Jesus were accepted as sacred Scripture alongside the Scriptures of Israel, the Old Testament. The first quotation is from Deuteronomy 25:4, where the law prevented muzzling an ox while it was threshing grain. The point of this prohibition is that oxen need to be nourished while they work, and should be fed from their labors. Similarly, Paul suggests that these Christian leaders should receive their maintenance from their own labors. He made the same argument, quoting the same Old Testament text, in 1 Corinthians 9:8-12. The second quote, "The worker deserves his wages," comes from Jesus' words in Luke 10:7. The point is self-evident; workers should be paid for the work they do. The congregation must compensate its elders fairly. Those who carry out their roles faithfully, who devote much time to the congregation (when they could have spent it on income-producing activities), should be doubly honored, especially those involved in the demanding, labor-intensive activities of preaching and teaching. An echo of Acts 6:1-6 can be heard here; there, the apostles (being preachers and teachers) needed time to devote themselves to studying the word and praying, so that they could properly do their work. So also the elders here; their financial needs were met so that they might work to help the community as it ministered to the needs of others.

Paul next turns to the matter of erring elders (5:19). The principle of requiring two or three witnesses to convict someone of wrongdoing was established in the Old Testament law (e.g., Deut 19:15), and is clearly an attempt to protect the innocent against false accusations. Those in leadership might face attacks and accusations from people unhappy with decisions the leaders had made. Timothy and his church were to afford these leaders protection against these questionable assaults. Elders were not to "get a free pass" if the accusations were based in fact, however. Those who had indeed sinned (or those who persisted in sin after the offense was uncovered; the present participle *hamartanontas* emphasizes ongoing or habitual action) should be rebuked (*elegche*, which also occurs in 2 Tim 4:2; Titus 1:9, 13; 2:15) in front of the church, so that all the church will know and accept the seriousness of sin and the need for leaders who are "above reproach" (3:2; cf. Titus 1:6). The humiliation of such a rebuke would also discourage other leaders from similar behavior. (See also the discussion of church discipline at Titus 3:10 and 1 Tim 1:19.)

Having set down "these things" (*tauta*), Paul uses an oath formula in 5:21 to emphasize their seriousness and gravity. He reminds Timothy that he is in the presence "of God and of Christ Jesus and of the elect angels," all of whom he calls to witness these words. The language has a liturgical ring to it, and may come from the worship of the Pauline churches. In worship, it is as if the heavens are opened and the worshipers see God on his throne, Christ Jesus at his right hand, and the angels in attendance (Isaiah 6; Revelation 5–6). The combination of these elements in an oath is found only here in the New Testament, as is the phrase "elect angels" (*eklektōn angelōn*). The adjective *eklektos* is derived from the verb, "to choose." The implication is that these angels, who are the chosen messengers of God, are witnesses to these instructions. Because the entire heavenly court is watching, Timothy must "keep" (*phylaxēs*) these commands and teachings "without prejudice, doing nothing from partiality." Paul uses *phylassō* five times in the Pastoral Epistles; four of the five deal with the way instructions and traditional material are received and treasured (here; 6:20; 2 Tim 1:12, 14; cf. 2 Tim 4:15).

Paul continues his instructions regarding elders with a clear warning. "Do not be hasty in the laying on of hands" (5:21). This instruction refers to the New Testament practice of setting people apart for leadership by ordination (the laying on of hands). Timothy must be careful about the kinds of people he places in leadership. It is important that they measure up to the standards of belief and character that would enable them to lead faithfully. Paul continues: "nor participate in the sins of others; keep yourself pure." The connector *mēde* ("nor," or "and do not") does not introduce new topics, but always points back to a preceding prohibition. This connector indicates that this command is connected with the command about being deliberate in the choice of leaders. Thus if Timothy hastily chooses people for leadership without first proving their character, and those leaders subsequently commit gross or damaging sins against the church (such as sexual sins, introducing heresy, stealing money), then Timothy has participated in those sins and bears some responsibility for the damage done.

Paul inserts personal instructions in 5:23, in a brief parenthetical digression. "Do not drink only water, but use a little wine because of your stomach and your frequent illnesses" (5:23). Perhaps Timothy has stomach problems that are related to the stress brought on by hastily chosen leaders? At any rate, fermented wine was used in water to purify it for drinking; remember, safe drinking water was often not available in the ancient world. The care of the church leader begins with the leader taking care.

After the digression, Paul returns to the problem of hastily chosen leaders, and the necessity of proving someone's character over time before entrusting responsibility to them (5:24-25). Some people have obvious character issues that make them unfit for leadership; such people's sins "precede them to judgment" (judgment over their character; salvation is likely not in view here). But other people appear to be of high character at first, and their true colors appear only over time. "There is nothing hidden that will not be revealed, nor anything secret that will not become known" (Luke 8:17); "Be sure that your sin will find you out" (Num 32:23). But if Timothy will continue to prayerfully watch, and not be in a rush to push responsibilities onto people, then the good works and character traits that mark those who are fit for leadership and responsibility will show themselves. Then he will with confidence be able to entrust leadership to them.

Slaves (6:1-2a). Since the Christian message had a special appeal to poorer segments of society, many slaves appear to have embraced the gospel, finding freedom in the midst of bondage. Two Pauline letters have sections in household codes addressed to Christian slaves and masters (Ephesians and Colossians), and Philemon addresses and redefines the master/slave relationship. In 1 Timothy, however, only the slaves are addressed. Speculation has surrounded the lack of instructions addressed to masters here; 6:2a clearly refers to believing masters.

Paul here speaks to all Christian slaves (6:1), and then specifically to the slaves of Christian masters (6:2). He refers to all slaves as being "under the yoke," an agrarian image which originally referred to the wooden frame placed over the necks of animals to join them for plowing, pulling a cart, etc. Similar yokes were sometimes used on people who had been captured in battle or sold into slavery. This background led to the use of "yoke" as a symbol for subjection and dependence, slavery. A slave was the property of another person, and had no rights. He or she was expected to show complete loyalty and obedience to the master. Paul commands all Christian slaves to "regard" (*hēgeisthōsan*) their masters as "worthy of all honor" (6:1); in other words, to give them the respect and honor due them as masters. As with the practical instructions in 1 Timothy 2, Paul's purpose revolves around witness: they are to do this "so that the name of God and the teaching of the church may not be blasphemed." The phrase "the name of God" refers to God's reputation, particularly among those who are not in a covenant relationship with him (see Rom 2:24, which quotes Isa 52:5). "Blasphemy" is insulting or damaging speech or actions, speech that defames. Paul's concern is that disrespectful behavior will cast a negative shadow on the gospel and be a stumbling block to its reception by others.

Paul then focuses on Christian slaves who had "believing" masters. They must not "despise" their masters (6:2). "Despise" translates *kataphroneitōsan*, which refers to showing contempt or scorn, or to "be unafraid of" someone (BDAG). Some Christian slaves of Christian masters may well have thought that their shared faith gave them the right to misbehave or disobey. Paul commands them not to presume on the faith they share with their owners. Instead, the shared faith should motivate them to serve these believing masters more diligently, out of love. Again, Paul's concern is for the witness of the church, and would be the same whatever socioeconomic system he was addressing. No matter what setting Christians find themselves in, their calling is to live in ways that show respect and grace, and draw people to the gospel rather than turning them away.

Paul closes the section with another anaphoric *tauta*: Timothy must "teach and command these things." Again, the Christian faith is not just a system of beliefs. It requires actions and obedience to the example and law of Christ.

False Teachers Contrasted with Paul and Timothy (6:3-10)

Paul here returns to the topic of false teachers, previously addressed in 1:3-7 and 4:1-3. Once again, their identity is not specified. In the earlier references Paul emphasized their teachings. Here, the focus turns to their behavior and its damaging effects on the church. Paul sees these behaviors (and the damage they do) as the inevitable result of teaching false doctrines. The first part of this section (6:3-5) is one long conditional sentence, with 6:3 describing the condition (the "if" clause) and 6:4-5 outlining the results of the condition (the "then.")

Paul organizes his argument against the false teachers around three standards for measuring a teacher's truth and acceptability (or the lack thereof). Teachers are false if:

1. They teach something other than what Paul has taught in this letter. The text simply reads, "if someone teaches otherwise," which may refer to the instructions in 5:1–6:2, but likely has the larger object in view.
2. They "do not adhere to the sound words concerning our Lord Jesus Christ." "Sound" (*hygiainousin*) refers to something being healthy or solid, uncorrupted. Here, the false teachers are those who disagree with Paul's gospel, his teachings about Jesus' life, death, and resurrection, and what it achieved.
3. They reject "the teaching that leads to godliness." Whoever rejects or teaches things that detract from people's devotion and obedience to God is a false teacher.

Such a person is "conceited, understanding nothing, with a twisted desire for controversies and debates about words" (6:4). "Twisted desire" translates *nosōn*; Josephus applies this word to people who stir up rebellion and dissension for their own selfish, manipulative purposes (*Ant* 16.244; 18.25). (For "controversies" [*zētēseis*], see the discussions at 2 Timothy 2:23 and Titus 3:9. For "debates about words" [*logomachies*], see also Titus 3:9.)

Next, Paul highlights the inevitable effects on the life of the community. "From these [their obsessions with controversies and arguments about words? Or their activities as described in 6:3?], the following things arise":

- "Envy" (*phthonos*), the desire to have or attain what belongs to others;
- "Strife" (*eris*), schisms and divisions that undermine the unity of the community;
- "Slander" (*blasphēmiai*, plural), blasphemies on the horizontal plane (between people) rather than the vertical (aimed at God). This would

include both character assassination and harsh, abusive language directed at or against others.
- "Evil suspicions," "suspicions" (*hyponoiai*), refers to thinking ill of other people based on little or no evidence; such unfounded opinions often spread throughout the church, doing much damage. These suspicions are "evil" (*ponērai*).

The false teachers' activities also result in "constant arguments" for their victims—as opposed to the love and health that the gospel produces (6:5; cf. 1:4-5). The minds of the victims of the false teachers have been corrupted (*diephtharmenōn*, which refers to being depraved or wasting away). Further, they have been robbed or defrauded (*apesterēmenōn*) of the very truth that could be producing good things in their lives.

Finally, they "suppose they can make a profit by religion." "Religion" here translates *eusebeia*, normally rendered "godliness." The focus in 6:5 is on the external appearances of religion rather than the internal realities. The false teachers believe they can "turn a buck" by acting and sounding religious—and indeed, many did and continue to do so.

The topic of money and the unhealthy desire for it causes Paul to digress in 6:6-10. In this digression, he is concerned with demonstrating the proper relationship between godliness and gain/profit. "There is indeed great gain in godliness" (6:6)—but not the false godliness that the false teachers practice, nor the material gain they and their followers think will bring peace and satisfaction. The godliness Paul has in view is true godliness, God-directed, "with contentment." Contentment (*autarkeias*) was a favorite Greek virtue, especially prized by the Stoics (of Epicurus in *Diogenes Laertius* 10.130; *Sextus Empiricus* 98). *Autarkeia* could refer to self-sufficiency, having resources so that one lacked nothing. It could also refer to being content with one's status or condition in life. The fact is, "we brought nothing into the world, so that we can take not a single thing out of it" (6:7). This means that the gathering of wealth and possessions beyond what one needs is meaningless (cf. Job 1:21); this statement has parallels in Stoic philosophy as well. The mention of "food and clothing" (*diatrophas kai skepasmata*) in 6:8 echoes both Stoic teachings and the words of Jesus himself (Matt 6:25-34; Luke 12:22-32), which Paul may well have in mind. If Job 1:21 is the background of 6:7, and Jesus' words from the Sermon on the Mount the background of 6:8, then the structure here mirrors the structure in 5:18, where both the Old Testament and the words of Jesus serve as warrants and are treated as Scripture.

Nevertheless, there are some "who want to be rich" (6:9). These people "fall into temptation, and a trap, and many senseless and harmful desires." "Fall" translates *empiptousin*; figuratively, the word refers to being defeated, succumbing to something, or being overcome. The desire for wealth and all it brings leads people into temptation (the desire to sin) and a trap (the devil's trap? See the discussion at 3:7) and "senseless" (*anoētous*, lit., "mindless" or "thoughtless") and harmful desires. These desires "plunge people into ruin and destruction." "Plunge" translates *bythizousin*, which refers to drowning a person or sinking a vessel; figuratively, it refers to causing someone "to experience disastrous consequences" (BDAG). "Ruin and destruction" (*oltheron kai apōleian*) are synonyms that refer to violent and extensive destruction; the two together may mean "total destruction," stressing the severity and intensity of the damage.

Paul concludes, "for the love of money [*philargyria*; cf. 2 Tim 3:2] is the root of all kinds of evil" (6:10). The Stoics taught that *philargyria* was one of the chief expressions of vice. Likewise the Cynics; Diogenes of Sinope once said that the love of money was "the mother city of all kinds of evils" (*Diogenes Laertius* 7.111, 6.50). In the same vein, Josephus said that this vice motivated Noarus (Varus) to betray and kill an official delegation of seventy innocent Jews, without Agrippa's approval or knowledge (*J.W.* 2.483; Kasher 1988, 197). The fact that the root of all kinds of evil is "the love of money" (rather than money itself) does not weaken Paul's case against the love of money. In fact, it strengthens Paul's case when we realize that evil things with no apparent connection with money may, after all, result from the love of money. The love of money has resulted in two things, according to Paul. First, "some people, striving for money, have wandered away [*apeplanēthēsan*] from the faith." *Apoplanaomai* refers to wandering from true teaching, to stop believing in what is true and turn to what is false, "exchange the truth of God for a lie" (Rom 1:23). Further, they have "pierced themselves through [*periepeiran*] with many anxieties." *Peripeirō* literally refers to impaling something (Josephus, *J.W.* 3.296); in this instance, it figuratively refers to self-imposed agony. Paul uses the word here translated "anxieties" (*odunais*) to refer to his agony over the fate of the Jewish people (Rom 9:2).

In 6:3-10, Paul again describes the false teachers and the destructive results of their activities. Because of a twisted, selfish core to their character, they reject the teachings of the gospel and all it involves and produces. They pursue their own teachings—not even convinced of the truth of their words, but simply as a way to make money—and sow chaos and dissension and division in the church.

Paul's Charge to Timothy, Continued (6:11-16)

Having described the false teachers, the effects of their activities, and the dangers that await them and those who follow them, Paul in 6:11 returns to his charge to Timothy: "But you, man of God, flee these things [*tauta*]." "Man of God" is an expression often used for prophets in the Old Testament: Moses (Deut 33:1), an unnamed prophet (1 Sam 2:27), Samuel (1 Sam 9), Shemaiah (1 Kings 12:22), Elijah (2 Kings 1:12-13; 4:7). It characterizes the person as one who belongs to God and represents God. Paul has previously talked of Timothy's gifts in contexts where it would be logical to assume that prophecy was Timothy's spiritual gift. Paul gives Timothy two directives, one negative and one positive. First, the negative: "flee these things." "Flee" (*pheuge*) is a present imperative, which suggests continuing, habitual action. It is not enough to flee once from the love of money and the vices that accompany it. Timothy's rejection of these things must be a constant pattern in his life.

Second, Paul commands Timothy to pursue six virtues. Each of these is found in virtue lists elsewhere in the New Testament. The first three virtues are directed toward God. The second trio of virtues is directed toward people. They are

- "righteousness" (*dikaiosunē*), an ongoing right relationship with God and the life/behavior that result from that relationship;
- "godliness," true reverence for God and actions, especially religious actions, that express that devotion;
- "faith," trusting God in a way that produces obedience;
- "love" (*agapē*), self-sacrificial actions in the best interests of others;
- "patience" (*hypomonē*), leading and ministering with *agapē* and tenderness, even when people are being immature and wayward; and
- "gentleness" (*praupathian*), restraint, the quality of not being harsh in dealing with others.

The pursuit of these virtues will allow Timothy to "fight the good fight for the faith" (6:12). Paul frequently used metaphors from the world of military (e.g., 2 Tim 2:3-4) and athletics (e.g., Phil 3:13-14; 2 Tim 2:5), often weaving them together. *Agonizō* ("to fight") and *agōna* ("the fight") can refer to military conflict, a boxing match, a race, or any other contest. Here, the fight is for the good of the gospel. This is a good (*kalos*) fight, because the combatant (Timothy) does not seek riches or his own glory, but to keep the life-changing message of the gospel pure and effective. Timothy's goal is also to "take hold of eternal life." "Take hold" translates *epilabou*, from *epilambanō*, which refers to grasping an object. If the image in 6:12a is athletic (and not military), then the picture here is of the victor in a contest being handed the champion's trophy, and "taking hold of eternal life" is a way of saying, "win eternal life for yourself and your people by fighting to keep the gospel pure and effective" (cf. 4:16). This phrase calls to mind the final victory of God and his people's participation in that victory. It also points to the present experience of believers, who are called to demonstrate that eternal life is part of their lives in the here and now. As part of his calling to this life, Timothy "confessed the good confession before many witnesses." "Confessed" (*hōmologēsas*) refers to a public agreement with or acknowledgment of some monumental truth or fact; here it refers to Timothy's public acknowledgment that "Jesus Christ is Lord" at his conversion. Paul was likely a part of Timothy's conversion and baptism (Acts 16:1-6). Here, he is encouraging Timothy to continue his service to Christ with the same kind of faithfulness as he aspired to at the beginning (Knight 1992, 264–65).

Paul adds a third imperative to the two commands of 6:11-12: "I charge you, in the presence of God who gives life to all things, and of Christ Jesus, who himself testified to the good confession before [*epi*] Pontius Pilate, to keep this command . . ." (6:13-14a). The language is solemn (cf. 5:21). Paul reminds Timothy again that this charge is carried out with God and Christ as its witnesses. The reference to Pilate is the only mention of this Roman governor in the letters. Pilate ruled Palestine from 26–36 CE, and presided over Jesus' trial in Jerusalem. If the preposition *epi* is translated "before," as above, then Paul is referring specifically to that trial. Thus Jesus' steadfastness and adherence to the truth before Pilate, under the threat of crucifixion, was a testimony to the truth ("the good confession"). So also now Timothy must adhere to the truth, in spite of opposition. However, if *epi* is translated "during the time of" (cf. Mark 2:26), then the confession refers to the witness of Jesus' life and ministry, particularly his suffering and death, all of which took place while Pilate ruled. Whatever the case, Jesus' confession (6:13) obviously parallels Timothy's confession (6:12). In both cases, Paul emphasizes faithfulness that overcomes opposition.

What is the commandment that Paul charges Timothy to keep? It is the command (*parangelia*) with which Paul began the letter, where Paul urged Timothy to command the false teachers to stop their subversive activities, the command to guard the teaching of the gospel and all it involves. All the intervening instructions flow from this command, and thus are included in this charge. Timothy must keep this command perfectly and completely, in a way that guards the gospel's reputation (and thus the church's reputation and witness) from slander and reproach (*anepilēmpton*; cf. 3:2; 5:7).

Timothy must keep the commandment in this way "until the appearing of our Lord, Jesus Christ." "Appearing" translates *epiphaneia*; this word is used in the Pastoral Epistles to refer to both the earthly ministry of Jesus (2 Tim 2:10) and the second coming (2 Tim 4:1; Titus 2:13). Hellenistic writers used this word to refer to a god or semi-divine being (even a king or emperor) being revealing himself, or making himself visible by an act of power. In Hellenistic Judaism, the word referred to the way God revealed himself by manifestations of his power. Here it clearly refers to the second coming of Christ, which God will reveal "at the right time" (6:15; "time" here translates *kairos*). This reference to God bringing all history to a close causes Paul to spring into praise, with a hymnic description of God:

> The blessed and only sovereign,
> The King of kings
> And Lord of lords,
> Who alone possesses immortality,
> Dwelling in unapproachable light,
> Whom no human has ever seen or can see. (6:15b-16)

"Sovereign" translates *dynastēs*, "ruler" or any other powerful official (for God as "blessed" [*makarios*], see the discussion above at 1:11). As the "only sovereign," God is the only true ruler who deserves the title, no one else compares. "King of kings" and "Lord of lords" are used in the New Testament for both God and Jesus (Rev 17:14; 19:16). God is the only one who possesses (and therefore can share) "immortality," the power to transcend death and decay, and thus live forever. The idea of God dwelling "in unapproachable light" refers to the idea, common in the Old Testament, that God reveals himself by means of an intense and dazzling light that no human eye can withstand (Exod 24:16-17; 33:20; 34:29-35). The inability of people to look on God points to God's holiness and separateness from his creation.

Paul closes this hymn with a powerful statement of praise: "To him be honor and eternal power! Amen." Instead of the usual "honor and glory" (see 2 Tim 4:18), Paul ascribes to God "eternal power" or "eternal dominion." The notion of God ruling forever is prevalent in the Old Testament (e.g., Exod 15:18; Ps 146:10; Lam 5:19). Thus Paul summarizes the motif of God's sovereignty that runs throughout the hymn.

In 6:11-16, Paul juxtaposes Jesus' faithful life with his coming appearing. Timothy lives between these events and must look back to the example of Jesus' faithful witness even as he looks forward to the day when God's rule is completely realized. In this sense, Christians live between memory and hope; both define the Christian life. The God who created and who initiated salvation does not stand outside history, a spectator to its destruction. He takes up residence in history to redeem it: "The word became flesh and dwelt among us" (John 1:14).

Here, Paul also holds two realities side by side. The first is the inevitability of struggle and opposition. Timothy, like Jesus, must cling to his confession of the truth of God, even when truth and conviction are not popular things. He must "fight the good fight" by refusing to compromise the truths of the gospel, even when such compromise would win him popularity and reduce the animosity he faces. At the same time, Timothy must continue in obedience and faithfulness to the only ruler truly deserving of being called ruler, the God who called Timothy to salvation and vocation, the only one with eternal and unbounded power. Then Timothy can win eternal life for himself and his people by keeping himself (and helping keep them) on the path of the true gospel.

Final Instructions and Reiteration of the Charge (6:17-21)

Before his last charge to Timothy, Paul must say one more word about affluent Christians: "Regarding those who are rich in the present age . . . " (6:17). Paul emphasizes their having stored up wealth for this age rather than the age to come (cf. Matt 6:19-24, 33). Timothy is to command them "not to be haughty" (*hypsēlophronein*). This word carries the picture of "having too elevated an opinion of oneself," a person who gives the impression that he or she is more important than everyone else. Rich believers are also not to "set their hope on the uncertainty of riches"; financial wealth ebbs and flows and cannot be depended on. Instead, they are to "set their hopes on God, who richly provides us with everything for our enjoyment." Notice in 6:17 the play on words: "set hopes on riches [*ploutou*] which are unreliable" is opposite "set hope on God, who provides us with all richness [*panta plousiōs*] for our enjoyment." God is the source of true riches; what he provides is true wealth; godliness with contentment is great gain (6:6-8). Paul then gives Timothy commands to pass on to these wealthy Christians:

- "They are to do good, being rich in good works" (6:18). The second phrase repeats the theme of the first, but more emphatically. "Good works" are

actions done on behalf of other people; this phrase serves as a shorthand description of the Christian life in the Pastoral Epistles. The point here is that rich Christians, instead of focusing on their own interests and pleasures, must focus on meeting the needs of others, doing good for other people.
- They must "be generous givers, willing to share." As with the previous pairing, the second phrase unpacks or adds emphasis to the first, while repeating the main idea. The Greek word translated "willing to share" (*koinōnikous*) is related to the word for "fellowship," *koinōnia*. Generosity and sharing have been hallmarks of the church since the earliest days (Acts 2:42-47; 4:32-37). These virtues motivated Paul's desire to deliver the collection to the saints in Jerusalem.

If rich Christians obey these commands, and pursue these virtues, they can—in spite of the handicap their wealth poses—"store up" a different kind of treasure. They will "store up for themselves a good foundation for the future, so that they can take hold of the life that is truly life" (6:19). "Store up for themselves" translates *apothēsaurizontas*, which refers to building up a store of something, hording weapons (Josephus, *J.W.* 7.299) or financial resources, food, etc. This treasure is establishes a good foundation for the future, enabling them to find *true life*. This life extends beyond the riches of the present age, and it lasts into eternity. Wealth is a trap for these believers; it deceives them into thinking that they provide for themselves, and thus have no need for God. Too often, this self-deception is not realized until it is too late (Luke 12:13-21; 16:19-31; Acts 4:32-5:11; Jas 5:1-6). Jesus clearly warns his people not to be deceived by the illusion of self-sufficiency and security that wealth projects (Matt 6:19-21; Luke 16:31). True wealth is not measured by how many possessions are stored, but by readiness to do good for others, being "rich in good works, generous, ready to share." Again, Paul juxtaposes the present and the future of the Christian life. By being faithful, "doing good, being rich in good works, generous, ready to share," Christians "store up for themselves a good foundation for the future" (cf. Matt 6:20) so that they can "take hold of the life that really is life," both now and in the future.

Paul closes the letter with one last charge to Timothy. The charge involves two commands. First, "Guard the deposit which has been entrusted to you" (6:20). Again, Paul uses succession language to describe the command and authority that he has given Timothy through this letter: "the deposit which has been entrusted to you" translates a single Greek word, *parathēkēn*. Paul uses this word in 2 Timothy 1:12 and 14, where he also explicitly refers to the gospel and the authority and responsibilities that accompany it. Timothy must "guard this deposit" by faithfully executing the directions given him in the letter, and by keeping the teaching of his churches pure. Second, Timothy must "reject profane, empty noises" (for "reject" [*ektrepomenos*], see the discussion at 1:6; 5:15; 2 Tim 4:4). "Profane" (*bebēlous*) refers to something that has no room or concern for God or spiritual things (see the discussion at 2 Tim 2:16). "Empty noises" (*kenophōnias*) refers to talk which has no value (BDAG; cf. 2 Tim 2:16).

Paul here joins this useless, damaging talk with "contradictions that are falsely called knowledge." "Contradictions" translates *antitheseis*, which refers either to teachings that contradict the gospel or to teachings that are internally contradictory. In either case, the fact that a teaching is contradictory means that it is false. "Falsely called knowledge" refers to the false teachings described throughout the letter (1:3-7; 4:1-4). The reference to knowledge (*gnōsis*) may suggest that some form of early Gnosticism may be present; this may be of a piece with the emphasis on genealogies in 1:4. Sadly, by "professing" these teachings, "some have abandoned the faith." "Professing" (*epangellomenoi*) refers to claiming to be an expert in something (BDAG; cf. *Diogenes Laertius* 1.12, where this word refers to self-appointed experts in philosophy). Here, the false teachers have claimed expertise in the teaching of the law (1:7) and other spiritual matters. Because of these claims, and their lack of humility, they have abandoned the true gospel of salvation. Like Hymenaeus and Alexander, who shipwrecked their faith (1:20), these people have turned from the true faith to a counterfeit masquerading as the truth, exchanging the truth of God for a lie.

The letter closes with the simplest benediction: "Grace be with you." As in everything, Paul begins this letter with grace (1:2), closes it with grace, and draws out the meaning(s) of grace in the teaching in between. "You" is plural, indicating that the letter's message is not just for Timothy; the letter was to be read to the entire church. As with Titus and 2 Timothy, the letter is personal, but it is not private. It spoke to them, as it speaks to us today.

2 Timothy

2 Timothy: Triumphant Ministry

Outline

1. Salutation, Greeting, and Prayer of Thanksgiving (1:1-5)
2. Paul's Charge to Timothy (1:6–4:8)
   A. A Model to Emulate: Paul the Sufferer (1:6–2:13)
      1. Join in suffering (1:6-18)
      2. Be strong (2:1-7)
      3. Theological foundation (2:8-13)
   B. Images of Ministry (2:14–3:9)
      1. A worker who passes the test (2:14-19)
      2. A vessel fit for noble use (2:20-26)
      3. Theological foundation (3:1-9)
   C. A Model to Emulate: Paul the Triumphant (3:10–4:8)
      1. What Timothy knows and how it benefits him (3:10-17)
      2. Paul's charge, Paul's victory (4:1-8)
      3. Personal notes, final greetings, and benediction (4:9-22)

Salutation, Greeting, and Prayer of Thanksgiving (1:1-5)

Second Timothy begins with a typical Pauline letter opening. The standard Graeco-Roman letter opening consisted of the name of the sender, the name of the recipient, and a brief greeting. This brief greeting was usually followed by a short prayer or blessing. Paul characteristically expands each element with descriptive material, giving his letter openings a distinctively Christian (and distinctively Pauline) flavor. His letter openings are much longer than was customary for Graeco-Roman letters. Further, these expansions to the parts of the openings have a rhetorical purpose.

Here, Paul describes himself as "an apostle of Christ Jesus by the will of God" (1:1; cf. Rom 1:1; 1 Cor 1:1; 2 Cor 1:1; Gal 1:1). An apostle (*apostolos*) was someone sent as a delegate or envoy, carrying a message or performing a task for the person who sent him/her. Here, Paul's apostleship is "by the will [*thelēmatos*] of God." In the openings of each of the Pastoral Epistles, Paul emphasizes his apostolic authority. The circumstances in Paul's churches make this emphasis necessary: opponents of Paul are at work in his congregations, questioning his authority. In 2 Timothy, this emphasis on authority is also necessitated by the circumstances in Paul's own life: Paul is imprisoned and facing death. How will his churches survive and thrive after his execution? In this letter, Paul ensures their continued health and effectiveness by making Timothy his successor, passing on his ministry into Timothy's care (see Introduction to the Pastoral Epistles).

"Will" carries both the idea of "desire" and "purpose." Paul's place as an apostle is in accordance with God's desires and purposes. The next phrase, "for the promise of life," unpacks God's desire/purpose for Paul's apostleship. God has sent Paul to fulfill his promise by carrying the gospel message and doing the work that makes eternal life available to those who hear (cf. 1 Tim 1:16; 4:8; 6:12, 19; Titus 1:2; 3:7). For Paul, this promise both defines the future and shapes the present. It is experienced "in Christ Jesus," that is, in a relationship with Jesus Christ that is so close and so intimate that people experience themselves to be united with Christ. "In Christ" is, perhaps, Paul's favorite definition of the Christian life; this phrase and its equivalents appear more than seventy times in the letters attributed to Paul. He uses this language to describe the believers' participation in Jesus' death and resurrection life, and the benefits—past, present, and future—that come to those who are so joined to Jesus Christ.

Timothy, the recipient of the present letter, is Paul's "beloved child" (1:2). Rather than the masculine *huios*, Paul here uses the generic term for child, *teknon*. The generic terminology may be part of an effort on Paul's part to echo the tone of testamentary literature. The testament is a recognized ancient literary genre, common both in Graeco-Roman and Jewish circles, in which a leader conveys his last words and wishes to his followers/children. Second Timothy is not a testament *per se*, but it uses some of the features of the genre (Richards 2002, 133). "Beloved" (*agapētō*) is an intimate term of endearment (cf. 1 Tim 1:1 and Titus 1:1, where Paul describes the recipients as his "*true*" [or "legitimate," *gnēsios*] children). By referring to Timothy as his beloved child, Paul echoes other biblical references to beloved children: Abraham and Isaac (Gen 22), Jesus (Mark 1:9-11 par.; John 3:16), etc. Timothy has been Paul's faithful companion and fellow-worker through thick and thin (see the introduction above).

2 Timothy: Triumphant Ministry

As in 1 Timothy, Paul adds "mercy" (*eleos*) to his customary greeting of "grace [*charis*] and peace [*eirēnē*]." Each element of this greeting has special significance (see the discussion of 1 Tim 1:2).

In 1:3-5, Paul follows the greeting with a prayer of thanksgiving. In most of his letters, Paul includes some kind of prayer or benediction after the greeting; this was customary in Graeco-Roman letters. Paul breaks this pattern in the Pastoral Epistles, however; only here, in 2 Timothy, do we find such a prayer. Paul omits the prayer of thanksgiving from 1 Timothy and Titus primarily for rhetorical effect. By moving directly from greeting to admonition, Paul heightens the urgency of the instructions. By contrast, 2 Timothy is much more personal that 1 Timothy and Titus; 1 Timothy and Titus are more official in tone than 2 Timothy.

For Paul, the prayer of thanksgiving in his letters fills an important function. First, Paul uses the prayer to fulfill the rhetorical purpose of *philophronesis* or *captatio benevolentiae*, an appeal for the reader's good favor. Second, Paul here typically introduces themes or concerns from the body of the letter. In 1:4, Paul describes his concern for and longing to see Timothy, an expression of their goodwill toward each other. In 1:3 and 1:5, he makes reference to the foundations of faith that he and Timothy share, a theme that will resurface in this letter (3:14).

In 1:3, we catch a glimpse of Paul's deep commitment to prayer. He exhorts the Thessalonians to "pray without ceasing" (1 Thess 5:17). Likewise, he "remembers" Timothy in his prayers "constantly, night and day" and his every remembrance is wrapped in prayer on Timothy's behalf. While he makes no attempt to explain the mysteries and mechanics of prayer, Paul is clearly committed to its practice. Prayer was the fuel that drove Paul's work, not an interruption to his busy schedule but the foundation on which that schedule was built. We also see here, as in other places, that Paul's prayers included giving thanks. He was grateful to God for Timothy and for all the others with whom he shared the work of ministry. Praying for his colleagues was a crucial dimension of Paul's prayer life. He prayed both for their needs, and to thank God for the way God blessed him through them. Note the strong similarities with Philippians 1:3-5, where Paul's prayers are filled with joy because of the Philippians' participation in his work.

Paul begins the prayer, "I thank my God every time I remember you." "I thank" translates the Greek verb *eucharisteō*, which is a cognate of *charis*, "grace," from 1:2. Paul's audience would have noted the repetition of *charis*; for Paul, the repetition serves as a reminder of his gospel, which centers on God's grace. The God to whom Paul gives thanks is also the God whom Paul worships. "Worship" (*latreuō*) can refer to any kind of service done by one person, slave or free, for another. For Paul, worship and service are integrally related, for true worship always results in the service of others (cf. Rom 12:1-2). Paul worships "with a clear conscience" (*kathara syneidēsei*). In the Hellenistic world, the "conscience" refers to a way of thinking and of self-examination that allows a person to make right moral and ethical decisions. Those who are "in Christ" no longer make such decisions on the basis of the values of the world. Instead, their basis for moral choices is the new creation (2 Cor 5:16-17). When Paul refers to a "clear conscience," he might mean that he has made the right choices, morally and ethically; therefore, his conscience is clear. He could also use the phrase to mean, "with undivided attention," referring to his single-minded devotion to God and God's people. Jesus clearly taught that single-mindedness is crucial for those who would be his disciples: "Blessed are the pure in heart . . ." (Matt 5:8); "Seek first his kingdom and his righteousness . . ." (Matt 6:33). Likewise, Kierkegaard said, "To be pure in heart means to desire only one thing" (Kierkegaard 1956).

Furthermore, Paul, in his consistent and single-minded worship, has followed in the footsteps of his Jewish "ancestors" (*progonōn*). What Paul has experienced in Christ and the work that he is now about are in direct continuity with what God has been doing since he called Abraham and began his redemptive work. Paul highlights this emphasis again in 1:5, with his reference to the history of Timothy's faith, how it was passed to him by his mother Eunice and his grandmother Lois.

In these verses, Paul highlights the significance of the church, the community of faith. Paul sees himself as part of a tradition, in which his ancestors worshipped before him. The writer of Hebrews, after giving a long list of faithful servants of Yahweh from the past, reminds believers that they are surrounded by a "great cloud of witnesses" (Heb 12:1). Paul thinks of his ancestors as models (not objects) of proper worship and service. In the development of Christian tradition, these "ancestors" in the faith came to be referred to as "the communion of saints."

Paul further expresses the depth of his relationship with Timothy in 1:4. He longs to see Timothy; this desire is echoed in 4:9, 11, and 21, thus framing the entire letter with Paul's concern for and desire to see Timothy. Paul remembers Timothy's tears, perhaps prompted by his grief over Paul's imprisonment and suffering for the gospel (1:8). Timothy is likely also aware that Paul has been abandoned by some of his coworkers (1:15; cf. 4:10, 16). Paul was deeply concerned for Timothy, and longed to see him so that he could encourage Timothy and prepare him for the work ahead. Paul's joy is in some way dependent on Timothy's joy. Similarly, Paul calls upon the Philippians to "make my joy complete" by living a life "worthy of the gospel"

(Phil 2:2; 1:27). The implication here is the same. Paul's joy is dependent on the joy and faithfulness of others. According to Paul, this is what it means to be part of the Body of Christ: "If one part suffers, every part suffers with it; if one part is honored, every part rejoices with it" (1 Cor 12:26).

Paul's concern with Timothy's tears is heightened by his memory of Timothy's "sincere faith" (*anypokritou pisteōs*) (1:5). Here, "faith" refers to Timothy's trust in and confidence in Jesus Christ, which results in obedience (Eph 2:6-10; Rom 1:5 and 16:25-27). Timothy's faith is "sincere"; it is not polluted by pretense or hypocrisy. As with Paul himself (1:3), Timothy's faith is in keeping with that of his forebears, Timothy's grandmother Lois and his mother Eunice. "Lois" and "Eunice" are both Greek names, found nowhere else in the New Testament. According to Acts 16:1, Timothy's father was Greek but his mother—unnamed in Acts—was Jewish. If so, it is likely that Lois, Eunice's mother, was also Jewish. Greek names were not uncommon for Diaspora Jews.

Timothy's faith first "lived" (*enōkēsen*) in Lois and Eunice; the verb literally means "to be at home," likely indicating the depth and extent to which their faith was integral to their lives. Timothy had no doubt been deeply impacted by their faith. In Judaism, the family was and is the primary locus for passing on the traditions of faith, from generation to generation. Timothy's case makes it clear that both women and men are crucial to the chain of tradition. Now it is Timothy's turn to pass on what he has received from Lois and Eunice and Paul, so that his people may also have a genuine faith.

Paul's Charge to Timothy (1:6–4:8)

In 1:6, Paul's attention turns from his past to his present, and Timothy's future. The remainder of the body of the letter (1:6–4:8) contains a series of charges or orders for Timothy. These commands rest on the foundation of Timothy's faith and place in Paul's work, for which Paul gave thanks in 1:3-5. They encourage and empower Timothy as he succeeds Paul as the leader of Paul's churches (see Introduction to the Pastoral Epistles). One of the chief functions of both succession and testamentary literature was to encourage and empower those being left behind to carry on the work begun by the departing leader (Stepp 2005; Collins 2002, 196; see Introduction to the Pastoral Epistles).

In terms of structure, the body of the letter falls into three large sections (cf. the similar structure in Van Neste 2004, 224–32). The first large section,

1:6–2:13, centers on Paul's suffering and Timothy's response to it. Throughout this section, Paul uses the language of shame and endurance:

- *epaischynomai*, "to be ashamed," in 1:8, 12, 16;
- *apostrephomai*, "reject" or "abandon" (due to shame), 1:15;
- *sygkakopatheō*, "join in suffering," 1:8; 2:3;
- *endynomoomai*, "be strong, 2:1;
- *hypomenō*, "endure," in 2:10.

The question in this section is, will Timothy be ashamed (or afraid) of sharing Paul's imprisonments and the persecution that he faced, and so fail to faithfully lead Paul's churches? Paul is calling Timothy to follow in his footsteps. The successor cannot expect to escape the fate that befell his predecessor; Timothy must be prepared for the opposition he will face as he takes up Paul's mantle.

The second large section, 2:14–3:9, centers on images of ministry. In the first half of this section, Paul paints two new pictures of ministry (the workman who has passed the test in 2:15, and the vessel fit for noble use in 2:20-21; cf. the pictures of ministry in 2:1-7). Both 2:1-7 and 2:14-26 center on such images, but Paul uses the pictures differently in 2:14-26. In 2:1-7, Paul strung several illustrations of ministry together and left Timothy to draw the meaning from them. Here, Paul introduces the image and then immediately turns to explicit practical instructions about the life and work of ministry. Note:

- *Image*: a workman who has passed the test (2:15);
- *Instruction*: avoid useless talk and disputes (2:16-19);
- *Image*: vessels fit for noble use (2:20-21); and
- *Instruction*: flee youthful lusts, and stay away from the things that can make you unfit for use (2:22-26).

In the last part of this section (3:1-9), Paul describes factors that make the instructions in 2:14-26 so urgent. The kinds of people ministers will encounter in the last days, in and out of the church, make this special, careful approach necessary. Only ministers who live according to these instructions, who keep themselves pure from the venal, treacherous habits and practices of the false teachers and their followers, are adequate to the task.

2 Timothy: Triumphant Ministry

The third large section, 3:10–4:8, focuses again on Paul's example and the way it benefits Timothy. In the first half of the section, Paul lists several things that Timothy knows:

- Paul's example of faithfulness in the face of suffering (3:10-13);
- The legacy of Timothy's own faith (3:14);
- The Scriptures, their use, and the benefits they bring (3:14-17).

In the midst of this half of the large section, Paul inserts a warning about persecution and treachery in the last days.

In the second half of this section (4:1-8), Paul solemnly charges Timothy to be ready to articulate faithfully the message of the gospel, no matter what he faces. Timothy must live a life that is in harmony with the gospel he preaches, so that his message and ministry will be effective. Paul has lived such a life, and now—even as his life is taken from him—he is victorious, and will receive the victor's crown. Again, Paul inserts a warning about the perils of ministry in the last days.

A Model to Emulate: Paul the Sufferer (1:6–2:13)
Join in suffering (1:6-18)

In 1:6-14, Paul's encouragement to Timothy takes both negative and positive forms. Positively, Paul exhorts Timothy to faithfully use and administer the spiritual gift that God has given him. Negatively, Paul encourages Timothy not to be ashamed of the testimony of the gospel, and not to be afraid of suffering for it.

Paul tells Timothy to "rekindle the gift of God" that was within him. "Rekindle" (*anazōpyrein*) literally refers to fanning something into flames. The New Testament writers use fire imagery to refer to the gifts of the Holy Spirit (Acts 2:3-4, 19; 1 Thess 5:19). "Gift" (*charisma*) refers to the result of *charis* ("grace") (*TDNT* 9.402), a gift in evidence of a relationship with a benefactor. Paul's most extensive discussion of these gifts is in 1 Corinthians 12–14, where he asserts that they are the means by which God is building up the church and accomplishing his purposes in the world. To say that this gift is "within you" is a figurative way of speaking about someone possessing something to such a degree that it becomes part of that person's nature.

Paul does not identify the gift Timothy received. The gift of prophecy seems a reasonable suggestion: this is the only gift to be found in each of Paul's lists of spiritual gifts (Rom 12:6; 1 Cor 12:10, 28-29; Eph 4:11). In both the Old and New Testaments, prophecy refers to speaking forth the word of God to the people of God. The prophet speaks to the people of God's will in particular situations: "Thus saith the Lord," forth-telling, more than foretelling. This gift would be essential for the church in Ephesus, where Timothy may still be stationed, as it would be for every community of faith. Paul says that Timothy possesses this gift through the laying on of Paul's hands. The practice of the laying on of hands dates back at least to the time of Moses. In 1 Timothy 4:4, Paul alludes to the fact that the group of elders (in Ephesus? in Lystra, Timothy's hometown?) had laid hands on Timothy. Here Paul suggests either that he participated in that event—a fact not mentioned in 1 Timothy 4:4—or that a second ceremonial laying on of hands had taken place. At any rate, Paul understands the laying on of hands to be something that sets Timothy apart for ministry. He further sees Timothy's ministry as a continuation of his own. For an ancient Mediterranean audience, the laying on of hands was part of the imagery of succession, symbolizing the transfer of authority or power from a leader to one who comes after. So also here; the laying on of hands in 2 Timothy 1:6 is part of a succession from Paul to Timothy. Timothy is Paul's successor in the care of and administration of the gospel. The laying on of hands symbolizes and enacts a transfer of power and responsibility from Paul to Timothy, which will be complete when Paul finishes his course.

Again, note the importance of the church as a community of faith. The gifts of the Spirit function best within this community. In the early church, the laying on of hands was practiced when the church set someone apart for a special ministry or service (e.g., Acts 6:6; 13:3). In this way, the community both affirmed the call of God on people's lives and charged them to fulfill the ministry to which they had been called. Similarly, note the central role that memory plays in this section: Paul remembers (1:3), he recalls (1:4), he is reminded (1:5), and he reminds (1:6). Believers must acknowledge their debt to those in Christ who came before, and learn from their examples of faithfulness. And as part of the community of faith, they are responsible for affirming God's calling and gifting on those among them.

In 1:7, Paul employs the classical rhetorical technique of antithesis or contrast, juxtaposing what is not with what is. "For God has not given us a spirit of timidity but of power and love and self-discipline." Paul begins with the negative "cowardice" (or "timidity," *deilias*), in order to emphasize the positive "power [*dynameōs*] and love [*agapēs*] and self-discipline [*sōphronismou*]." "Spirit" here can refer to the Holy Spirit and thus the strength that he gives to the believer. It could also refer to the human spirit, the inner being of a person or the state in which one finds oneself. "A spirit of cowardice" thus refers to "a cowardly spirit."

In the honor/shame culture of the first-century Mediterranean world, *deilias* was universally condemned. In the light of the military imagery Paul uses in 2 Timothy, (e.g., 2:3; 4:7), "cowardice" is an especially loaded idea. According to *The Martyrdom of Polycarp*, just before his death Polycarp heard a voice from heaven charging him, "Be strong, Polycarp, and play the man" (9.1). And so Polycarp did. The coward may be unwilling to do what must be done, and so is unacceptable as a soldier for Christ. After all, God gave believers "a spirit of power and love and self-discipline." "Power" is the spiritual strength that enables believers to be faithful and victorious in the midst of adverse circumstances. In Ephesians 3:20, Paul reminds his readers that God's "power which is at work within us is able to accomplish far more abundantly than all we can ask or imagine." Such power must always be grounded in love, which determines how that power is used. *Sophronismos*, the word translated "self-discipline" (or "self-control") is found only here in the New Testament. This virtue was highly praised in the first-century Hellenistic world (see Sirach 37:11; Philo, *Moses* 1.233, 236; Dio Chrysostom, *Discourses* 11.101; 71.7; Epictetus, *Discourses* 1.24.3). *Sophronismos* is often translated "moderation," and refers to being characterized by good judgment and prudence. Imperial documents use cognates of this word to refer to administrators who show good judgment and discretion in the execution of their duties. Words from the same root are found throughout the Pastoral Epistles, suggesting a kind of self-discipline that is modest, chaste, and restrained in behavior (Collins 2002, 200; Titus 1:8; 2:2, 4, 5, 6, 12; 1 Tim 2:9, 15; 3:2). For Paul, self-discipline (like power) results from and is determined by love. Timothy is to live in the reality of God's love for him that manifests itself in his love for others, to live in the power of love which overcomes the world, and to exhibit self-discipline that enables him to be faithful so that love can become manifest to all.

God has given believers this "spirit of power and love and self-discipline." Paul suggests that there will be times, however, when they must "rekindle the gift," and (like Timothy) work to keep it active.

In 1:8, Paul instructs Timothy, "Therefore, do not be ashamed of the testimony of the Lord" (1:8). This spiritual fire of the previous verse is necessary because of the difficult situations that Timothy will be facing. "Testimony of the Lord" may refer to the gospel message (testimony about Jesus, who he was and what he accomplished). Here, however, it more likely refers to Jesus' testimony—his earthly ministry, arrest, trial, humiliation, and crucifixion (cf. 2:6). Crucifixion was a distinctly cruel and horrible Roman punishment, usually reserved for insurrectionists and slaves and the worst criminals. In Timothy's world, making a victim of crucifixion into the object of one's faith would be shameful and nonsensical; the Jewish world likewise, "Cursed is everyone who is hung on a tree" (Deut 21:23; Gal 3:13). No one in his/her right mind would want to serve such a master! Yet Paul calls Timothy to refuse to be ashamed of this testimony. "Do not be ashamed" (*epaischynthēs*) translates the same verb used by Paul in Romans 1:16 when he makes his own bold confession of faith: "I am not ashamed of the gospel." Timothy need not be ashamed of the cross, for while its testimony makes no sense to the human mind, it is the power and wisdom of God, which offers salvation to all who believe (1 Cor 1:18-25). Further, both Paul and Timothy will participate in and complete (cf. Col 1:24) the sufferings of Jesus on behalf of the church. If they are not ashamed of Jesus' suffering, then they—as his successors in the care of the gospel—can expect to suffer as Jesus suffered. This shared suffering is part of the evidence that they are indeed Jesus' successors (cf. my earlier conclusions in Stepp 2005, 154).

Some people in the churches might also see Timothy's association with the imprisoned Paul as something shameful. Some of Paul's churches seem to have believed that prosperity and a lack of persecution were signs of God's favor (e.g., 1 Cor 4:8-13). Because of this sense of over-realized eschatology (here the idea that heaven comes on earth for the truly spiritual), the persecution that Paul faced brought him suspicion from some quarters of the church.

Paul exhorts Timothy to not be ashamed, but rather "join with me in suffering for the gospel." "Join with me in suffering" is literally "suffer together for the gospel" (*sygkakopathēson tō euangeliō*). Suffering for the sake of the gospel is a prominent theme in Paul's letters (see especially the catalogs of suffering in 1 Cor 11:23-27 and 2 Cor 6:3-10; cf. also Rom 16:6, 12; 1 Cor 15:10; 16:16; 2 Cor 1:6; Gal 4:11; Phil 2:16; Col 1:24; 1 Thess 1:15; 5:12). Here as elsewhere, Paul is not commending suffering *per se*. He commends suffering that advances the work/cause of the gospel. Paul never sought suffering, and indeed used various means to avoid it when he could (e.g., the use of his Roman citizenship in Acts 16:37; 22:25-29; 25:10-12). He had no martyr complex. His concern was always to be faithful to the call of God in his life and faithful to those to whom he had been sent.

Paul and Timothy will overcome suffering "by relying on the power of God." Paul understood that God empowered his servants to stand up under suffering. Note the reappearance of the word "power" (*dynamis*) from 1:7. God's power is dynamic, earthshaking, transforming, explosive power. In Ephesians 3:20, Paul speaks of God "who by the power at work within us (cf. 1:7) is able to accomplish abundantly far more than all we ask or imagine." It is a power that does not aim to rescue believers *from* suffering, but rather sustains them *through* suffering. The earliest church understood this well. In Acts 4:23-31, Luke describes how the Jerusalem church prayed in the midst of persecution and suffering. Their prayer was not to be rescued from persecution, but rather that they be enabled to speak the word with boldness in the face of it. They were willing to rely on God's power and be faithful in suffering for the gospel, just as Paul was doing and Timothy would do.

The New Testament warns Christians that conflict with the world is inevitable: "In this world you will have trouble, but take heart! I have overcome the world" (John 16:33). Here, Paul reminds Timothy and all who read/heard this letter of this conflict, and that they triumphed over suffering by relying on the power of God. Believers may miss this note as they seek to live faithful lives: left to their own devices, they may be overwhelmed by circumstances, but by relying on the power of God, believers can remain faithful, even in the face of suffering. Before his ascension, Jesus promised his disciples that they would "receive power" so that they could be his witnesses (Acts 1:8). It is on this power that Paul relies, and it is this power that enables Paul to proclaim, "I can do all things through him who gives me strength" (Phil 4:13). Christians do not face suffering, pressure, or persecution alone. They have the power of God at work in and through them, and can be faithful "through the help of the Holy Spirit who dwells in us" (1:14).

In 1:9-10, Paul breaks into a doxology, a statement of praise motivated by the mention of the "power of God" at the end of 1:8. It is not unusual for Paul to make such statements of praise (e.g., Eph 3:20-21; Rom 11:33-36; see the discussion on doxologies at 2 Tim 4:18). The grammar of 1:9-10—the piling up of participles and uniform phrase lengths—suggests that these verses are an early Christian hymn describing God's saving work in Christ. The editors of the United Bible Societies Greek New Testament arrange these verses in poetic format. They can be rendered as

> The one who saved us
>> And called us to a holy calling,
> Not because of our works
>> But because of his own purpose and grace,
> Which he gave to us in Christ Jesus
>> Before time began,
> And which he has now revealed
>> Through the appearing of our Savior, Christ Jesus,
> Who has both destroyed the power of death
>> And brought life and immortality to light through the gospel.

This hymn represents the faith of the early Christian communities. From the beginning, Christians created confessions and hymns that expressed the essence of the faith, and taught and encouraged one another with these materials. The nature of the gospel cries out for such expressions. Scholars have isolated many examples in the New Testament. (For an introduction to this area of study, see Hunter 1961; Gloer 1984.)

The theological force of these verses is prominent and striking. Paul encourages Timothy by reminding him that the God whose power sustains him in suffering is the God "who saved us and called us to a holy calling." Paul often refers to God's call (Rom 8:30; 9:6-26; 1 Cor 1:9, 7:15, 17-24; 15:9; Gal 1:6-15; 5:8; 1 Thess 2:12; 4:7; 5:24). In Paul's mind, God's call includes both salvation and service. "Calling" (*klēsis*) refers to the role or position in God's plans to which he calls Christians.

The Christian's calling is a "holy calling" in that it involves being set apart for God's specific purposes. In the New Testament, being "holy" (*hagia*) does not refer to some level of super-piety. Instead, the word describes ordinary people who are set apart by God for extraordinary purposes. Christians are to be holy because God is holy, set apart or consecrated to God's purposes because God is consecrated to his own purposes (1 Pet 1:15; Lev 11:44; Exod 19:6). Our holiness is not first a matter of our character or accomplishments. It is rather a matter of our calling. The next phrase clearly rules out defining holiness as super piety: we have this holy calling "not because of our works but because of his purpose and grace." Our calling is not our doing, or something we've earned. It is a result of God's grace (Rom 3:24-25; Eph 2:8-10). This grace is given "in [*en*] Christ Jesus" (Rom 12:3, 6; 1 Cor 1:4; 3:10; Gal 2:9). The preposition *en* here can be translated "through," in which case Christ Jesus is the agent God uses to give grace. Paul further affirms that this grace originated in the heart and purpose of God "before time began" (*pro chronōn aiōniōn*); this phrase is the Greek translation of a Semitic expression that refers to a period before time existed.

For Paul, God is the one who is at work in all of this. Before the beginning of time, God determined to give grace to his people through or by means of Christ Jesus, "selected before the creation of the world" (1 Pet 1:20). This gracious work of God is "now revealed through the appearing of our Savior, Christ Jesus." Paul uses this same word, *epiphaneias* ("appearing"), in 1 Timothy 6:14 to refer to Jesus' second coming. Here, however, it refers to his first coming, his earthly ministry and all it involved and produced. The word group from which *epiphaneia* derives sometimes carries the sense of "shining," as a light shining illuminates or makes visible the thing that is appearing. By Jesus' appearing (his first coming), the nature of God's gracious purposes is made visible for all to see. God's purpose for humanity is not death but life and immortality.

In Christ, God has "destroyed the power of death." Elsewhere, Paul uses this verb, *katargēsantos*, to mean "make nothing," "invalidate," or "destroy." Implicit here is Paul's understanding of the resurrection. Without Jesus' resurrection, death is the end and nothing good outlasts it. But because of Christ's resurrection, life has the final word—not death. Biblically, life is a core attribute of God. He creates and gives life through his breath, his essence. This life God brings is not just biological, temporary life, but immortal life, "incorruptible" or "imperishable." This is the life *after* life after death, which Paul writes about in 1 Corinthians 15:42-55, when he proclaims,

> This perishable body must put on imperishability, and this mortal body must put on immortality. When this perishable body puts on imperishability, and this mortal body puts on immortality, then the saying that is written will be fulfilled: "Death has been swallowed up in victory." "Where, O death, is your victory? Where, O death, is your sting?"

Because the proclamation of the gospel *is* the announcement of the resurrection of Jesus Christ from the dead, it brings this new life—new in both quality and chronology—to light (1 Tim 1:11; 2 Tim 1:8, 10; 2:8).

In 1:11-12, Paul describes his own relationship to the gospel: "of this gospel [lit., "of which," pointing back to 1:11] I was appointed a herald and apostle and teacher." Paul understands his main task to be proclaiming this gospel. Faithfulness to this task has brought him suffering, but entrusting himself to the person at the center of the gospel enables him to press on. He calls Timothy to follow in these steps.

"Appointed" (*etethēn*, from *tithēmi*) is commonly used in succession contexts (2 Kings 2:24 LXX; cf. 1 Tim 1:12). Thus Paul again describes himself as a successor of Jesus Christ in the care of the gospel. Here, in language identical to 1 Timothy 2:7, Paul reminds Timothy of his appointment. At the same time, he takes up the theme of suffering and shame introduced in 1:8; this echo is further evidence that 1:9-10 is a hymn which Paul has placed in the center of his discussion. The suffering that Paul has experienced results from his faithfulness to his appointment as herald, apostle, and teacher. The verb *etethēn* is a divine passive: Paul did not take up these titles on his own, or appoint himself to these tasks. He was appointed to them by God (cf. the contrast Paul draws between himself and the self-appointed would-be teachers in 1 Tim 1:3-7 and 11).

Each of the titles is significant. Paul uses two titles ("herald," "teacher"), which would have been familiar to Hellenistic audiences, to explain a third, less familiar title ("apostle"). A "herald" announced *euangelion* ("good news") to the public, proclaiming things like a victory in battle or the birth of an heir to the emperor or even an imperial edict that brought relief or restoration. In Hellenistic religious literature, the herald played the role of prophet and teacher. For example, heralds served in the Temple of Artemis in Ephesus. The "teacher" was also a well-known figure in the Hellenistic world, one who expounded ideas in a systematic fashion. Teachers were generally respected for their intelligence and regarded as figures of authority. Luke's Gospel, traditionally associated with a non-Jewish Hellenistic audience, often refers to Jesus as a teacher. For Paul, teaching was an important spiritual gift. Its place in 1 Corinthians 12:28 ("In the church, God has appointed first apostles, second prophets, third teachers, then . . .") might suggest that Paul viewed it as one of the three most important gifts for the life of the church. And, as noted in the discussion of 1:1, "apostle" refers to a person sent by some authority as a delegate or envoy, carrying a message or performing a task for the person who sent him/her, carrying the sender's authority.

"It is as a result of my faithfulness to this appointment," Paul writes in 1:12, "that I suffer as I do." Paul likely has in mind not only his circumstances as he writes—a prisoner in Rome, facing execution—but all the suffering he has experienced in service to the gospel. But Paul is "not ashamed" (*epaischynomai*, the same verb as in 1:8) because he knows (*oida*) the one in whom he has put his faith (*pepisteuka*, from *pisteuō*). In 1:8, Paul set himself before Timothy as an example of one who is "not ashamed" of his own suffering. For Paul, and now for Timothy, shame is replaced by trust and confidence. Paul's trust and confidence are not in himself or his own abilities, convictions, rightness, etc. Paul's trust and confidence are in the God he serves, of whom he is an apostle. His knowledge is not just information, it is knowledge born of an intimate relationship with someone, and a confidence based on his experience that the one he trusts has been faithful in the past, is faithful in the present, and will be faithful in the future. Further, Paul asserts, "I am sure [*pepeismai*, from *peithō*] that he [God] is able to guard what he has entrusted to me." The form of *peithō* used here is in the perfect tense, emphasizing a continuing sense of confident assurance. Paul is sure that God is able "to guard" (*phylaxai*) what has been entrusted to Paul. "To guard" refers to keeping something secure, protecting something, or keeping ones attention focused on something so that it produces the desired effect (e.g., Hesiod, *Works and Days* 263, 491, 561).

What is God protecting in this verse? "What he has entrusted to me" translates *parathēkēn mou*, literally "my deposit" or "my trust." Generally speaking, this phrase refers to an object that has been handed over to another for safekeeping. The object might be money, property, a portion of one's harvest, etc. *Parathēkēn mou* here can refer to something that Paul has entrusted to God (a subjective genitive), such as Paul's life or security or future. Taken this way, the verse reads, "I am sure that he is able to guard what I have entrusted to him . . . ." This is the traditional translation of this passage, found in the NIV, NRSV, and KJV.

However, the phrase *parathēkēn mou* can also refer to something that has been entrusted to Paul (an objective genitive), such as his gospel or apostleship. Taken this way, the verse reads, "I am sure that he [God] is able to keep what he has entrusted to me." This reading fits the context better than the traditional translation; compare 1:14, where *parathēkēn* also refers to the teaching that God has entrusted to Paul and then to Timothy. The RSV and NET translate the verse in this way. (A third reading of *parathēkēn mou* has it referring to the gospel that Paul is entrusting to Timothy via this letter. This reading fits the larger context of the letter well, reflecting in a nutshell the overarching story of 2 Timothy. But in the immediate context, Paul is focusing on his own confidence and how it serves as a model for Timothy. Thus the second reading is the best.)

In the Hellenistic world, the careful preservation of a deposit was a sacred duty, and the gods were often invoked on such occasions (Collins 2002, 213). Philo wrote,

> The most sacred of all the dealings between human beings is the deposit on trust. . . . He who repudiates a deposit acts most wrongfully. . . . He has set at nought both the human and the divine and repudiated two trusts, one that of him who consigned the property, the other that of the most voracious of witnesses, who sees and hears all whether they intend or do not wish to do what they say. (*Special Laws* 4.30, 32)

Elsewhere, Philo writes that the knowledge of divine rites is a deposit that must be preserved (*Abel and Cain* 60).

Even as Paul suffers, God keeps watch over his gospel so that it will not lose its effectiveness. Indeed, even though Paul will die and his ministry will end, God will keep that gospel vital and effective "until that day." The demonstrative "that" indicates that Paul is referring to "the Day of the Lord," the end of this present age. Paul's confidence is set in an eschatological framework. He knows that Jesus will be revealed as Lord of all in the end. He must be faithful to this Jesus because this Jesus has been, is, and will be faithful to him. This confidence enables him to carry on in the face of persecution and death, and it will do the same for Timothy.

Having set out his own relationship to the gospel, Paul in 1:13-14 calls Timothy to follow his example. In 1:6-7, Paul urged Timothy to rekindle the gift of God that he had received. Now, he challenges Timothy to "hold on to the pattern of sound teaching that you heard from me" (1:13). "The pattern" translates *hypotupōsin*, which can be translated "model" or "paradigm." Paul sees his teaching as a paradigm to which Timothy must adhere because it is "sound teaching." "Sound teaching" is literally "sound words." "Sound" (*hygianontōn*) describes something that is healthy or solid. In the Pastoral Epistles, Paul uses this word and its cognate adjective *hygiēs* to modify "words" (here; 1 Tim 6:3; Titus 2:8), "teaching" (2 Tim 4:3; 1 Tim 1:10; Titus 1:9; 2:1), and "faith" (Titus 1:13; 2:2). Thus "sound teaching" is a shorthand description of the gospel message and its essence. Paul's emphasis on "sound teaching" implies the existence of "unsound teaching." The Pastoral Epistles give evidence that unsound teaching was in fact a problem in Paul's churches, a problem Timothy had to deal with as he assumed leadership.

Timothy must adhere to this sound teaching by "the faith and love that are in Christ Jesus." Paul also uses this phrase in 1 Timothy 1:14. For Paul, faith and love are the essence of the Christian life (Gal 5:6; 1 Cor 13:13; 1 Thess 1:3; 3:6; 5:8; Phlm 5; cf. 2 Tim 2:22; 3:10; 1 Tim 1:14; 2:15; 4:12; 6:11; Eph 6:23). "Faith" here, without the definite article (i.e., not "*the* faith," the body of teaching that made up Paul's gospel), refers to the relationship of trust leading to obedience that one enters upon accepting the gospel message. This faith is founded upon the love that is "in Christ Jesus," in a deep and abiding relationship with Jesus Christ. This love defines both our relationship to Jesus and, as a result, our relationship to others. If Timothy faithfully follows Paul's example, he will live a life grounded in and determined by trusting obedience and Christ-like love.

Confident that Timothy has heard this sound teaching, Paul exhorts him to "guard the good treasure entrusted to us, with the help of the Holy Spirit living in us" (1:14). The phrase "treasure entrusted to us" translates the single word *parathēkēn*. This verse echoes the language of 1:12:

- "I am sure that he [God, the one to whom Paul has entrusted himself] is able to guard [*phylaxai*] what he has entrusted [*parathēkēn*] to me" (1:12);
- "Guard [*phylaxon*] the good treasure entrusted to us [*parathēkēn*]" (1:14).

As in 1:12, the *parathēkēn* is the teaching that God had entrusted to Paul, for which he had been appointed herald, apostle, and teacher. Now, through this letter, Paul entrusts this teaching and all that goes with it into Timothy's keeping. Timothy will be able to faithfully keep and administer this teaching through the Holy Spirit's presence in his life. Paul writes often of the indwelling Spirit (e.g., Rom 8:11; 1 Cor 3:16). The Holy Spirit sets people apart for the purposes of God, and it is God's Spirit that enables God's people to be faithful to God's purposes. This Holy Spirit enables Paul to be faithful to his appointment, and he (the Spirit) will likewise enable Timothy to be faithful to his own vocation. Indeed, the God who calls also empowers the called to be faithful. Timothy does not face his vocation or the suffering that accompanies it alone. God does not call people and then abandon them, closing the door behind himself on his way out. He is faithful to empower them by the Spirit so that they may faithfully fulfill the roles to which he appoints them, whatever they may be.

In 1:13-14, Paul employs near-parallel statements to impress on Timothy the nature and importance of his task. The "sound teaching" and "good treasure" represent the understanding of the gospel that Paul has entrusted to Timothy. To "adhere to it" and to "protect" or "guard" it are pictures that help Timothy understand his task. He must hold to the gospel as Paul has given it to him, not letting go, even if an angel from heaven should proclaim a gospel contrary to it (Gal 1:8-9). He must protect it because "there are some . . . who want to pervert the gospel" (Gal 1:7) by turning it into another gospel—when in fact there is no other gospel! Paul struggled against those who would have perverted the gospel throughout his ministry, as is evident in his letters. Paul calls Timothy—and others who fill the pastoral role—to protect the teaching of the church. The world was and is filled with counterfeit gospels, institutions and individuals claiming to be the source of security and peace. But there was and is only one source of true security, salvation, and peace.

Reflecting on his own suffering leads Paul to the first of four autobiographical passages in this letter, 1:15-18 (see also 3:11; 4:6-8; 4:16-18). Here we learn more about Paul's situation at the time of writing. He describes his relationships with Christians, Phygelus and Hermogenes and Onesiphorus, none of whom are mentioned elsewhere in his letters. By mentioning these men, Paul draws a contrast between two ways early Christians responded to his imprisonment and suffering. He uses the contrast to push Timothy (and indeed all who read the letter) to respond appropriately to the suffering of fellow Christians.

The picture Paul draws of himself in these verses is a poignant one. Alone in prison, he awaits his death. This passage reflects a clear chiastic pattern:

A. Timothy's knowledge of the Asian churches (including Ephesus) and their response to Paul's chains (v. 15)
   B. Prayer for Onesiphorus and his household (16a)
      C. Paul's shameful situation in prison (16b) (the focal point of 1:15-18)
   B'.Prayer for Onesiphorus and his household (18a)
A'. Timothy's knowledge of Ephesian church (18b)

Paul is certain that Timothy knows that "all who are in Asia have turned away" from him, including Phygelus and Hermogenes. "All have turned away" might refer to the time of an arrest in Asia when no one came to his aid. It might also refer to the fact that the Christians in Asia were no longer mindful of Paul during his final (traditionally Roman) imprisonment. This "turning away" can refer to their physically abandoning Paul, no longer visiting or supporting him. It could also refer to an act of repudiation, in which they neglected Paul or refused to acknowledge or help him. "Asia" refers to the Roman province (now a part of Turkey); Ephesus, one of Paul's most important bases, was the provincial capital. "All" is clearly an exaggeration since neither Timothy nor Onesiphorus (mentioned in the very next verse) have abandoned Paul. Yet many, evidently including the leaders of churches where Paul had poured himself out sacrificially, had deserted him. This group of deserters included Phygelus and Hermogenes. Phygelus is not mentioned elsewhere in early Christian literature. However, the apocryphal *Acts of Paul* mention a coppersmith named Hermogenes, a friend of Paul's one-time coworker Demas (who also deserts Paul, according to 2 Tim 4:10). The *Acts of Paul* depicts Demas and Hermogenes as opponents of Paul's teaching on celibacy and resurrection from the dead. These men represent the kind of people Timothy must be prepared to deal with in his own ministry—false friends, opportunists who see in Paul's misfortune an opportunity to indulge themselves (Collins 2002, 217).

By the end of the first century, various stories about Paul were circulating. Some would give rise to apocryphal literature about Paul. One of the most interesting and significant of these is the second-century *Acts of Paul and Thecla*. According to this work, Paul was bound, imprisoned, scourged, and expelled from Iconium because of a female convert named Thecla (*Acts of Paul* 3.17, 21). Demas (2 Tim 4:10) and Hermogenes (2 Tim 1:15; cf.

4:14), who had been with Paul when he escaped from Antioch, were the instigators of this trouble *(Acts of Paul* 3.4, 12, 14, 16). These turncoats are described as being "full of hypocrisy" and as having "flattered Paul as if they loved him" (*Acts of Paul* 3.1).

Paul's suffering was not just physical. He also experienced the mental and emotional suffering that comes from being deserted by friends and coworkers. So painful was his sense of abandonment that he felt like every Christian in Asia had turned away from him, including Phygelus and Hermogenes. These verses show us Paul's humanity and are a reminder of the fact that even the most committed Christians are not immune to the pain that comes from broken relationships.

In contrast to the defectors, Onesiphorus "often refreshed" (*anapsyxen*) Paul and was not "ashamed" (*epaischunthē*, cf. 1:8, 12) of Paul's "chains." Instead, he searched for Paul and found him. "Refreshed" suggests both the easing of anxiety and the meeting of physical needs. "Often" (*pollakis*) suggests that this is something Onesiphorus did on multiple occasions, over and over (cf. 1:18b). In fact, 1:18b may be a reference to the acts of repeated support in 1:16. Or the verse may refer to other acts of service Onesiphorus has rendered to Paul's church in Ephesus (where Timothy has served and may still be serving), about which Timothy has detailed knowledge. Paul's point is that Onesiphorus has been consistently faithful in his service both to Paul and to the Ephesian church. Timothy should seek to be as faithful.

Paul also mentions "Onesiphorus," whose name means "profit bearer," in 4:19. Here, Paul prays that "the Lord grant mercy to the household of Onesiphorus." This prayer is similar to prayers Paul offered for people in the thanksgiving sections of his letters (Rom 1:9-10; Phil 1:3-4; 1 Thess 1:2-3; Phlm 4-6). It echoes the central phrase of the Aaronic blessing, "The Lord make his face shine upon you and be gracious to you" (Num 6:25).

Paul calls upon the Lord, who is rich in mercy (Num 14:18; Joel 2:13; Ps 86:5, 15), to grant this mercy to Onesiphorus's "household." The importance of the household in early Christianity cannot be overestimated. The household was both the nucleus of Graeco-Roman society and the nucleus of the early church. Early congregations gathered in homes. Their hosts provided hospitality and preaching opportunities for itinerant missionaries like Paul (e.g., the hospitality of Lydia and the Philippian jailer in Acts 16; on the household, see the discussion of Titus 2).

Paul here does not further describe the nature of Onesiphorus's service. However, his faithfulness became legendary in the early church, as the apocryphal *Acts of Paul* demonstrates. In that document, Onesiphorus played a significant and heroic role in Paul's ministry as a resident of Iconium.

Together with his wife Lectra and his sons Simmias and Zeno, Onesiphorus welcomed Paul to the city and hosted him during his stay there. Paul's appreciation for Onesiphorus's hospitality prompted Hermogenes and Demas to oppose Paul there. After listening to Paul preach in Onesiphorus's house for three days and nights, a woman named Thecla broke her engagement to be married and became a disciple of Paul. She was later imprisoned, and on her release followed Paul to Myra. Paul subsequently sent her back to Iconium to preach; there she delivered an impassioned doxology, again in the house of Onesiphorus (3:2-7, 25, 23-26, 42).

Onesiphorus was "not ashamed" of Paul's chains. The mention of chains is a clear reference to imprisonment, which often included the binding of both hands and feet with heavy iron chains. Imprisonment was a shame-filled situation, and to be identified with a prisoner would be shameful as well. Nevertheless, Onesiphorus identified with Paul in his shame, and was not only willing but eager to care for Paul's emotional and physical needs. Such behavior was clearly counter-cultural.

In 1:8, Paul urged Timothy not to be ashamed of Paul, but to follow Paul's example instead. Now, Paul holds Onesiphorus up as the example Timothy is to follow. The contrast between Onesiphorus and Phygelus and Hermogenes could not be more sharply drawn, nor could Timothy's choice be clearer.

In 1:18a, Paul's prayer focuses on Onesiphorus himself. It is essentially the same prayer as in 1:16a: "that he will find mercy from the Lord on that day." An eschatological dimension is added by the allusion to "the Day of the Lord" (see 1:12). The themes of "shame" and "that day" run throughout 1:12-18.

In 1:15-18, Paul draws a sharp contrast between Onesiphorus's faithfulness and the unfaithfulness of Phygelus and Hermogenes. Onesiphorus refused to be swayed by the shame of Paul's imprisonments and suffering. He not only ministered to Paul in Rome, he also rendered "much service" in Ephesus. Paul sets him before Timothy (and before believers today) as a model to be emulated.

Be strong (2:1-7)

Having set himself and Onesiphorus before Timothy as examples of faithfulness in the face of suffering and potential shame, Paul returns to exhortation and illustration. In 2:1-7, he urges Timothy to be strong in the faith, to follow Paul's example in ministry, to teach and train faithful leaders/teachers, and to endure suffering. He draws illustrations from military life, athletics, and agriculture.

Paul writes, "You then, my child" (2:1). The "you" is emphatic. In Greek, the pronoun is included in the verb. Therefore, the repetition of the pronoun here heightens the urgency of the instructions that follow. This emphasis also heightens the contrast between Timothy's contemplated behavior and that of Phygelus and Hermogenes. Paul again shows his affection for Timothy by again referring to him as Paul's child (*teknon* again; cf. 1:2). Paul's first charge to Timothy is to "be strong in the grace that is in Christ Jesus." "Be strong" (*endynamou*) is a present imperative verb, which commands an ongoing or habitual behavior. It could be rendered, "Keep on being strong." The passive voice suggests that the source of strength is not Timothy himself, but something outside him: he finds it "in the grace that is in Christ Jesus." "Grace" (*charis*) is the unearned, undeserved favor and love that God freely gives to those who are united with Christ. As we are united with Christ, we dwell in the sphere of grace. The first "in" is instrumental: "Let God strengthen you *by means of* his grace, which is found in Christ Jesus."

Paul again highlights the centrality of grace in the Christian life. The strength that Timothy needs for faithful ministry is not of his own making, but is found in God's grace. "Be strong in the Lord, and in his mighty strength" (Eph 6:10). Human strength can only take Timothy so far.

Paul's second charge to Timothy (2:2) echoes 1:13, where Paul spoke of his own "sound words" that Timothy had heard. Here, Paul writes of the "many witnesses" through whom (or "in the presence of whom") Timothy had heard Paul's teaching; "to be a hearer of" is a Greek expression for being a student of someone. Again, this points us to the importance of the church as a community of faith. Western culture emphasizes the individual and downplays the significance of community; not so the ancient Mediterranean culture of the New Testament world. From the beginning of his ministry, Jesus called out a community that would learn from him, his life and example and teaching, and then, in its own life and example and teaching, call others to join the community (Mark 1:16-20; 2:13-14; Matt 28:18-20). A healthy faith community has always been the best context for hearing and being nourished in the faith.

Now Timothy is to "entrust" that which he heard from Paul into the care of others, who will themselves be able to prepare the next generation of teachers and servants. This verse describes multiple generations of succession.

- Paul received his ministry as a succession of tradition (i.e., his gospel and all that it involves and produces) from Jesus Christ;
- Paul passes on that tradition to Timothy;

- Timothy passes that tradition on to faithful leaders;
- These faithful leaders are themselves able to pass the tradition on to others.

"Entrust" (*parathou*) is a form of *parathēkē* (the thing that was entrusted to Paul and then to Timothy in 1:12 and 14). Paul also used this word in 1 Timothy 1:18, to refer to his entrusting to Timothy his command against false teaching in the Ephesian church. This is a strong succession term; see Introduction to the Pastoral Epistles. But note that this is not a succession of office: Timothy does not become an apostle, nor does Paul (as Jesus' successor) become a Messiah. It is a succession of tradition. Both Paul and Timothy receive the care and administration of the gospel from their predecessors, and along with the tradition they receive the power to carry out these duties properly.

That which Timothy has heard from Paul has now been entrusted to Timothy (1:14), so that he may in turn entrust it to others. The verb translated "entrust," *paratithemai*, is another succession term. The word refers to "passing something along," which can imply teaching and unpacking the material, not just handing it down. Those to whom Timothy passes Paul's gospel are to be "faithful"; the accent here is on reliability and dependability, although they are also (to be sure) to be people of faith. They must be committed to the truth of the message, so that they will be competent and acceptable as teachers of the next generation. Notice also that Timothy is to pass Paul's gospel on to faithful *people*, not faithful *men*: the noun *anthrōpos* is generic, not specifically male (which would require *anēr*, not *anthrōpos*). The focus here is on faithfulness, truth versus heresy, not gender.

Paul's third charge to Timothy is to "share in suffering" or "endure suffering" (*sygkakopathēson*, 2:3). Paul is thinking of the kind of suffering that he himself has faced and is facing, suffering for the sake of the gospel. He has already called Timothy to join him in this suffering (1:8).

In 2:3b-6, Paul extends this discussion by using three parallel metaphors to illustrate Christian life and ministry. The "good soldier" illustration (2:3b-4) is the first of the three. Paul elsewhere uses military life as a metaphor for Christian life and ministry (1 Cor 9:7; 2 Cor 10:3-4; cf. Rom 13:12; Phil 2:25; 1 Thess 5:8; Phlm 2). Here, a good soldier suffers with fellow soldiers for the sake of the cause, so that the victory might be won for the common good. Not only must the soldier share in suffering with fellow soldiers. The soldier must also demonstrate a single-minded devotion to the commander, by not becoming entangled in civilian affairs. "Commanding officer" (*stratologēsanti*) refers to a military commander; it *can* refer to the one who enlists soldiers, which might lead some to think Paul is demanding Timothy's loyalty for himself. But that is not the force here; Jesus is the commanding officer, not Paul.

"Entangled" (*emplekomai*) is a rare verb, referring to becoming so involved in something that one is restricted or controlled by it, therefore no longer free to do what should be done. Military life demanded total commitment. Roman soldiers were not allowed to marry, or to pursue businesses outside their military duties (Dio Cassius, *Roman History* 60.24). Service in the Roman army meant total devotion and commitment to the emperor. Nothing less would suffice.

Two things seem clear about a good soldier, as Paul describes it. First, good soldiers are prepared to accept the consequences of doing their duty, even if those consequences involve suffering (1:8; 2:3; etc.). Second, good soldiers are so focused on doing their duty that they will not let anything stand in the way. They refuse to be diverted or sidetracked. Paul calls Timothy to a similar commitment to the gospel of Jesus Christ.

In 2:5, Paul shifts to the second metaphor, the athlete. As was the case with the metaphor of the good soldier, Paul uses this illustration elsewhere (1 Cor 9:24-27; cf. Phil 3:14). Paul was no doubt familiar with the Isthmian games, which were held in Corinth every two years, and were second only to the Athenian Olympics in importance. He knew that only those who faithfully followed the rules of competition could wear the victor's crown. For example, if a runner failed to go around the post at the turn in a race, an umpire would strike him with a stick (cf. *2 Clem* 7). The rules covered not only the competition itself, but also involved approved means and methods of training. Athletes were required to spend months in rigorous preparation for the events. Athletes who did not compete according to the rules were disqualified from winning the prizes; the winners, who did not disqualify themselves by their behavior, would be crowned with a wreath of pine or laurel or celery (Collins 2002, 223).

The third image, the farmer, is the topic in 2:6. Again, Paul uses this metaphor elsewhere to describe Christian life and ministry (1 Cor 3:6-9; 9:7; Gal 6:7-10). In 1 Corinthians, Paul likens the church to "God's field," in which both he and Apollos labored so that they would receive their appropriate rewards. Here Paul reminds Timothy that the laborer is worthy of his wage (see 1 Tim 5:17-18; 1 Cor 3:8; 9:7-10; Luke 10:7). The phrase "hardworking [*kopiōnta*] farmer" points to the farmer who is wholehearted in devotion to the work: *kopioō* refers to *hard* work, labor, toil through difficulties and trouble. "The hardworking farmer should receive the first of the harvested crop": the farmer who works both hard and smart, through fatigue and trouble, is more likely to harvest from a good crop. The farmer who is lazy or who ignores the cycles of seasons, planting and harvest, soon grows hungry, and his family with him. Both the images of "farmer" and "harvest" are used in the New Testament as metaphors for evangelism.

The idea that draws the three images together is that all three, soldier, athlete, and farmer, must seriously attend to the rules governing their work. If they ignore the principles of their vocation—if the soldier ignores the rules of the battlefield, if the runner does not run the proper course, if the farmer plants in the wrong season—then they fail at their task. Likewise, Timothy's calling is a high and serious calling. If he does not minister and serve and lead in ways faithful to Paul's gospel, he will fail at his task. Gifts and talents are not enough; believers can disqualify themselves from service by behavior that damages the work of Christ, by selfish ambition, by compromises that gut their faithfulness to the truth of the gospel.

Paul challenges Timothy: "Mind the things I say, for the Lord will give you understanding of all these things" (2:7). The verb "mind" (*noei*) refers to carefully considering something, thinking it through. If Timothy is mindful of Paul's charge, carefully thinking through these instructions, then the Lord will give him "understanding of all these things," referring to the instructions of 2:4-7.

Theological foundation (2:8-13)

In this paragraph, Paul offers a theological justification for his exhortations to Timothy. This exhortation begins with fragment from an early Christian hymn/confession (2:8). The hymn fragment underscores the nature of the gospel that sustains Paul amidst suffering and imprisonment (2:9-10). Paul follows this statement of confidence and purpose with a second hymnic statement, which he declares to be a "faithful saying" (2:11-13).

Paul begins, "Remember Jesus Christ . . ." (2:8). "Remember" (*mnēmoneue*) does not imply something that has been forgotten. Paul is rather pointing to something significant for the faith that should be given greater attention. The name "Jesus Christ" together with the phrases "raised from the dead, descendant of David" have a marked confessional sound and rhythm. Paul spoke frequently of the resurrection of Jesus, and always emphasized that God was the one who acted to raise Jesus from the dead. Here, God's role is implied by the divine passive (see Rom 6:4, 9; 7:4; 1 Cor 15:12, 15-17, 20; compare with the active voice with God as subject, Rom 4:24; 8:11; 10:9; 2 Cor 4:14; Gal 1:1; 1 Thess 1:10).

"Jesus Christ, raised from the dead, descendant of David" captures the essence of the gospel in highly compressed form (cf. Rom 1:3-4 as part of the longer summary, 1:2-5). Paul emphasizes Jesus' humanity by using the order "Jesus Christ" (rather than "Christ Jesus," which is more common in the Pastoral Epistles). That this Jesus was raised from the dead implies, of course, that Jesus died (and was therefore flesh and blood, human; perhaps Paul has some Docetic denial of Jesus' humanity in mind here?). In "from the dead," "the dead" is plural. This suggests that the phrase is better rendered "from among the dead," a partitive genitive. Paul understands the resurrected Jesus to be the first fruits of the resurrection, the sign that those who are united with him will also be raised. It is this hope that sustains Paul, and it is this message and hope that Timothy must faithfully proclaim.

"Christ" is the Greek equivalent of the Hebrew "Messiah." Both words mean "anointed one." This term refers to the long-anticipated King of Israel who would reestablish the throne of David and restore prosperity and *shalom* to the nation. Paul further underscores this expectation, and the unexpected way God began fulfilling it, by the phrase "descendant of David" (lit., "of the seed of David"). In Romans 1:3, as Paul begins explaining his message and ministry to the Roman church, he uses this expression to emphasize Jesus' Davidic origins in fulfillment of messianic expectations. The New Testament underscores this relationship elsewhere, primarily in the Synoptics (Matt 12:1, 6, 17; Mark 12:35-37; Luke 1:32; 3:31) and Johannine writings (John 7:42; Rev 5:5; 22:16).

Jesus was Israel's Messiah, God's means of blessing the entire world in fulfillment of his promises to Abraham (Gen 12:3). God kept this promise in an unexpected way—by Jesus' death. But death did not have the final word—Jesus was raised from among the dead. And because he was raised, the power of sin is broken, death itself is undone, the dead too will rise. This message is Paul's gospel. It affirms both Jesus' humanity and his glorification. Both are essential to Paul's gospel, and as Timothy ministers he must keep these things in mind. This message is the basic essence of the Christian faith. It is the content of what Paul preaches and calls Timothy to preach faithfully as well.

Memory is a powerful thing. In 2:1, Paul called on Timothy to be strong. In 2:8, he calls on Timothy to be mindful of the things that will help him be strong. One of the hallmarks of the Judaism in which Paul was raised was its emphasis on constantly remembering the mighty works of God in history. Israel's worship was wrapped in family history. Each of the major festivals of Israel was a celebration of these memories. In times of distress and trouble, they remembered what God had done, how he had been faithful in difficult circumstances in the past. This kept alive the expectation that God will act again. Christians live between memory and hope; remembering Jesus

Christ is to live in the expectation of his return, which strengthens the believer in the midst of suffering.

In 2:9-10, Paul returns to the subject of his suffering. He introduced this topic in 1:8. Here, he emphasizes the nature of the hardship he suffers. "Suffer hardship" (*kakopatheō*) refers to being in distress, physical suffering. Paul suffers this hardship to the point of "being chained [*desmōn*] as a criminal [*kakourgos*]." *Kakourgos* refers to "one who customarily does what is wrong," an evildoer (*LN* 88.114). Luke uses this word to refer to the criminals who died with Jesus. Paul continues to point to his own fate as a way of reminding Timothy of what he may face if he follows in Paul's footsteps, faithfully carrying out his ministry.

Still, whatever Paul's situation, no matter what he suffers, "the word of God is not chained." In Paul's mind, the gospel that he proclaims is the word of God, because the message he received as Jesus' successor comes from God and summarizes and enacts God's saving plan. This gospel "*is* the power of God for salvation" (Rom 1:16, emphasis added). To the Corinthians, Paul wrote, "the message of the cross is foolishness to those who are perishing, but to us who are being saved it is the power of God" (1 Cor 1:17). Throughout the Bible, the word of God is viewed as a powerful thing. By God's word, creation came into being (Gen 1). God's word has power to create something from nothing. Once spoken, it actively moves toward fulfillment. Nothing can stop God's word, or keep it from realizing God's purposes for it. And that word is personified in Jesus (John 1:1-18; 1 John 1:1-4; Rev 19:13), whom even death and the grave could not restrain. Paul may be in chains, but God's word is not bound (cf. Acts 28:31, where Paul, though imprisoned, preaches the gospel "with complete boldness, unhindered").

Paul writes, "Therefore, I endure [*hypomenō*] all things for the sake" of his churches (2:10). The fact that God's word is not chained gives meaning to Paul's suffering, enabling him to endure everything. "Endurance" was one of the highest virtues in both Jewish and Hellenistic thought. Both Plato and Aristotle considered it among the noblest of virtues. Stoic moralists, for whom resistance to passion was the ideal of the ethical life, extolled the virtue of endurance. Philo described it as a manly virtue (*Change of Names* 153, 197; *Moses* 2.184; see also 4 Macc 1:11; 5:23; 17:4, 23), a characteristic of athletes (*Abel and Cain* 46; *Every Good Man Is Free* 26), and one of the mightiest virtues (*Cherubim* 78). Rebekah, whose name in popular Hebrew etymology meant "strong confidence," is the symbol of endurance for Philo (*Cherubim* 47; *Preliminary Studies* 36; Collins 2002, 227).

Paul's endurance is not endurance for endurance's sake, however. Nor is it endurance for Paul's sake. Paul's endurance is for the benefit of others. Paul suffers, but he understands that his suffering can have positive results for other people. This distinguishes suffering for the gospel from suffering for the sake of suffering. Suffering for the sake of the gospel is a form of witness that might benefit others by bringing them to faith. Paul assures the Philippians that his imprisonment has actually

> . . . helped to spread the gospel, so that it has become known throughout the whole imperial guard and to everyone else that my imprisonment is for Christ. And most of the brothers and sisters, having been made confident in the Lord by my imprisonment, dare to speak the word with greater boldness and without fear. (Phil 1:12-14)

Paul did not set out to suffer, but he believed in a God who could transform the cross (the epitome of brutality and inhumanity) into the vehicle for mankind's redemption. This God could likewise turn Paul's own suffering into something redemptive (cf. Col 1:24).

Paul's endurance is "for the sake of the elect," those chosen by God, whose faith God foreknew (cf. Rom 8:28-30). If salvation results from the proclamation of the gospel (Rom 10:13-14; 1 Cor 1:17-18), then Paul (and Timothy) must endure in spite of every adversity, including suffering and imprisonment, so that others "may obtain the salvation that is in Christ Jesus, with eternal glory." The salvation to which Paul refers is "in Christ." This statement points to the relationship where salvation is found, the believer's relationship with Christ. It includes the experience of being in union with Christ and all that this relationship brings in the present. It also looks forward to the future, to that relationship's consummation in eternal "glory." In the Old Testament, God's "glory" was the manifestation of his presence. Paul here points to that presence as the believer's eternal home.

"The saying is sure" (2:11) is literally, "the saying is faithful." Paul uses this formula three times in 1 Timothy (1:15; 3:1; 4:9), once (here) in 2 Timothy, and once in Titus (3:8). The formula indicates that Paul is quoting or using traditional material, which he may or may not have authored himself and which the audience may already know. The formula may precede the material (e.g., 1 Tim 1:15), or it may follow (e.g., 1 Tim 3:1a; 4:9; Titus 3:8). Here, the formula precedes the traditional material to which it points (2:11b-13); some argue that, since 2:8 is also traditional material, the formula points back to the christological statement there.

The material in 2:11-13 is a well crafted, tightly knit balanced poetic structure, characteristic of Greek hymns and Hebrew psalms. It is composed of two couplets (2:11b-12a, 12b-13a) in four clauses, demonstrating both parallelism and antithesis. Each clause consists of a conditional sentence ("if ... then"), which is assumed to be true. The "if" in each clause deals with an attitude that a person might have or an action that a person might take, followed by the description of the results ("then"). The first couplet (2:11b-12a) deals with positive aspects of the Christian experience. The second couplet (2:12b-13a) treats negative matters, the consequences of unfaithfulness. Thus positive and negative matters are contrasted side by side; this was a popular rhetorical device.

The hymn reads,

> If we died with him, we will also live with him;
> If we endure, we will also reign with him.
>
> If we renounce him, he will also renounce us;
> If we are not faithful, he will remain faithful,
> For he cannot renounce himself.

The synonymous parallelism of the first couplet ("If we died . . . if we endure . . . ") highlights the present state and future hope of the Christian. The grammar makes it clear that what is being proposed (the "if" statement) is assumed to be true. Thus the phrase could be translated, "Since we died with him." "We" refers to all Christians, those who have died with Christ (cf. Rom 6:3-11; Col 3:1-3; cf. Col 2:20). "Died with him" translates a rare compound verb (found only here; Mark 14:31; 2 Cor 7:3). In the aorist tense, this verb depicts the Christian's death with Christ as a completed action in the past, a definite event that has taken place in the life of the believer. The result, "we will also live with him," is another rare compound verb (here; Rom 6:8; 2 Cor 7:3). In the future tense, this verb points to the believer's eternal hope, which is now present (but incomplete). Only in solidarity with Christ is this death and future life possible. With Jesus we die, and with Jesus we will live. This language is characteristically Pauline; compare Romans 6:8, where Paul (in a discussion of the effects of baptism) writes, "if we have died with Christ, we believe that we will also live with him." As believers enter into solidarity with the humanity and death of Jesus, they also come to share in his life (Rom 6:5-11; 2 Cor 4:14; 1 Thess 4:14-17).

The present tense verb rendered "if we endure" (1:12) could also be translated, "if we continue to endure," or "if we keep on keeping on." In 2:10, Paul portrays himself as the model of such endurance (cf. 4:7-8). "We will reign with him" translates another rare compound verb (lit., "we will reign together"). In the New Testament, this word is found only here and in 1 Corinthians 4:8. It appears in Polybius, *Histories* 30.2.4, where it refers to a proposal that rule be shared by two brothers. Again, the future tense suggests an eschatological focus. "To reign together with Christ" is to share in the kingdom of God, the traditional symbol for God's eschatological reign at the center of Jesus' preaching (Mark 1:15 and para).

The second couplet (2:12b-13a) deals with the consequences of unfaithfulness. The structure here is worth noting. The first part of each line describes an unfaithful action: "we renounce [or deny] him." The second part of each line describes a consequence of that offense by repeating the offense from the opposite direction: "he will deny us." Such statements describe an eschatological law of retribution, "sentences of holy law" (Schmidt 1977, 518; Käsemann 1969). Here, Paul sets denial and faithlessness over against endurance and faithful suffering, making a sharp and stark contrast. In both 2:12b and 2:13a, "he" translates *ekeinos* ("that one"), referring to Jesus at his return. Collins suggests that this verse "speaks enigmatically of 'that one' rather than of the Lord because the Lord is a Savior, a beneficent figure, whereas 'that one' is a vindicator" (Collins 2002, 220).

The faithful saying of 2:11-13 echoes the teachings of both Paul and Jesus. In 2:11, Paul echoes his declaration from Romans that "if we have been united with him like this in his death, we will certainly be united with him in his resurrection" (Rom 6:5). Verse 2:12a is echoed in Revelation 20:4 ("They came to life and they reigned with Christ . . ."), and 2:12b echoes Jesus' teaching in Mark 9:38a.

The final phrase of the second couplet is unexpected. Based on the three previous clauses, the reader would expect to read, "If we are faithless [to him] he will refuse to be faithful [to us]." Instead, Paul writes, "he will remain faithful." Two explanations for this dramatic shift have been offered.

1. God remains faithful in his sense of justice, which requires that he pronounce judgment on the faithless just as he will deny the deniers. The final clause, "for he cannot deny himself," is added to explain why this will be the case. God, being just, must be just in all matters, for that is who he is; he cannot deny his character. While this reading makes sense logically, it appears to be the opposite of what Paul says elsewhere about God's gracious justice.
2. He remains faithful in the sense of his loyalty that transcends human frailty and failures. This sense is the primary way in which the Old Testament depicts God's faithfulness. He keeps his covenant with his

people, even though they fail to perfectly keep their end of the agreement (Gen 15:17; Ps 32; 103; Jer 31:31-34). What he cannot deny about himself is his faithfulness to his people.

The second reading is clearly the better way to understand the passage. Thus this hymn celebrates the gospel of salvation by grace through faith that Paul and Timothy were commissioned by God to proclaim. The faithfulness of God is not thwarted, even by the failures of his people's faith. This good news is not based on who or what they are. Nor is it based on what they deserve. It is instead based on who God is. He will be faithful, and keep his promise of grace, because he cannot deny who he is.

Images of Ministry (2:14–3:9)

The second large section in the body of the letter, 2:14–3:9, differs in character from sections before it and after it, because it makes no reference to Paul's personal example. The first large section (1:6–2:13) used Paul's suffering (his imprisonment and the desertion of coworkers) as its foundation for building a model of ministry as triumph over suffering. The last large section (3:10–4:8) also depends heavily on Paul as the example of one who triumphed over suffering and persecution.

By contrast, 2:14–3:9 makes no mention of Paul's suffering, with two tacit exceptions:

- 2:7, which mentions the false teachers Hymenaeus and Philetus; and
- 2:24, where Paul refers to "the Lord's slave." Paul applies this language to himself several times in his letters (e.g., Titus 1:1; Rom 1:1), but not elsewhere in 2 Timothy.

This section centers on two images of ministry: the workman who has passed the test and the vessel fit for noble use. Paul follows both illustrations with practical instruction about the life and priorities of ministry. Then in the last part of this section, Paul describes the kinds of people and problems that ministers encounter in the last days; these constitute a minefield that careful ministers must safely navigate, if their ministries are to be triumphant and successful.

A worker who passes the test (2:14-19)

With another exhortation, Paul returns to the everyday realities of Timothy's ministry and the nature of his task (2:14). Timothy must "remind them of these things": "remind" echoes the memory motif, introduced in 2:8. "These things" (*tauta*) refers to the theological teaching in 2:8-13: Throughout the Pastoral Epistles, *tauta* refers to Paul's teachings (1 Tim 3:14; 4:6; 11, 15; 5:7, 21; 6:2b; 2 Tim 2:2; Titus 2:15; 2:8; see the discussion under 1 Tim 3:14). Here, it refers particularly to the "faithful saying," the traditional material in 2:8-13. Furthermore, Timothy is to "solemnly warn them" (*diamarturomenos*) against "disputing about the meaning of words" (or "engaging in verbal warfare," *logomachein*). He is to warn them "before God," that is, in the presence of God or calling on God as his witness. This phrase contributes to the solemnity of the task and the seriousness of the charge Timothy must make (cf. 2 Tim 4:1; 1 Tim 5:21; 6:13). Paul fleshes out the warning, employing a rhetorical argument of advantage. He describes the dangers associated with such disputes in terms of the disadvantages they bring and the advantages they do not bring. These arguments "do nothing helpful" (*chrēsimon*), nothing of value. They are useless exercises, futile. Worse, "they bring ruin [*katastrophē*] on the listeners." *Katastrophē*, source of our English word "catastrophe," refers to total ruin or destruction. Second Peter 2:6 applies this word to the fate of Sodom and Gomorrah.

Paul next (2:15) provides Timothy with a standard for examining his own life and conduct: the Christian leader's life must always be an examined life. Timothy must "make every effort" (*spoudason*; see the discussion at Titus 3:12) "to present [himself] before God as a proven workman [*ergatēn*] who has no cause for shame." "Proven" (*dokimon*) describes something or someone that has passed the test. Hellenistic writers used this adjective to mean "qualified" or "competent." Philo applies it to a competent craftsman (*Heir* 158), mathematicians and astronomers (*Creation* 128), physicians (*Unchangeableness of God* 65; *Special Laws* 3.117), and priests (*Special Laws* 1.166). The one before whom Timothy must present himself is God. Paul may be Timothy's mentor, but Timothy must answer to God, to whom he owes his ultimate allegiance.

"Having no cause for shame" (*anepaischynton*) translates a single adjective, a negative cognate of *epaischunomai*, "to be ashamed," from 1:8, 12, 16. The shame motif has already played a prominent role in this letter. In the honor/shame culture of the Graeco-Roman world, people would do whatever was necessary to avoid shame. Shame before one's fellow human beings was a serious thing. Paul's concern is even more serious, that Timothy not be ashamed before God.

How does Timothy avoid this shame? He must "pass on the word of truth without deviating." Here, Paul defines how Timothy is to teach. "Pass on without deviating" translates *orthotomounta*, a participle that literally refers to cutting something in a straight way, "plowing a straight row." It carries the connotation of "exactness and precision, without error or flaw." It was used figuratively to describe the accurate passing on of teaching that does not distort the message, explaining something correctly. It looks back to the succession of tradition in 2:2, the faithful passing on of Paul's gospel from one generation to the next. In a context where Paul's churches were dogged by false teaching, this admonition was doubly important.

Paul also defines what Timothy is to teach. The worker who is "proven," who "has no cause for shame," is the one who accurately passes on the message (*logos*) of the gospel. "Word of truth" is a succinct characterization of Timothy's message. It echoes Paul's description of his own preaching (e.g., 2 Cor 6:7). Paul frequently refers to his message as *logos* (1 Cor 14:36; 2 Cor 5:19; Phil 2:16; 1 Thess 1:8; 2:13). He also refers to his message as "truth" (*alētheia*; Gal 2:5, 14; 5:7; 2 Cor 4:2; 6:7). The "word of truth" is a shorthand expression for the gospel Paul charges Timothy to preach.

Timothy's ministry, like that of pastors who follow him, centers on the word of truth. He must preach, teach, illustrate, and apply the gospel message; this is both a great privilege and a grave responsibility. The health of the church depends on people having a clear understanding of God's word. The work is labor-intensive, and requires time for preparation. Paul knows that the work in the Ephesian church—like any other busy church—will expand to fill whatever space Timothy allows it. So he urges Timothy to keep his priorities in order, and make sure he has time to study and prepare. Likewise, in Acts 6, the Apostles chose the Seven "to minister at tables" in the daily distribution of food (or money for food), rather than dealing with that problem directly. This enabled the Apostles to devote themselves "to prayer and ministry of the word" (Acts 6:4). Both ministries were essential—the serving of physical food to nourish the body and the serving of the word to nourish the mind and spirit.

Paul immediately contrasts the "word of truth" with "profane chatter" (*bebēlous kenophōnias*), which Timothy must "avoid" (*periistaso*) (2:16; cf. 1 Tim 1:9; 6:20). The structure of the Greek text here is powerful. Following the word order in the text, the passage reads ". . . explaining without deviation the word of truth. But profane chatter you must avoid." By placing "word of truth" and "profane chatter" next to one another, Paul draws a strong contrast between the two. The word translated "profane" was used to describe something irreligious or godless. Similarly, our English verb "profane" means to take something that is acceptable to God and render it unacceptable to God. This is close to Paul's meaning here; something "profane" stands in sharp contrast to something holy, dedicated to God, acceptable to God. Thus "profaneness" is the antithesis of godliness (*euse-*

beia). The word translated "chatter" is plural, "chatterings," which suggests there was no lack of such chattering in Ephesus (assuming that Timothy continued to serve there). This godless talk likely includes false teaching; it may go beyond false doctrine and unsound words into other areas of frivolous or damaging speech.

Profane chatter is to be avoided because of its destructive effects: it causes those who engage in it to "progress further and further in ungodliness [*asebeia*]." "Godliness" (*eusebeia*) is a cardinal virtue in the Pastoral Epistles. It refers to appropriate attitude and conduct toward divine things. In a Christian context, *eusebeia* is a life lived in and from reverence for God. Its opposite quality, *asebeia* (ungodliness), must be avoided at all costs. In addition to the progress in ungodliness that it fosters, "their talk [profane chatter] will spread like gangrene" (2:17). In the same way that an infection spreads its poisons throughout the body, so ungodly talk metastasizes and spreads destruction through the church.

In 2:17b, Paul focuses on two specific parties who are guilty of engaging in or promoting "profane chatter," Hymenaeus and Philetus. Hymenaeus appears in the New Testament only here and in 1 Timothy 1:20, where Paul describes him (alongside a man named Alexander) as someone who has "suffered shipwreck in the faith." Paul then "hands them over to Satan" so that they will be brought to repentance. Hymenaeus shares his name with the Greek god of wedding ceremonies. Philetus, whose name means "amiable," appears only here in the New Testament.

According to Paul, these two "have strayed from the truth by claiming that the resurrection has already taken place" (2:18). "Have strayed" translates *ēstochēsan*, which Hellenistic writers used to refer to serious errors in understanding (Plutarch, "On Listening to Lectures," *Moralia* 46A; "Obsolescence of Oracles" 10, *Moralia* 414F; "Table Talk" 7.5, *Moralia* 705C; Josephus, *J.W.* 4.2.5 §116). The word is synonymous with *hamartanō*, which the Septuagint and New Testament use as their default term for "sin."

Paul identifies one aspect of the serious error being taught by Hymenaeus and Philetus. They proclaim that the resurrection has already taken place. Christians from a Hellenistic background brought with them a worldview that disdained the body and the physical universe. Paul's teaching on the resurrection came from a different worldview, a Jewish worldview, which emphasized the goodness of the physical universe (at least as it had been created by God), and thus the bodily nature of the resurrection. This difference in worldviews led to misunderstandings and even rejections of Paul's teaching on resurrection in several places. One such misunderstanding gave rise to Paul's extended treatment of the resurrection in 1 Corinthians 15; so also the treatments of the topic in 1 Thessalonians 4:13–5:11 and 2 Thessalonians 2:1-12 (cf. Acts 17:32).

Influenced by ideas such as these, the false teaching mentioned here may have arisen from misunderstanding of Paul's teaching about conversion as a kind of dying and rising with Christ (cf. Rom 6:1-11 and Col 2:11-12; 2:20–3:4). Some concluded if the believer dies and rises with Christ at baptism, then the resurrection has already occurred. This would lead to spiritualizing the idea of resurrection so that it came to be understood as a metaphor for conversion, without any future bodily resurrection. Clearly, Christians from a Hellenistic background had difficulty accepting the notion of a physical resurrection. Add to this the way that Hellenistic thought separated the physical from the spiritual, and the last thing anyone from that perspective wanted after death was another body (e.g., see Acts 17:18, 32)! This kind of "demythologizing" would have sounded reasonable to Hellenistic ears, making the Christian message more attractive.

Paul clearly describes the results of this teaching: "they are overturning some people's faith." The verb *anatrepousin* means "to overthrow" or "destroy." It can be understood in the sense of "subverting" or "undermining" something. The Gospel of John uses this word to describe Jesus overturning the moneychangers' tables (John 2:15). Elsewhere in the Pastoral Epistles, Paul uses this word to refer to the effects that false teachers have on households (Titus 1:11). Here, what they are undermining or destroying is some people's faith. "Faith" here refers either to a person's relationship with God or their adherence to the content of the gospel, or both. By their perverted teaching about the resurrection, Hymenaeus and Philetus are undermining people's adherence to the clear teaching of Paul's gospel (2:8), the word of God (2:9), the trustworthy saying (2:11), and the word of truth (2:15). In so doing, they are damaging their hearers' relationship with God as well.

In spite of the subversive teaching of people like Hymenaeus and Philetus, "God's solid foundation stands firm" (2:19). Paul sets up another clear contrast here. God's firm foundation (the message of the gospel and the church which springs from it) is solid and can never be overturned or subverted. Paul here uses both the verb "to stand firm" (*histēmi*) and the adjective "firm" (*stereos*). The image of a building is one of Paul's favorite metaphors for the church (Rom 15:20; 1 Cor 3:10-12; Eph 2:20). Paul knows that the building is only as strong as its foundation (1 Cor 3:9b-17). Here, the foundation bears an inscription, which contains three allusions from the Septuagint.

- *"The Lord knows those who are his"* is from Numbers 16:5. This quote points Timothy to God's promise to protect his people from those who would corrupt them, and punish the corrupters. Numbers 16 tells the story of the revolt of Korah, Dathan, and Abiram against Moses. Using the language of the royal court, where only the king's own men are allowed to stand in his presence, Moses said, "In the morning the Lord will make known who are his, and who is holy, and who will be allowed to approach him." The next day, the ground opened up and swallowed the leaders of the rebellion, and fire consumed those who had followed them.
- *"Stay away from unrighteousness, everyone who claims the name of the Lord"* combines two allusions from the Septuagint. The first is Sirach 17:26, *"turn away from unrighteousness."* The second is from Isaiah 26:13, where the people proclaim their allegiance to the one God after having followed other gods: *"we claim the name of the Lord."* In both Isaiah 26:13 LXX and 2 Timothy 2:19, "claim" translates *onomazomai*, which refers to pronouncing a name in a ritual or ceremony.

Taken together, these materials from the Septuagint state a clear message. To have lives built on this solid foundation, people must make genuine conversions, repudiating other gods and calling on the name of the Lord alone, turning from a life of unrighteousness to a life of faithfulness. Nothing less will do. God will not be mocked by pretension; he knows the ones who belong to him. "Let us not talk falsely now, the hour is getting late" (Dylan 1968).

<u>A vessel fit for noble use (2:20-26)</u>

Having examined the foundation, Paul now turns to the house itself. "In a wealthy [*megalē*, lit., "great" or "large"] home, there are implements [*skeuē*] not only of gold and silver but also of wood and clay" (2:20). The mention of silver and gold utensils suggests the translation of *megalē* adopted here: not "large" but "important" or "wealthy." *Skeuos* is a generic term, referring to any kind of object or container, bowl, or basket (*LN* 6.1; 6.118). Poor people would have used utensils made of wood or crockery, but even the poor would have some familiarity with items made from richer materials. Paul's extended metaphor here distinguishes between the materials from which the utensils are made and their uses. Objects made of gold and silver are for special use (lit., "honorable use," *timēn*), while objects made of wood and clay are for ordinary use (lit., "dishonorable," *atimian*).

In 2:21, Paul shifts attention to the necessary washing of utensils so that they may be used for special purposes. This metaphor points to the necessity of cleansing oneself in order to be of special ("honored") use in the household of God. The cleansing (*ekkatharē*) may be a reference to baptism, a physical enactment of the spiritual reality of conversion. More likely, Paul's reference to cleansing summarizes and extends instructions from throughout the chapter:

- it parallels the reference to good soldiers not becoming entangled in civilian affairs, athletes competing according to the rules, etc., in 2:3-6, and
- it amplifies the instructions of 2:15 and the reference to fleeing from unrighteousness in 2:19.

Thus Timothy must keep himself clean of things that will distract him from his ministry or detract from its effectiveness. Timothy then will be "an object for honorable use, consecrated [*hēgiasmenon*], helpful [*euchrēston*] to the master of the house, prepared [*hētoimasmenon*] for every good work." "Consecrated" is cultic language for being set apart for God's use. "Master of the house" translates *despotē*, which is a common designation for God in the Septuagint and in Hellenistic Jewish writings (e.g., Gen 15:2, 8; Jonah 4:3; Jer 1:6; 4:10; Job 5:8; Dan 9:15; Tob 8:17; Philo, *Heir* 22; Josephus, *Ant* 8.4.3; *J.W.* 7.8.6 §32; cf. Jesus' use of *oikodespotēs* ["master of the household"] in his parables, Matt 13:27; 20:1, 11; 21:33; 24:43; Luke 12:39; 13:25; 14:21). The household in this metaphor is, of course, the church. In 1 Timothy 3:15, Paul referred to the church as "the household [of God]." Early Christians commonly used household language to refer to the church. The master of this household is God, and those who would enter this household must answer to this master. Christians must keep their lives and hearts in line, so that they are ready for the master's use, "ready for every good work." They have become a new creation, committed to the tasks God has been preparing for them (and which God has been preparing them for) (2 Cor 5:17; Eph 2:8-10).

The challenge Paul has for Timothy in these verses is clear. Timothy must choose the kind of servant he will be. To be consecrated and useful to the Master, his conversion must be a present thing, not just an event in his own private salvation history. Conversion and salvation are ongoing processes, a continuous pattern of turning away from and turning toward. Therefore, Timothy must "flee youthful passions" and "chase after righteousness, faithfulness, love, and peace" (2:22). The two verbs translated "flee" (*pheuge*) and "chase after" (*diōke*) draw a sharp and dramatic contrast. This same construction, with the same two verbs, appears in 1 Timothy 6:11.

1 Timothy 6:11	**2 Timothy 2:22**
Flee from these things (the catalog of vices in 6:3-10): *chase after* righteousness, godliness, faithfulness, love, endurance, gentleness.	*Flee from* youthful passions *chase after* righteousness, faithfulness, love, and peace

The phrase "youthful passions" (*neōterikas epithymias*) picks up a motif found elsewhere in the Pastoral Epistles (2 Tim 3:6; 4:3; 1 Tim 6:9; Titus 2:12; 3:3). Timothy, though a young man, must shun the passions of youth (cf. Titus 2:6). Leaders in the household of God are to be mature individuals (such as the *presbyteroi* of 1 Timothy 3, 5 and Titus 1, 2) who can control their passions. While "passions" are usually seen as sexual urges and desires (cf. 1 Cor 6:18), other desires and compulsions also come into play. Indeed, the Stoics taught that passion itself, whatever its object, should be avoided, for it only serves to disturb one's sense of peace. In contrast, Paul suggests that passion should not be avoided; it must rather be redirected into the pursuit of righteousness, faithfulness, love, and peace!

The list of things that Timothy is to pursue is one of twenty such "virtue lists" in the New Testament (e.g., 2 Cor 6:6-7a; Gal 5:22-23; Phil 4:8). Writers of Paul's day commonly used such lists to spell out the qualifications and characteristics of leadership. "Righteousness," "faithfulness" (or faith), and "love" also appear in 1 Timothy 6:11, and the pairing of "faith" and "love" is a classic Pauline description of the Christian life (e.g., 1 Thess 3:6; Gal 5:6). Both terms describe the essence of the Christian's relationship to God, and (as the biblical definition of faith includes loyalty/faithfulness) the essence of the Christian's relationship with others, as well.

- "Righteousness" (*dikaiosunē*) is found in other Pauline virtue lists (Phil 4:8; 1 Tim 6:11; Titus 1:8; Eph 5:9; cf. 6:14). Hellenistic Jewish writers used *dikaiosunē* to refer to being in right relationships with other people, therefore rightly relating to God.
- "Peace" (*eirēnē*) is also found in Galatians 5:22. The Hellenistic world generally thought of *eirēnē* in terms of the absence of armed conflict, or the absence of personal pain. In Hellenistic Jewish writers, however, use the word as the equivalent of the Hebrew shalom, God's full blessing on his covenant people, the wholeness of life that only God can give. Shalom

refers to a life where everything is good and right and healthy—and *not* just the absence of violence or pain. Biblically, shalom is synonymous with salvation. Sin brings alienation, hostility, and suspicion toward God (e.g., Gen 3:6-10, where the man and the woman hide because they are afraid of God and ashamed of their nakedness). Jesus came to bring shalom with God, a relationship without fear or anger or suspicion or animosity. And this peace with God transforms all other relationships (see the salutations in Paul's letters, "grace and peace"; Rom 5:1; 8:6; 14:17, 19, etc.; cf. the "reconciliation" motif in Rom 5:10; 2 Cor 5:16-21; Eph 2:14-20; Col 1:19-23).

The admonition ("flee from youthful passions") is not for Timothy alone, but is also for "all who call on the name of the Lord with a pure heart." Again, Paul points to the importance of the community of faith. The continuing process of conversion and salvation is one that Timothy shares with all the faithful. He is not alone in the adventure of faith. He shares this adventure with the household of God. The New Testament makes no room for "Lone Ranger" Christianity. Faith inevitably joins us to the community of the faithful.

Paul and Timothy are among those who call on the name of the Lord (1 Cor 1:20). This description reflects a common biblical idea (cf. the allusion to Isa 26:13 in 2:19 above; Gen 12:8; 13:4; 21:33; 26:25). "Calling on the name of the Lord" refers to acknowledging Jesus' lordship (Phil 2:9-11). Believers acknowledge his lordship, calling on his name, at conversion (Rom 10:12-14; Acts 22:16), and the converted continue to acknowledge his lordship by calling on his name, individually and corporately. This acknowledgment must be made "with a pure [or "cleansed," *katharas*] heart." In both the Old and New Testaments, the "heart" is the core of a person's being. A "pure heart" is a heart that is not polluted by alien convictions and commitments. It possesses an undivided loyalty to God, a single-minded commitment to God and his purposes. Both the Old and New Testaments warn against double-mindedness (e.g., Ps 119:113; Jas 1:8, 4:1-10). Likewise, Jesus warns against trying to serve two masters (Matt 6:24; see also the discussion under 1:3). The biblical message is clear: faithfulness is born from purity of heart.

Having admonished his community to "avoid disputing over the meanings of words" (2:14), Timothy must also set an example in another area: "avoid foolish, senseless arguments." "Foolish" (*mōras*) means without understanding. "Senseless" describes an argument that reveals a lack of education, thought, or training. In 1 Timothy 6:4, Paul associated such "controversies" (*zēteseis*) with verbal warfare, people attacking one another through words. In Titus 3:9, Paul uses the same word to refer to forceful disagreements where there is no interest in seeking a solution. Such controversies "give birth to quarrels" and inevitably lead to further conflict, which is the opposite of the peace that Timothy is to pursue.

The specific phrase "the Lord's slave" (*doulon kuriou*) is found only here (2:24) in the New Testament, but Paul does refer to himself as a slave of Christ (e.g., Rom 1:1; Gal 1:10) and a slave of God (Titus 1:1; see the discussion there). "Slave" and "lord" are terms that go together. Every lord has slaves, and every slave has a lord/master. As a slave of the master of the household of God, Timothy must avoid quarrels and "be kind toward all, able to teach [rather than quarrel], tolerant, correcting opponents with gentleness" (2:24b-25). "Kind" (*ēpion*) has the primary sense of not being cruel or harsh. This word works in combination with its synonym "gentleness" (*prautēti*) in the final phrase of the translation (2:25a) to form an inclusio, which describes how Christian leaders should deal with those who oppose them.

> Kind (or gentle)
>   Teaching
>   Tolerating evil attacks
>   Correcting
> Gentle

The gentleness Paul commands is undergirded by the ability to teach. "Tolerant" (*anexikakon*) is a compound word, which literally means "putting up with evil." Those who would effectively act to correct opponents must be willing to "take the hits" that will come their way, without complaining or returning fire, and respond in gentleness. They must also be well schooled in Scripture, which gives them the ability to correct. The picture of such a leader is of one who teaches, tolerates the ignorant attacks of evil people, and corrects in a spirit of gentleness.

"Perhaps God will allow them to repent, leading them to knowledge of the truth" (2:25b). Kindness and gentleness must surround all efforts to teach and correct, because people frequently react harshly to teaching and correction. A gentle demeanor when responding to such attacks may open the door for God to lead the opponents to repentance. "Perhaps" (*mēpote*) is a word of hope, implying that something is possible through it might be unlikely. Paul does not guarantee that Timothy's behavior, even if consistent and aboveboard, will produce a happy outcome. Indeed, Paul himself was rejected by people more than once. There is no guarantee, but there is hope, and hope makes such behavior a risk worth taking. To the Hellenistic mind, "repentance" (*metanoian*) referred to changing one's mind. The biblical understanding is broader than this. In the Old Testament, "repentance" means "to change directions," "to reorient oneself." Biblically, repentance involves nothing short of a total reorientation of one's life, such as the conversion Paul experienced and the conversion of the Thessalonian Christians, who "turned to God from idols, to serve a living and true God" (1 Thess 1:9). The Thessalonians' experience also illustrates the result of such repentance: it produces an ability to come to know the truth. As noted above, conversion is always a turning toward as well as a turning away: Paul here accents the positive side of conversion, what the convert is turning toward. In the Pastoral Epistles, Paul frequently uses "knowledge of the truth" as a shorthand designation for his understanding of the gospel upon which his mission and community is founded (3:7; 1 Tim 2:4; Titus 1:1). Repentance "leading to knowledge of the truth" implies that they will "come to their senses" (2:26). "Come to their senses" translates *ananēpsōsin*, a verb that refers to sobering up, returning to one's right mind. Hellenistic writers link repentance with coming to one's senses. Philo says that, after his drunkenness (Gen 9:21), Noah became "sober again, that is to say, he repents and recovers from an illness" (*Allegorical Interpretations* 2.18; cf. *Sobriety* 38; *Migration of Abraham* 219).

In the remainder of 2:26, Paul shifts from the language of Hellenistic moral philosophy to the language of apocalyptic. Apart from repentance, the opponents are caught "in the devil's trap [*pagidos*]," "held captive [*ezōgrēmenoi*] to do his will." *Zōgreō* refers to being trapped (or captured) alive, and was often used in reference to hunted animals or prisoners of war. Paul refers to "will" (*thelēma*) twice in this letter. In 1:1, he refers to the will of God, which made him an apostle. Here, he refers to the will of the devil—two dramatically different wills, resulting in dramatically different lifestyles. Liberation from captivity to the devil and the lifestyle that results from that captivity is a result of the conversion that Paul describes here. Once a slave of the devil, by repentance one transfers allegiance and becomes a slave of the Lord (cf. 2:24). First Timothy 3:6-7 also speaks of the necessity of being freed from the snares of the devil. In explaining why overseers should not be recent converts, Paul writes: "He must be well thought of by outsiders, so that he may not fall into disgrace and the devil's trap [*pagida*]."

In sum, this paragraph (2:14-26) begins and ends with warnings. It begins with Paul pointing to the dangers of "disputing over words, which does nothing good but only ruins those who listen" (2:14). It ends with Paul warning Timothy to have "nothing to do with foolish controversies . . . the Lord's slave must not quarrel" (2:24). These warnings frame a collection of teachings about the worker whom God approves. A third warning sits at the center of the paragraph: "avoid profane chatter" (2:16). According to Paul, there are discussions that may go over the line into what is useless and even dangerous. How will Timothy know where the line is drawn? Paul gives two indicators here. First, there are dangers in any discussion with someone whose theological views are radically unorthodox. When there is no search for understanding, such talks cease to be profitable. Second, if a discussion damages the community, if it upsets or subverts faith, or breeds quarreling, then leaders are wise to avoid it.

On the positive side, Paul describes how Timothy can make his teaching and speech beneficial. First, he must be a faithful interpreter of Scripture, one who seeks to communicate the heart of the text (2:15). Second, he must be a useful instrument in the household of faith, one that is cleansed and dedicated to the owner's purposes (2:20-21). Third, he must look for opportunities to be involved "in every good work," a life dedicated to the way of Jesus (2:21). Fourth, he must "flee from youthful passions" (2:22): as a mature follower of Jesus Christ, he must live a life of self-control and restraint. Fifth, Timothy must "chase after righteousness, faithfulness, love, and peace, along with all those who call on the Lord from a pure heart" (2:22). He must live a life characterized by these virtues, as part of a faith community that pursues the same. Sixth, he must be "gentle toward all, able to teach, tolerant, correcting opponents with gentleness" (2:24). As a result, "God perhaps will allow them to repent, leading them to knowledge of the truth" (2:25).

Theological foundation (3:1-9)

In 3:1-9, Paul warns Timothy about the kind of opponents God's servants will face "in the last days." Again, this warning reflects an apocalyptic worldview, but with an interesting twist. The classic Jewish (and developing Christian) apocalyptic worldview held that the last days, before the establishment of a messianic kingdom, would be filled by unprecedented evil and catastrophic events. Mark 13 describes cosmic cataclysm. The book of Revelation describes war, famine, disease, and cosmic upheaval (6:3-8; 8:6-13). In 2 Timothy 3:1-9, however, Paul focuses not on cosmic upheavals or natural catastrophes, but on moral upheaval. To describe this upheaval, Paul uses another well-known Hellenistic literary device, the vice list.

While this passage is clearly descriptive, it is also prescriptive. It strongly resembles 1 Timothy 4:1-5, not only in subject matter but in style; Paul in both places describes the present situation in terms of future events. The future tense verbs throughout are logical futures, warning about both the future and the present. To be sure, as the end draws near the evil will become more intense, but this evil is already present: "Children, it is the last hour. As you have heard that antichrist is coming, so now many antichrists have come" (1 John 2:18).

Paul opens with the command, "know this" (3:1), which emphasizes both the urgency and necessity of this knowledge for Timothy and his community. According to Peter's sermon in Acts 2, the coming of the Holy Spirit on Pentecost fulfilled the prophecy of Joel 3:1-5 LXX, and inaugurated "the last days" (Acts 2:17; Heb 1:2). Earlier in 2 Timothy, Paul referred to "that day" (1:12, 18; cf. 4:8), the day of the Lord, to which the Old Testament prophets pointed as the day of God's judgment and deliverance. The days leading up to "that day" are "the last days," in which believers now live. Those days will be "terrible times" for people of faith in the household of God. Their distress is a result of the moral and spiritual depravity that characterizes the lives of those living around them.

Paul's vice list in 3:2-4 resembles those of 1 Corinthians 6:9-10, Galatians 5:19-21, Romans 1:29-31, and 1 Timothy 1:9-10. Paul does several things to give the list coherence:

- The Greek words for nine of the eighteen vices begin with an alpha privative (the Greek *a-*, a prefix like our English "non-" or "anti-". This indicates that people will lack the virtues opposed by each of these vices.
- Paul uses the root *phil-* ("love") in two pairs of words, one pair at the beginning of the list (*philautoi*, "lovers of self"; *philargyroi*, "lovers of money") and another pair at the end of the list ("lovers of pleasure [*philēdonoi*] rather than lovers of God [*philotheoi*]). Another word built on the same root is placed in the middle of the list: *aphilagathoi*, "haters" (lit., "anti-lovers") of what is good.
- Notice also the sharp contrast between "lovers of self" at the beginning of the list and "lovers of God" at the end.

Paul warns Timothy: "Terrible times will come, because people will be . . ."

1. "lovers of themselves" (*philautoi*)—This word appears only here in the New Testament. It speaks of a love that is selfish, emphasizing self-importance and self-centeredness. It is a love that considers neither God nor

others. Nowhere is this vice more powerfully portrayed than in Jesus' parable of the rich fool (Luke 12:13-21). Read this parable carefully and notice how many times the first-person pronoun "I" appears. In contrast, Paul seeks to flesh out the call of Jesus, who demanded that his disciples deny themselves, take up their crosses, and follow him (see Mark 8:34-35). Paul clearly understood the perils of a life centered in self rather than God. Believers cannot live for Christ without dying to self (2 Cor 5:14-15; Gal 2:20).

2. "lovers of money" or "lovers of wealth" (*philargyroi*)—In 1 Timothy 6:10, Paul described "the love of money" as "a root of all kinds of evil." Then as now, examples of this truth are myriad. The juxtaposition of the first two vices is important: being a "lover of self" produces a life of greed and selfishness.

3. "boastful" (*alazones*)—This term refers to a person brags with empty words, because his/her pride has no basis in fact.

4. "arrogant" (*hyperēphanoi*)—Meaning shameless, contemptuous of others. These people forget that "God opposes the proud [*hyperēphanois*] but gives grace to the humble" (Jas 4:6; Ps 138:6; Prov 3:34; Matt 23:12; Luke 18:14; 1 Pet 5:5).

5. "abusive" (*blasphēmoi*)—This word is often found in Hellenistic vice lists. Literally "blasphemers," the word describes a person who defames, disparages, or ridicules other people. In biblical and Jewish literature, of course, God is usually the object.

6. "disobedient to parents" (*goneusin apeitheis*)—In a culture that viewed the family as the most important unit in society, disobedience or disrespect for parents was a grave sin. This word refers both to children who refuse to obey parents and adult children who rebel against the head of the household. *Apeitheis* is the first of an alliterative group of five successive vices, all of which begin with the alpha privative. For example, *peitheis* means "obedient," *apeitheis* signifies the opposite.

7. "ungrateful" (*acharistoi*)—Refers to a lack of thankfulness, a spirit of ungraciousness.

8. "unholy" (*anosioi*)—Something that is not devoted to or of service to God.

9. "heartless" (*astorgoi*)—This word refers to a lack of affection for others, especially for family or others to whom one should be close. Paul includes this characteristic in the vice list in Romans 1:29-31. Early Christians applied this adjective to the Roman practices of abortion and exposing unwanted children (i.e., abandoning them to die or be stolen by slavers, etc.).

10. "unforgiving" (*aspondoi*)—This word refers to a person who refuses to seek peace or reconciliation with another. A *sponde* was originally an offering of wine poured out to the gods prior to a banquet in celebration of peace or a truce. Gradually, the term came to refer to the truce itself. These are people who are incapable of making peace, who hang onto and meditate on every offense.
11. "slanderers" (*diaboloi*)—A plural form of the adjective *diabolos*, from which we get the English word "devil." This word frequently appears in Hellenistic vice lists, and is found in all three of the vice lists in the Pastoral Epistles (1 Tim 3:11; 2 Tim 3:3; Titus 2:3). The devil is the slanderer/accuser *par excellance*.
12. "self indulgent" (*akrateis*)—This word describes a lack of self-control. *Kratos* refers to power; here the power that is lacking is the power to restrain oneself. This word introduces a second group of vices that begin with the alpha privative.
13. "brutal" (*anēmeroi*)—This term was used to speak of wild animals or uncultivated plants, growing wildly. With reference to people, it has the force of "uncivilized" or "savage."
14. "haters of good" (*aphilagathoi*)—Those who prefer the evil and hate the good, or oppose anything that is wholesome.
15. "treacherous" (*prodotai*)—This term refers to a person who betrays another, or breaks a trust by handing someone over to an enemy. Luke uses this word to describe Judas in Luke 6:16 and the Jewish leaders involved in Stephen's death in Acts 7:52.
16. "reckless" (*propeteis*)—Could also be translated "impetuous." This word carries the idea of acting without thinking. It appears frequently in philosophical and biographical literature to refer to people whose impulsive actions lead to suffering or injustice (Philo, *Abraham* 208; Josephus, *Ant.* 19.6.3 §300).
17. "conceited" (*tetyphōmenoi*)—This verb is related to *typhoō*, which originally meant "wrapped in smoke or fog," then metaphorically "senseless," "shrouded in conceit" (*LSJ*). It is related to *typhos*, "pride." Philo uses *typhos* to describe an orator who is so caught up with the art of his own rhetoric that he could no longer perceive the truth, and suggests that such pride is the source of many kinds of evil, including contempt for God/the gods (*Decalogue* 4–6).
18. "lovers of pleasure rather than lovers of God" (*philēdoni mallon hē philotheoi*)—Most Hellenistic thinkers considered lust for pleasure (*hēdonē*), especially sensory or sexual pleasures, to be the most shameful passion and the source of many other vices (TLNT 3.189–90). For

Paul, such lovers of pleasure were on a collision course with destruction. "Lovers of God" is a term that goes back to Aristotle, who used it to describe the religious or pious (*Rhet* 2.17.6). This phrase's placement at the end of the list is no accident; it clarifies Paul's design for the vice list. The list began with a reference to "lovers of self," people whose lives are oriented toward self, self-worship, selfish values. At the end of the list, Paul says that all of these vices spring from a refusal to love and acknowledge God. In Christ, however, believers live lives oriented toward God (not self) and others. This orientation produces a life that blesses others.

In 3:4-5, Paul moves from the generic description of 3:1-4 (which might fit any ungodly person, to some degree) to a specific description of the false teachers and troublemakers in his churches, people who opposed him throughout his ministry. These people "adhere to an outward form of godliness, but disregard its power." "Adhere" translates *echō*, "possess" or "hold to" (cf. 1:13, where Paul uses the same word to tell Timothy to "adhere to/hold on to the pattern of sound teaching that you heard from me"). These people cling to an outward kind of godliness: "form" (*morphōsin*) refers to mere appearance, with no relation to inner reality. "Godliness" is one of the chief designations for the Christian life in the Pastoral Epistles, a life lived in and from reverence for God. "Disregard" (*ērnēmenoi*) refers to "paying no attention to something," "being unconcerned with something." Luke had Jesus use this same word when he said, "If anyone wants to follow after me, that person must deny himself, take up his cross daily, and follow me" (Luke 9:23).

With the phrase "outward form of godliness," Paul *may* be referring to the legalism of the Judaizers, which prized external signs of righteousness, such as diet and circumcision. Or he may be aiming toward any kind of religiosity that focused on outward appearances without concern for inward reality. There is an "outward form of godliness" which has nothing godly about it. It is a sham, like a grand façade constructed to hide the true condition of a decrepit building. These people's religion is not really part of them. It is religion for appearances' sake; the story of Ananias and Sapphira illustrates this well (Acts 5:1-11). The power of godliness is found in the reality of an authentic Christian life. Pious pretensions yield none of this power. Paul commands Timothy: "Have nothing to do with them."

Paul describes these pseudo-Christians more fully in 3:6-9. They "creep into the households" of believers. "Creep into" translates *endynontes*, which implies furtiveness, secrecy; "they sneak into" or "insinuate themselves," under false pretences. "Households" is literally "houses" (*oikias*), which may imply that the troublemakers Paul has in view are teachers who make use of people's hospitality to corrupt the teaching of the church. On the other hand, the Pastoral Epistles use household language throughout, and congregations met in houses, therefore this may refer to the false teachers creeping into house church congregations. In the phrase, "they captivate silly women," "captivate" translates *aichmalōtizontes*, which literally referred to taking a prisoner, and metaphorically to taking control of someone. "Silly women" translates *gynaikaria*, a diminutive of *gyne*, "woman." *Gynaikarion* literally means, "silly little women" (BGAD). Paul's use of the tem, which reflects the cultural prejudices of the New Testament world, is likely aimed at the fact that the false teachers were teaching things that appealed to the "new Roman woman" (Winter 2003).

The term *gynaikarion* and the description that follows reflect a stock pattern or "topos" in the writings of Hellenistic moralists. These women are

- "overwhelmed by their sins";
- "swayed by all kinds of passions"; the kinds of passions are not specified;
- "always studying, yet never able to come to knowledge of the truth." The issue is not whether the women can learn; Paul has in fact already affirmed that women can and should be taught (1 Tim 2:11-12). The issue is not even whether such women can ever come to "knowledge of the truth" (see the discussion at 2:25). The problem is that *these* women (and other such women and men) cannot or will not come to know (experience) the truth under the guidance of these teachers.

In 3:8, Paul further describes the character of these teachers by use of the story of Jannes and Jambres. Jewish tradition gave these names to the Egyptian magicians (unnamed in the biblical text) who opposed Moses (Exod 7:11–8:19). The church Fathers often mention these two. According to Origen, at some point the traditions about them were written down in a book he refers to as the book of Jannes and Jambres (Mambres) (*Celsus* 41.51, PG 11.1111–1112; *Commentary on Matthew* par 117, PG 13.1769). According to the traditions, even after their defeat in Pharaoh's court, these two continued to oppose Moses. They used their demonic powers in an effort to keep Israel from crossing the Red Sea, and caused Israel to worship the golden calf (Exod 32:1-20).

Like Jannes and Jambres, Timothy's opponents "oppose the truth" by opposing the message and work of the gospel. Their minds are "corrupt" (*katephtharmenoi*): this word has the force of corruption that leads to collapse, "rottenness." This is an intense form of the verb *phtheiro*, "to corrupt." Paul uses this form to emphasize the depth of their corruption. Further, "their faith is counterfeit [*adokimoi*]." Here, "faith" appears to refer to their personal trust in Jesus Christ, or the lack thereof. They have no real relationship with God through Jesus Christ, because their faith is "counterfeit." *Adokimos* means "failing the test" or "unacceptable." The word describes something that doesn't measure up to standards, something worthless. Etymologically, the term implies a judgment (*doki-*) on the part of an appropriate authority. For example, officials might declare that a person is unqualified to hold a certain job or office. These characteristics set the false teachers in opposition to the truth.

"But they will not make much progress" (3:9): "progress" (*prokopsousin*) often referred to moral and intellectual growth. Paul could here be saying that these people's growth in the faith will be stunted. He could also be saying that their selfish plans to corrupt others for profit will fail. Just as Jannes and Jambres were eventually stopped, these people will be stopped, "for their folly [*anoia*] will become plain to everyone." *Anoia* can be translated "ignorance"; etymologically, the word refers to mindlessness. Luke 6:11 uses *anoia* to refer to the Pharisees' mindless, murderous rage toward Jesus, after he healed on the Sabbath. Paul says, in the end, that the corruption and hollowness of these false teachers will shine through, and they will be exposed for what they really are: charlatans!

A Model to Emulate: Paul the Triumphant (3:10–4:8)

In the first half of the third large section of the letter, Paul follows the vice list and negative descriptions of 3:1-9 with a kind of virtues list, made up of qualities from his own experiences, things about which Timothy has personal experience. In the second half of this section, Paul solemnly charges Timothy to be ready to articulate faithfully the message of the gospel, no matter what he faces. His life must be in harmony with that message, so that it will be effective. Paul's example, central to the first major section of the letter (1:6–2:13) and absent from the second major section (2:14–3:9) returns to the fore and remains there for the rest of 2 Timothy. He points to himself as one who has lived a life consistent with the truth of the gospel, and now—even as his life is poured out—he triumphs, and wins the victor's crown.

What Timothy knows and how it benefits him (3:10-17)

In 3:1-9, Paul described the evil that would threaten and infect the community. In 3:10-17, he describes his own life as an example for Timothy to follow as he seeks to lead Paul's churches. Again, Paul uses contrast to make a dramatic point; cf. 1:7, 15-18; 2:11-13: Timothy must pattern his life after Paul, the apostle. He must seek to imitate Paul. In the Graeco-Roman world, imitation was one of the primary modes for teaching. Paul's references to his own example, etc., are not egotism; instead, this is an accepted form of instruction (see the discussion of imitation under Titus 2:7).

Knowing that Timothy will suffer persecution, Paul reminds him of the suffering and persecution that he himself has suffered. Paul's goal here is both to encourage and to instruct. He continues to take the apocalyptic tone of 3:1ff. One idea central to apocalyptic is the belief that the faithful will suffer in the "last days" (Matt 24-25; cf. Mark 8:34-35 par., Matt 5:3-12). In the same way, Peter writes, "Do not be surprised by the fiery ordeal that is taking place among you . . ." (1 Pet 4:12).

Paul reminds Timothy of that which he has "observed" (*parēkolouthēsas*); the verb literally means "to accompany," and was used by the Stoics to refer to the relationship between teachers and disciples. The word later came to mean "making a careful study" or "a diligent investigation" of something. Luke uses this word to describe the careful research that he did in preparation for writing his gospel (Luke 1:3). Epictetus uses this word to describe someone who closely follows an argument or philosophical demonstration, and the notion of conforming to a particular model of behavior or belief by following the model faithfully. Timothy has had the opportunity to observe Paul in such a way. Now Paul is able to present himself as a pattern for the ministry to which Timothy has been called.

First, Timothy has closely followed Paul's "teaching" (*didaskalia*). *Didaskalia* refers to both the content (the "what") of Paul's teaching and the method (the "how"). To be an effective teacher, Timothy will need to pay attention to both. Timothy knew the content of Paul's teaching, some of which is summarized in the "faithful sayings" of the Pastoral Epistles (2:11; 1 Tim 1:15; 3:1; 4:9; Titus 3:8). Timothy also knew the methods of Paul's teaching, and he is to follow Paul's example with regard to both the "what" and the "how." (Interestingly, fifteen of the twenty-one New Testament appearances of *didaskalia* are in the Pastoral Epistles, where there may be a distinction between the singular "teaching" and the plural "teachings." Paul uses the singular term as a technical term for the authentic apostolic teaching as a whole, as delivered to and through Paul and Timothy [1 Tim 1:10; 4:6, 13, 16; 5:17; 6:1, 3; 2 Tim 3:10, 16; 4:3; Titus 1:9; 2:1; 2:7; 2:10]. In the one place where he uses the plural term "teachings," however, Paul is referring to the false teachings of his opponents [1 Tim 4:1].)

Second, Timothy has closely followed Paul's "conduct" (*agōgē*, literally "way of life," the way Paul conducted his daily life, his consistent pattern of behavior). At times, this word was used in Hellenistic writings to refer to a person's training or reputation, suggesting that one has adopted a particular lifestyle in imitation of a teacher or master. Paul certainly saw himself as having adopted the way of life modeled by Jesus, and he called those he taught to imitate him as he imitated the Lord (1 Cor 11:1). The Pastoral Epistles repeatedly affirm that belief must be accompanied by action, likewise, "faith by itself, if it has no works, is dead" (Jas 2:17; cf. Eph 2:10). Paul modeled a way of life, and called on Timothy to follow his pattern.

Third, Timothy has closely observed Paul's "purpose" (*prothesei*). *Prothesis* was often used to refer to someone's plan, a statement of purpose, or a thesis to be demonstrated. For Paul, God clearly demonstrated his purpose for humanity in Jesus Christ (e.g., 2 Cor 5:18-21). Paul understood that his ministry, his gospel, and his work were not about him but rather about the fulfillment of God's purposes in him and through him. Thus his purpose was at one with God's purpose.

Fourth, Timothy had observed Paul's "faith" (*pistei*). Here, *pistis* can be either objective (the content of what Paul believed and taught) or subjective (Paul's personal commitment to Jesus Christ). Since he has already mentioned his teaching, which would focus on the content of his faith, it seems more likely here that Paul is referring to his personal commitment to Jesus Christ. Come what may, Paul trusts the God who saved him and called him to ministry. He trusts God to the point of obedience, even when obedience costs him his life. This is the essence of New Testament faith. Biblically speaking, *faith* is never reduced to agreement with propositional statements: even the demons believe on that level (Jas 2:19)! They believe, but their agreement with propositions does not lead to commitment, repentance, or obedience. In the New Testament, faith refers to trusting God in a way that produces obedience. This is what Paul has done, and what Timothy must continue to do in the difficult times that lie ahead.

Fifth, Timothy has observed Paul's "patience" (*makrothymia*). *Makrothymia* refers to the ability to control anger or other negative responses, forbearance. This characteristic is found throughout the virtue lists in Paul's writings (2 Cor 6:6; Gal 5:22; 1 Thess 5:14; Eph 4:2; Col 1:11; 3:12). It is a vital virtue for one who teaches, and a result of love.

Sixth, Timothy has observed Paul's "love" (*agapē*). For Paul, love was the essential Christian virtue, the epitome of all Christian virtues (1 Cor 13). Paul frequently expressed his love for all those to whom he had preached the gospel (1 Cor 4:14; 10:14; 15:58; 16:24; 2 Cor 7:1; 12:19; cf. Phil 2:12; 4:1; 1 Thess 2:8; Phlm 1, 16). For Paul, Christian love is not limited to a love for God. It is never just a vertical love; it is always and inevitably love for others as well, a horizontal love (cf. 1 John 4:20). Because of his familiarity with Paul's life and ministry, Timothy has seen how Paul loved God and others, and which shows him how he too must love.

Seventh, Timothy had witnessed Paul's "endurance" (*hypomonē*). *Hypomonē* refers to steadfastness. It is synonymous with patience (*makrothymia*). However, patience refers to something internal, the ability to control anger, etc., remaining inwardly calm in the face of adversity. Endurance refers to an external response, the ability to cope with difficulties, persevering and continuing to give effort in the face of obstacles. Philo used *hypomonē* to describe an athlete who puts up with pain and opposition (*Every Good Man Is Free* 26). Philosophers frequently used this word to speak of people who faced difficulties, even death, with courage. Timothy had witnessed Paul's endurance, the steadfastness with which he carried on in the face of the obstacles that lay before him.

In 3:10-13, Paul follows this description of his example with a reminder of the realities that Timothy will face. As with 1:10, Paul points to his own example, here with a short recitation of the sufferings that his work for the gospel has brought him. Paul includes similar lists of his circumstances in 1 Corinthians 4:10-14, and 2 Corinthians 6:4-10; 11:23-27; 12:10 (see Collins 2002, 257). These lists demonstrate that Paul has suffered much as a servant of God. They remind his readers that they can and should expect the same. Paul uses these lists to make two points. First, they underscore his endurance, his steadfastness. No matter what circumstances he faced, no matter how difficult the task, no matter what it cost him in terms of persecution and hardship, Paul pressed on. So must all faithful servants of God. Second, these lists are a clear testimony to the power of the gospel that Paul proclaimed. Time and again, Paul discovered that nothing could stop the advance of the gospel. The gospel overcame every obstacle that human beings could put in its way. The word of God *will* achieve its desired effects (Matt 13:18-23; Mark 4:13-20; Luke 8:11-15). Luke's narrative of the Pauline mission demonstrates this dramatically, ending with a depiction of Paul in Rome, chained and yet free, preaching the gospel (from his prison!) without hindrance (Acts 28:31). The very existence of Timothy's community is clear testimony to this truth.

Timothy knew of Paul's "persecutions" (*diōgmois*) (3:11). This word speaks of systematic harassment. It refers to hardships, usually of a physical nature, endured at the hands of people persistent in their opposition (cf. 1 Cor 4:12; 2 Cor 11:23-32; 12:10; Rom 8:35; Acts 8:1; 13:50; 2 Thess 1:4). Timothy also knows of the sufferings Paul experienced at three cities in the province of Asia: Antioch, Iconium, and Lystra (Acts 13–14). Luke describes Paul's persecution at the hands of Jews in Antioch (of Pisidia) in Acts 13:50. When Paul moved on to Iconium, some ninety miles away, similar persecution awaited him (Acts 14:1). When Paul then moved to Lystra, Jews from Antioch and Iconium followed. They stoned Paul and dragged him outside the city, leaving him to die there (Acts 14:19). In his summary of this mission, Luke described how Paul returned to each of these cities, telling his people, "It is through many persecutions that we must enter the kingdom of God" (Acts 14:21-22). According to Luke, Timothy was himself from Lystra (Acts 16:1-2), so he likely knew these stories well.

The mention of his sufferings in these cities leads Paul to exclaim, "What persecutions I endured!" implying that these were but a few of many. But Paul does not dwell on the persecutions, for he immediately turns to emphasize that "the Lord rescued me from all of them." This rescue is testimony of the Lord's faithfulness. It is also part of Timothy's knowledge of Paul; he knew about the persecution, and he also knew about the ways God delivered Paul. These words, therefore, were inherently encouraging to Timothy and (along with him) all the servants of God who faced persecution and suffering. As God had been faithful to Paul, who had himself been steadfast and faithful, so God will be faithful to Timothy and to all who serve faithfully. While these words continue to reflect Paul's apocalyptic view of the "last days" as a time of persecution and suffering for the faithful (see 1 Thess 3:3-4; 1 Cor 11:19), they are also born from his own life experience. He knows from experience that "all who want to live a godly life in Christ Jesus will be persecuted" (3:12). Again, this statement is not mere speculation about a possible future. It is the reality that Paul and Timothy faced in their daily lives.

In 3:12, we meet two of Paul's favorite ways to describe the Christian life. First, it is a "godly" life, a life lived in and from reverence for God. Second, it is a life lived "in Christ Jesus" (see Rom 3:24; 1 Cor 1:2; Gal 2:4; Phil 1:1; 1 Thess 2:14; Phlm 23; 2 Cor 2:14; 1 Tim 1:14; 3:13). This expression, or the shorter "in Christ," is found in all of Paul's letters. As used by Paul, it has both a mystical sense and a practical sense. To live "in Christ Jesus" is to live in union with him (mystical) and to live in union with him is to live his life in the world (practical: this is the real "what would Jesus do?"). For Paul, the mystical and the practical could not be separated. Christian ministers must "want to live" (or "desire to live") this life. The verb translated "want" (*thelontes*) refers to choosing something. The life of ministry is not a life people live by accident, or fall into. This is a life lived by conscious choice, and those who make this choice must be prepared for the things that go along with the choice, even persecution and suffering.

At the same time that the faithful are making this choice, "wicked people [*ponēroi*] and imposters [*goētes*] will go from bad to worse" (3:13). *Ponēros* refers to being morally corrupt; *goēs* describes a swindler, someone who deceives people by pretending to be what he/she is not. Lucian uses *goēs* to refer to fraudulent doctors/healers, "quacks" (Lucian, *Alexander* 5). Dio Chrysostom described the need for citizens who were willing to speak and act out of good will and concern for their fellow human beings: "to find such a man as that is not easy . . . so great is the dearth of noble, independent souls and such the abundance of toadies, imposters [*goētan*], and sophists" (*Discourses* 32.11).

In the "last days," these wicked people and imposters will go from bad to worse. They will continue to lead people astray, "deceiving and being deceived." The notion of "going astray" was a classic *topos*, and implied some sort of seduction—moral, intellectual, or both. Dio Chrysostom describes how false teachers, having been led astray themselves, lead others into error and confusion (4.33; 4.37). The Bible, from beginning to end, describes Satan as a deceiver (Gen 3; Rev 12:9, 14). "Deceit" is a cardinal characteristic of the "last days." As Jesus warned in the "little apocalypse" (Mark 13 para), things will not be getting better and the path of faithfulness will not get easier. Deceivers will proliferate. Christians must beware, lest we also be deceived (Mark 13:5-6). Tragically, the downward spiral away from God will continue for the "wicked." As they continue to live lives based on "the Lie" (Rom 1:25), they continue to propagate this deception. Adding to the tragedy is the fact that some believe they are serving the truth.

In 3:14-17, Paul reminds Timothy of his foundation. Paul urges, "But you, you continue in what you learned and firmly believe" (3:14). The second person pronoun, repeated alongside the imperative verb, is emphatic. This draws a sharp contrast between Timothy and the people Paul has just described: "As for them: they will go from bad to worse, deceiving and being deceived. But as for you, you continue in what you have learned." Timothy cannot stray, "deceiving and deceived"; he must continue (*mene*), or remain grounded in, the things he learned.

The teachings that Timothy has received came from reputable sources; this knowledge also gives Timothy incentive to continue in what he has been taught. The plural "from whom" (*para tinōn*) suggests that Timothy has had more than one teacher. While Paul served as Timothy's primary teacher, Timothy's own mother and grandmother are also singled out (1:5) as part of this chain. No doubt others, unknown today, also played an important role in teaching Timothy the faith.

Paul adds another fact that Timothy is aware of: since he was a child (*apo brephous*, literally "from infancy"), Timothy has known "the sacred writings, which are able to instruct [him] for salvation through the faith which is in Christ Jesus" (3:15). "You have known" (*oidas*) is a perfect tense verb, indicating past action with present effect. What he has known from his earliest years continues to impact his life in the present. The phrase, "sacred writings" (*hiera grammata*) was used in Hellenistic Judaism to refer to the Jewish Scriptures, our Old Testament. Philo writes, "Either you have not the genuine feelings of the nobly born or you were not reared and trained in the sacred writings," reflecting the assumption of pious Jews that young men should be trained in the Scriptures from a very young age (*Gaius* 195; cf. Ps 71:17; Matt 19:20). According to the rabbis, "at five years old [one is fit] for the scripture; at ten for the Mishnah, at thirteen for [keeping] the commandments, at fifteen for the Talmud" (*m. 'Abot* 5.21). These Jewish Scriptures were able to make Timothy wise, to instruct him, for salvation. The Jewish Scriptures, read in the light of Christ Jesus, had power to change lives and bring people to faith. Paul has come to read the Scriptures in this new way, and here he emphasizes the importance of the Old Testament for understanding the Christian faith. Paul is following the example of Jesus. In the synagogue in Nazareth, Jesus explained the nature of his mission through the Jewish Scriptures (Luke 4:16-30). On the road to Emmaus, he explained his death and resurrection from the same sources (Luke 24:13-35). Similarly, Matthew presents Jesus as the fulfillment of the Jewish prophetic writings. Clearly, the early Christians turned to the Jewish Scriptures to understand and proclaim their message about Jesus. These writings, then, played a central role in teaching people how to find and live out salvation. Timothy's lifelong familiarity with these Scriptures is for Paul but another testimony to their importance for Christians.

Paul here describes one of the purposes of Scripture: it instructs the believer "for salvation through the faith which is in Jesus Christ." Properly read, Scripture points to Jesus Christ, what he has done for believers, how they can know him and through him know the life for which God created them. Improperly read (i.e., not read as something that points to Jesus Christ), the Scriptures are something else entirely—an intellectual puzzle, a fascinating object for scientific study, but powerless to save. Carson writes, "Jesus insists that there is nothing intrinsically life-giving about studying the Scriptures, if one fails to discern their true content and purpose" (Carson, 1991, 263, commenting on John 5:39). "The faith which is in Christ Jesus" refers to the gospel of Jesus Christ, which makes this new life available to those who believe.

Paul further describes the importance of the Jewish Scriptures for Christians in 3:16-17, as he turns his attention to the nature and use(s) of these writings. He describes both the "what" (what the Scriptures are) and the "what for" (their purpose). He begins with the "what," describing the nature and importance of these writings: "Every scripture is inspired by God" (*pasa graphē theopneustos*) (3:16). These three Greek words have been the subject of much debate. The discussion focuses on three basic issues. First, what is the meaning of "every scripture" (*pasa graphē*)? Second, what does Paul mean by saying that these writings are *theopneustos*, "inspired by God"? Third, the phrase has no verb. How should we supply the phrase with a predicate?

First, the word rendered "every" in "every scripture" is singular. Thus, in spite of the traditional translation "all," the phrase is literally, "every scripture." This can be taken collectively, however, as a reference to the Scriptures as a whole, thus "all" Scriptures. Or the word can be taken distributively to refer to "every," thus to each and every part of Scripture. While both arguments can be made, the rabbis taught that each and every part of Scripture was important, no matter how small. This suggests that the phrase is best rendered, "each and every part of scripture." Second, "inspired by God" translates a single Greek word, *theopneustos*. This is a rare verbal adjective, a compound of the words "God" (*theos*) and "to breathe" (*pneō*). Thus the phrase is literally, "God-breathed" (cf. Paul's expression "God-taught," *theodidaktoi*, in 1 Thess 4:9). This word echoes the creation stories from Genesis, where God breathes the breath of life into Adam's nostrils (Gen 2:7). The picture is that God inspires, breathes his thoughts and words and motivations, into the minds of the prophets who serve as his mouthpieces. The picture is also that God's words have life in them, and therefore give life.

Third, the phrase is elliptical in that it does not have a principal verb. The normal practice with such phrases is to supply a being verb, "is," but where does the verb go? Interpreters have suggested two possibilities. First, the verb can be placed after *theopneustos,* so that the phrase is rendered, "Every scripture [which is] inspired by God is useful . . ." (so NEB, REB). The remainder of 3:16-17 then describes the various ways the inspired Scriptures are useful. This reading distinguishes between inspired and noninspired Scripture, implying that only parts of the Bible are inspired and therefore useful (and other parts are not). This distinction conflicts with the way Paul interpreted the Old Testament. Further, it is not consistent with the ways the rabbis interpreted Scripture. Second, the verb can be placed after *graphē*, "scripture," so that the phrase reads, "Every scripture is inspired by God, and is useful . . ." (so AV, RSV, NIV, NRSV, revised NAB). This is the better reading. By this reading, Paul is making a point about both the nature and function of Scripture.

Next, Paul returns to the purpose of inspiration. These Scriptures are "useful for teaching, for rebuking, for correcting, and for training in righteousness, so that the person of God may be competent, equipped for every good work" (3:16-17). In addition to the function of Scripture earlier described by Paul—it guides us to salvation through the new life made available by the gospel of Jesus Christ—Scripture is useful for four things:

1. "for teaching" (*didaskalian*)—The Scriptures nourish and inform spiritually. They convey information to believers about how they should understand God and his actions, and how they should see themselves and their world. Jesus' teaching was based on Scripture, and Paul quotes and alludes to Scripture again and again.
2. "for rebuking" (*elegmon*)—The Bible shows us our errors, and helps us understand where we've gone wrong. This Greek word refers to reproof, confronting someone who is doing something wrong or accepting error or falsehood.
3. "for correcting" (*epanorthōsin*)—Scripture corrects believers in their errors. *Epanorthōsin* refers to taking someone who has fallen down or strayed from the correct path, setting them back on their feet on the right path again (BDAG). This word was used to refer to restoring, repairing, or rebuilding, correcting the written text of papyri, and people who speak of change for the sake of improvement (TLNT 2.30–31). Here, it refers to restoring someone to a better state, with the implication that some error or fault needs to be corrected.
4. "for training in righteousness" (*paideian tēn en dikaiosunē*)—*Paideia* ("training") is a broad term, and was applied to everything involved in properly rearing an individual to be a mature member of society. Hellenistic thinkers heavily stressed the importance of *paideia*. For Paul, this training aims toward a right relationship with God and all that that relationship entails. According to the rabbis, the Scriptures are the place to begin such training. This training began with the Scriptures, moved on to the oral Torah (which became the Mishna), and finally to the Talmud. Rabbinic rules of interpretation were intended for the development of *halakah*, which enabled people to live as they ought (on *halakah*, see the discussion under Titus 1:14).

Note the structure of this unit: Paul begins with teaching and ends with training. Between the two poles are two tasks that teaching and training inevitably involve:

Teaching
    Rebuking
        Correcting
Training

Training in righteousness aims at a particular goal: "so that the person of God may be competent, equipped for every good work." It makes God's people "competent" (*artios*), "proficient," "able to meet all demands" (BDAG), adequate and sufficient to the task of doing good works. "Equipped" (*exērtsmenos*) refers to having everything one needs to perform a particular job or task. "Good works" is a constant theme in the Pastoral Epistles. God's people, as members of the household of faith, are to be committed to doing good works. Ephesians 2:10 reminds us, "We are his workmanship, created in Christ Jesus for good works, which God prepared beforehand for us to walk in them."

In 3:10-17, we see the importance of two crucial components of the Christian life. In 3:10-13, we see the importance of the community of faith. Paul, Lois, Eunice, and all the others from whom Timothy learned about faith played a vital rule both in his coming to faith and in his continued growth. The community of faith powerfully shapes and nurtures the faith and life of those brought up in it. In 3:14-17, Paul points to the vital role the Bible plays in both coming to faith and continued growth in the faith. Both tradition (community) and Scripture are essential to the building of healthy Christians.

Paul organizes 3:14-17 into a chiasm that gives further emphasis to the teaching:

A. Tradition, the teaching of the community (3:14)
    B. The Scriptures, knowing them (3:15a)
        C. Reaching wisdom that leads to salvation through faith in Christ (3:15b)
    B'. The Scriptures, their nature (3:16a)
A'. Tradition, the teaching of the community (3:16b-17)

The nature and purpose of Scripture are more fully set forth in these verses than anywhere else in the Bible (with the possible exception of Psalm

119). As to its nature, Scripture is "God-breathed," inspired, and filled with life by God. Paul attempts no explanation of how this inspiration took place (cf. 2 Pet 1:21); it is enough for him to say that Scripture is *theopneustos*, and to describe the purposes of Scripture:

- It points toward a saving relationship with Jesus Christ, and feeds and strengthens that relationship (3:15);
- It guides God's people in how to be God's people by giving them information and shaping their worldviews and actions, and by showing them where they've gone wrong and how to get right (3:16b);
- It does these things so that believers will be prepared for the lives, actions, and deeds that God desires from them (3:17).

Paul's charge, Paul's victory (4:1-8)

Paul continues his charge to Timothy in 4:1-2: The language Paul uses—"I charge you, in the presence of God and Christ Jesus"—emphasizes the seriousness of the charge. The fact that the charge is both preceded (3:1-13) and followed (4:3-5) by descriptions of the troublemakers who will dog the church in the last days underlines the urgency with which Timothy must respond, as does the imminence of Paul's execution.

Paul writes: "I charge you, in the presence of God and Christ Jesus" (4:1). The formula is reminiscent of a solemn oath before a royal tribunal (see 2:14; 1 Tim 5:20, 21; 6:12, 13). "In the presence of God" (*enōpion tou theou*, lit., "before God") echoes the biblical expression that refers to making offerings and worship "before the Lord" (1 Sam 7:6; Pss 56:13; 61:7; 68:3 [LXX 55:14; 60:8; 67:4]). This formula was frequently used to describe judgment or rites of atonement. Hellenistic writers use similar formulas to refer to legal acts of succession. The addition of "Christ Jesus" brings this idea clearly into the realm of the Christian gospel. Paul continues the eschatological tone of this section of the letter by his description of Jesus, "who is about to judge the living and the dead." The phrase "the living and the dead" uses a set of antitheses to refer to a single thing. Here, "the living and the dead" refers to "all people"—all people will be judged, not by some emperor or some other deity, but by Christ Jesus.

The eschatological tension is heightened by the next phrase of Paul's description of Jesus: "and in view of his appearing [*epiphaneian*] and his kingdom." It is before God and Christ Jesus, who will judge the living and the dead, and in view of Jesus' return, that Timothy is charged (*diamarturomai*).

Paul's charge to Timothy falls into two sections, 4:1-2 and 4:5, with an apocalyptic description of the times sandwiched between. The first part of the charge consists of five imperative verbs. Timothy must

1. "Preach the word" (*kēryxon ton logon*): throughout the New Testament, preaching is central to the Christian mission. Mark 1:14 summarizes Jesus' ministry as a ministry of preaching, and Mark refers to Jesus' preaching no fewer than nine times. In Acts, Luke describes the preaching of the early Christians in Jerusalem/Judea (2:14-36; 10:34-43), Samaria (8:5), and wherever Paul went (9:20; 19:13; 20:25; 28:31). He summarizes Paul's ministry as "preaching the kingdom" (20:25; 28:31). Paul alludes to preaching in almost every letter, emphasizing its importance in Romans 10:14-15: Now Paul charges Timothy to perform this action that has been so characteristic of his own ministry: "preach the word." In the Pastoral Epistles, "the word" is a shorthand expression for the Christian message: word of God (2:9; 1 Tim 4:5; Titus 1:3; 2:5); message of truth (2:15); words of faith (1 Tim 4:6). These are linked to and summarized in the "faithful sayings." Preaching the word is essential for evangelizing and nurturing the community of faith.
2. Timothy must "be persistent, whether the time is favorable or unfavorable." The verb "persist" (*epistēthi*) suggests continuing in an activity, in spite of opposition. "Whether the time is favorable or unfavorable" renders two Greek words, *eukairōs* ("convenient," "at a favorable time") and *akairōs* ("inconvenient," "out of season"). Again, note Paul's use of antitheses for poetic and rhetorical effect. The language reflects the Hellenistic concern for seizing the opportune moment to speak. Timothy will have to preach the word persistently, in spite of opposition, whether circumstances are ideal or not. Paul has already warned Timothy about the difficult times that lie ahead (3:1-9, 12), and returns to this same topic in 4:3-5.
3. Timothy must "correct" (*elegxon*; cf. 3:16), convincing people of the truth and persuading them to turn away from error.
4. Timothy must "rebuke" (*epitimēson*), denouncing error and warning people against false paths.
5. Timothy must "encourage" (*parakaleson*) his people to conduct their lives in ways appropriate to the calling that they have received (cf. 1 Thess 2:12; Phil 1:27).

These three final imperatives, "convince, rebuke, encourage," were frequently used by Hellenistic writers to describe the activities of a wise teacher.

Timothy must carry out these orders with "the utmost patience [*makrothumia*] in teaching [*didachē*]." *Makrothumia* and *didachē* form a hendiadys, where two items are joined by "and" and the second item describes or unpacks the first. Here, "teaching" describes the place where Timothy is to exercise patience, and patience is the quality that characterizes the teaching. Paul has already reminded Timothy of his own patience in teaching (3:10; cf. 1 Tim 1:16). Now Timothy's teaching must exhibit the same quality.

The urgency with which Timothy must carry out this charge is heightened by the problematic times in which he serves (4:3-4). The future tense verbs throughout these verses seem to point to the author's and reader's future. However, the problems Paul describes were already troubling the church, and would only get worse (cf. 3:1-5; 1 Tim 4:1-2). At the beginning of 2 Timothy 3, Paul described these difficult times, paying special attention to the false teachers who led the gullible away from the true path. Here, in 4:3-4, the emphasis falls on those who will be led astray.

Paul writes, "For the time will come when people with not accept sound teaching, but will collect teachers to meet their own desires, wanting to scratch their itching ears" (4:3). All three finite verbs (*estai*, "will come" or "will be"; *ouk anexontai*, "will not put up with" or "will not accept"; and *episōreusousin*, "will collect") are future tense, but point to present realities that were (and are) escalating toward a future climax. Paul uses two metaphors to describe the response of these people who are so easily led astray. What causes this tendency? First, they "collect teachers to meet their own desires." They shop for teachers who will say what they want to hear, affirm their whims and lusts and human wisdom (1 Cor 1:20-25) in their arguments with the teachers of the true gospel (cf. 1 Tim 2:7; 2 Tim 1:11). Second, they collect these teachers so as to "scratch their itching ears." This suggests a kind of insatiable, shallow curiosity that is always looking for bits of information and interesting theories, but never puts what is taught into practice (cf. Acts 17:21, where Luke describes the Athenians as dilettantes ["dabblers"] who spent all their time doing nothing but talking about or listening to new ideas).

Thus the picture: these people will seek out teachers who tell them the kinds of things they want to hear, stroke their egos, affirm their prejudices and lusts. They will "collect" these teachers; they won't become disciples or followers, or adhere to a particular way of life. They will move from teacher to teacher whenever the newness wears thin, looking for the next person who will scratch them where they itch.

This picture implies a negative conversion. These people "will turn away from hearing the truth, and turn aside to follow myths" (4:4). "Truth" (*alētheias*) in the Pastoral Epistles refers to the gospel message (e.g., 1 Tim 6:5). The word "myths" (*mythous*), used in the New Testament only in the Pastoral Epistles (cf. 1 Tim 1:4; 4:7; Titus 1:14) and 2 Peter (1:16). However, Hellenistic writers spent much time discussing the differences between "myth" and "truth." Pindar wrote, "Sometimes the sayings of mortals leave truth behind; fables [*mythoi*] ornamented with clever fictions deceive us" (*Olympian Odes* 1.28–29; cf. the discussion at Titus 1:14). Eager to satisfy their own desires, these people gladly turn away from the truth and turn (or return) to believing myths. Elsewhere in the Pastoral Epistles, the same language is used to refer to "endless genealogies" (1 Tim 1:4) and "old wives' tales" (1 Tim 4:7). Interest in spiritual things does not necessarily equate to interest in the things of God.

In 4:5, Paul returns to the charge to Timothy with four more imperative verbs. Continuing a pattern found elsewhere in the Pastoral Epistles, Paul follows a description of apostasy with an exhortation to appropriate action: "But you, be sober in all situations." Again (cf. 3:10, 14), the second person pronoun is emphatic, marking a strong contrast between the attitudes and behaviors just described and the attitudes and behaviors required of Timothy. Timothy must

1. "be sober [*nēphe*] in all circumstances [*en pasin*]"—The qualification "in all circumstances" suggests that the sobriety here is figurative and generic, not merely abstaining from too much wine. New Testament paraenesis uses "be sober" in this figurative sense to mean being alert and in control with regard to both speech and conduct (e.g., 1 Thess 5:6, 8; 1 Pet 1:13; 4:7; 5:8). In the Hellenistic world, sobriety was highly valued, and "sober" was sometimes synonymous with "self-disciplined." Plato taught that sobriety was a necessary quality of public servants, who must exercise sober judgment within a context of moderation and the restraint of their own personal desires (*Laws* 11 §918). Philo describes sober people as those who have set "training" (*paideia*) as their head (*Drunkenness* 153; see the discussion under Titus 2:2). As in 1 Thessalonians 5:6-8, the admonition to be sober seems to include an eschatological element. This reflects Jesus' frequent admonitions to his disciples that they be alert and ready (see Mark 13:5, 9, 33, 34, 35; see also *TDNT* 4:937).

2. "endure suffering" (*kakopathēson*; cf. the discussion of this word at 2:9)—Throughout this letter, Paul emphasizes the inevitability of suffering. In 1:8, he calls Timothy to join him in suffering for the gospel: cf. 2 Corinthians 11:23-28. In 2:3, Paul exhorts Timothy to "share in suffering like a good soldier of Jesus Christ." In 2:9, Paul reminded Timothy that the hardships that he (Paul) was suffering were the result of his faithfulness to the gospel. Clearly, Paul is not commanding Timothy to suffer for the sake of suffering, or for the sake of being obnoxious, etc. Rather, he is to be willing to suffer evil for the sake of the gospel. Remember the words of Jesus:

> Blessed are those who are persecuted *on account of righteousness*, for theirs is the Kingdom of Heaven. Blessed are you when people revile you and persecute you and utter all kinds of evil against you falsely *on my account*. Rejoice and be glad, for your reward is great in heaven, for in the same way they persecuted the prophets who were before you. (Matt 5:10-12, emphasis added)

3. "do the work of an evangelist" (*ergon poiēson euaggelistou*)—This work is the preaching of the good news. "Evangelist" was a function/office in the early church. Evangelists apparently focused on taking the gospel message into areas where it had never gone before. In Ephesians 4:11, "evangelists" is listed among the functions God gave to the church as part of Jesus' universal victory. This is one of the terms Paul uses to describe his ministry (1:8; 2:15; cf. 1 Cor 1:17), work he did without shame or regard for his own personal safety. This also is the work that Timothy must do.

4. "fulfill your ministry" (*tēn diakonian sou plērophorēson*)—Just as God appointed Paul to his ministry (1:1; cf. 1 Tim 1:12, etc.), so also God has appointed Timothy to a ministry of his own. Even though Timothy's ministry would differ in some respects from Paul's (and overlap greatly in others), it is *his* ministry, *his* calling, that is in view.

Note the structure of 4:1-5:

A. Introduction, solemn formula (4:1)
   B. Charge to Timothy: preach; be persistent; correct, rebuke, encourage (4:2)
      C. Factor that makes the charge urgent (4:3-4)

B'. Charge to Timothy: be sober; endure suffering; do the work of an evangelist; fulfill your ministry (4:5)

This frame emphasizes the link between the work outlined in the charge and the times in which the work is to be performed. The passage presents in capsule form the basic role of the pastor in any age or situation, ancient or modern; the urgency will always be the same. Timothy and those who follow him must

1. Preach the gospel faithfully and persistently, regardless of circumstances and reception;
2. Teach patiently so as to convince, rebuke, and encourage;
3. Be alert to the circumstances in which they minister, and alert to the ways the gospel addresses these circumstances;
4. Be prepared to suffer for the sake of the gospel, for suffer they will;
5. Be about the business of advancing the kingdom: this is the task of an evangelist, to herald news of the king and the kingdom.

By obeying these admonitions, Timothy and all who follow carry out their ministry faithfully.

In 4:6-8, Paul returns to his own example and how it can benefit Timothy. Paul fulfilled his ministry faithfully (4:6-8); Timothy must now do the same. As elsewhere, Paul's example is crucial both to Timothy's understanding of his charge and to his faithfulness in carrying it out. Notice how Paul's "I" in 4:6 compares to the imperatives of 4:2 and 4:5, and the emphatic repetitions of "you" earlier in the letter (2:1; 3:10, 14; 4:5).

Paul begins: "As for me" (4:6), echoing 4:5 and calling for Timothy to apply Paul's example to his own life: "I am already being poured out as an offering." Here, Paul uses a cultic image that would resonate powerfully in both Jewish and Greek minds. In the Old Testament, drink offerings of wine were to be poured on or at the foot of the altar at the time of sacrifice (Num 15:5; 28:7; 2 Kings 16:13; Jer 7:18; Hos 9:4; Sir 50:15). In the Hellenistic world, drink offerings of wine were often added to a sacrifice or poured out to the gods before drinking or after eating a meal. Drink offerings also played a prominent role in the solemn meals of Hellenistic religious associations and trade guilds, where they were offered to the divine patron between the meal itself and the lecture or discussion that followed.

Here, Paul's language points to the transience of life: Paul is ready to die, his life like an offering already poured out and evaporating. Yet his life is not poured out for nothing; it is poured out in service/sacrifice to his Lord and Master (cf. Phil 2:17). This also implies Paul's impending death: indeed, "the time of my departure is at hand." The word translated "departure" (*analuseōs*) was a popular metaphor for death in Paul's day. It may have originally been a sailing term, referring to the loosing of a boat from its moorings (*luō* refers to releasing or loosing the bonds that hold an object).

Paul's impending death causes him to see his ministry in a particular way. He sums up this view in three poignant and powerful declarations:

1. "I have fought [*ēgōnismai*] the good fight [*kalon agōna*]." Here, Paul again employs military imagery. Hellenistic writings commonly speak of soldiers or armies as having fought the good fight. The adjective "good" can refer to the way the soldier fought (fighting nobly) or the purpose of the fight (fighting for a noble cause). In the Pastoral Epistles, "fighting the good fight" refers to fighting for the work, integrity, and proper use of the gospel, Paul's struggle against those who would oppose the work of the gospel from within the church (false teachers) and from without (persecution, arrest, etc.).
2. "I have finished the race" (*ton dromon teteleka*). Paul has run the race that God set before him. He has been faithful to follow and complete the course. Paul here follows the military metaphor with an athletic one, as he did earlier (2:3-6). Hellenistic moralists often used the image of a race to describe the struggle for truth and moral life (e.g, Seneca, *Letters* 34.2; 109.6; Philo, *Allegorical Interpretations* 3.14).
3. "I have kept the faith" (*tēn pistin tetērēka*). "Faith" here probably refers to the Pauline gospel, which Paul has faithfully kept (see the discussion on 1:11-12 above). Paul has preserved the teaching and message of the gospel, administering it according to his calling, and keeping it free from error. When Paul spoke to the Ephesian elders, during his trip to Jerusalem just prior to his arrest, he said: "I do not count my life of any value to myself, if only I may finish my course [*teleiosai ton dromon mou*] and the ministry that I received from the Lord Jesus, to testify to the good news of God's grace" (Acts 20:24). Now, in 2 Timothy, he writes that he has finished that course and been faithful to that ministry.

"From now on" (*loipon*) often appears as a closing formula in Paul's letters (2 Cor 13:11; 1 Thess 4:1; cf. Phil 3:1; Eph 6:10; 2 Thess 3:1). Paul, like the victors in the Hellenistic games, receives a crown. Generally, the winners of athletic contests received a crown made from a wreath of flowers; on rare occasions, the crown was made of precious metal. Paul, however, receives a "crown of righteousness" (*ho tēs dikaiosunēs stephanos*). "Righteousness" in the Pastoral Epistles refers to a life lived in a right relationship with God and with others. The crown of righteousness is bestowed upon Paul by "the Lord, the righteous judge." Paul draws a clear connection between the crown and the one who bestows it. The One who is righteous recognizes the righteousness of others. In the Old Testament, the one who judges righteously is the Lord of hosts (e.g., Jer 11:20). Philo and other Hellenistic Jews affirmed that God alone was just and the absolutely righteous judge (*Dreams* 2.194; *Moses* 2.279; cf. Josephus, *J.W.* 7.8.6 §323; *Ant* 2.6.4 §108; 11.3.6 §55). "On that day" refers to the Day of the Lord (cf. the discussion at 1:12; cf. 1:18). Paul sometimes refers to this same event as the day of the Lord, of Christ, or of Jesus, or simply "that day" (1 Thess 5:2; 1 Cor 5:5; 2 Cor 1:14; Phil 1:6, 10; 2:16; cf. 2 Thess 2:2 and 1:10).

Paul will not be the lone recipient of this crown, for it will be rewarded "not only to [him] but to all who have longed for his appearing." Unlike athletic competitions, which have only one winner, Paul here affirms the solidarity of the faithful in salvation. The crown of righteousness awaits Paul, and Timothy, and all who are faithful to fight the good fight, finish the race, and keep the faith—the community of the faithful, the church.

Personal Notes, Final Greetings, and Benediction (4:9-22)

Paul's final instructions to Timothy serve as another reminder of the importance of community for living the Christian life and fulfilling one's calling. Three times in this brief section, Paul urges Timothy to come to him soon (4:9, 11, 13). Paul then repeats the request a fourth time, in 4:21. Paul also tells Timothy to bring Mark with him: Paul needs the support of his community, his friends, more than ever. These instructions present information about people not found elsewhere in the New Testament. The place names, however, highlight the scope of Paul's ministry: Thessalonica, Dalmatia, Ephesus, Troas, Corinth, Miletus, and the provinces of Macedonia, Galatia, Illyricum, Asia, and Achaea.

Paul pleads, "Make every effort to come to me soon" (4:9). "Make every effort" translates *spoudason*, "do your best" or "do everything you can" (see the discussion at Titus 3:12). Paul explains the urgency of this plea: "For Demas has deserted me and returned to Thessalonica, because he loved the present age" (4:10). The mention of "the present age" (*aiōna*) reflects Paul's apocalyptic worldview, in which the present age is evil, transitory, and opposed to God (in contrast with the coming age, where God's rule is universal; see 1 Cor 1:20; 2:6, 8; 3:18; 2 Cor 4:4; Gal 1:4; Eph 1:21).

This phrase not only contrasts the two ages. It also draws a distinction between Demas on the one hand and Paul and those who with him eagerly await Christ's appearing: you cannot eagerly await Jesus' return and the transformation brought by the coming age if you are in love with the present age. Demas had "deserted" (*egkatelipen*) or "forsaken" the imprisoned Paul, in his time of need, and gone to Thessalonica. Thessalonica was the Roman provincial capital of Macedonia, and the place where Paul preached the gospel and established a church (Acts 17:1-9). This church struggled with questions about eschatology and the resurrection.

Demas's desertion was both physical and spiritual, for he had not only abandoned Paul, he had also abandoned the truth of the gospel. The second-century apocryphal *Acts of Peter* describes Demas as Paul's companion as Paul fled from Antioch to Iconium (Acts 13:49-51). While pretending to love Paul, he became extremely jealous of him and conspired with Hermogenes (mentioned already in 1:15) against Paul, teaching that the resurrection had already taken place in the birth of children, and that Christians "are risen again in that we have come to know the true God" (cf. 2 Tim 2:18; Col 2:12; 3:1). It is easy to see how such a story could have arisen from Paul's comments in this letter.

Paul continues, "Crescens has gone to Galatia, and Titus to Dalmatia." This is the only mention of Crescens in the New Testament. Galatia is a Roman province in Asia Minor, modern-day Turkey. In Acts 13:14–16:5, Luke describes Paul's mission travels in the southern part of this province, focusing on his preaching in Antioch of Pisidia, Iconium, and Lystra. Titus was a Gentile Christian (Gal 2:3), described in Paul's letters as a trusted coworker (see Introduction to the Pastoral Epistles). He accompanied Paul to Jerusalem at one point (Gal 2:1, 3) and played an important role in Paul's ministry with the Corinthian church (2 Cor 2:13; 7:6). When writing to the Corinthian church, Paul described Titus as his "partner and coworker in your service" (2 Cor 8:23). The letter to Titus indicates that, after a preaching mission on the island of Crete, Paul left Titus behind to organize the leadership of new congregations. Dalmatia, mentioned only here in the New Testament, consisted of the southern part of the Roman province of Illyricum (present-day Albania) on the northeast coast of the Adriatic Sea. This area was an important tax base for Rome. In Romans 15:19, Paul indicates that he had preached the gospel from Jerusalem to Illyricum. According to the apocryphal *Acts of Paul* 11.1, Titus was from Dalmatia. The mention of Crescens and Titus together with Demas suggests that they too had deserted Paul, or at least left without Paul's approval. Furthermore, Paul seems to be contrasting these three men with Luke (4:11), who alone remained with Paul. It is clear that Crescens and Titus left Paul physically. It is not clear, however, whether they deserted him spiritually or not. The continued existence of the letter to Titus suggests that, at least as far as Titus is concerned, either this was not the case or Titus was somehow restored.

With the departure of Demas, Crescens, and Titus, "only Luke" remains with Paul (4:11). Beyond this verse, the New Testament mentions Luke twice. According to Philemon 1:24 and Colossians 4:14, Luke was present with Paul in his imprisonment as he wrote those letters. According to Colossians (where he is mentioned alongside Demas, both in a positive light), he is known as "the beloved physician." Tradition associates Luke with the writing of Luke and Acts. Acts contains several sections where the author moves from third-person narrative to first-person plural, the "we" sections (16:10-17; 20:5-15; 21:1-18; 27:1-28:16). These sections (if not the entire narrative of Acts) appear to have been written by a travel companion of Paul. If the traditional attribution of Acts to the pen of Luke is correct, then the most logical reading is that Luke accompanied Paul on these portions of his journeys, which included his journey to Rome. Origen suggested that Luke be identified with the Lucius of Romans 16:21 (*Commentary on Romans* 10.39 [*PL* 14.1288]).

Deserted by his comrades, Paul does not have the support around him that he needs. He instructs Timothy to "get Mark, and bring him with you, for he is useful [*euchrēstos*] to me in my ministry." Mark is probably John Mark, the cousin of Barnabas, who traveled briefly with Paul and Barnabas on their first missionary journey (Acts 12:25; 15:37-39). Tradition associates this Mark with the writing of the gospel that bears his name. According to Luke, Mark was the reason the partnership of Paul and Barnabas ended. Paul evidently did not have a high regard for Mark at the time. But here, at the end of Paul's life, he describes Mark as being "useful" or "helpful." As we've seen previously with the story of Onesimus and Philemon, even those who seem useless can find redemption and restoration. Furthermore, even Christians can experience broken relationships, but broken relationships don't have to remain broken. They can be restored. In 2 Corinthians 5:18-19, Paul proclaims that "God was in Christ, reconciling the world to himself," and that this God who reconciles "has given to us the ministry of reconciliation." Here we see an example of Paul practicing what he preached.

Paul has sent Tychicus (whose name means "fortunate") to Ephesus. Tychicus appears frequently in relation to Paul. Acts 20:1-5 identifies him as a Gentile Christian from Asia who accompanied Paul on his last journey to Jerusalem. In Ephesians 6:21, Paul calls him "a dear brother and a faithful minister in the Lord." Likewise, in Colossians 4:7, he is "a beloved brother, a

2 Timothy: Triumphant Ministry

faithful minister, and a fellow servant in the Lord," whom Paul was sending to encourage the Colossians. He would fill in the Ephesians and Colossians on the news about Paul, and may well have carried those letters. In Titus 3:12, Paul plans to send Tychicus to Crete so that Titus can move on to join Paul in Nicopolis. In every case, Tychicus appears to be Paul's trusted coworker and confidant. It would not be surprising to find him on another mission to Ephesus.

Paul further instructs Timothy: "When you come, bring with you the cloak which I left in Troas, with Carpus, and the books, especially [*malista*] the parchments" (4:13; for *malista*, see Towner 2006, 311, 695; Skeat 1979; R. A. Campbell 1995). It is not clear whether Paul's books have been left with Carpus along with the cloak, or if they are in Timothy's possession. The cloak (*phailonēs*) was likely the equivalent of our overcoat or topcoat, a warm robe that Paul would wear over his regular clothing. Paul later mentions the onset of winter (4:21); perhaps this motivates his desire for the cloak.

In the New Testament, "book" (*biblion*) generally meant a scroll, a document made of sheets from papyrus leaves or animal skin. These smaller pieces were sewn together in one long sheet, rolled up like a tube, and tied or sealed to keep them from unraveling. These books might contain many things, of course, but the logical assumption—given the importance of the Jewish Scriptures both to Paul and his communities—is that they contain Paul's copy of these Scriptures, or digests/catenas from these Scriptures. The frequency with which Paul quotes the Old Testament in his letters makes it likely that he owned his own copy of at least parts of the Jewish Scriptures.

Paul is especially concerned with retrieving "the parchments" (*membranas*). Parchment was a special kind of paper made from sheepskin. As a leatherworker (Acts 18:3), Paul may have had occasion to make such paper and use it for writing letters or for a notebook. Perhaps he used such a notebook for his own theological journaling, or to take notes about the various communities as he traveled, or even author's copies of his correspondance. Documents in a *membrana* may have taken the form of a codex, what we think of as a book today. Whatever these scrolls and parchments contained, they were obviously important to Paul, and he wanted them with him as soon as possible. The fact that he left them behind, as important as they were to him, may suggest that he had been taken away, perhaps arrested, before he was able to gather all his belongings.

Paul warns Timothy by name about another opponent, "Alexander the coppersmith," who had done Paul "a great deal of harm" (lit., "showed me many evils") (4:14). The name "Alexander" was quite common in the Hellenistic world. First Timothy 1:20 mentions an Alexander who, together with Hymenaeus had "suffered shipwreck in the faith." This suggests that these two were at one time among the faithful in Ephesus, but were no longer. If the Alexander mentioned in 2 Timothy 4:14 is the same as the Alexander in 1 Timothy 1:20, then his "shipwreck in the faith," whatever form it took, resulted in great harm to Paul.

The description of Alexander as a coppersmith (*chalkeus*, which refers to someone who works in various kinds of metals, in addition to copper), and the likelihood that Timothy is still in Ephesus when this letter is written, brings to mind the riot that broke out in Ephesus as a result of Paul's ministry there (Acts 19:21-41). Luke indicates that this riot was the result of agitation caused in the community by a man named Demetrius, a silversmith who resented the effects that Paul's ministry had on his trade in silver shrines and idols. If Alexander is identified with the same group, then the nature of the many evils he inflicted on Paul is clear. At any rate, Paul is confident that God will repay Alexander for opposing the gospel (cf. 1 Tim 1:20, where Paul "turns over" Hymenaeus and Alexander to Satan, "in order that they may be taught not to blaspheme").

It is indeed possible that both passages refer to the same Alexander. If so, he was someone who at first violently opposed Paul in Ephesus. He then was converted and became a member of the church, then suffered "shipwreck in the faith," and became an implacable opponent of Paul.

Paul describes Alexander as one who "strongly opposed" (*lian antestē*) the gospel message as preached by Paul and his coworkers (4:15). "Strongly opposed" could be translated "vehemently" or "violently" opposed. Paul emphatically warns Timothy to "beware of him" (*hon kai su phylassou*, lit., "for this one, you yourself indeed be on guard"). As far as Paul is concerned, Alexander poses a serious threat to Timothy's ministry and the message of the gospel. At the same time, Timothy and his people must remember that the Lord, the righteous judge (4:8) would repay Alexander for his treachery and opposition to the gospel. Paul has pointed to the Day of the Lord as the time when the faithful will be vindicated and rewarded. Here, he reminds Timothy of the other side of "that day," that it will also be a day of judgment. In 1 Thessalonians 4:6, in a discussion of the coming of the Lord, Paul echoes Psalm 93:1 LXX, speaking of the Lord as the avenger of evil. The fact that the wicked will not always prosper is an encouragement to Christians. The fact that God alone is the righteous judge, and that judgment belongs to him, is a caution.

Paul turns again to his example and how it may benefit Timothy. "No one came to support me at my first defense, but everyone deserted me" (4:16). "At my first defense [*apologia*]" is legal terminology, suggesting a formal judicial hearing. Paul gives no indication of where and when this hearing took place. The clear implication is that there has since been a second hearing, which ended with Paul under a death sentence (4:6-8). These are the words of a man who spent his life for others and now finds himself all but alone. The contrast between "no one came to support me" and "everyone deserted me" is dramatic; for emphasis, Paul uses the first person singular pronoun in both phrases. While we know that this language is hyperbolic—Luke is with him and only Demas is explicitly said to have deserted him—it does give a strong sense of the abandonment that Paul felt at this crucial time. For all the similarities between 2 Timothy and Philippians, several factors make the letters different:

- Paul's tone of abandonment (cf. Phil 1:7-8);
- Paul's resignation to his own death (cf. Phil 1:20-26);
- Paul's confidence that his ministry will continue after his death, through the faithful work of Timothy his successor (cf. Phil 1:24).

Paul prays for the coworkers who deserted him: "May it not be reckoned against them." This prayer heightens the pathos of the situation. "May it not be reckoned" translates an expression (*mē logistheiē*) from the world of commerce, which literally means "do not charge to one's account." Using the expression in a figurative sense, Paul prays that no record of his coworkers' wrongdoing be kept, so that they will be exempt from the consequences. Paul here obeys Jesus' command to pray for his enemies and persecutors (Matt 5:43-48). Like Stephen (Acts 7:59) and Jesus before him (Luke 23:34, or the ancient tradition behind that disputed verse if it was not part of the original text of Luke), Paul prays for the benefit of those who have harmed him. The strong parallels here as Paul stares into the face of death are not accidental: "imitate me as I imitate Christ."

Others may have deserted Paul, "but the Lord stood by me and gave me strength" (4:17). The word "but" draws our attention to the contrast between the faithlessness of people and the faithfulness of God. God demonstrates his faithfulness to Paul in two ways. First, the Lord stood by him, in contrast to those who deserted him. Second, the Lord strengthened (or "empowered" or "enabled," *enedynamōsen*) Paul. In Ephesians 3:20, Paul speaks of the kind of empowering given by God, "who by the power [*dynamis*] at work within us is able to accomplish far more than all we can ask or imagine . . . ."

This presence and empowering resulted in two things for Paul. First, it made it possible for the message of the gospel to be "fully proclaimed" through Paul. "Fully proclaimed" translates *plērophorēthē*, which is literally "completely fulfilled." This implies that Paul is saying that the gospel was consistently proclaimed by him in this situation, not only with his words but with his actions as well. Saint Francis famously said, "Go into the world and preach the gospel; if necessary, use words." Because God empowered him, even under this trying circumstance, Paul was able to communicate the life-changing truth of Jesus Christ in both word and deed.

Second, God demonstrated his faithfulness to Paul by giving Paul opportunities, even as he was being tried, to preach the gospel to the Gentiles so that everyone in earshot heard it. From the beginning of his career, Paul understood himself to have been specifically called to be an apostle to the Gentiles. According to Galatians 2:1-10, the leaders of the Jerusalem church endorsed this understanding of his call when he described it to them. The early church remembered Paul in these same terms, "apostle to the Gentiles" (see Acts 9:15; 22:21; 26:12-18). Paul's faithfulness to this call brought him to the circumstances under which he wrote this letter, and the Lord's faithfulness to Paul empowered him once again to live and proclaim the gospel so that all the Gentiles would hear it. To outsiders, Paul's circumstances must have seemed bleak, perhaps even hopeless. But Paul had learned that God could use even the most negative of circumstances for his purposes (cf. Phil 1:12-14). As far as Paul was concerned, his present circumstances were no exception.

Third, God rescued Paul "from the lion's mouth." Elsewhere, Paul refers to fighting the wild beasts in Ephesus (1 Cor 15:32). He also refers to the affliction he had experienced in Asia when so utterly, unbearably crushed that he despaired of life itself, sure that he had received a sentence of death (2 Cor 1:8-11). These references lead some to believe that Paul here is referring to these experiences, and that they should be taken literally. Thus they conclude that Paul had been sentenced to die in the arena, to be torn apart by wild animals for public entertainment, and that God had delivered him. Others suggest a metaphorical reading of the phrase. The image of being snatched from the jaws of a lion was a popular image for being rescued or escaping from serious conflict with one's enemies. The psalmist uses a similar image to speak metaphorically of the same kind of deliverance: "Save me from the mouth of the lion" (Ps 22:21; cf. 22:13, 16). The early church used this psalm to reflect on the isolation of Jesus, deserted by his friends as he faced death on the cross (Matt 27:46; Mark 15:34). Paul likely made a similar connection as he faced the threats of enemies throughout his ministry.

In 4:18, Paul expresses the same kind of confidence: "The Lord will deliver [*rhysetai*] me from every evil attack and save me for his heavenly kingdom." This confidence has seen Paul through so much. Second Corinthians 11:23-28 contains an incredible list of the struggles Paul had faced by the time that letter was written. With 2 Timothy, written perhaps ten years after 2 Corinthians, Paul is still confident. His attitude is reminiscent of Winston Churchill, who once commented on his experiences in the Boer War with the famous line, "There is nothing quite as exhilarating as being shot at, with no ill effect." In 4:18, Paul echoes Jewish and Christian prayer traditions, which assert that God delivers his people from evil (Gen 48:16; Ps 17:12-13; Prov 2:12; *b. Ber* 16b; *b. Sanh* 107a; *b. Qidd* 81b; *b. Sukk* 52b; the seventh of the *Eighteen Benedictions*). Paul's affirmation, "the Lord will rescue me from every evil attack," is similar to the language of prayer that Jesus taught his disciples in Matthew 6:13, "rescue us from the evil one" (cf. *Didache* 8.2). Paul is confident that God is both rescuing him "from" and saving him "for." That for which he is being saved is God's "heavenly kingdom." Once again, the language of the Lord's Prayer is reflected: "Let your kingdom come" (Matt 6:10). Already in 4:1, Paul spoke of the kingdom in an eschatological context. Everything that Paul has done and that Timothy must now do is done in the light of the reality of this kingdom *and* as preparation for their participation in this kingdom. Paul's faith in the reality of this kingdom sustains him and drives him in his ministry. Such a faith is necessary for those who would carry on in the face of rejection and persecution from those who reject and oppose the kingdom.

Hellenistic letters do not commonly contain doxologies. Paul's letters frequently contain several such statements, however (Rom 11:36; 16:25-27; Gal 1:5; Phil 4:20; Eph 3:20-21). Here, Paul expresses gratitude and praise at the way God has provided for him throughout his ministry and the perils that he faced. "To him be glory forever, amen." This same doxology is found in Galatians 1:5 (cf. Hebrews 13:21). Such doxologies quickly found their way into early Christian worship, and have traditionally played a central role in the liturgies of the church. Like the doxology of 1 Timothy 1:17, this statement contains the basic elements of traditional Jewish/Christian doxologies. Paul offers praise to God; "glory" (*doxa*, the Greek word from which doxologies receive their name) is a theme in every New Testament doxology, with the exception of 1 Timothy 6:16b. Second, the offering is "forever," literally "to the ages of ages." This is also a common theme in New Testament doxologies (e.g., Gal 1:5; Phil 4:20; 1 Tim 1:17; Heb 13:21; 1 Pet 4:11; Rev 1:6; 5:13; 7:12). Finally, "amen" (*amēn*, lit., "so be it") came to be the standard congregational response in worship, affirming the community's participation in the offering of praise and glory to God.

Paul follows the doxology with the kinds of personal greetings that typify the endings of his letters. Here we meet a few familiar characters, and a few who are otherwise unknown.

- "Priscilla and Aquila" (4:19) are among the best known of Paul's coworkers. Like Paul, they were leatherworkers by trade. They were expelled from Rome by the edict of Claudius (49 CE), and provided Paul with hospitality and a place to work his trade during his eighteen-month stay in Corinth (Acts 18:1-17). Leaving Corinth with Paul, they eventually landed in Ephesus where they hosted a congregation in their home (Acts 18:18; 1 Cor 16:19). In Romans, Paul describes them as his coworkers and notes that they had risked their lives for him (16:3-4). Always interesting when their names are mentioned is the fact that Priscilla's name is normally listed before the name of her husband, Aquila (Acts 18:18, 19, 26; Rom 16:3-4; 2 Tim 4:19; but see Acts 18:2 and 1 Cor 16:19, where Aquila is named first). The normal order of their names, which goes against Graeco-Roman custom, may indicate that Priscilla was the leader of this husband and wife ministry team, or at least more assertive in personality or in spiritual gift than her husband. On the other hand, the order might also indicate that Priscilla was from a higher socio-economic class than her husband. The fact that they hosted a congregation in Corinth may indicate that they were a couple of some wealth.
- The "household of Onesiphorus," obviously significant to Paul, was mentioned in 1:15-18, where Paul describes how Onesiphorus was of assistance to him in Rome. Paul there points to Onesiphorus as an example for Timothy's own response to Paul's suffering.
- "Erastus" (4:20) is another familiar figure in the Pauline circle. Paul established a church in Corinth during an eighteen-month stay there, around 51 CE (Acts 18:1-18). In Romans 16:23, Paul (writing from Corinth) identifies Erastus as the Corinthian city treasurer. In Acts 19:22, Luke describes Erastus as one of Paul's helpers in Ephesus. Erastus went with Timothy to Macedonia to prepare for a visit from Paul. Now, during the writing of 2 Timothy, Erastus is back in Corinth. (An inscription still visible in Corinth, from the middle of the first-century, reads, "Erastus, in return for his position of leadership, laid this pavement at his own expense." The fact that the Erastus mentioned in the inscription held office in Corinth at about the same time as Paul's ministry there, and the uncommonness of

Erastus as a name, all suggest that the Erastus of the inscription and the Erastus of Paul's letters are one and the same man).
- "Trophimus" (whose name means "nourishing") was a Gentile Christian from Ephesus. Together with Tychicus (2 Tim 4:12), Trophimus worked with Paul in Troas and Macedonia. Later, he accompanied Paul to Jerusalem (Acts 20:4; 21:29). His presence in Jerusalem triggered a riot, when Jews from Asia assumed (wrongly) that Paul had taken him into the Temple. This riot led to Paul's incarceration, and ultimately to his trip to Rome. During the writing of 2 Timothy, Trophimus is apparently in Miletus, where Paul left him when he (Trophimus) was ill.

Paul expresses again his strong desire for Timothy to join him quickly: "Make every effort to come here before winter" (4:21). The onset of winter would make travel dangerous or impossible. If Paul is in Rome, Timothy might have only a small window of time for making this journey, and any delay would mean the trip could not be safely taken until the next spring. At this point, with execution literally hanging over his head, such a timetable was unthinkable for Paul.

Finally, Paul includes third-person greetings from individuals to Timothy. This list resembles similar greetings in Romans 16:16, 21-23; 1 Corinthians 16:19-20; Philemon 1:23-24; Colossians 4:10-14 (cf. 1 Pet 5:13). None of the individuals listed here—Eubulus, Pudens, Linus, Claudia—appear elsewhere in the New Testament. Traditions about them did develop in the early church, however.

- According to the apocryphal *Acts of Paul* 8.1.1, "Eubulus" was a presbyter and companion of Stephanus, one of Paul's first converts in Achaea (1 Cor 16:15-18). He devoted himself to the service of the saints, and was one of three Corinthians sent to serve Paul.
- "Pudens" was the son of a Roman senator and a woman named Prisca.
- Irenaeus (d. 200 CE) and Eusebius (d. c. 330) identify "Linus" as Peter's successor as overseer of the church in Rome, the second Pope in Catholic tradition.
- "Claudia" was a common name during this period. It may suggest that the woman was a member of the royal household, a slave or member of the household (*gens*) of the Roman emperor Claudius. According to Suetonius, Claudius had a penchant for freeing slaves, particularly slaves of the royal household. Many of these expressed their gratitude by taking the emperor's name for themselves or members of their family, resulting in a sort of extended family known as the *gens* Claudia.

- A general third-person greeting from "all the brothers and sisters" closes this section. This greeting resembles the greetings at the ends of other Pauline letters (1 Cor 16:20; Phil 4:22; cf. 2 Cor 13:12; Titus 3:15; 3 John 15). The language is thoroughly Pauline, as he often addresses his readers as "brothers and sisters" (*adelphoi*), reflecting his view of the church as a household in which all the members are family.

As do all of Paul's letters, 2 Timothy ends with a benediction: "The Lord be with your spirit; grace be with you all" (4:22). This two-part blessing reflects the basic elements of Pauline benedictions. In "The Lord be with your spirit," the second-person pronoun is singular, suggesting a focus on Timothy only. "The Lord be with your spirit" is a Semitic expression, equivalent to "the Lord be with you."

Grace appears as a theme in all of Paul's benedictions, and here Paul takes up one last time this central theme. Appropriately, the letter begins with grace (1:2) and ends with grace (4:22). The plural pronoun *humōn*, translated "you all," indicates that even this most personal of letters was not private, not intended for Timothy alone. Paul expected Timothy to read this letter to his church, and the grace and blessing he prays for is for them as well as for Timothy.

Paul has written to Timothy to describe his own ministry, and to pass the care of that ministry on to Timothy, making him Paul's full successor. He writes this letter to be overheard by Timothy's people, so that they, too, will better understand Timothy's calling, and the nature of his ministry. By learning about the nature of Timothy's calling and ministry, they come to better understand their own, as do we.

Works Cited

Arichea, Daniel C., and H. A. Hatton. *Paul's Letters to Timothy and Titus*. UBS Handbook. New York: United Bible Societies, 1995.

Aune, David. *The New Testament in Its Literary Environment*. Library of Early Christianity. Philadelphia: Westminster, 1987.

Baldwin, H. Scott. "A Difficult Word: *Authenteō* in 1 Timothy 2:12." In A. J. Kostenberger, ed., *Women in the Church: A Fresh Analysis of 1 Timothy 2:9-15*. Grand Rapids: Baker, 1995.

———. "Appendix 2. *Authenteō* in Ancient Greek Literature." In A. J. Kostenberger, ed., *Women in the Church: A Fresh Analysis of 1 Timothy 2:9-15*. Grand Rapids: Baker, 1995.

Barrett, C. K. *The Pastoral Epistles*. New Clarendon Bible. Oxford: Oxford University Press, 1963.

———. *Signs of an Apostle*. London: Epworth, 1970.

Bassler, Jouette M. *1 Timothy, 2 Timothy, Titus*. Abingdon New Testament Commentaries. Nashville: Abingdon, 1996.

Bauckham, Richard J. "Pseudo-Apostolic Letters." *JBL* 107 (1988): 469–94.

———. *Jesus and the Eyewitnesses*. Grand Rapids: Eerdmans, 2006.

Beker, J. Christiaan. *Heirs of Paul*. Philadelphia: Fortress, 1991.

Bonhoeffer, Dietrich. *The Cost of Discipleship*. New York: Collier Books, 1963.

Bultmann, Rudolf. *History of the Synoptic Tradition*. Oxford: Blackwell, 1963.

Campbell, R. Alastair. *The Elders: Seniority within Earliest Christianity*. Edinburgh: T&T Clark, 1994.

———. "A New Look at 1 Timothy 5:8." *New Testament Studies* 41 (1995): 157–60.

Campenhausen, Hans von. *Ecclesiastical Authority and Spiritual Power in the Church of the First Three Centuries*. Stanford: Stanford University Press, 1969.

Carson, D. A. *The Gospel according to John*. Pillar New Testament Commentary. Grand Rapids: Eerdmans, 1991.

Charles, J.D. "Vice and Virtue Lists." In Stanley E. Porter and Craig A. Evans, *Dictionary of New Testament Background: A Compendium of Contemporary Biblical Scholarship*. Downers Grove IL: InterVarsity Press, 2000.

Collins, Raymond. *1 & 2 Timothy and Titus: A Commentary*. New Testament Library. Louisville: Westminster/John Knox Press, 2002.

Coupland, Simon. "Salvation through Childbearing? The Riddle of 1 Tim 2:15." *Expository Times* 112 (2001): 302–303.

Danker, F. W. *Benefactor: Epigraphic Study of a Graeco-Roman and New Testament Semantic Field*. St Louis: Clayton, 1982.

Davies, W. D. *The Setting of the Sermon on the Mount*. Cambridge: Cambridge University Press, 1977.

Deissmann, Adolf. *Light from the Ancient East: The New Testament Illustrated by Recently Discovered Texts of the Graeco-Roman World*. Rev. ed. Grand Rapids: Baker, 1965.

Dibelius, Martin, and Hans Conzelmann. *The Pastoral Epistles*. Hermeneia. Philadelphia: Fortress, 1972.

Donelson, Lewis R. *Pseudepigraphy and Ethical Argument in the Pastoral Epistles*. HUT 22. Tübingen: Mohr [Siebeck], 1986.

Dylan, Bob. "All Along the Watchtower." *John Wesley Harding*. Capitol Records, 1968.

Easton, B. S. *The Pastoral Epistles*. London: SCM, 1947.

Evans, Craig A. "Mark's Incipit and the Priene Calendar Inscription: From Jewish Gospel to Greco-Roman Gospel." *Journal of Greco-Roman Christianity and Judaism* 1 (2000): 67–81.

Ferguson, Everett. "*Topos* in 1 Timothy 2:8." *Restoration Quarterly* 33 (1991): 65–73.

Gerhardsson, Birger. *Memory and Manuscript*, revised ed. Grand Rapids: Eerdmans, 1998.

Gloer, W. Hulitt. *An Exegetical and Theological Study of Paul's Understanding of New Creation and Reconciliation in 2 Cor 5:14-21*. Lewiston NY: Mellen Biblical Press, 1996.

———. "Hymns and Homologies in the New Testament." *Perspectives in Religious Studies* 1984.

Gray, Patrick. "The Liar Paradox and the Letter to Titus," *CBQ* 69 (2007): 302–14.

Hanson, A. T. *The Pastoral Epistles*. New Century Bible Commentary. Grand Rapids: Eerdmans, 1982.

Harrison, P. N. *The Problem of the Pastoral Epistles*. Oxford: Oxford University Press, 1921.

Holmes, J. M. *Text in a Whirlwind: A Critique of Four Exegetical Devices at 1 Timothy 2:12-15*. JSNTS. Sheffield: Sheffield Academic Press, 2000.

Hunter, A. M. *Paul and His Predecessors*. Philadelphia: Westminster, 1961.

Johnson, Luke T. *The First and Second Letters to Timothy*. Anchor Bible. Garden City NY: Doubleday, 2001.

Karris, Robert J. *The Pastoral Epistles*. Wilmington DE: Michael Glazier, 1979.

Käsemann, Ernst. "Sentences of Holy Law in the New Testament." *New Testament Questions of Today*. Philadelphia: Fortress, 1969.

Kasher, Aryeh. *Jews, Idumaeans, and Ancient Arabs: Relations of the Jews in Eretz-Israel with the Nations of the Frontier and the Desert During the Hellenistic and Roman Era (332 BCE–70 CE)*. Tübingen: Mohr [Siebeck], 1988.

Kelly, J. N. D. *A Commentary on the Pastoral Epistles*. Harper's New Testament Commentaries. New York: Harper & Row, 1963.

Kierkegaard, Soren. *Purity of Heart Is to Will One Thing: Spiritual Preparation for the Office of Confession*. New York: Harper, 1956.

Knight, George W. *Commentary on the Pastoral Epistles*. New International Greek Testament Commentary. Grand Rapids: Eerdmans, 1992.

Malherbe, Abraham J. *Moral Exhortation: A Greco-Roman Sourcebook*. Library of Early Christianity. Philadelpia: Westminster Press, 1986.

Marshall, I. Howard. *The Pastoral Epistles*. International Critical Commentary. Edinburgh: T&T Clark, 1999.

Meade, David G. *Pseudonymity and Canon*. Wissenschaftliche Untersuchungen zum Neuen Testament 39: Tübingen: Mohr (Siebeck), 1986.

Meeks, Wayne A. *The First Urban Christians: The Social World of the Apostle Paul*. New Haven: Yale University Press, 1983.

Merkle, Ben. *The Elder and Overseer: One Office in the Early Church*. New York: Peter Lang, 2003.

Metzger, Bruce M. "Literary Forgeries and Canonical Pseudepigrapha." *Journal of Biblical Literature* 91 (1972): 3–24.

Miller, James D. *The Pastoral Epistles as Composite Documents*. SNTSMS. Cambridge: Cambridge University Press, 1997.

Mounce, William D. *The Pastoral Epistles*. Word Biblical Commentary. Dallas: Word, 2000.

Oden, Thomas C. *First and Second Timothy and Titus*. Interpretation: A Bible Commentary for Preaching and Teaching. Louisville: Westminster/John Knox Press, 1989.

Osiek, Carolyn, and David L. Balch, *Families in the New Testament World: Households and House Churches.* Louisville: Westminster/John Knox, 1997.
Peacock, Charlie. "Experience." *The Secret of Time.* Sparrow Records, 1990.
Perriman, Andrew C. "What Eve Did, What Women Shouldn't Do." *Tyndale Bulletin* 44 (1993): 129–42.
Prior, Michael. *Paul the Letter-Writer and the Second Letter to Timothy.* JSNT Supp 23. Sheffield: JSOT Press, 1989.
Quinn, Jerome D. "The Last Volume of Luke." In *Perspectives on Luke–Acts,* Charles H. Talbert, ed. Perspectives in Religious Studies, Special Studies Series No. 5. Danville VA: Association of Baptist Professors of Religion, 1978.
———. *The Letter to Titus.* Anchor Bible. Garden City NY: Doubleday, 1990.
Richards, William A. *Difference and Distance in Post-Pauline Christianity: An Epistolary Analysis of the Pastorals.* Studies in Biblical Literature 44. New York: Peter Lang, 2002.
Roloff, Jurgen. *Der Erste Brief an Timotheus.* EKKNT. Zurich: Benziger, 1998.
Schmidt, Daryl. "The LXX Gattung 'Prophetic Correlative,'" *JBL* 96 (1977): 517–22.
Scholer, David. "1 Timothy 2:9-15 and the Place of Women in the Church's Ministry." In A. Mickelsen, ed., *Women, Authority & the Bible.* Downers Grove IL: InterVarsity Press, 1986. Reprinted in A. J. Levine, ed., *A Feminist Companion to the Deutero-Pauline Epistles.* Cleveland: Pilgrim Press, 2003.
Skeat, T. C. "'Especially the Parchments': A Note on 2 Tim 4:13." *Journal for Theological Studies* n.s. 30 (1979): 173–77.
Stepp, Perry L. *Leadership Succession in the World of the Pauline Circle.* New Testament Monographs 5. Sheffield UK: Sheffield Phoenix Press, 2005.
Stiefel, J. H. "Women Deacons in 1 Timothy: A Linguistic and Literary Look at 'Women Likewise.'" *NTS* 41 (1995): 442–57.
Talbert, Charles H. *Ephesians and Colossians.* Paideia. Grand Rapids: Baker Academic, 2007.
———. *Reading Corinthians.* Revised ed. Macon GA: Smyth & Helwys, 2002.
———, and Perry L. Stepp. "Succession in Mediterranean Antiquity, Part 1: The Lukan Milieu," and "Succession in Mediterranean Antiquity, Part 2: Luke–Acts." 1:148-68, 169–79 in *Society of Biblical Literature Seminar Papers, 1998.* Atlanta: Scholars Press, 1998.
Thiselton, A. C. "The Logical Role of the Liar Paradox in Titus 1:12, 13: A Dissent from the Commentaries in the Light of Philosophical and Logical Analysis." *BibInt* 2 (1994): 207–23.
Thurston, Bonnie. *The Widows: A Women's Ministry in the Early Church.* Minneapolis: Fortress, 1989.
Towner, Philip. *The Letters to Timothy and Titus.* Grand Rapids: Eerdmans, 2006.
Trobisch, David. *The First Edition of the New Testament.* New York: Oxford University Press, 2000.
———. "Let the Context Interpret: A Narrative-Critical Approach to the Letters of Paul." Paper presented at the annual meeting of the Society of Biblical Literature, San Antonio TX, November 23, 2004.
Van Neste, Ray. *Cohesion and Structure in the Pastoral Epistles,* JSNTSS 280. London: T&T Clark, 2004.
———. "Looking Through a Literary Lens at a Pastoral Epistle." Paper presented at the annual meeting of the Evangelical Theological Society, San Diego, CA, November 2007.
Waters, Kenneth L., Sr., "Saved through Childbearing: Virtues as Children in 1 Tim 2:11-15." *JBL* 123 (2004): 703–35.

Winter, Bruce W. "The New Roman Wife and 1 Tim 2:9-15." *Tyndale Bulletin* 51 (2000): 283–92.
———. "Providentia and the Widows of 1 Timothy 5:3-16." *Tyndale Bulletin* 39 (1988): 83–99.
———. *Roman Wives, Roman Widows: The Appearance of New Women and the Pauline Communities.* Grand Rapids: Eerdmans, 2003.
Witherington, Ben III. *Letters and Homilies for Hellenized Christians: A Socio-Rhetorical Commentary Titus, 1–2 Timothy, and 1–3 John.* Downer's Grove IL: IVP Academic, 2006.
———. *Conflict and Community in Corinth: A Socio-Rhetorical Commentary on 1 and 2 Corinthians.* Grand Rapids: Eerdmans, 1995.
Wright, N. T. *Surprised by Hope: Rethinking Heaven, the Resurrection, and the Mission of the Church.* San Francisco: HarperOne, 2008.
Young, Frances M. "On EPISKOPOS and PRESBUTEROS." *Journal of Theological Studies* 45 (1994): 142–48.

Other available titles from SMYTH & HELWYS

Reading the New Testament

Reading Matthew
A Literary and Theological Commentary
David E. Garland

Reading Matthew provides thorough guidance through Matthew's story of Jesus. Garland's commentary reveals the movement of the story's plot while also highlighting the theology of Matthew. Reading Matthew is an essential book for students and ministers studying the first Gospel.
978-1-57312-274-0 296 pages/pb **$22.00**

Reading Mark
A Literary and Theological Commentary on the Second Gospel
Sharyn Dowd

Dowd examines the Gospel of Mark from literary and theological perspectives, suggesting what the text may have meant to its first-century audience of Gentile and Jewish Christians. Mark is a Greco-Roman biography of Jesus written in an apocalyptic mode. Its theology is based on the message of the prophet Isaiah— the proclamation of release from bondage and a march toward freedom along the "way of the Lord."
978-1-57312-288-7 200 pages/pb **$22.00**

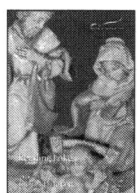

Reading Luke
A Literary and Theological Commentary on the Third Gospel
Charles H. Talbert

Reading Luke concentrates on the literary and theological distinctives of the third Gospel. Charles Talbert's effective and insightful commentary enables its reader to see and feel the full force of the literary masterpiece that begins the Christian story in the birth of Jesus Christ and continues in the Acts of the Apostles. Reading Luke is an essential book for students and ministers studying Luke-Acts.
978-1-57312-393-8 304 pages/pb **$23.00**

To order call 800-747-3016 or visit www.helwys.com

Reading John
A Literary and Theological Commentary on the Fourth Gospel and the Johannine Epistles (revised edition)
Charles H. Talbert

Reading John concentrates on the literary and theological distinctives of the Fourth Gospel and the Johannine Epistles. New Testament scholar Charles Talbert's unique commentary considers the entire scope of these works attributed to John, their literary settings and particularities, and their continuing theological importance to the Christian story. Thoughtful and engaging, *Reading John* is essential to students and ministers studying the New Testament and the Johannine writings.   978-1-57312-278-8 322 pages/pb **$23.00**

Reading Acts
A Literary and Theological Commentary (revised edition)
Charles H. Talbert

Answers to the usual introductory questions do not yield sufficient harvest to enable an intelligent reading of Acts. The approach of *Reading Acts* is to ask how ancient Mediterranean auditors would have heard Acts when it was read in their presence. To be successful Talbert divides this approach into two parts— how Acts would have been heard in its precanonical context and in its canonical context.

978-1-57312-277-1 302 pages/pb **$22.00**

Reading Romans
A Literary and Theological Commentary
Luke Timothy Johnson

The Epistle to the Romans is considered to be the classic of Reformation theology. Luke Johnson, a scholar from the Roman Catholic tradition, invests this commentary with breadth of perspective and clarity of expression. He focuses on understanding the key themes and their relationship to the whole of Pauline writings and the shaping of Christianity.   978-1-57312-276-4 260 pages/pb **$22.00**

Reading Corinthians
A Literary and Theological Commentary
Charles H. Talbert

Paul's letters to the Christians in Corinth portray a young church struggling to live out the demands of the gospel amid the life of a thoroughly urban setting. In *Reading Corinthians*, biblical scholar Charles Talbert helps his reader to grasp what was at stake in the conversations between Paul and the Corinthians. What we find there is not only a word for the struggling faithful in Corinth, but an always truthful word for the church today.

978-1-57312-386-0 258 pages/pb **$22.00**

To order call 800-747-3016 or visit www.helwys.com

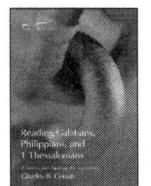

Reading Galatians, Philippians, and 1 Thessalonians
A Literary and Theological Commentary

Charles B. Cousar

Cousar interprets three Letters of Paul, each showing Paul in a different light. The commentary traces the movement of the letters, paragraph by paragraph, and pays particular attention to the literary character of the writing and the theological implications of the text for the church today.

978-1-57312-323-5 264 pages/pb **$24.00**

Reading Colossians, Ephesians and 2 Thessalonians
A Literary and Theological Commentary

Bonnie Thurston

Like other volumes in this unique series, *Reading Colossians, Ephesians, & 2 Thessalonians* focuses on comprehending the major themes of the epistles and their relationship to the understanding of the early Christian communities. With the focus on the work in its entirety rather than a verse-by-verse methodology, this volume will appeal to the professional and nonprofessional alike, as well as to college and seminary students.

978-1-57312-500-0 216 pages/pb **$22.00**

Reading Paul's Letters to Individuals
A Literary and Theological Commentary on Paul's Letter to Philemon, Titus, and Timothy

W. Hulitt Gloer and Perry L. Stepp

In their study of the Pastoral Epistles, Gloer and Stepp describe the continuation of Paul's missionary work, the internal and external conflicts, and Paul's gradual withdrawal from the work that has defined his life.

978-1-57312-519-2 306 pages/pb **$23.00**

Reading Hebrews & James
A Literary and Theological Commentary

Marie E. Isaacs

Reading Hebrews and James provides a clear path through the unique and often divisive Letter to the Hebrews and Letter of James. Isaacs's commentary on these two letters expertly considers questions of authorship and historical context while also making both Hebrews and James undeniably relevant for today's faith. Preachers and teachers alike will benefit from the essential study that *Reading Hebrews and James* offers.

978-1-57312-318-1 268 pages/pb **$22.00**

To order call 800-747-3016 or visit www.helwys.com

Reading 1 Peter, Jude, and 2 Peter
A Literary and Theological Commentary
Earl J. Richard

This volume is dedicated to the study of three late, little-known biblical works that historically have been relegated to the lesser works of the New Testament. *Reading 1 Peter, Jude, and 2 Peter* underscores the light that these letters shed upon one another and focuses on the snapshots they provide of early Christian communities as they encountered the social and religious environment in which they were situated.

Careful reading of 1 Peter reveals the complex world of the post-apostolic period. Jude and 2 Peter provide a sober look at the early community's evolution in doctrinal and moral terms.   *1-978-57312-314-3 416 pages/pb* **$25.00**

Reading Revelation
A Literary and Theological Commentary
Joseph Trafton

Biblical scholar Joseph Trafton considers one of the most enigmatic of biblical books. Examining the Revelation to John in its literary and theological contexts, Trafton finds a text that works through its cultural bounds to offer a word to believers in the here and now.

978-1-57312-289-4 242 pages/pb **$22.00**

To order call **800-747-3016** or visit **www.helwys.com**

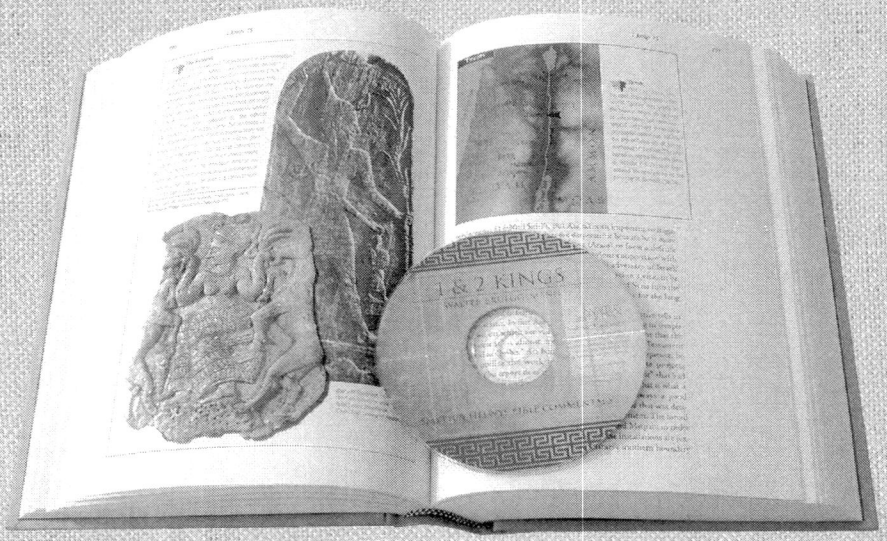

THIS SERIES WILL MAKE AN ENORMOUS IMPACT ON THE LIFE AND FAITH OF THE CHURCH.

Walter Brueggemann, author of *1 & 2 Kings*

The *Smyth & Helwys Bible Commentary* includes "commentary" and "connections" information within each chapter. The *Commentary* provides an analysis of the passage, consisting of interpretation of the passage, its language, history, and literary form, and discussion of pertinent theological issues. *Connections* offers application of analytical insight for (1) teaching of the passages, including suggested approaches for instruction and additional resources for further study, and (2) preaching based on the passage, including suggested approaches, themes, and resources. Most Bible commentaries are limited to providing only "commentary," without the helpful "connections" included in this series.

Additional Features

- CD-ROM with powerful search & research tools
- Unique hyperlink format offers additional information
- Includes maps, photographs, and other illustrations relevant for understanding the context or significance of the text
- Quality craftsmanship in printing and binding
- Distinctive sidebars/special interest boxes printed in color
- Footnotes that offer full documentation

OLD TESTAMENT
GENERAL EDITOR
Samuel E. Balentine
*Union Presbyterian Seminary
Richmond, Virginia*

PROJECT EDITOR
R. Scott Nash
*Mercer University
Macon, Georgia*

NEW TESTAMENT
GENERAL EDITOR
R. Alan Culpepper
*McAfee School of Theology
Mercer University
Atlanta, Georgia*

Choose our **Standing Order Plan** and receive a **25% discount** on every volume. To sign up or for more information call **800-747-3016** or visit **www.helwys.com/commentary**

Made in the USA
Lexington, KY
25 May 2014